PROPHETS & PROFESSORS:

ESSAYS ON THE LIVES AND WORKS OF MODERN POETS

BRUCE BAWER

STORY LINE PRESS
1995

ISBNs: 1-885266-05-7 cloth, 1-885266-04-9 paper

Published by Story Line Press, Inc., Three Oaks Farm, Brownsville, OR 97327

Book design by M. Rae Thompson

This publication was made possible thanks in part to the generous support of the Nicholas Roerich Museum, the Andrew Mellon Foundation, the National Endowment for the Arts and our individual contributors.

ACKNOWLEDGMENTS

I wish to thank the following editors, past and present: at *The New Criterion*, Erich Eichman, Donna Rifkind, and the late Eva Szent-Miklozy; at *The Hudson Review*, Frederick Morgan, Paula Deitz, and Ronald Koury; at *The American Spectator*, Joseph Epstein; at *The Washington Post Book World*, Michael Dirda; at *Poetry*, Joseph Parisi. I also wish to thank Dana Gioia and William Logan, who edited the special section of the issue of *Verse* in which my essay on Donald Justice first appeared.

Library of Congress Cataloging-in-Publication Data
Bawer, Bruce 1956
    Prophets & professors: essays on the lives and works of modern poets / Bruce
        Bawer.
        p. cm.
    ISBN 1-885266-05-7 cloth   ISBN 1-885266-04-9 paper
    1. American poetry—20th century—History and criticism. 2. Poets, Ameri
    can—20th century—Biography. 3. Poetry—History and criticism. I. title.
    PS323.5.B37 1995   95-19562
    811'.5—dc20   CIP

TABLE OF CONTENTS

in memoriam
CAROL SALTUS
poet, critic, friend

PREFACE

In the 1980's, I spent a few years on the board of a national organization that awards annual literary prizes in several categories. Every year at the nominating meeting, twenty-five or so of us would sit around a large table and proceed from category to category, each of us, in his or her turn, praising certain books and denouncing others. Almost everyone had strong opinions, and the arguments were many and sometimes bitter. The one exception was in the category of poetry. When we came to poetry, there tended to be a sudden palpable feeling of discomfort in the room, a certain awkward silence. As we went around the table, four or five people would say "Pass," some of them adding by way of explanation that they didn't read contemporary poetry and felt incompetent to pass judgment. The first time this happened, I was shocked. Even I—who had complained in print about the way contemporary poetry had alienated educated readers—was surprised to discover that people who made their living as literary critics (and, in many cases, as book-review editors for major American newspapers) considered contemporary poetry to be out of their league. "You either have the critical vocabulary to deal with this stuff or not," said one of my fellow directors, a critic and fiction writer of no mean distinction.

This discovery troubled me. I respected my fellow critics for admitting their unfamiliarity with and sense of alienation from contemporary poetry. But as a professional critic who also happened to be a poet and who cared deeply about the future of the art, I was dismayed that colleagues of mine—who, I gathered, read and revered the great poetry of earlier periods—had given up poetry in our time as a lost cause. They were unwilling to read it, unwilling to form opinions about it and to say in print what was wrong with it. Why? One reason, I think, was that they were insecure—afraid that, to some extent, the explanation for their indifference to contemporary poetry lay in a failure in themselves, not in the work. Certainly some professors who have made a specialty of contemporary poetry have encouraged non-specialist critics to think this way—encouraged them, that is, to distrust their own judgment of recent poetry and to defer to academic specialists. Non-specialist critics who disobey, openly dissenting from academic orthodoxy, can expect to be viewed in many faculty lounges as having done something base, low, dishonorable; can expect to see their arguments twisted, their motives impugned. Little wonder that so many of my fellow critics kept contemporary poetry at arm's length!

Another reason for my colleagues' disregard for contemporary poetry was doubtless that they considered poetry so ailing and marginal a genre that criticism was beside the point, or even cruel—like kicking an invalid. In this they were perhaps like the majority of literate people today, who tend to treat contemporary poetry the way Victorian England treated women—namely, they put it on a pedestal and say pretty things about it and speak of it only in the most gentle and complimentary of terms. But they don't really take it *seriously*. For when a society takes an art seriously, it argues about it. If television is crowded with programs on which talking heads inanely debate the merits of new movies, giving this one a thumbs-up and that one a thumbs-down, it is because our society takes its movie entertainment seriously. Go to Lincoln Center and you'll see balletomanes arguing passionately during intermissions about the relative merits of the dancers and choreographers; they do this because they take the ballet seriously. But those who read contemporary poetry—which, in our society, basically means poets—shy away from criticism. Such poets, as I have written elsewhere, tend to see poetry less as an art than as a means of personal expression ("love me, love my poems") or as a sort of interest group whose members are all working for the same cause—virtue and sensitivity in all things—and are supposed to help each other out; for a poet to write a negative review of another poet is seen by many members of the poetry world as treason—a betrayal of the tribe, a violation of the corporate spirit, a breach of the fraternity code. They think that all reviews should be positive, and that the only legitimate purpose of reviews of poetry is to encourage people to buy books; what they don't realize is that this insular, self-protective stance has helped poetry to become marginalized, to be turned into something that only poets read—and read, in many cases, only for the same practical, professional reasons (i.e., the desire to see what the competition is up to) that some English professors read papers by other English professors.

We live in an age when good poets routinely sell out their art by conferring M.F.A. degrees on bad poets; an age when purported admirers of poetry churn out insipid Poetry Videos that turn the art into something that it is not; an age when nobody blinks an eye at the cheerful admission by the nation's most influential poetry critic, Helen Vendler, that she has "no ear." (This admission, in a *Harvard Magazine* interview, came in response to a charge leveled in my essay "Helen Vendler, Poetry Critic," which is reprinted in these pages.) And we live in an age, finally, when poetry criticism has all but withered away, replaced largely by blandly favorable reviews, sycophantic interviews of one poet by another, and other forms of discourse that are barely indistinguishable from publicity. If the essays in this book sometimes seem intemperate, this is why: because the present critic takes poetry very seriously, seriously enough to have strong opinions about it, and seriously enough to be quite exasperated about the various ways in which many of those who claim to love it have let it down.

THE AUDACITY OF EMILY DICKINSON

One day late in 1881, the young wife of a recently hired instructor at Amherst College wrote to her parents in Washington about her impressions of her hometown. Among other things, she told them about a mysterious woman who was "the *character* of Amherst":

> It is a lady [she explained] whom the people call the *Myth*. She is a sister of Mr. [Austin] Dickinson [the college treasurer], and seems to be the climax of all the family oddity. She has not been outside of her own house in fifteen years, except once to see a new church, when she crept out at night, & viewed it by the moonlight…. Her sister, who was at Mrs. Dickinson's party, invited me to come & sing to her mother sometime…. People tell me that the *myth* will hear every note—she will be near, but unseen…. Isn't that like a book? So interesting.
>
> No one knows the cause of her isolation, but of course there are dozens of reasons assigned.

The "*Myth*," of course, was none other than Miss Emily Dickinson, who at the time of the young lady's gossipy missive was fifty years old, had never married, and had spent much of her life writing poems, hundreds of them, of which only a handful had been published. Even now, a century after her death (in 1886), critics and biographers, like her Amherst contemporaries, are unable to agree upon an explanation for her refusal, during the last seventeen years of her life, to leave her family's house or to receive visitors. Nearly every Dickinson scholar, however—certain that in the explanation, whatever it may be, lies the key to her mind and character and poetry—has put forward a solution to the puzzle. Clark Griffith, for example, theorizes in *The Long Shadow: Emily Dickinson's Tragic Poetry* (1964) that the poet was emotionally crippled by her tyrannical father, Edward Dickinson, a distinguished lawyer, civic leader, and a one-term representative to Congress. John Cody, alternatively, proposes in *After Great Pain: The Inner Life of Emily Dickinson* (1971) that Dickinson was incapacitated by the conviction that she had been failed, in some way, by her simple, submissive, and affectless mother, Emily Norcross Dickinson. Rebecca Patterson argues in *The Riddle of Emily Dickinson* (1953) that the poet secluded herself because of her friend Kate Scott Anthon's "cruelty"; Vivian R. Pollak, in *Dickinson: The Anxiety of Gender* (1984), argues that she was the victim of "a crisis of sexual identity"; and William R. Sherwood, in *Circumference and Circumstance: Stages in the Mind and Art of Emily Dickinson* (1968), maintains that her isolation was the consequence of a supposed affair with the Philadelphia minister Charles Wadsworth. And Ruth Miller, in *The Poetry of Emily Dickinson* (1968), offers what may be the most cogent explanation, given the fact that Dickinson's poetry was the most important thing in the world to her: namely, that after having sent her poems for years to two distinguished men of letters—Samuel Bowles of the *Springfield Republican* and Thomas Wentworth Higginson of the *Atlantic Monthly*—and endured the failure of both men to recognize her greatness (while they regularly published the work of stunning mediocrities), Dickinson simply gave up hope of being understood and appreciated in her own time, and withdrew.

Cynthia Griffin Wolff, in her respectable but seriously flawed new critical biography of Dickinson,[1] refrains from overemphasizing her own theory on this matter. Wolff thinks that Dickinson's trouble with her eyesight—trouble that became acute in the early 1860s and abated permanently after a few years—may help to explain her retreat into isolation. But the eyesight trouble, in Wolff's view, was less a real cause than a precipitating factor, an excuse that Emily took advantage of to avoid the sort of events that she had never really enjoyed attending anyway; and once the pattern of withdrawal had begun, it simply developed naturally and by slow degrees. "Vinnie [Lavinia, Emily's sister, who also never married and lived with Emily in the family manse] always claimed that her sister's retirement was 'only a happen'—a slow process, the result not of one dramatic tragedy, but rather of many separate, small decisions."

Actually, when seen in the light of Dickinson's unique perspective on things and her revolutionary concept of poetry—to which I will return presently—the isolation of her last years seems almost an inevi-

---

[1]*Emily Dickinson*, by Cynthia Griffin Wolff; Knopf, 638 pages, $25.

tability; how such an extraordinary sensibility managed to come into being in nineteen-century Amherst, Massachusetts, however, is another question. It is a question that much concerns Wolff, who, by means of an interpretation that is by turns revealing and highly dubious, purports to explain Dickinson's vision and poetics as the product of her familial and religious background.

The lives of her father and paternal grandfather do in fact seem to shed light on Emily Dickinson's life and art. Her grandfather Samuel Fowler Dickinson—a lawyer, politician, and orator of considerable local reputation, and the builder of the "Old Homestead" (the first brick house in Amherst) in which Emily Dickinson would spend her life—was a strikingly obsessive man. Observes Wolff: "The notion of a 'Father' in the Dickinson household—particularly as it related to 'Kingdom' and 'Power' and 'Glory'—was complex and fraught with conflicting emotions." Samuel Dickinson's Amherst was a center of conservative Trinitarian belief at a time when, in many parts of Massachusetts, liberal Unitarianism was in flower. The wealthy, ambitious Samuel, who served for forty years as the deacon of Amherst's West Church, was (in the words of his great-granddaughter) "a flaming zealot for education and religion," a man who wanted "to hasten the conversion of the whole world." To this end, he dedicated several years of his life and the bulk of his considerable fortune to the establishment of Amherst College, a bastion of Trinitarianism that would serve to counterbalance the liberal Unitarianism of Harvard.

Four of Samuel's five sons left Amherst in their twenties to make careers elsewhere, apparently unwilling to compromise their prospects by maintaining too close a tie to their by then financially ailing father; only one son, Edward, remained dutifully in Amherst, where he practiced law like his father and—purely out of filial loyalty—allowed himself to become involved in Samuel's desperate and ill-advised money-making schemes. Not until after Samuel's death in 1838, in Hudson, Ohio (where, having lost his money and honor in Amherst, he was attempting a new start as the treasurer of the newly founded Western Reserve College), did Edward manage to rehabilitate the family's reputation and fortune. He succeeded, furthermore, in becoming what his father had been at the height of his career: the quintessential Amherst public man with a special interest in, and a close relationship to, Amherst College. Yet whereas Samuel had been zealous in his support of the college, and all but fanatically devoted to its spiritual mission, Edward was prudent and circumspect in his dedication, interested in the institution less out of any real enthusiasm for its purpose, it would seem, than out of a sense of civic obligation and family pride. Edward's pet project was the railroad: he was celebrated as the man who brought it to Amherst. "In many ways," writes Wolff,

> the father's force had been surpassed by the son's; in one significant way, however, [Samuel] remained supreme. Nothing in Edward's life could match the emotional and spiritual vitality of Samuel Fowler Dickinson's original vision. Ultimately, Edward's life was pinched and compromised and unsatisfying: he never yielded himself entirely to any beckoning phantom of heroic grandeur, though he seems to have had many poignant glimpses of some glory that might have been; and the ghosts of this drama haunted the Dickinson family throughout the poet's lifetime.

If Emily Dickinson's paternal grandfather had been a man of almost poetic vision, her father was, by comparison, all prose—a proud and self-important man who took politics more seriously than culture and philosophy, his son (who would maintain the ascendancy of the Dickinson dynasty in Amherst) more seriously than his daughters. He was away on business much of the time, and even when he was at home, the Old Homestead was essentially "a house of isolation," in Wolff's words, "a house where the children's independence could be maintained only if easy intimacy and spontaneous affections were sacrificed." Emily viewed her father with both warmth and bitterness, genuine respect and ironic amusement; she once asked Higginson to explain to her "what home is"—as if she had never had one—yet could write to her brother, Austin, that "Home is a holy thing."

Yet for all her differences from her family she was, at bottom, very much a Dickinson. Her poetry—which unquestionably was far more important to her than anything else in life—was in a sense her version of the Great Dickinson Enterprise, a sort of obsessive visionary project in the tradition of her father's railroad and her grandfather's college; just as Samuel and Edward sought, by their grand acts of civic improvement, to lead Amherst into a better future, so Dickinson sought, by her poetry, to lead her readers to a clearer understanding of the truths of nature. She conceived of herself as having superior insight

into these truths—a conceit of which she might never have been ca-
pable had she not been the daughter and granddaughter of such asser-
tive and audacious men. (And a conceit, too, that distinguishes her
from the Transcendentalists, who felt that all men have equal access to
the ultimate truths and partake equally of what Emerson called the
Oversoul.) Among the many Dickinson poems that take poetry itself
as their theme, and thus help to illuminate her approach to the art,
perhaps the following is most famous:

> This was a Poet—It is That
> Distills amazing sense
> From ordinary Meanings—
> And Attar so immense
>
> From the familiar species
> That perished by the Door—
> We wonder it was not Ourselves
> Arrested it—before—
>
> Of Pictures, the Discloser—
> The Poet—it is He—
> Entitles Us—by Contrast—
> To ceaseless Poverty—
>
> Of Portion—so unconscious—
> The Robbing—could not harm—
> Himself—to Him—a Fortune—
> Exterior—to Time—

A poet, then, is a person who can see great truths in ordinary things,
truths that, upon disclosure, seem so obvious that we wonder why we
never noticed them ourselves; so conversant is she with the Infinite
that she may be said to live outside of time and beyond the material
concerns of this world, sufficient unto herself. Yet the truths she tells
should not be presented too bluntly, too directly. Ambiguity is a vir-
tue. "Tell all the Truth," she wrote,

> but tell it slant—
> Success in Circuit lies
> Too bright for our infirm Delight

The Truth's superb surprise

As Lightning to the Children eased
With explanation kind
The Truth must dazzle gradually
Or every man be blind—

The reference to blindness is significant. Words like *seeing* and *eyes* and *blind* fill her poems, and they rarely carry only their usual meanings. *Seeing* means perceiving the truths hidden in nature; the poet "sees," and she enables her readers to "see" as well.

Dickinson's definition of the poet is clarified in another poem:

Essential Oils—are wrung—
The Attar from the Rose
Be not expressed by Suns—alone—
It is the gift of Screws—

The General Rose—decay—
But this—in Lady's Drawer
Make Summer—When the Lady lie
In Ceaseless Rosemary—

This poem, perhaps better than any other, succinctly summarizes Dickinson's poetic theory. The lesson of its first stanza is that there are essential truths ("Oils") in nature that do not communicate themselves to most people automatically; rather, they must be distilled from nature, as attar is distilled ("expressed," or pressed out) in a screw press, by the conscious action of a person with a particular gift—that is, a poet. Yet, as the second stanza of the poem makes clear, the art of writing poetry is superior not only to that of the distiller of attar, but to that of the God Himself who created the rose. For a real rose will decay when summer passes; but a rose that exists in a poem—specifically, in *this* poem—will preserve summer forever, even if it remains in the poet's drawer, where no one will see it. The poet may be dead and buried, resting in a grave under a bed of rosemary, but because she has left the poem behind she will lie in the "Ceaseless Rosemary" of remembrance ("Rosemary: that's for remembrance"—*Hamlet*).

As she can turn out longer-lasting roses than God, so she can turn out two sunsets to his one (and more portable sunsets, for that matter):

I send Two Sunsets—
Day and I—in competition ran—
I finished Two—and several Stars—
While He—was making One—

His own was ampler—but as I
Was saying to a friend—
Mine—is the more convenient
To Carry in the Hand—

Yet if she can compare herself (favorably) to God in some poems, in others she characterizes the poet's role more modestly, even touchingly:

This is my letter to the World
That never wrote to Me—
The simple News that Nature told—
With tender Majesty

Her message is committed
To Hands I cannot see—
For love of Her—Sweet—countrymen—
Judge tenderly—of Me

Indeed, in the following poem, she presents the poet as a mere slave of nature, whose function is to supply the "oil" to light nature's "lamp":

The Lamp burns sure—within—
Tho' Serfs—supply the Oil—
It matters not the busy Wick—
At her phosphoric toil!

The Slave—forgets—to fill—
The Lamp—burns golden—on—
Unconscious that the oil is out—
As that the Slave—is gone.

Thus even after the poet ceases to write (and, for that matter, even after her death), the "Lamp" continues to "burn"—that is, the poem continues to speak to the world.

Through poetry, then, Dickinson sought to gain immortality. But it was a special sort of immortality: she would perish and her poems would live. The metaphor of lights and lamps and wicks reappears in another poem:

> The Poets light but Lamps—
> Themselves—go out—
> The Wicks they stimulate—
> If vital Light
>
> Inhere as do the Suns—
> Each Age a Lens
> Disseminating their
> Circumference—

The light of poetry, in other words, endures even longer than that of lamps; it is eternal, like the sun. The word *circumference*, it should be noted, is extremely important to Dickinson. In a letter to Higginson, she notes elliptically, "My Business is Circumference—." An examination of the poems in which the word appears suggests that she adopted it as a sort of umbrella term to designate at once all the varieties of infinitude—Immortality, Eternity, Heaven, the endless vastness of space and time—all of which seem incomprehensible to us, and seem at the same time to surround and overwhelm us, here in our finite world. In the above poem, Dickinson makes it plain that poetry itself partakes of circumference; as a poem passes from generation to generation, it presents the mortal beings who read it with a glimpse of eternal things.

Apparently, by telling Higginson that her business was circumference, Dickinson meant that she saw it as her function to mediate between the known and the unknown, between the limited and the limitless. She was fascinated by the notion that just beyond the homely things of this life lay a magnificent, mysterious, and immutable Hereafter; the idea of immortality obsessed her (it was, she wrote Higginson, "the Flood Subject"). One poem after another touches upon the contrasts between the brevity of life and the amplitude of historical time, between the humble stillness of the grave and the promised circumferential glory of the Afterlife. A poem that begins by contemplating the graves of anonymous housewives concludes as follows: "And yet, how still the Landscape stands! / How nonchalant the Hedge! / As if the 'Resurrection' / Were nothing very strange!" And another poem strikingly captures the antithesis between the passivity of death and the vibrancy with which life charges on through the centuries:

> Safe in their Alabaster Chambers—
> Untouched by Morning—
> And untouched by Noon—
> Lie the meek members of the Resurrection—
> Rafter of Satin—and Roof of Stone!
>
> Grand go the Years—in the Crescent—above them
> Worlds scoop their Arcs—
> And Firmaments—row—
> Diadems—drops—and Doges—surrender—
> Soundless as dots—on a Disc of Snow—

Since her role, as she saw it, was to describe the infinite world, and the only language available was one that had been designed to describe a finite world, Dickinson resorted to symbolism. In her poems, she assigned new (and not necessarily consistent) meanings—meanings associated with the passage of time, the journey from life to death, and the visionary power of the poet—to words like *morning, day, sunrise, bird, sun, flower, purple, glad, victory, kingdom, crown, monarch, jewel, gem, pearl, snow, sea,* and *music.* These double meanings are often based upon the Trinitarian doctrine of "type" and "antitype"—the belief, in other words, that certain phenomena on earth foreshadow events in the hereafter. The idea that the coming of morning prefigures the awakening on Judgment Day, for example, informs several Dickinson poems:

> Will there really be a "Morning"?
> Is there such a thing as "Day"?
> Could I see it from the mountains
> If I were as tall as they?
>
> Has it feet like Water lilies?
> Has it feathers like a Bird?
> Is it brought from famous countries

19

Of which I have never heard?

Oh some Scholar! Oh some Sailor!
Oh some Wise Man from the skies!
Please to tell a little Pilgrim
Where the place called "Morning" lies!

Here (as in many Dickinson poems) the Pilgrim is a traveller not from England to Plymouth, but from this world to the other. Similarly, in the following lines, the ascent of a soul into heaven is "coronation," while those who remain back on earth are "peasants": "Smiling back from Coronation / May be Luxury— / On the Heads that started with us— / Being's Peasantry—."

If Dickinson's poetry concerns itself with the paradox of life after death, its method, too, partakes heavily of paradox. Dickinson typically combines exotic diction and hyperbolic imagery with a severely spare style and a refreshingly colloquial tone; in most of her poems, she borrows the characteristic meter of Christian hymns ("common meter," with alternating four- and three-foot lines) in order to say things that many "good Christians" might consider blasphemous. She combines a romantic's love of beauty and truth and nature, and a natural gift for piety and devotion, with a sharp (though exquisitely controlled) sense of irony and a profound awareness of the inexcusable evil of which both men and their Maker are capable; she combines an Emersonian Transcendentalist's conviction that all the essential truths are contained in nature, ready to be perceived, with a poetics based upon the anti-Transcendentalist notion that only some men—poets—are capable of perceiving those truths. In an age when Americans were becoming less interested in religion, though they continued to pay it lip service, she combined a Puritan's seriousness about death and salvation with a truly subversive attitude toward Trinitarian orthodoxy. Indeed, she writes about man and God, sex and death, this world and the other, romantic love and Christian belief, in identical ways, and often in terms of one another, so that in some poems ("Wild Nights— wild nights," for instance, or "Title divine—is mine!") it is not clear— and perhaps is not supposed to be clear—whether her theme is religious fervor or sexual ecstasy. She personifies objects of nature and, conversely, represents people as natural objects; she describes simple objects with an unmistakable reverence for their innate holiness, and brings grand abstractions down to earth by talking about them as if they were people or places one could find in the Amherst town directory or on a map. Take, for example, the opening stanza of her most famous poem of all, in which the narrator—as in many Dickinson poems—speaks, as it were, from beyond the grave: "Because I could not stop for Death— / He kindly stopped for me— / The Carriage held but just Ourselves— / And Immortality."

To write such a poem was an act of imaginative liberation; it was to redefine God's world in her own way, to illuminate his mysteries by rendering them from her own perspective, in terms of the world she knew. This preoccupation with redefining explains why so many of her poems take the form of definitions:

> "Hope" is the thing with feathers—
> That perches in the soul—
>
> . . .
>
> Exultation is the going
> Of an inland soul to sea,
> Past the houses—past the headlands—
> Into deep Eternity—
>
> . . .
>
> Experience is the Angled Road
> Preferred against the Mind
> By—Paradox—the Mind itself—
> Presuming it to lead.
>
> . . .
>
> Publication—is the Auction
> Of the Mind of Man—

Her dictionary, to which Dickinson refers several times in her poetry and letters, gave her the accepted definitions of words; these poems presented her own definitions. She saw herself as audacious, and audacious she was: God provided the Bible, man her lexicon, and she in her poetry spat back her own versions of both. Many of her poems, as a matter of fact, are direct responses to, wholesale rewrites of, or witty elaborations upon texts both sacred and secular. "Essential Oils—are wrung—," for instance, was inspired by a sentence in Higginson's essay "Letter to a Young Contributor": "Literature is attar of roses, one drop distilled from a million blossoms."

Cynthia Griffin Wolff places great emphasis upon Dickinson's audacity. It is her thesis, in fact—and she rides it tirelessly—that Dickinson, though she never did convert, nonetheless consciously perceived poetry as a means of wrestling with God, on her own ground and on her own terms. (The theory compels Wolff to regard an obscure Dickinson poem, "A little East of Jordan," which is about Jacob's fateful wrestling match, as something of a touchstone for the entire *oeuvre*.) There is, to be sure, some truth in this characterization; many of Dickinson's poems, far from being conventionally reverent, often challenge God pugnaciously, describe him as cold and uncaring, and generally take his name in vain: "Of Course—I prayed— / And did God Care?" And doubtless Dickinson's dichotomous view of her father influenced the mixture of disparagement and reverence, love and rage, with which her poetry regards God. In Dickinson's poetry, as Wolff observes, "rage is entirely separated from 'my father, Edward Dickinson': it finds expression only in the poetry, directed toward a 'Father' in Heaven Whose face we never see and Whose voice we never hear." In a letter to Higginson, Dickinson writes of her father that "His Heart was pure and terrible and I think no other like it exists." She might well be speaking of God.

This is not to suggest, of course, that to Dickinson God was a rhetorical device, a stand-in for an earthly father against whom she could not bring herself openly to rebel. Far from it. Throughout her life, the deity was a searingly real presence to Dickinson. Though the power of Christ was fading elsewhere in the country, in Amherst the old-time religion remained strong; the Dickinson children attended church regularly, read the Bible daily, and, at the Amherst Academy, followed a curriculum of which religion formed the core. But churchgoing and Bible-reading and religious education were not considered sufficient. All good Trinitarians were expected, at some point (often, but not necessarily, as the result of a local religious revival or a death in the family), to undergo a "conversion experience" and tender a public "profession of faith." To convert, one had to accept one's subordination to God, had to set aside reason and logic and independent thought of all kinds when they conflicted with the Word of the Lord. The Biblical prototype (or, to use the Trinitarian jargon of the day, the "type") of the convert was Jacob, who had wrestled with the Lord at Peniel (Genesis 32:24, 26) and won "a royal estate" for his sons in return for his eventual submission. As Jacob had wrestled with God, so every Christian, it was felt, must face God (and his own conscience) in a confrontation, and emerge having lost his autonomy but having gained Life Everlasting. Yet, though virtually everyone around Dickinson eventually bowed down before the Lord, and though her letters demonstrate that she was sorely troubled by her own inability to do so—particularly during the Great Revival of 1850, in which her father and Lavinia were both converted—Dickinson never succumbed. Just as she chose never to take a husband, Dickinson refused to become the bride of Christ; if God would not give her immortality, then her poetry would do so.

For Dickinson was simply too much of an intellectual, a thinker, to be able to put aside independent thought and submit herself entirely to God. Certainly the idea of faith preoccupied her; but she battered her own faith with questions and doubts, and it continually wavered. She could write that "To lose one's faith—surpass / The loss of an Estate— / Because Estates can be / Replenished—faith cannot—," and could describe faith as "the Pierless [sic] Bridge / Supporting what We see / Unto the scene that We do not— / Too slender for the eye." But she could also write, with a fine, scientifically savvy wit, that

> "Faith" is a fine invention
> When Gentlemen can *see*—
> But *Microscopes* are prudent
> In an Emergency.

Ultimately, independence—from both man *and* God—seems to have been a necessary condition of life to Emily Dickinson. In a number of her poems she writes about self-sufficiency:

> On a Columnar Self—
> How ample to rely
> In Tumult—or Extremity—
> How good the Certainty
>
> That Lever cannot pry—
> And Wedge cannot divide
> Conviction—That Granitic Base—
> Though None be on our Side—
>
> Suffice Us—for a Crowd—
> Ourself—and Rectitude—
> And that Assembly—not far off

From furthest Spirit—God—

In her own way, Dickinson was as much of a lone trailblazer as any Western homesteader of her day, as dedicated a practitioner of self-reliance as any disciple of Emerson, as zealously monomaniacal a visionary as her grandfather Samuel.

Wolff's thesis, then, strikes one as valid, and relatively fresh. But the idea of Dickinson as a battler against God, in its broadest sense, is hardly original: William R. Sherwood, to cite just one critic, speaks of Dickinson's poetry as an act of self-assertion, "a movement of resistance against God and man, a campaign of guerrilla warfare, subversive and underground, that countered brute and blatant power with covert wit." And the picture of Dickinson that results from this concentration upon the idea of poet-as-wrestler is a distorted one. The poetry is simply more varied in its tone—and, specifically, in its attitude toward God and the Hereafter—than Wolff wants us to believe. Dickinson is alternately irreverent and worshipful, skeptical and secure in her belief; sometimes she bemoans her solitude, employing prison, cage, and coffin metaphors, and sometimes she celebrates it; she is by turns angry, joyful, afraid, ironic, morose. The Dickinson in whom Wolff would have us believe is tiresomely predictable in her concerns and monotonous in her approach.

Nor does it help that, after devoting 150-odd pages of this supposed critical biography to portraits of the poet's grandfather and parents, to discussions of life in nineteenth-century Amherst and of the theory and practice of Massachusetts Trinitarianism, and to the childhood and schooling of the poet, Wolff turns to Emily's adult life and makes it clear at once that she has no intention of going into the subject. "Dickinson's 'life,'" Wolff explains, "served her poetry precisely in its simplicity, in the *absence of significant event*." Therefore, "as the woman becomes Poet, biography must shift its principal focus from the person to that Voice of the verse, for it was in her poetry and not in the world that Emily Dickinson deliberately decided to 'live.'" Having thus justified her failure to chronicle the poet's life, Wolff proceeds, for most of the remaining three hundred or so pages of the book, to explicate one poem after another. This procedure might not be so unfortunate, except for the fact that Wolff chooses so many mediocre poems, leaves out so many important ones, and repeats herself so terribly much—and all because she is mainly interested in supporting her argument that Dickinson was the poet-as-wrestler.

Wolff's discussion of the poet's childhood, moreover—a discussion upon which her entire reading of Dickinson is based—consists largely of dubious and utterly speculative psychoanalytical theorizing. For instance, Wolff maintains (and her only real evidence is that Emily Norcross Dickinson was shy and uncommunicative with adults) that the poet's mother failed her during the child's "preverbal stage." "When mother and baby are able to engage successfully in nonverbal communication," Wolff writes, "the infant will derive immense emotional strengths from the process.... When this stage of communication is skillful and loving, the infant learns to feel good both about her mother and about her own emergent self, acquiring a fundamental sense that the universe is on the whole benign." The result is "a strong and confident sense of self, an ability to interact gracefully with others, and the conviction that the world is a good place." If the mother botches it, however, the child emerges with a weak sense of self, an inability to sustain relationships, a fear of separation from loved ones, and a sense that the world is "governed by an indifferent or hostile God." What's more, when the child learns to talk, he may construe the switch from visual to verbal communication as a "Fall into Language," "verbal discourse seeming a second-best alternative to some other, loosely defined, transcendent intimacy" that he has never been able to achieve—with the result that he may nostalgically "overvalue *seeing* (as opposed to saying)." Strangely enough, however, "just because language has been forced to perform so critical a task in the early life of such an infant, verbal formulations may also seem to have a unique sovereignty. No Power will compare to the Power of the Word." To be sure, this hypothetical case history seems to jibe well enough with the known facts of Dickinson's life; but there are simply too many *unknown* facts about Dickinson's life to permit such an analysis. Wolff concludes her foray into infant psychology by saying that it was as a result of Dickinson's "Fall into Language" that "words became her refuge and her one great love." But what about the poets whose mothers did not deprive them of affection, and who grew to love words anyway? And what if Dickinson's mother had not deprived her of love (assuming that Wolff is right about this)—would Dickinson never have become a poet?

Sometimes it seems as if the dissemination of inane ideas in nearly self-parodic jargon is Wolff's specialty: "In sum, [Dickinson] wanted to make the terms of existence that were meaningful to the Voice of her poetry relevant to the terms of existence by which her readers defined their own lives—whoever those readers might be, in no matter what time or place. And the miracle is, she succeeded." Frequently, when she is speaking of Dickinson's wrestling match with the Lord, Wolff's rhetoric is overheated. She describes the poet as "fashion[ing] [a] destiny of heroic conquest for herself," of "engag[ing] in an Armageddon of her own making against the God of death," with "Kingdom, Glory, and above all Power" as her "wagers." Sometimes Wolff's view of Dickinson is so skewed that one feels as if one has stumbled into the wrong seminar:

> [It] was grandeur, only grandeur—and Power—that Dickinson wanted. She wanted to be America's Representative Voice, and she wanted that Voice to challenge God Himself and wrestle for dominion. Yet even Emerson, in his greeting to Whitman, had welcomed the younger poet to a "great *career*." By the mid-nineteenth century, poets had to content themselves with precisely this kind of success—circumscribed and limited to this world. What would it have meant to Emily Dickinson to be merely a published poet, perhaps even a *minor* published poet? With the vision of transcendent heroism that she had formulated, how could Emily Dickinson settle for a "career"?

Clearly Wolff is misreading here, is interpreting Dickinson's rhetoric about poetry and immortality in too literal-minded a manner. Certainly Dickinson did not want to be America's Representative Voice in the way that Whitman did; rather, she wanted to be a voice of nature, indifferent to international boundaries and historical divisions.

In truth, it is Wolff, not Dickinson, who is preoccupied with the supposed ugliness of materialism and careerism in late nineteenth-century America. She has opinions about America's history and culture and wants us to believe that Dickinson felt the same way she does. She suggests more than once, for example, that in the difference between Samuel Dickinson's visionary faith and Edward and Austin's prosaic concern with business and politics, Emily Dickinson must have seen an emblem of a major nineteenth-century shift for the worse in American character. The only certainty here, of course, is that *Wolff* sees such a parallel and such a shift—which she attributes, one might add, to the fading of religious enthusiasm and the advent of the Gilded Age. She describes mid-to-late-nineteenth-century America as "a diminished thing" (not only using the phrase from Frost's "The Oven Bird," but also borrowing the poem's title for her prologue), and says—in what is patently a projection of her own romantically conceived political opinions onto her subject—that "It was the end of our glory and the beginning of our sorrow that Emily Dickinson could see in Amherst, Massachusetts, during those years surrounding our Civil War." But Wolff seems a bit inconsistent on this topic, ridiculing Edward Dickinson on one page for not being bold enough to become a *really* big business success, and faulting him on the next page for "driving hard bargains and living ostentatiously." And though she is patently charmed by the mythic glory of Samuel Dickinson's fervent Christianity, she seems to find the religion itself inimical.

Finally, and perhaps most oddly of all, Wolff comes across as blaming Edward Dickinson for the "subordination" of woman prior to the age of Gloria Steinem. After quoting his view that the education of men and women should be based upon an assumption of equal ability as well as upon a recognition of their different roles in society, Wolff gripes: "If it is 'best' to assume that in the 'natural abilities' women *are* 'exactly equal' to men, why ought their 'sphere' be 'different from that of men'?" A valid question, to be sure, but what is it doing in a biography of Emily Dickinson?

But then, of course, this 638-page tome is not really a biography of Dickinson; rather, it is a work of literary criticism—part Freudian, part biographical, part feminist, part archetypal—which is sometimes illuminating and intelligent and often foolish. Perhaps its fundamental defect is that Wolff is not enchanted by Dickinson so much as she is enchanted by an idea about Dickinson. One cannot help but wonder what Emily Dickinson herself—who dealt in tiny poems about great truths—would have made of this bulky farrago of misconceptions.

JANUARY 1987

H.D.: MOTHER OF US ALL?

If the father of modern American poetry was Ezra Pound, its mother was Hilda Doolittle, and its place of birth—in a rare real-life instance of poetic rightness—was English poetry's glorious crypt, the British Museum. The time was late in 1912. The tall, striking, introspective (though not particularly intellectual) Miss Doolittle had offered to bring some of her new poems to the Museum so that Mr. Pound, who at the age of twenty-seven was already a notorious figure in London's literary underworld, might pass judgment on them.

Doolittle was twenty-six, and a complete nobody. Indeed, her only claim to fame was that, years ago, when she had been a sweet young slip of a thing at Bryn Mawr, Pound (then William Carlos Williams's roomie at the University of Pennsylvania) had been her fiancé. On Hilda's part, at least, it was real love. The crude and charismatic Pound had played Heathcliff to her Cathy. Utterly earthy and living and *real*, he had breathed raw humanity into her ultramundane household (Father Doolittle was a University of Pennsylvania astronomer, Mother Doolittle a pious Moravian). Hilda's announcement that she intended to marry her post-Byronic avant-garde neo-pre-Raphaelite made her parents frantic. But they needn't have worried: Pound had other plans. Or, rather, he had no plans, including marital ones; he went where his instincts drove him. In this case they drove him straight out of his engagement to Hilda and into the transatlantic literary swim. Hilda, however, did not give up. She followed him to New York. She followed him to London. With the financial backing of her philistine father, she rejected philistinism forever and became a bohemian, just like Ezra. He wrote poems, so she wrote poems. And finally, on that day in 1912, approximately a year after she had pursued him to the capital of Empire, she showed them to him. The first one he looked at—and the one that did it, according to legend—was "Hermes of the Ways," which begins as follows:

The hard sand breaks,
and the grains of it
are clear as wine.

Far off over the leagues of it,
the wind,
playing on the wide shore,
piles little ridges,
and the great waves
break over it.

But more than the many-foamed ways
of the sea,
I know him
of the triple path-ways,
Hermes,
who awaits.

Dubious,
facing three ways,
welcoming wayfarers,
he whom the sea-orchard
shelters from the west,
from the east
weathers sea-wind;
fronts the great dunes.

Wind rushes
over the dunes,
and the coarse, salt-crusted grass
answers.

Heu,
it whips round my ankles!

The absorption in a natural world devoid of humans (except, natu-
rally, for the author) and free of human conflict; the seashore setting;
the fascination with the awesome physical power of nature; the
Homeric epithets ("many-foamed," "salt-crusted") and Olympian

name-dropping; the liberal drawing upon a severely (and intention-
ally) limited working vocabulary (her short list: *sea, stream, wind, wave,
sand, wine, grass, rose, flower, rock, stem, leaf, red, pink, white, violet*)—all
are prime characteristics of the *oeuvre* of which "Hermes of the Ways"
constitutes the beginning.

These were not, however, the characteristics that mattered to
Pound. What struck him, rather, when he read this and Hilda's other
poems, was their brevity, their directness, and their natural rhythm. In
those first moments, the three famous principles of Imagism, which he
later set down in an essay in *Poetry*, must already have begun forming
in his mind:

> 1. Direct treatment of the "thing" whether subjective or ob-
> jective.
> 2. To use absolutely no word that does not contribute to the
> presentation.
> 3. As regarding rhythm: to compose in the sequence of the
> musical phrase, not in sequence of a metronome.

Suddenly, Pound had a literary movement, and he had a disciple. And
who could have been a better one? Hilda was devoted to him, com-
pletely willing to be made an example of whatever theory he might
come up with, willing even to change her poems around to fit his theory
better. Best of all, she had no ideas of her own to muck things up. You
could count the ideas in her poems on one finger. "Sea rose," for ex-
ample, was a paean to a tough flower able to withstand the assaults of
a rough world.

> Rose, harsh rose,
> marred and with stint of petals,
> meager flower, thin,
> sparse of leaf,
>
> more precious
> than a wet rose
> single on a stem—
> you are caught in the drift.
>
> Stunted, with small leaf,
> you are flung on the sand,

lected its works in a magazine, *The Egoist*, edited by Pound and Aldington, and an anthology, *Des Imagistes*. And that, as it happens, was pretty much that. Before the spring was over, Pound had left H.D. at the altar of Imagism as he had left her previous incarnation, poor old Hilda, at the altar of marriage; and he had founded another poetic movement, Vorticism (which, incidentally, didn't even make it through the summer). The position of patron of Imagism passed to Miss Lowell, the corpulent heiress from Boston whom H.D. called "the hippopoetess"; the position of man in H.D.'s life passed to Aldington, who (on orders, one half suspects, from Pound) had married her in the fall of 1913. Under Lowell, the movement (which a disgruntled Pound claimed had degenerated into a flabby, self-indulgent "Amygism") lasted a couple more years, then rolled over and died. The Imagist poem was simply too restricted a form to capture the interest of any good, original poet (or good, original reader, for that matter) for very long. As for the Aldington union, it didn't last much longer. Although the two stayed legally married until 1938, and H.D. signed herself "Mrs. Hilda Aldington" until her death in 1961, the two never lived together after 1919.

Aldington's place in H.D.'s life was taken by a woman who was as practical, tough, independent, intellectual, political, and businesslike as H.D. was not. Like H.D., she published (for she too was a writer) under a name which was not her natural one. The difference, however, was that Bryher (born Winifred Ellerman, daughter of one of the richest men in England) had made up her own name, and for her own reasons. H.D. didn't love Bryher, wasn't even attracted to her, but because Bryher—with her take-charge attitude, her efficiency, her devotion to H.D., and her huge fortune—made life very easy, H.D. stayed with her for a while. Forty-three years, to be exact. During these decades, H.D. wrote a number of books, most of them volumes of autobiographical prose that she called novels and that were published by Bryher. (She seems to have been the financial angel behind half the small literary presses functioning in Europe between the wars.)

Reading through these uniformly slack, sloppy, self-indulgent books one realizes that this most celebrated practitioner of the narrowest of poetic forms—"our gracious Muse, our cynosure and the peak of our achievement," Ford Madox Ford called her in his 1930 *Imagist Anthology*—was possessed of an extremely limited gift. Limited by what? Ironically, by the same dogged non-intellectuality that made her a successful Imagist. H.D. liked nothing better than an op-

portunity not to cerebrate, and it is largely because of this that she was
so good at being an Imagist and so bad at being anything else. The sad
fact is that, freed of the discipline of Pound and his movement, H.D.
grew lazy. Her work lost its tightness, its control, its rhythm, and often
descended into banal self-parody:

> O which of the gifts of the gods
> is the best gift?
> this,
> this,
> this,
> this;
> escape
> from the power of the hunting pack
> and to know that wisdom is best
> and beauty
> sheer holiness.

But all this doesn't matter to Barbara Guest, whose unrelenting focus
in her biography, *Herself Defined: The Poet H.D. and Her World*,[2] is on
H.D.'s relationship with Bryher and the almost diary-like prose works
that grew out of that union. So strong is this emphasis that the book is,
by Guest's own admission, almost a double biography, with H.D.'s
involvement in a handful of cheap, obscure films that Bryher produced
in the Twenties receiving as much attention as her involvement in
Imagism. *Herself Defined* is clearly a labor of love—but just as clearly,
the object of love is not H.D.'s work, nor even her real inner life. Rather,
what Guest is in love with is the idea of H.D. and Bryher's seemingly
perfect little *ménage*. She is in love, that is, with an image. She is
absolutely charmed for example, by H.D.'s endless, neurotic "I-am-
an-ancient-Greek" conceit, which was a major facet not only of her
poetry but of her day-to-day life. H.D. called herself "Dryad." Aldington
was her Roman. Havelock Ellis was "Chiron" (after Achilles's teacher).
And so on. Even when she was nearly dead with pneumonia, H.D.
managed to keep up the game: "If I could walk to Delphi," she groaned
to Bryher, "I should be healed." Guest never pauses in her apparent

---

[2]*Herself Defined: The Poet H.D. and Her World*, by Barbara Guest; Doubleday, 360
pages, $18.95.

admiration of this pretentious nonsense to attempt even the slightest explanation of it. She acknowledges, to be sure, that H.D. "was fond of making entrances" and that such writers as Louis Wilkinson and John Cournos found her "a natural target for satire." But Guest—in a highly characteristic failure to say anything negative about H.D. without smothering it in qualifications—decides that such satires "are tributes to the power of H.D.'s personality. She had charisma, a special ability to project." That Guest is so intrigued by this charisma, and so uninterested in what it masked, is a source of frustration throughout *Herself Defined*. For we never feel, while reading this book, that Guest has even come close to defining H.D. (unless we believe, with Vonnegut, that "we are what we pretend to be"). Unfortunately, to Guest's mind, her duty as a biographer of H.D. is not to explain but to celebrate, not to understand but to pay homage, not to leap over the wall of willful mystery surrounding her subject but simply to worship at it. Indeed, one senses at times that Guest would consider it a betrayal of her idol to make that leap.

Thus the reader of *Herself Defined* is constantly in the position of being surprised. One has no inkling that Bryher might be living on the edge until Guest mentions a 1920 suicide attempt. One has no inkling that H.D. might be living on the edge until Guest dutifully reports, "Then came H.D.'s mental breakdown...." To give Guest her due, she does attempt to account for this event, but the explanation, such as it is, comes as an afterthought. "There is no written evidence of events leading up to the breakdown," she writes; "however, interpretations can be drawn from her writing. It is apparent that H.D. had overextended herself...." Guest goes on to explain later that H.D.'s mounting euphoria and increasing participation in séances, both previously discussed and buried amid a barrage of other, irrelevant matters, may well have marked the approach of a psychological crisis. To mention such facts and not suggest their possible significance until several pages—or even chapters—later, when they have been completely forgotten, is spectacularly ineffective biographical writing. Such a procedure, unhappily, is something of a habit with Guest, whose favorite phrase, one begins to believe after a while, is "This reveals that...." Guest does not seem to have any rational system of selecting facts; she presents the details of H.D.'s life haphazardly, routinely paying more attention to the trivial than to the crucial, and not even making it clear most of the time which is which. She forgets, for example, to mention that H.D. was being neglected on the European poetry scene—a rather important piece of information—until she tells us that H.D.'s appearance in Bryher's magazine *Life and Letters Today* was intended to counteract this neglect.

As all of this might suggest, *Herself Defined* is an incredibly confused piece of work. Guest does not tell us about the childhood of H.D.'s daughter Perdita until near the end of the book, when Perdita has already reached adulthood. We do not learn until page 247—it should have come a hundred pages earlier—that "it may even have been Yeats who first encouraged H.D.'s interest and reliance on horoscopes, her gropings into the occult." Not until after the section of the book covering World War I do we begin to hear how emotionally devastated H.D. was by the war. And there are some gaps Guest never does fill in. One will not learn from *Herself Defined*, for example, how H.D. and Aldington came to be an item, or how she managed to pull off what Guest describes as a complete recovery from her nervous breakdown. Oddly enough, if answers to such questions as these are omitted from the book, some facts are trotted out again and again. Guest tells us more than once, for instance, that H.D. "rarely expressed herself on the subject of other poets"; that there were "several H.D.s: the schoolgirl giggling with her friend, the faun startled in a brake, the priestess of letters" (and once, in this case, is plenty); that "H.D. was a powerful presence"; that H.D. was rich but thought of herself as impoverished; that H.D.'s friends formed something of "a deferential family circle" and that she "wished to maintain her position as a solitaire with her solitude inviolate, yet with friends within calling distance." Most frequent of all, perhaps, are Guest's out-of-the-blue litanies of praise for the steadfastness of "Bryher, the firmest of foundations." One has the sense sometimes that Guest is lost at sea in this book and must repeat these formulas—H.D.'s solitariness, Bryher's devotion—in order to regain her bearing.

Whether or not Guest is lost at sea, the reader certainly is. One never feels oneself to be witnessing the growth of H.D.; one never (as in the best biographies) feels the subject changing, undergoing the subtle shifts that occur over the course of years. Guest takes one around H.D. in the manner of a tour guide who leads one breathlessly from one room of a great mansion to another, never letting one pause to look around and take one's bearings, never explaining which room is which and who inhabits it and what its history is, but simply spewing out random facts about whatever happens to catch her eye. This may well be meant as a reaction against every ponderous, time-anchored biography ever written; but it just doesn't work. Guest has collected the parts of a puzzle but has not fitted them together—she has only handed them to the reader in a box.

Worst of all, the puzzle pieces aren't even well wrought. Reading *Herself Defined*, one continually feels the urge to rewrite Guest's prose:

> *Beowulf* [a book by Bryher] is delightful. It brings out the human suffering amid the vivid scenes of wartime; above all, it is a story of survival, just as H.D.'s *Walls* survived. Bryher had summoned all her knowledge of London wartime street life to incorporate in this book, and she does it simply and sparsely, but there is a scent of the common smell of the devastation of London and the desperate attempts of the ordinary people to survive.

Guest says *infers* at least twice when she means *implies*; she puts whole sentences in italics for dubious reasons; her punctuation is often bizarre. And her affection for the exclamation point makes the book read, in places, like copy for a tabloid:

> [H.D.'s grandfather] proceeded in 1852, a year before H.D.'s mother's birth, to invent a machine to manufacture paper bags!

> William Carlos Williams...sent her an acrostic for her birthday, although neglecting the actual birthdate!

> Looking around the room at his other friends there to greet him, Hilda guessed that one of them was a baronet!

> Harriet Weaver..."loved and admired people whose gifts were in some sense or other, for self-celebration." This would indeed explain her attraction to Ezra Pound!

> Just as she had depended on Pound the first years in England, so she turned to Cournos when the war separated her from Richard, whom she had turned to upon the "desertion" of Pound!

The book is a medley of comments on the American West together with Bryher's ideas on education; its heroine is Marianne Moore!

She also had become very India-conscious, and after visiting Campione on the lake was under the illusion that the town of nesting villas was like a Ganges village!

Sometimes Guest seems to be modeling her style on that of H.D., whose prose is typically rough, rambling, and slightly hysterical. At other times Guest's prose has the precise, affected quality of H.D.'s poetry. In her preface, for example, she writes that "I am grateful for those moments when H.D. with a blithe generosity permitted me to stumble on her rituals, her magic stones." (Guest is not the first to ape her idol's style; a predecessor in the field of H.D. studies, Susan Stanford Friedman, writes in the preface to her 1981 book *Psyche Reborn* of "the emergence of *Psyche Reborn* from the chrysalis of my own life.") It is interesting to observe that Guest's prose is disorganized in the same way that H.D.'s is. Like *Herself Defined*, H.D.'s *End to Torment*, a memoir of Pound, shifts constantly, and nervously, from year to year, apparently dictated by nothing except the idle meanderings of the author's memory. One senses that both H.D. and Guest are more interested in creating something arresting than something truly magnificent, more concerned with style than substance. When H.D.'s book *Bid Me To Live* first appeared, *Newsweek*'s reviewer described it as a piece of "quivering impressionistic prose." The same description could, one supposes, be applied fairly to Guest's book, only the prose quivers altogether too much, and the impressions never come into focus.

MARCH 1984

THE POETIC LEGACY OF
WILLIAM CARLOS WILLIAMS

So conscious are we nowadays of the extraordinary influence upon postmodern American poetry of William Carlos Williams—the second and concluding volume of whose collected poems has now been published—that it can be easy to forget that, during the heyday of the modernist movement, Williams was widely regarded as, at best, a second-tier figure.[1] Even Ezra Pound, who had known Williams since their college days and had helped secure publication for much of the poet-physician's early work, made it clear (to Williams's chagrin) that his old friend's poetic career interested him less than that of Pound's fellow expatriate T.S. Eliot. Indeed, it was not until the waning years of the modernist era—1937, to be exact—that James Laughlin and New Directions entered Williams's life, finally providing him with a steady publisher and effective distribution, and thus offering him some hope, at least, of a large audience for his verse. And it was not until the Forties and Fifties, when he began to win the allegiance of a widely influential younger generation of poets—whose aesthetic ideas were, in many instances, dramatically at odds with those of Williams's modernist confreres—that his name unquestionably joined those of Eliot and Pound in the pantheon of first-rank modern American poets.

And yet even to juxtapose his name with that of T.S. Eliot is to be reminded how utterly different Williams was from the man who, during both their lifetimes, came to be regarded as the very personification of literary modernism. If Eliot expressed his subtle, sophisticated philosophy of modernism in a prose that was crafted with rare precision and meticulousness, Williams proffered essentially uncomplicated ideas about poetry in a prose whose wordiness and lack of rigor often made those ideas seem confusing and contradictory. If Eliot saw mod-

---

[1] *The Collected Poems of William Carlos Williams*, edited by A. Walton Litz and Christopher MacGowan; New Directions. Volume I (1909-1939), 579 pages, $35; Volume II (1939-1962), 553 pages, $37.

ernism as a means of re-affirming literary tradition and of asserting the value of civilization, Williams (though a suburban homeowner and a family man) saw himself as a primitive, an aesthetic rebel. If Eliot, in his poetry, labored over lines that were more dense, allusive, comprehensive, and symbolic than anything in living memory, Williams churned out poems that were deliberately flat, talky, trivial, and naturalistic. If Eliot was supremely conscious of the weight of the past, Williams dwelled upon the evanescent moment. If Eliot was the intellectual, exalting the value of the mind, Williams was the anti-intellectual, exalting the values of the heart and flesh and muscle, and calling for "no ideas but in things." If Eliot was High Church, Williams was an observer of the Common Man. If, finally, Eliot identified himself unashamedly with *literature*, Williams despised the word and all that it connoted. Each in his own way sought to liberate poetry from late Victorian sentimentality, banality, and degraded romanticism; to that extent they were allied in the modernist cause. But the directions in which they sought to take twentieth-century poetry were strikingly divergent.

There was one other important distinction between them. Eliot, born into a Protestant St. Louis family that had been in America for two centuries, left America, wrote polyglot verse, and turned himself into the consummate Englishman. Williams—whose parents had lived in Puerto Rico, whose father was English, and whose French-speaking Catholic mother was descended from Basques and Dutch Jews—not only remained in America during the expatriate days of the 1920s but made Americanness and the American language the very foundation of his poetic principles. Americans, Williams argued, spoke a different language from the English—a language with its own vocabulary, rhythms, and inflections—and should therefore write a different poetry. He maintained in particular that the trappings of traditional form—rhyme, meter—were inappropriate to America in the twentieth century. "I say we are through with the iambic pentameter as presently conceived," he declared in a 1948 lecture, "through with the measured quatrain, the staid concatenations of sounds in the usual stanza, the sonnet." As he saw it, modern American poets should not work patiently to make a poem as distant, lean, and polished as possible (as Eliot and the New Critics might have suggested) but should rather regard it as a "field of action." Eliot's austere verses, Williams insisted, reflect a perverse, reactionary conviction that poetry "increases in virtue as it is removed from contact with a vulgar world"; Williams proposed that American poetry should, on the contrary, be close to the ground, democratic, "local." It was wrong, therefore, for American poets to remove themselves from their native soil: in order to write truly American poems, they had to live in America, among Americans.

Williams set himself, in short, in direct opposition to the man from St. Louis. Indeed, as Paul Marini observes in his exhaustive, reverent 1981 biography *William Carlos Williams: A New World Naked*, Eliot was "Williams' bete noir [*sic*], Williams' most celebrated literary antagonist. It was a battle in which Williams was consistently on the offense and in which Eliot, from his established vantage, chose simply to ignore Williams—at least publicly." To read Mariani's biography is to recognize that Williams's hostility toward Eliot, and his well-nigh fanatical insistence that modern American poetry should reject old forms and rhythms (a notion that has, of course, become strongly ingrained in the minds of succeeding generations of American poets), was largely a defense mechanism—in part a means of Freudian rebellion against his English father, and in part a means of adjusting psychologically to his own feeling of neglect by his expatriate colleagues, his sense of isolation in his hometown of Rutherford, New Jersey, and his deep resentment of the attention and praise accorded to Eliot by Pound (and, later, by the entire civilized world). To read Mariani is to appreciate the truth of Pound's observation, in a letter of the early Twenties, that if Williams did not join the exodus to Europe it was not because of any theory about American poetry but because he didn't have the nerve to leave home.

For the fact is that Williams was never a reckless, adventurous spirit, like Pound; nor could he ever have utterly transformed himself, as Eliot did. Born in 1883, Williams was a timid and naïve young man who spent many years in the shadow of his younger brother Ed, an architect and winner of the Prix de Rome; it was, indeed, his beloved Charlotte Herman's preference for Ed that prompted the twenty-five-year-old Williams to propose marriage to Charlotte's less attractive sister, Florence (Floss), with whom he would live, for a full half-century, in the town of his birth. The young Williams comes across in Mariani's pages—and in those of Williams's own slapdash, episodic *Autobiography* (1951)—as good-natured but pathetic, devoted to poetry but lacking a sense of identity, confused and directionless and desperate for guidance. Though he had his share of innate ambition, aggression, and rebelliousness, his mother's nearly fanatical moral idealism seems to have led him, as a young man, to adopt standards of virtue that succeeded only in immobilizing him. Reading about his youth, one can picture his rebelliousness building up inside him, awaiting an outlet; reading about his adult life, one wonders at its conspicuous monotony and conventionality: how could this numbingly settled middle-class life have been led by so rebellious a poet?

Yet if Williams was so rebellious in his poetry, perhaps it was, in large part, because poetry was the only realm in which he could bring himself to be audacious, to perform a major act of will. It was poetry, in other words, that provided a lifelong escape valve for Williams's otherwise powerfully suppressed rebellious instincts. And it was a college friend two years his junior who first showed him the way. Soon after entering the medical school at the University of Pennsylvania, the nineteen-year-old Williams met a flamboyant, egocentric seventeen-year-old sophomore named Ezra Pound, who was already full of radical, outrageous ideas about poetry. Pound was eager to recruit disciples, and he found one in Williams; almost overnight, Pound became Williams's mentor. For the next several years, to be sure, Williams continued to write in traditional forms: he spent years polishing a breathtakingly bad medieval epic in blank verse, and his first, privately published book, *Poems* (which he compiled in 1909, soon after receiving from London a copy of Pound's debut volume, *A Lume Spento*), was a collection of insipid late-Victorian verses in rhyming couplets and the like ("Innocence can never perish; / Blooms as fair in looks that cherish / Dim remembrance of the days / When life was young..."). But when Pound—who by then was in London, working for William Butler Yeats—informed him that this would not do, and advised him to read Yeats, Browning, Thompson, Swinburne, and Rossetti, the twenty-five-year-old Williams obediently changed direction. Or, at least, began to. Williams's next book, *The Tempers*—issued in 1913 by Pound's own London publisher, Elkin Mathews—was not all that Pound wanted it to be, and when he reviewed it for *The New Freewoman* he praised Williams more for his "vigour" than for his artistry. But Williams, who would become as zealous a modernist as he had once been a moralist, was doing his best to please his mentor: in these poems he solemnly imitates Pound's own imitations of that period, variously mimicking Pound as Elizabethan ("Lady of dusk-wood fastnesses, / Thou art my Lady..."), Pound as Browning ("Miserly, is the best description of that poor fool / Who holds Lancelot to have been a morose fellow…"), and Pound's protégé H.D. as ancient Greek ("O, prayers in the dark! / O, incense to Poseidon! / Calm in Atlantis").

After *The Tempers*, Williams might conceivably have developed in any direction. It was doubtless, to a considerable degree, the early poetry of T.S. Eliot—whom Pound met, and began to promote tirelessly, sometime between *The Tempers* and Williams's next book, *Al Que Quiere!* (1917)—that helped Williams to determine the precise course his development did take. From the beginning, the salient fact about Pound's fair-haired boy from St. Louis was that he was *literary*: while Williams had been studying pediatrics and obstetrics, the future author of *The Waste Land* had been studying philosophy and languages, reading Laforgue and Dante and the Metaphysical poets, and taking courses taught by Irving Babbitt and Henri Bergson. He had learned to despise Romanticism, which celebrated the raw, untutored, and spontaneous, and to admire reason and discipline; even such early Eliot poems as "La Figlia che Piange" mirror their author's belief that the more intelligent a modern poet was, the better, and that it was good for poems to reflect subtlety of thought, breadth of knowledge, and a thorough acquaintance with the classics. But though most of Eliot's literary contemporaries would gradually come to accept this judgment—and though an entire generation of poets, on both sides of the Atlantic, would labor to produce verses that satisfied Eliot's criteria—Williams patently knew from the start that he could never hold his own against Eliot on such grounds. "Since I cannot compete with him in knowledge of philosophy," he wrote in a surprisingly candid letter of the late Twenties, "nor even technical knowledge of the conned examples of English poetry which he seems to know so well—what is left for me but to fall back on words?" To fall back, that is, on a species of modern poetry which eliminated all the things Eliot did better than Williams, a poetry characterized by plain, flat, and even (in Wallace Stevens's phrase) "anti-poetic" language. A poetry, in short, utterly antithetical to that of T.S. Eliot.

The beauty part was that Pound—whom Williams would call "our greatest and rightest poet," and whose eccentric epistolary style he often imitated in his own missives—had already identified such a species. In 1912 Pound had founded the Imagist school of poetry, and (with H.D. and Richard Aldington) had set forth three supreme poetic principles: directness, concision, and natural rhythm. A good Imagist poem—Pound held up his two-line "In a Station of the Metro" as an example ("The apparition of these faces in the crowd; / Petals on a wet, black bough")—was a short, tightly focused representation of a single sensual experience; it was common for such poems to have a vaguely Oriental or Hellenic flavor and metaphorically to equate human images with natural ones. To be sure, Pound's Imagist phase didn't last long; within two years his poetry had changed drastically, and though he would continue to write for another half-century he would never again produce an Imagist poem. Brief though it was, however, it had been during this phase that Pound's manner was at its furthest remove from that of T.S. Eliot. Given Williams's fervent admiration for Pound and his loathing for Eliot, it is not surprising that Williams made Imagism the *point d'appui* in his quest for a mature style. One thing seems relatively certain: if Eliot, in the words of an astonished Pound, had "modernized himself *on his own*," Pound's influence played a crucial role in Williams's development into a modernist poet.

There were, of course, other influences in these early years. The New York Armory Show of 1913, for instance, brought to America the paintings of many modern artists—including Picasso, Braque, and Duchamp—whose work would later be described as influential upon Williams's poetry; during World War One, moreover, Williams became one of a group of artists and writers associated with the avant-garde New York literary magazine *Others*, among them Wallace Stevens, Marianne Moore, Maxwell Bodenheim, and Alfred Kreymborg. But Pound's Imagist phase remained the foundation of Williams's verse. *Sour Grapes* (1921) consists largely of modest, Imagist-style poems in which unsentimental images of man and nature are brought together. "Spring" is all of two lines long: "O my grey hairs! / You are truly white as plum blossoms." The collection also contains, however, at least one poem that belongs to what Williams's admirers might call his major phase, "The Great Figure":

> Among the rain
> and lights
> I saw the figure 5
> in gold
> on a red
> firetruck
> moving
> tense

unheeded
to gong clangs
siren howls
and wheels rumbling
through the dark city.

Williams tells the story behind this poem (which inspired Charles Demuth's 1928 painting *I Saw the Figure 5 in Gold*) in the *Autobiography*. Walking one summer day down West Fifteenth Street in Manhattan, headed for the painter Marsden Hartley's studio, Williams "heard a great clatter of bells and the roar of a fire engine passing the end of the street down Ninth Avenue. I turned just in time to see a golden figure 5 on a red background flash by. The impression was so sudden and forceful that I took a piece of paper out of my pocket and wrote a short poem about it." "The Great Figure" is a typical major-phase Williams poem: a quickly scribbled description of a brief experience. Though its roots are in Imagism, this poem abandons the timeless natural subjects, the refined style, and the slightly stylized tone typical of Imagism for the purpose of rendering in plain, telegraphic language a "sudden and forceful" impression of a modern, urban, technological phenomenon. It is one of many familiar poems in which Williams does not shrink from, but rather observes carefully, celebrates, and expresses a childlike wonder at, the mechanical, the grubby, the vulgar, the trivial, the homely, the banal, or the grossly physical. One thinks, for instance, of "The Attic Which is Desire:" (1930), in which the word *SODA* is printed vertically, surrounded by asterisks, as a means of representing a neon sign visible from Williams's attic window; of "Poem" (1930), which offers a step-by-step description of a cat climbing "over / the top of / the jamcloset"; of "This is Just to Say" (1934), in which Williams apologizes to Floss for eating some plums she had left in the icebox; of "To a Poor Old Woman" (1935), a description of a woman on the street, enjoying a bag of plums ("They taste good to her / They taste good / to her. They taste / good to her"); and of "Between Walls" (1938):

the back wings
of the

hospital where

nothing

will grow lie
cinders

in which shine
the broken

pieces of a green
bottle

As an obstetrician and pediatrician to the lower and middle classes, moreover, Williams was in a position to observe ordinary Americans at close range and in their most natural state; he had an ear for the way these people talked, and some of his more effective poems are, in large part, transcriptions of their conversation. A typical example (though it is based on the testimony not of a patient but of a nurse) is "The Raper from Passeneck," first collected in *An Early Martyr and Other Poems* (1935):

...if I get a
venereal infection out of this
I won't be treated.

I refuse. You'll find me dead in bed
first. Why not? That's
the way she spoke,

I wish I could shoot him. How would
you like to know a murderer?
I may do it.

I'll know by the end of this week.
I wouldn't scream. I bit him
several times

but he was too strong for me.
I can't yet understand it. I don't
faint so easily.

When I came to myself and realized
what had happened all I could do
was to curse

and call him every vile name I could
think of. I was so glad
to be taken home.

I suppose it's my mind—the fear of
infection. I'd rather a million times
have been got pregnant.

But it's the foulness of it can't
be cured. And hatred, hatred of all men
—and disgust.

Such poems as this benefit from Williams's willingness to contemplate less than uplifting varieties of experience. In some Williams poems, however, the graphic naturalism seems gratuitous. Frequently he seems to take a small boy's delight in Anglo-Saxon words for bodily functions, writing in "Turkey in the Straw" (1950), for instance, that "On my 65th birthday / I kissed her [Floss] while she pissed." In a lesser known poem, "April Is the Saddest Month" (1948)—whose title, needless to say, is a variation on the first line of *The Waste Land*—Williams deliberately emphasizes the contrast between his own attention to earthy detail and Eliot's high seriousness by bluntly describing two dogs mating: "There they were / stuck / dog and bitch." There is an air of contrivance about such poems, an almost adolescent need to shock.

Having entered his major phase with *Sour Grapes*, Williams spent the remainder of the Twenties concentrating on prose. Among his principal publications of this decade were a volume of radically experimental "improvisations" called *Kora in Hell* (1920); an anti-novel, reminiscent of Gertrude Stein's *The Making of Americans*, called *The Great American Novel* (1923); a historical survey, reminiscent of Lawrence's *Studies in Classic American Literature*, called *In the American Grain* (1923); and the first of several largely autobiographical novels, *A Voyage to Pagany*

(1928). With the exception of the novel—which, though less than exquisitely shaped, is at least coherent and readable, and possesses a degree of human interest—these books are all sloppy, self-conscious, and inchoate. A similar type of prose finds its way into Williams's poetry volumes of this period: in both *Spring and All* (1923) and *The Descent of Winter* (1928) Williams alternates prose and verse. The prose in the earlier book consists mostly of discursive notes on the nature of imagination, poetry, and their relation to reality. It is divided into "chapters," all of which are numbered (but not sequentially) and some of which are exceedingly short. The tone can be strident, at times sardonically so: "The imagination, freed from the handcuffs of 'art,' takes the lead! Her feet are bare and not too delicate. In fact those who come behind her have much to think of. Hm. Let it pass." And the book is positively rife with flippancies: "I realize that the chapters are rather quick in their sequence and that nothing much is contained in any one of them but no one should be surprised at this today."

The governing theme of *Spring and All* would seem to be that imaginative writing exists in its own realm, in some sense apart from the world of physical reality, in some sense connected to it. As ever, though, Williams's prose doesn't do a very good job of explaining these matters. Contradictions abound. At one point, for instance—in a clumsily worded allusion to Pater's graceful observation that "all art constantly aspires towards the condition of music"—Williams states, "I do not believe that writing is music. I do not believe writing would gain in quality or force by seeking to attain to the conditions of music." Two sentences later, however, he seems to be operating from the assumption that it is a good thing for writing to be like music:

> According to my present theme the writer of imagination would attain closest to the conditions of music not when his words are dissociated from natural objects and specified meanings but when they are liberated from the usual quality of that meaning by transposition into another medium, the imagination.

Williams was not the only modern American poet to concern himself with the relationship between the imagination and reality. In a number of essays, Wallace Stevens discussed this relationship with insight and eloquence; every time he took the trouble to write another essay on the topic, it was clear that he did so because he felt he had brought his understanding of it into somewhat sharper focus. Williams, alas, is a different case: he doesn't seem to have any idea what he thinks about imagination and reality, and the passages on this theme in *Spring and All* show him flailing about helplessly, grabbing at one analogy after another in an attempt to hit on something that sounds close to the truth.

Spring and All is concerned also with the advent of spring. Among Williams's goals here, plainly, is to write about this most hackneyed of poetic topics without resorting to the usual literary clichés and associations. He does this with some success, most notably in the familiar opening poem:

> By the road to the contagious hospital
> under the surge of the blue
> mottled clouds driven from the
> northeast—a cold wind. Beyond, the
> waste of broad, muddy fields
> brown with dried weeds, standing and fallen
>
> patches of standing water
> the scattering of tall trees
>
> All along the road the reddish
> purplish, forked, upstanding, twiggy
> stuff of bushes and small trees
> with dead, brown leaves under them
> leafless vines—
>
> Lifeless in appearance, sluggish
> dazed spring approaches—
>
> They enter the new world naked,
> cold, uncertain of all
> save that they enter. All about them
> the cold, familiar wind—
>
> Now the grass, tomorrow
> the stiff curl of wildcarrot leaf
>
> One by one objects are defined—

It quickens: clarity, outline of leaf

But now the stark dignity of
entrance—Still, the profound change
has come upon them: rooted, they
grip down and begin to awaken

As Donald Davie has noted, this poem is effective largely because Williams's characteristic weaknesses—a blunt, graceless style, an inability to effect smooth transitions—happen to be exactly what are called for here; the very point of the poem is to celebrate the season without romanticizing it, without falling into the lilting rhythms and false diction of the conventional paean to spring.

But much of the verse in *Spring and All*—like much of Williams's poetry in general—is of slender merits. A number of the poems I have mentioned, such as "The Great Figure" and "This Is Just to Say," fall into this category. At their best, such poems are snapshots, effectively recording stray moments, capturing small gestures, and calling attention to some of the more mundane moments of life. But they are little more than that, whatever else Williams's admirers may claim for them. Let us consider a specimen poem from *Spring and All*, one of his most well known and widely anthologized, "The Red Wheelbarrow":

so much depends
upon

a red wheel
barrow

glazed with rain
water

beside the white
chickens

Plainly, the speaker here feels that the wheelbarrow and chickens have some importance in the universe. But what is the nature of that importance? It's unclear. Nor does the poem succeed in making the reader feel this importance. The pictorial details alone, as Williams gives them, are hardly enough to evoke an experience that would sensibly explain why "so much depends upon" this wheelbarrow and these chickens. Williams himself explained that the theme of "The Red Wheelbarrow" was "the perfection of new forms as additions to nature"; and surely one can imagine that a fascination with the way man-made objects integrate into nature might have been the inspiration for this poem. But one can't really say that the poem communicates much of anything. What, then, does it have to offer? Some critics claim to find a "purity" in such poems as this. Perhaps there *is* a purity here, but if so, it has less to do with the sense or the sound of the words Williams has chosen, or with the way he has strung them together, than with all that clean white space surrounding the text. So little innate significance does this poem have, in fact, that it would seem to be deliberately inviting the reader to force some meaning upon it.

Now, throughout most of Williams's career, serious poetry critics had little patience for such gambits; since the foremost purpose of interpretation was to try to understand how an effective work of art manages to achieve its effect, a poem had to prove itself aesthetically deserving before a critic would take the trouble to dissect it. The postwar era, however, has seen a rise in the influence of a kind of academic critic who typically discusses a poem at exhaustive length without even addressing the question of what makes it worth analyzing; the attitude of such critics seems to be that whatever observations they make are self-justifying, that because it is possible to say certain things about a poem, they are necessarily worth saying. Such critics love a poem like "The Red Wheelbarrow" because its very brevity and simplicity pose little challenge to their actually quite modest critical skills, while at the same time allowing them to show off their ingenuity by "finding" an abundance of hidden meaning in eight tiny lines of poetry. Even a very good critic who works exhaustively at explicating a long, complex, brilliant poem—such as, say, Auden's "In Praise of Limestone"—will still find himself, at the end, in the shadow of the poet's magnificent intelligence; but a mediocre critic who manages to fill two or three pages with fanciful interpretations of "The Red Wheelbarrow" will end up impressing a lot of readers. *Imagine*, people think, *being able to get so much out of so little!* Academic poetry critics love Williams because he makes it easy for critics to look more important than the poems they're writing about.

Poems like "The Red Wheelbarrow" have accordingly become staples of the classroom and the scholarly essay. In a typical treatment, Majorie Perloff (perhaps the most prominent Williams critic in the academy today) explains in *The Dance of the Intellect* that what's important in "The Red Wheelbarrow" is not the poem's subject but "the interaction of lines":

> "Wheel" is separated from "barrow," "rain" from "water," using cuts that make us rethink the meaning of these compound nouns. Further, the morphemes "bárrow," "wáter," and "chíckens" each constitute a trochee, the "weight" of the red wheelbarrow being what "so much (the food supply? the farmer's survival? the pastoral order?) depends upon." Like a hard-edged painting, "The Red Wheelbarrow" is a composition in simple, primary colors—red and white— a red offset just slightly by the "glaze" of rainwater. The white chickens beside the red wheelbarrow: a synecdoche for an image of "the farm." And the picture is "framed" neatly by its stanzaic structure: the syllable count is 4/2, 3/ 2, 3/2, 4/2.

Similarly, after devoting a page or so to an analysis of the "visual pattern" of "Between Walls" (Williams's poem about pieces of green glass among cinders), Perloff maintains that although Williams said the poem is about how "in a waste of cinders loveliness, in the form of color, stands up alive,"

> what we admire in "Between Walls" is surely less the idea that beauty can be found even among trash, than the way this small observation is turned into a "field of action" in which line plays against syntax, visual against aural form, creating what Charles Olson was to call an energy-discharge, or projectile. Words are "unlink[ed] from their former relationships in the sentence" and recombined so that the poem becomes a kind of hymn to linguistic possibility.

To read the sort of criticism that Perloff perpetrates in these lines is to wonder whether such a critic has ever had a genuine aesthetic experience. Does Perloff really believe that "Between Walls" creates an "energy discharge"? Does she really think that anyone who has ever read "The Red Wheelbarrow" has had a sense of the poem being "framed" by its first and last lines? In exactly what way do that poem's line breaks make *her* rethink the meaning of the words *wheelbarrow* and *rainwater*? Has it ever occurred to her that before a poem can succeed at being a "hymn to linguistic possibility," it has to be something else first—namely, a successful poem? Perloff is precisely the sort of critic who has made it possible for Williams to triumph in the academy: in her mind, the important thing about a poem is not its aesthetic value but its susceptibility to ingenious critical methods. To a critic like Perloff, the wonderful thing about a poem like "The Red Wheelbarrow" is that there's so little *poem* to get in the way of whatever she wants to make of it.

In his collections of the Thirties and Forties—among them *An Early Martyr and Other Poems* (1935), *Adam & Eve & the City* (1936), and *The Wedge* (1944)—Williams dropped the intercalated prose that had characterized *Spring and All* and *The Descent of Winter*. But he did introduce prose, in a big way, into the multi-volume poem he regarded as his *magnum opus*, his answer to Pound's *Cantos* and Eliot's *The Waste Land*. *Paterson*—which was originally planned as a four-volume work (1946-51), though Williams added a fifth book in 1958—is an attempt to mythologize both a man and a city; the city is Paterson, New Jersey, and the man is the poet, also called Paterson, whom Williams identifies with the city. His "Author's Note" to the poem is worth reproducing in full because it is murky in much the same way as the poem itself:

> *Paterson* is a long poem in four parts—that a man in himself is a city, beginning, seeking, achieving and concluding his life in ways which the various aspects of a city may embody—if imaginatively conceived—any city, all the details of which may be made to voice his most intimate convictions. Part One introduces the elemental character of the place. The Second Part comprises the modern replicas. Three will seek a language to make them vocal, and Four, the river below the falls, will be reminiscent of episodes—all that any one man may achieve in a lifetime.

Though *Paterson* (which is omitted from *The Collected Poems*) contains a number of fine passages and arresting lines, it simply doesn't add up to a cohesive work of art. If one may borrow from Horace and call *The Waste Land* an example of "inharmonious harmony," *Paterson* is, by comparison, thoroughly cacophonous. It is far less compelling than either *The Waste Land* or *Cantos*, and far less fastidiously composed, too; for a poem of its ambitions, it contains a shocking amount of bad, lazy, and pretentious writing. I am speaking of the poetry here, because most of the prose is not by Williams. Some of this prose—mostly concerning the history of Paterson—is borrowed from old newspapers, history books, and the like. Some is epistolary: Williams includes the complete, unadulterated texts of several letters which had been sent to him, including one from a young admirer named Allen Ginsberg. And there are miscellaneous items: Book Three, for example, contains a page-long chart detailing the kinds of stone that may be found at various levels of a 2,100-foot-deep Paterson artesian well. It is hard to defend, on aesthetic grounds, the inclusion of some of these materials; at times Williams seems utterly frivolous, and eventually one has the feeling that his major motivation for *Paterson* was nothing more than the desire to write a long, important modern poem. Even Williams seems to have recognized that the poem—especially in its later books—was a failure; but he argued (not very convincingly) that this was appropriate, since the poem was about a "failure of speech."

Williams never again wrote a poem as expansive as *Paterson*, but in his collections of the Fifties and Sixties he was considerably more successful at working in relatively long forms. It was in *The Desert Music and Other Poems* (1954)—a collection of poems that were, on average, much longer than his typical verses of earlier decades—that Williams introduced, on a large scale, his famous triadic stanza. As seen in the opening lines of the lovely poem "Asphodel, That Greeny Flower," the triadic stanza requires that every second line of a poem be indented so much, and every third line so much more:

> Of asphodel, that greeny flower,
>> like a buttercup
>>> upon its branching stem—
> save that it's green and wooden—
>> I come, my sweet,
>>> to sing to you.
> We lived long together
>> a life filled,
>>> if you will,
> with flowers. So that
>> I was cheered
>>> when I came first to know

that there were flowers also
in hell.

Williams trumpeted his invention of this stanza—which first appeared in Book Two of *Paterson*, and was used consistently not only in *The Desert Music* but in *Journey to Love* (1955)—as if he had made a discovery on the order of penicillin. Throughout his career he had sought to represent, in poetry, the stress patterns of American English, and in his mind this triadic stanza was the best answer he'd seen; it offered, he said, a "solution [to] the problem of modern verse." Manifestly, he liked it because it didn't look like free verse, a term he despised as implying a lack of discipline; though he never would have put it this way, the wonderful thing for Williams about the triadic stanza was obviously that it allowed him to write free verse that didn't *look* like free verse. Indeed, though the stanza made no metrical demands upon him, Williams described each line, paradoxically, as a "variable foot." And as the engaging first lines of "The Descent" demonstrate, a "variable foot" could consist of one word or ten, two syllables or seventeen:

The descent beckons
    as the ascent beckoned.
        Memory is a kind
of accomplishment,
    a sort of renewal
        even
an initiation, since the spaces it opens are new places
    inhabited by hordes
        heretofore unrealized,
of new kinds—

It is a mark of the dubious nature of much of Williams's literary criticism that one of his justifications for the use of the variable foot was that since the world is relativistic, the poetic foot should be, too.

For all Williams's talk of innovation, however, the triadic stanza— as some critics have noted—isn't really all that different from the short, unindented three-line stanzas in which Williams had written many of his earlier poems. (Interestingly, most of the new poems included in Williams's last poetry collection, the 1962 *Pictures from Brueghel and Other Poems*, don't make use of the stanza.) It may be said, as a matter of fact, that the more important distinction of these later volumes is the greater warmth, fullness, lyricism, sustained coherence, and even grace that characterize many of the poems in them; on the whole, they are both more abstract and more personal than the bulk of Williams's earlier work. It is as if Williams—who in his earlier poems seems usually to have been satisfied with brief glimpses of people—finally began to discover, late in life, that human beings and ideas can be at least as interesting as wheelbarrows, that the contents of a person's mind and soul can be every bit as compelling as the contents of his refrigerator. This is not to suggest that the ideas he introduced in these later poems are necessarily first-class; doubtless many an admirer of "Aspholdel" has winced at the well-known lines in its coda: "If a man die / it is because death / has first / possessed his imagination." (Likewise, the most impressive thing, to me, about Williams's famous refrain in *Paterson* on the role of ideas in poetry—"no ideas but in things"—is that it manages to break its own rule.)

But then one should not be surprised that most of Williams's poetry is less than profound. "Why do you write?" he once asked himself in print. His answer was: "To have nothing in my head." Alas, he was spectacularly successful in achieving this goal; there is no greater flaw in his poetry than its thoroughgoing, and sometimes almost aggressive, mindlessness. Whether this was the consequence of a deliberate suppression of intellect or was something he couldn't avoid, we can't know for sure. We do know that he bragged endlessly about his fuzziness of mind ("I exist in a matrix of confusion") and about his unreflecting approach to poetic composition ("Write carelessly," he advised in *Paterson*, "so that nothing that is not green will survive"); we also know that he was either incapable of, or uninterested in, writing coherent argumentative or expository prose. To read Williams's critical *oeuvre* is to get the feeling that, for all his fulminating about dead forms and English rhythms and the need for a modern American measure, he never really had a clear idea of *why* he wanted to be a modernist. Though some of his innovations (not only the variable foot, but also the notion of a poem as a field of action) and catchphrases ("no ideas but in things") were supremely influential, he was not particularly good at explaining any of them—not even, one suspects, to himself.

Consider, for instance, his dismissal of conventional poetic forms as artificial, antiquated, and unsuited to American verse. Williams even went so far as to call Auden a failure because of his attachment to form. But Williams's reasoning was, shall we say, less than airtight: he argued that modern American poets shouldn't write in rhyme or iambic pentameter because modern Americans don't talk in rhyme or iambic pentameter. That no people in history ever *have* talked in rhyme or iambic pentameter didn't seem to strike him as a flaw in his argument. The profoundly unfortunate fact about his crusade against poetic conventions is that while he thought of himself as a literary insurrectionist who sought to lead American poetry out of the prison of form, the ultimate consequence of his efforts was to reduce drastically the expressive options available to an entire generation of American poets. Thanks largely to Williams, any sort of formal trappings became *démodé* in American poetry in the Sixties and Seventies—so much so that a young poet who violated the norms was likely to face condescension from colleagues, automatic rejection from editors, and lectures from his teachers to the effect that form was pre-modern, irrelevant, and reactionary. As for the majority of young poets who were swept up in the post-Williams tide, a large number of them have grown into respected middle-aged poets—and, naturally, professors of creative writing—who are virtually incapable of writing in rhyme or meter, and who have passed their indifference to these skills along to their students. Many of these professor-poets have taken Williams's "no ideas but in things" doctrine as an authorization to set their minds aside when they write, and to celebrate as a philosophical virtue the intellectual vacuity, disunity, and self-indulgence of their own and their students' poems. Some of them, futhermore, taking their cue from Williams's most strictly descriptive poems, have made their reputations on unbearably monotonous verses that read like catalogues of plant names, land formations, and such; others, who trace their line of poetic descent back to Williams's "I kissed her while she pissed" mode, engage in relentlessly flat confession.

It is instructive simply to list the names of some of the now-venerated poets who began their careers as disciples of Williams. The members of the first wave—Louis Zukofsky, Charles Reznikoff, George Oppen—were associated with Williams from the 1930s on and called themselves Objectivists, attributing to Williams their preoccupation with physical objects and with the poem itself as an object. But it was a later group of disciples who began to spread Williams's fame, and to extend his influence, to the four corners of the earth. As late as 1945, Conrad Aiken had left Williams out of his *Modern Library Anthology of American Poetry*; five years later Williams had gathered into his fold the up-and-coming versifiers Allen Ginsberg, Charles Olson, and Robert Creeley, all of whom, within a few years, would be telling the world that Williams *was* American poetry. These young poets regarded Williams as a sort of spiritual father, the originator of ideas about poetry that seemed almost consonant with—that, indeed, seemed almost to confer a kind of legitimacy upon—their own unconventional approaches to the composition of verse.

A special case was that of Robert Lowell, who was more gifted by far than any of these other young poets. Lowell's splendid first book, *Lord Weary's Castle* (1946), had been written in a consummately Eliotic manner against which he was eager to rebel; Williams himself, in reviewing Lowell's second book, *The Mills of the Kavanaughs* (1951), sensed the younger poet's restlessness: "Mr. Lowell appears to be restrained by the lines; he appears to *want* to break them." And break them he did: by the time *Mills* was published, Lowell had already been encouraged by the success of Ginsberg's own Williams-influenced manner to loosen up his lines and lower his level of diction; and over the course of the 1950s, driven by a legitimate need for a more flexible, colloquial manner, Lowell shifted away from Eliot's end of the modernist spectrum and toward Williams's. And what he ended up with, of course, was his 1959 volume *Life Studies*, in which he managed to manifest Williams's influence while writing a kind of poetry—direct, personal, and profoundly affecting—that was distinctly different from the Rutherford physician's.

The other young poets—Ginsberg, Olson, and Creeley—were a different story. At once tin-eared, uncerebral, and egomaniacal, all three had been on the lookout, in the early postwar years, for ways to turn their variously eccentric, radical, and narcissistic plaints into poems without the interposition of, well, any of that *poetry* stuff. They wanted to create poems that consisted of nothing but their voices, their vital spirits, confronting a blank page. To them, Williams was the ideal model, and his chatter about "no ideas but in things" and about poems as "fields of action" was right up their anti-intellectual alley. What separates Williams from these poets, however—and, for that matter, from most of the poets (though certainly not all) who claim him as their master—is that, in his own way, he believed in literary standards.

He *had* standards, however ill-conceived they were, however incoherently explained, however ineffectively put into practice. Unlike many of his followers, he never behaved as if he thought that anything thrown on a page was poetry. If he didn't feel comfortable with the term "free verse," it was because to him it *wasn't* free; according to the poetics of an Allen Ginsberg, by contrast, poetry is not only free but licentious. It seems significant, in this connection, that though Williams enjoyed having disciples, Mariani notes that he privately found many of the younger poets woefully primitive, and that he described some Beat poems as "nutty experimentation."

Yet Williams, more than anyone else, was behind that nutty experimentation. Out of the work of his disciples grew the major American poetry movements of the postwar period: Ginsberg's Beats, Olson's Projectivists, Lowell's Confessional poets. To point this out is not to suggest that all the contemporary poets who have manifested Williams's influence are bad; but it does seem fair to say that the great majority of these poets who have made aesthetically successful use of his influence (Louis Simpson, for example) were first accomplished formal poets who brought to their free verse a sense of discipline that most of his followers have sorely lacked. To later generations of poets, indeed, Williams became the symbol of a number of related ideas which he would almost certainly have hated—namely, that anyone who can steal a pencil, a piece of paper, and a few moments alone in the corner of a coffeehouse is a poet; that one sincere poet is pretty much as good as another; that poetry is easy to do; that if you simply put the words down as they come to you, what you arrive at will be a poem; and that such a poem will be as valid as anything Keats or Browning or Shakespeare ever wrote—more valid, certainly, than anything so formal and polished, because it'll be *you* on that page and not some artificial arrangement of words.

The truth is that Williams, revolutionary though he was to the end of his days, was not quite the radical that many of his present-day followers would have him be. Williams read the classics; he believed that there was such a thing as an objectively good or bad poem; and though he allowed his words to pour "carelessly" onto the page, he fussed over those words, once they were in black and white, to make them—in his judgment—as good as possible. This is, by a considerable margin, the finer part of Williams's legacy—and the fact that it has been so blatantly ignored by so many of his self-styled disciples goes a long way, I think, toward explaining why young poets nowadays are, in increasing numbers, turning for inspiration and example not to Williams but to his old antagonist Eliot, and are again learning to work in those amaranthine forms that Williams spent a lifetime trying to bury.

SEPTEMBER 1988

THE FICTIVE MUSIC OF WALLACE STEVENS

Thirty-one years after his death, more people than ever are reading the sublime poetry of Wallace Stevens, and his critical reputation—which has grown steadily since 1950, the year he was awarded the Bollingen Prize—has never been greater. But even today, in the minds of many readers who feel perfectly at home with his contemporaries Eliot, Yeats, and Williams, the name of Stevens is, beyond all else, synonymous with enigmatic symbolism and abstruse epistemology. To a dismayingly large number of people, indeed, the most interesting thing about him is not his poetry but the fact that he wrote most of it while serving as vice president in charge of surety claims for the Hartford Accident and Indemnity Company.

The more consideration one gives to this disaffection for Stevens's work among certain types of readers, the more firmly one believes that their problem is not with its difficulty but with Stevens's monolithic impersonality—an impersonality that makes a good deal of Eliot's poetry look, by comparison, positively diaristic—and his devotion to abstraction. In an age when celebrated poets tend to glory either in simpleminded self-celebration or purposeless physical description, these unreceptive readers doubtless find the sort of poetry that Wallace Stevens wrote far from easy to digest.

Two recent books—one an oral portrait, the other a work of academic criticism—seem specifically designed to make the impersonal, intellectual Stevens more congenial to this sort of contemporary reader. The first book is Peter Brazeau's *Parts of a World: Wallace Stevens Remembered* (1983), which has just been reissued by North Point Press, and which is based on interviews with dozens of Stevens's surviving friends, relatives, and co-workers.[1] I say "oral portrait" and not "oral biography" because, unlike any number of other recent life studies

---

[1] *Parts of a World: Wallace Stevens Remembered*, by Peter Brazeau; North Point Press; 330 pages, $12.50.

that are constructed of a series of excerpts from interview transcripts, *Parts of a World* (whose title is taken from that of Stevens's fourth collection of verse) does not, strictly speaking, tell a story. Instead, Brazeau offers us a numbingly monotonous and generally unrevealing series of sepia-toned snapshots, as it were, of Stevens the business executive, Stevens the poet, Stevens the family man. In part, this monotony is unavoidable. Stevens, born in 1879 to an upper-middle-class family in Reading, Pennsylvania, went on to live a life that, on the surface, was extraordinarily uneventful. After attending Harvard College and New York Law School, he wed a hometown girl, Elsie Kachel, and spent the remainder of his life married to her and working in insurance. He never travelled to Europe, made virtually no intimate friends, probably never had an affair, and lived one day pretty much the same way as the next. But Brazeau's "oral portrait" format makes this book even more static and colorless than it had to be. Not only do his interviewees tell us precious little of value about Stevens; they almost invariably tell us every banal detail a dozen times.

The first of the book's three sections, for instance, which is devoted to Stevens the insurance man, consists largely of testimony wherein his former colleagues at the Hartford describe how "gentlemanly" he was (or—take your pick—"urbane," "charming," "courtly," "gracious," "civilized," "distinguished," "polished," "dignified," and "impressive," most of which crop up at least twice); what a "first-class" insurance lawyer he was considered to be (perhaps the best surety-claims man in the country—though one is not quite sure, for a while, precisely what a surety-claims man is); how wonderfully sarcastic (and, to those who misunderstood him, arrogant and insulting) his deadpan humor could be; how lucid, concise, and beautifully written were his business letters, how illegible his handwriting, how marvelous his vocabulary; what integrity he displayed in all business matters; and how much he loved imported tea, fresh fruit, good cigars, and cinnamon buns (of which he partook frequently at his desk).

Certainly, some of this material is of real interest. But Brazeau never seems to realize when he's reached the saturation point. For example, when his interviewees explain, one after the other, that they never really got to know Stevens (who believed in all work and no play at the office), Brazeau insists upon giving us every deathless word:

> I didn't see much of Stevens. He was generally tucked away
> somewhere in connection with his work. He wasn't the kind

of fellow, "Well, I'm Wallace Stevens!" He wasn't the blustery type. He just went quietly about his business and did what was necessary.

[Stevens] was a rather aloof person [who like to] hold people at arm's length.... Most executives, whenever they're free to do so, love to sit around and relax, unwind, lollygag. Stevens was not that kind of person. He was not receptive.... He was always, to most people who didn't understand him, formidably busy.

He had difficulty relating to people.... He was sort of a loner.... He was not what I call a hail-fellow-well-met person.

He was hard to get acquainted with.

I always had the feeling that here was a man you just didn't get to know too well. He was always somewhat of a stranger, in the sense that most of the company men that I met I became very friendly with. We had many things that we exchanged, personal things. But you didn't do that with Wallace Stevens. He was always aloof and pretty much his own man.

He was not a warm personality as far as those in the office went. He wanted his privacy and respected the privacy of others.

Not, mind you, that Stevens was a perpetual sobersides. If he steadfastly avoided chummy behavior at the office, he was equally adamant in his refusal to discuss business after hours. Indeed, at parties, and at his beloved Canoe Club (which, one gathers, was the sort of place where George Babbitt would have gone for a good time), he was, with a couple of drinks in him, "one of the boys"—a cutup, a teller of smoking-car jokes, the very picture of "Harvard-Yale football-game levity," who, upon arrival at a nightclub, would tell the orchestra leader to play "Did You Ever See A Dream Walking?" That such words as "playful," "jovial," and "jolly" recur as frequently in the interviews as "austere," "aloof," and "somber" simply affirms that Stevens's life was, as *Hud-*

son Review editor Frederick Morgan tells Brazeau, "neatly compart-mentalized."

And compartmentalized it was, right down the line. Stevens kept his insurance work separate from his home life, and his poetry separate from both. Rarely did he so much as breathe his wife's name at the office; never did he take her to business functions; and only two or three times, in his thirty-nine years at the Hartford, did he invite a colleague over to the house for dinner. "It was a standing matter of astonishment at the office," recalls one colleague, "that no one ever got to see his family." Nor, unless they took the trouble to hunt down one of his collections at the local bookstore, did more than a few of them get to see his poetry either. True, once he had published a couple of volumes, it was no secret at the Hartford that there was a poet on the premises. Far from it: he regularly sent his underlings to the *Oxford English Dictionary* to check the meanings of recondite words that he planned to use in his poetry, and on rare occasions even read poems in progress aloud to associates, asking their opinions. But most of the time he nipped in the bud any attempt on the part of a colleague to engage him in a discussion of poetry, or to persuade him to explicate a given poem.

In the second and third sections of the book, "The Man of Letters" and "The Family Man," Brazeau attempts to open up to us those areas of Stevens's life that he kept to himself at the office. Unfortunately, most of the people interviewed in Part Two—among them such familiar literary names as Richard Wilbur, Harry Levin, Cleanth Brooks, and Léonie Adams—knew Stevens no better than did the folks at work. One problem here is that most of the writers and editors with whom Stevens had extended relationships (William Carlos Williams, for example, and Harriet Monroe) are no longer with us; another problem is that Stevens had, it appears, only two really close literary-type friends in his entire life, neither of them a well-known writer, both of them now deceased: Henry Church (a denizen of an artsy New York clique of which Stevens was, for a time, a sort of associate member) and Judge Arthur Gray Powell of Atlanta (whose colorful conversation inspired the titles and some of the details of several of his poems, among them "A High-Toned Old Christian Woman" and "Decorations in a Nigger Cemetery"). We do learn, in Part Two, that Stevens loved Braque, Klee, Stravinsky, Berlioz, and Greta Garbo, that he highly esteemed Delmore Schwartz (whose work represented, to him, a hope for twentieth-century poetry), and that he disliked Hemingway, Cummings, and Frost (who, for his part, thought of Stevens as a "swell from Harvard"). On the admirable side, Stevens consistently refused to accept payment for lectures, readings, or magazine publication of his poems; on the unadmirable side, he was, alas, as full of the prejudices of his time as anyone else, criticizing a restaurant for catering to Jews and referring to Gwendolyn Brooks as a "coon."

It is not until the last (and briefest) section of the book that Brazeau covers what one feels should have come first—Stevens's parents, his upbringing, his life as husband and father. Since Elsie is dead and his only child, Holly, isn't one of Brazeau's interviewees, the picture of the poet as family man is based solely on the testimony of nieces, neighbors, and the like, who were vouchsafed only occasional glimpses of the Stevenses. Though vague, the picture they paint is a decidedly somber one. There was, unsurprisingly, "not much communication" in the Stevens home—no fighting, just silence at the dinner table and closed bedroom doors. Elsie is variously described as sweet and cruel, pathetic and strict, a naïve homebody, a willing serf; all witnesses agree that she was an excellent cook and an obsessive homemaker, and that neither she nor Stevens was a particularly affectionate parent.

It is in the description of the poet's father, Garrett Barcalow Stevens, that *Parts of a World* comes closest to suggesting an explanation for all this. Garrett Stevens was, as Brazeau explains, a corporate lawyer and amateur versifier who, by every account, was distant, domineering, and emotionally undemonstrative, not to mention highly conscious of his family's "respectability"—all characteristics for which Wallace Stevens would be noted. When young Wallace announced that he wanted to marry Elsie, an undereducated girl both literally and figuratively from "the other side of the tracks," Garrett objected and, when Wallace married her anyway, didn't speak to his son for years. A generation later, the pattern repeated itself almost exactly: Holly decided to marry, and Stevens objected on the grounds that the boy she had in mind, whom Stevens called a "Polack," was simply "not her equal." Holly married him anyway, and she and Stevens were, as a result, estranged for several years.

What is one to make of this? Why did Stevens, in so many ways, become a tintype of his father? Why was such an enlightened modern poet weighted down, psychologically, with so much philistine freight? It almost seems as if, in some sense, Stevens was paying his father homage—or, perhaps, penance. If he admired Delmore Schwartz so fervently, surely this admiration had a good deal to do with Schwartz's endless contemplation, in his poetry, of the theme of parents, children, and fate, and of the strong but subtle ties—of guilt and resentment, love and hatred—that bind sons inescapably to their fathers. In this connection, Stevens writes in "Esthétique du Mal" that

> It may be that one life is a punishment
> For another, as the son's life for the father's.

He speaks to the same theme, but takes an utterly different tone, in "Recitation after Dinner," a poem he read at a meeting of the Saint Nicholas Society (whose members all trace their lineage back to the early Dutch settlers). The poem—in which he borrows Virgil's image of Aeneas carrying his father Anchises on his back (an image Stevens used more than once)—helps to account for the keen interest in genealogy that Stevens developed in middle age; in it, he speaks of tradition as

> ...a clear, a single, a solid form,
> That of the son who bears upon his back
> The father that he loves, and bears him from
> The ruins of the past, out of nothing left,
> Made noble by the honor he receives,
> As if in a golden cloud. The son restores
> The father....

Here, then, Stevens sees the father—and, by extension, all the generations preceding him, and the entire past—not as a dreadful burden but as something marvelous and ennobling. There must be an illuminating story behind all of this. But it is not a story that any of Brazeau's interviewees is able to tell us.

Indeed, what *Parts of a World: Wallace Stevens Remembered* demonstrates more persuasively than anything else is the weakness of the composite oral portrait as a form of biography—or, at least, literary biography. With a relatively uncomplicated subject like Andy Warhol's starlet Edie Sedgwick, whose life provided the material for Jean Stein's book *Edie*, this weakness was not critical. With a more substantial subject, though, the oral form is less defensible, its fundamental superficiality far more manifest. If a book like Peter Manso's *Mailer* nonetheless succeeds to a considerable extent, it is because Mailer is a colorful personality who has led an unsettled and combative life, and because he wears his id on his sleeve. But applied to a man like Wallace Stevens— the turbulence of whose soul rarely, if ever, roiled his smooth surface, and who had nothing but contempt for the Hemingway or Mailer type of writer, who gives the impression that he has to throw himself into life in order to write about it—the oral form fails to provide either insight or entertainment in enough abundance to justify the endeavor.

It would be wrong to mention Ernest Hemingway without taking note, in passing, of Stevens's most dramatic—and out-of-character— literary encounter. So strong was Stevens's antipathy for Hemingwayesque prose that, in February of 1936, the insulting remarks that Stevens made at a cocktail party in Key West provoked the novelist to engage him in a fistfight, which Stevens lost and Hemingway magnanimously agreed to keep quiet about. The tussle is symbolic of the utter contrast between the two writers' approaches to their art. If Hemingway strained, in the best Conradian manner, to *present* objective phenomena rather than explicitly render his subjective reactions to them, Stevens considered the "mere rendering of an object or scene... an imaginative failure." So observes Milton J. Bates in *Wallace Stevens: A Mythology of Self*, our second recent book under consideration.[2]

The relationship between reality and the imagination, of course, is at the thematic center of Stevens's poetry, and is the subject of most of the lectures collected in his sole volume of prose, *The Necessary Angel: Essays on Reality and the Imagination* (1951). Of the seven pieces in this volume, it is the earliest, "The Noble Rider and the Sound of Words," in which Stevens most fully and coherently explains his aesthetic theory. Poetry, he writes, is a phenomenon characterized by "the interdependence of the imagination and reality as equals." It is not a sedate interdependence but an active, even an agitated, one: for the mind, wherein the imagination resides, "is a violence from within that protects us from a violence without. It is the imagination pressing back against the pressure of reality." Yet Stevens does not mean to suggest that, during the writing of poetry, these two entities are at war with one another; on the contrary, the creation of poetry is, to his mind, "not a choice of one

---

[2] *Wallace Stevens: A Mythology of Self*, by Milton J. Bates; University of California Press; 319 pages, $24.95.

over the other and not a decision that divides them, but something subtler, a recognition that here, too, as between these poles, the universal interdependence exists…they are equal and inseparable." The measure of a poet is "the measure of his power to abstract himself, and to withdraw with him into his abstraction the reality on which the lovers of truth insist. He must be able to abstract himself and also to abstract reality, which he does by placing it in his imagination." (For instance, a poet may write about creativity, "the maker's rage to order words," by writing about a woman singing on the beach at Key West.)

If twentieth-century poetry is not all that it could be, Stevens suggests, it is because not only poetry but all the arts have suffered, in modern times, from the "pressure of reality." Reality, in other words, has gained the upper hand over imagination. Why? Because the modern world, as Stevens sees it, is a world no longer able to maintain its belief in its chief imaginary construct (i.e. God), and therefore no longer able to wield the imaginative powers it once commanded. The things of the imagination, as a result, have become weakened, watered down, debased; "the idea of nobility"—to Stevens, a crucial element in poetry, and "imaginary" because it would not exist without a human mind to conceive of it—"exists in art today only in degenerate forms or in a much diminished state."

That Stevens does not consider such an abstract entity as nobility to be "real" does not mean that it is unimportant to him; without such "fictions" as nobility, it is clear, life would be meaningless. And this, in fact, is to him the essential function of poetry in the modern world: to provide us all with a "supreme fiction," a grand, subsuming illusion to take the place of God, and thereby to restore to life its meaning, or, rather, its semblance of meaning—which amounts, in his philosophy, to precisely the same thing. As he says at the end of "The Noble Rider," poetry seems "to have something to do with our self-preservation; and that, no doubt, is why the expression of it, the sound of its words, helps us to live our lives." Or, in the words of "The Man with the Blue Guitar,"

> The earth, for us, is flat and bare.
> There are no shadows. Poetry
>
> Exceeding music must take the place
> Of empty heaven and its hymns,

Ourselves in poetry must take their place....

I have used the word "philosophy," but Stevens, though he has been described as a philosophical poet, was no philosopher—at least not in the sense that the term is usually understood. His realm was not that of logic but of intuition; as the title of one of his essays, "The Irrational Element in Poetry," suggests, he saw poetry as a discipline that transcends the boundaries of reason. When, in a late poem called "The Sail of Ulysses," he writes of knowledge—the sort of knowledge, naturally, that poets deal in—he distinguishes it unambiguously from reason:

> ...knowing
> And being are one: the right to know
> And the right to be are one. We come
> To knowledge when we come to life.
> Yet always there is another life,
> A life beyond this present knowing,
> A life lighter than this present splendor.
> Brighter, perfected and distant away,
> Not to be reached but to be known,
> Not an attainment of the will
> But something illogically received,
> A divination....

In his preoccupation with the imagination, Stevens recalls Coleridge, who (along with the other English Romantic poets) was an important influence upon his conception of poetry. In an essay entitled "The Figure of the Youth as Virile Poet," Stevens describes Coleridge as "defining poetry all his life"; and the fact is that Stevens, in both his prose and his verse, was continually doing the same thing. But he did not do so in the manner of a professional philosopher: like Coleridge, he was both brilliant and unsystematic, at times inconsistent in his terminology, never proceeding from theory but always from feeling.

Coleridge is hardly the only poet or critic who helped to shape Stevens's literary theory and practice. Indeed, *Wallace Stevens: A Mythology of Self* is largely concerned with identifying the ways in which various writers influenced him. Among these influences are Walter Pater and the Aesthetes, who were all the rage at Harvard when Stevens

was an undergraduate there. Though Stevens patently had more re-
gard for everyday reality than did the Aesthetes, he believed, with them,
that the poet does not have a "social obligation" to anyone, that poetry's
purpose is not to "say something" about life but to attain the
nonreferential purity of music, and that the creation of a poem is no
less important than any other human activity. The Aesthetes, more-
over, must be given much of the credit for Stevens's often récherché
diction, bizarre wit, and sumptuous imagery, as well as his Wildean
affinity for paradox. The central idea of his *oeuvre*—that modern man
must believe in something he knows to be a fiction—is, needless to
say, paradoxical, and a number of his poems, like many of Wilde's
epigrams, derive their effectiveness largely from the device of saying
that X is not X, or X is the opposite of X:

> A. A violent order is a disorder; and
> B. A great disorder is an order....
> —"Connoisseur of Chaos"

> This is form gulping after formlessness....
> —"The Auroras of Autumn"

> We do not prove the existence of the poem.
> It is something seen and know in lesser poems.
> It is the huge, high harmony that sounds
> A little and a little, suddenly,
> By means of a separate sense. It is and it
> Is not and, therefore, is....
> —"A Primitive Like an Orb"

> It is possible that to seem—it is to be,
> As the sun is something seeming and it is.
>
> .   .   .
>
> It is a world of words to the end of it,
> In which nothing solid is its solid self.
> —"Description without Place"

> It must be visible or invisible,
> Invisible or visible or both:
> A seeming and unseeming in the eye.
>
> .   .   .

There was a myth before the myth began....
    —"Notes toward a Supreme Fiction"

A sunny day's complete Poussiniana
Divide it from itself. It is this or that
And it is not.
    —"Poem Written at Morning"

Along with the Aesthetic influence, of course, went that of the French Symbolists. From them Stevens, like most modern poets, learned a number of lessons, among them the value of mystery and ambiguity in poetry. Mallarmé's remarks on this subject, as quoted by Bates, might well have been written by Stevens himself, so well do they describe the way his poetry operates:

> The Parnassians take something in its entirety and simply exhibit it; in so doing, they fall short of mystery; they fail to give our minds that exquisite joy which consists of believing that we are creating something. To *name* an object is largely to destroy poetic enjoyment, which comes from gradual divination. The ideal is to *suggest* the object. It is the perfect use of the mystery which constitutes symbol. An object must be gradually evoked in order to show a state of soul; or else, choose an object and from it elicit a state of soul by means of a series of decodings.

By taking the Symbolist path in this regard, Stevens was, as Bates observes, rejecting not only the Genteel Tradition that had governed American poetry in his youth, but the Imagist revolution as well, whose principal criteria for effectiveness in poetry were simplicity and directness.

Stevens was never one to rush into print, and his first collection, *Harmonium*, did not appear till 1923, when he was forty-four. The book is distinguished by an air of modernist gloom, as exemplified by the final lines of its outstanding poem, "Sunday Morning":

> We live in an old chaos of the sun,
> Or old dependency of day and night,
> Or island solitude, unsponsored, free,
> Of that wide water, inescapable.

Deer walk upon our mountains, and the quail
Whistle about us their spontaneous cries;
Sweet berries ripen in the wilderness;
And, in the isolation of the sky,
At evening, casual flocks of pigeons make
Ambiguous undulations as they sink,
Downward to darkness, on extended wings.

This anguish about the godlessness of the universe, however, is sup-
planted in succeeding volumes by the conviction that poetry can and
must take the place of God as a principle of order and virtue. "I desire
my poem," Stevens once wrote in a letter, referring to "The Man with
the Blue Guitar," "to mean as much, and as deeply, as a missal." This
determination is evident in one poem after another—in "The Idea of
Order at Key West," for instance, wherein the woman singing creates a
world:

She was the single artificer of the world
In which she sang. And when she sang, the sea,
Whatever self it had, became the self
That was her song, for she was the maker. Then we,
As we beheld her striding there alone,
Knew that there never was a world for her
Except the one she sang and, singing, made.

In developing the notions that are implicit in this poem, Stevens
was in many respects a student of Nietzsche, who recognized the so-
cial and psychological benefit of the illusion of God and who said, as
Bates reminds us, that "Art is with us in order that we may not perish
through truth." Like Nietzsche, Stevens worried that the twentieth
century's loss of faith in God would mean, eventually, the loss of faith
in the virtues that God represented; thus, like Nietzsche, he was taken
with the notion of an imaginary hero, whom Nietzsche called
Übermensch and Stevens called "major man," who would embody the
paramount virtues of the race. The idea of "major man" was intro-
duced in Stevens's single longest poem, "Notes toward a Supreme Fic-
tion," but is elaborated upon in other poems, including "Paisant
Chronicle," wherein Stevens writes that the major men

...are characters beyond

> Reality, composed thereof. They are
> The fictive man created out of men.
> They are men but artificial men. They are
> Nothing in which it is not possible
> To believe....

To the influence of Nietzsche, we must add that of two philosophers closer to home: William James and George Santayana. Both were professors at Harvard when Stevens was a student there; James published his book *The Will to Believe* less than a year before Stevens entered Harvard, and Santayana published *Interpretations of Poetry and Religion* the year Stevens left. In a letter explaining the attitude that informs the book *Notes toward a Supreme Fiction*, Stevens invokes the title of James's book:

> Underlying it is the idea that, in the various predicaments of belief, it might be possible to yield, or to try to yield, ourselves to a declared fiction.
>
> This is the same thing as saying that it might be possible for us to believe in something that we know to be untrue. Of course, we do that every day, but we don't make the most of the fact that we do it out of the need to believe, what in your day, and mine, in Cambridge was called the will to believe.

Yet, as Bates observes, Stevens goes beyond James. The philosopher of pragmatism had declared that it is sensible to believe in something that is not known for certain to be true, but which might, indeed, be true; Stevens declared that it is a good idea to believe in something one knows to be false. In taking this position, he was less in line with James than with Santayana, who saw both poetry and religion as fictions of human manufacture—worthwhile, to be sure, but fictions nonetheless.

It was in the Thirties that the convictions Stevens had forged out of these influences—and the poetry that he, in turn, had forged out of these convictions—had the roughest time of it. During the Depression years, Marxist critics habitually condemned Stevens as an elitist, even a fascist, for his refusal to join the vanguard of Socialist Realism by writing poems about enchained workers and bloated capitalist bosses. In *Owl's Clover* (1936), he succumbed to this pressure, in a sense, by attempting, as he put it, "to make poetry out of commonplaces: the day's news"—or, as he explained in a letter to a reviewer of the book, "to dip aspects of the contemporaneous in the poetic." Aesthetically speaking, the results of this experiment were not conspicuously successful; most of the poems in *Owl's Clover* fell far beneath Stevens's usual standard, and did not merit reprinting in *The Palm at the End of the Mind*, the definitive selection from his poetic *oeuvre*.

Rather than regard these poems, however, with the majority of Stevens's critics, as an unfortunate temporary descent into the maelstrom, Bates, while recognizing their literary weaknesses, nonetheless appears to perceive them as a major step in Stevens's development. His extensive discussion of *Owl's Clover*, furthermore, is accompanied by a scholarly disquisition upon the subject of Stevens's attitude toward Marxists—whom Stevens despised not because they were idealists but because they were not his *type* of idealists. Stevens saw himself as a visionary idealist, proceeding "by fits of visionary insight rather than calculation." Marxists, on the contrary, were bound by theory, by their own brand of logic, and claimed to know what they were headed toward: a perfect communist state, as laid out in the *Manifesto*. Stevens found this sort of programmatic certainty to be at odds with reality as he knew it, not to mention at odds with his convictions regarding the proper function of the imagination. Yet at times, paradoxically, he seems to have seen his Marxist contemporaries as being far more in touch with reality and logic than he. Bates, in discussing these matters, sometimes appears disturbingly willing to accept this characterization of Thirties Marxism, seeing Stevens as the unrealistic, pure poet and the Marxists as the keen-eyed viewers of reality. One manifestation of this tendency is that Stanley Burnshaw—whose fatuous critique of Stevens "inspired" *Owl's Clover* in the first place, and provoked the contemplation of Marxism entitled "Mr. Burnshaw and the Statue"—is described by Bates as practicing "intelligent criticism." (In fairness it should be noted that Burnshaw, in later years, repudiated the views he held in the Thirties.)

These are not the only problems in Bates's book. He seems to look upon Stevens's poetic theory as being more rigidly and elaborately thought out than it really was, and to regard his poetic practice as having undergone a progressive development from one volume to the next in a fashion that—in one reader's opinion—is a bit too tidy to be thoroughly convincing. There are other flaws: Bates includes a substantial amount of biographical information but does very little with it; he goes on far too long about such matters as the history of leftist poetry in the early part of the century and the journalistic career of Richard Harding Davis (who he feels must have influenced Stevens's brief youthful foray into reporting); and he writes a plodding academic prose that makes reading this potentially absorbing study a wearisome chore. But these misgivings having been registered, it must be said that *Wallace Stevens: A Mythology of Self* does succeed, in many respects, in explaining how Stevens came to be the sort of poet that he was.

And what sort of poet, in the final analysis, was he? Decades ago, Yvor Winters labeled Stevens a "hedonist"—the idea being that Stevens's verse was solipsistic, that he was interested merely in his own sensations. Randall Jarrell, for his part, complained that Stevens had his head too far up in the heavens and not even one foot on the ground. But it is difficult for this critic, at least, to discover any justification for such complaints. Far from being preoccupied, in his poetry, either with himself or with dehumanized abstractions, Stevens is, rather, concerned throughout his work with celebrating the miracle of the human mind—its ability to create its own order, to conceive of beauty, to make moral discriminations, to take dominion over the things of the earth—the genius of the sea, the slovenly wilderness. His is not the undisciplined joy-seeking of the hedonist or of the wielder of disconnected abstractions, but, on the contrary, the joy of the artist in his own ability to discipline the physical world around him in a comprehensible whole, to find—as Stevens writes in "The Sail of Ulysses"—"meaning in design / Wrenched out of chaos."

FEBRUARY 1986

CONRAD AIKEN'S PILGRIMAGE

To the typical person of middle age or younger with any interest at all in American literature, the name of Conrad Aiken is likely to be familiar, but probably little more than that. It may be a name that one has skipped past once or twice in the *Norton Anthology of Modern Poetry* on one's way to Wilfred Owen or Hart Crane; or one may recognize Aiken as the author of one or more widely anthologized short stories. Or perhaps one's first thought upon hearing Aiken's name will be of T. S. Eliot, with whom Aiken studied at Harvard College and in the now almost mythic story of whose career he played a modest supporting role as percipient critic, occasional contributor (to Eliot's magazine *The Criterion*), and admiring (if somewhat patronized) friend. Even if one knows a bit about Aiken's life and work, his name will probably tend to evoke vague thoughts of his versatility, productivity, and endurance (his first book appeared in 1914, his last in 1971) rather than bring immediately to mind a particular novel or story or poem. Indeed, one reason for many readers' unfamiliarity with Aiken's *oeuvre* may well be that his bibliography is downright intimidating. For the first question that someone interested in reading Aiken must ask himself is: Where to start? With the twenty-nine volumes of poetry that he published in his lifetime? (The second edition of Aiken's *Collected Poems*, published in 1970, contains over one thousand pages.) With his five novels? With his criticism, his letters, his plays, his short stories? (*The Collected Short Stories* runs to nearly six hundred pages.) How about with *Ushant*, the notorious autobiographical "essay" he published in 1952?

And now there is yet another item bidding for a place on the Aiken student's must-read list: Edward Butscher's enlightening but deeply flawed new book, *Conrad Aiken: Poet of White Horse Vale*, the first installment of a projected two-volume biography which follows Aiken from his 1889 birth in Savannah, Georgia, to 1925, when, in the words of the jacket copy, "he stood on the threshold of both nervous breakdown and poetic success."[1] I shall return to this book—and to the subject of Aiken's tragic and troubled life—presently; suffice it for now to say that Butscher, whose heavily psychoanalytical approach to literary lives was manifested in his single previous contribution to the genre, *Sylvia Plath: Method and Madness* (1976), would seem to have found his ideal subject in Conrad Aiken. For Aiken, as much as Butscher, was fascinated by the theories of Freud, Jung, Adler, and company, and regarded literature as, above all, a means of exploring human consciousness. In this connection, a remark made by William Demarest, the protagonist of Aiken's highly autobiographical novel *Blue Voyage* (1927), may be of more than passing interest:

> It is my weakness as an author (so the critics have always said) that I appear incapable of presenting a theme energetically and simply. I must always wrap it up in tissue upon tissue of proviso and aspect; see it from a hundred angles; turn laboriously each side to the light; producing in the end not so much a unitary work of art as a melancholy *cauchemar* of ghosts and voices, a phantasmagoric world of disordered colors and sounds; a world without design or purpose; and perceptible only in terms of the prolix and fragmentary. The criticism is deserved, of course: but I have often wished that the critics would do me the justice to perceive that I have deliberately aimed at this effect, in the belief that the old unities and simplicities will no longer serve. No longer serve, I mean, if one is trying to translate, in any form of literary art, the consciousness of modern man. And this is what I *have* tried to do.

It was precisely to this end—the translation of the consciousness of modern man—that Aiken specialized for many years in an extremely long, loose, and repetitive kind of poem he called a "symphony." By nature a traditionalist, an admirer of Victorian verse, and (in his youth) an eager imitator of the simple, strong, and very popular narrative poems of John Masefield, Aiken nonetheless sought to participate in the modernist revolution, and he plainly felt that, by eschewing many of the structural conventions of poetry and adopting in their place some

---

[1] *Conrad Aiken: Poet of White Horse Vale*, by Edward Butscher; University of Georgia Press, 518 pages, $34.95.

of the structural conventions of music, he could represent the flow, the flux, the rhythms of human consciousness in a way that pre-modern verse had largely failed to do. The poems that he wrote in accordance with this theory—among them *The Jig of Forslin* (1916), *Senlin: A Biography* (1925), *The House of Dust* (1920), and *The Pilgrimage of Festus* (1923)—are notable for their graceful but prosy blank verse (which, like that in Eliot's "Love Song of J. Alfred Prufrock," often rhymes irregularly), their occasional lapses from this prosiness into clichéd "poetic" language and melodramatic imagery, and their dismaying lack of development. Reading these garrulous poems, one rarely feels as if one is getting anywhere; instead, one has the sensation of wandering back and forth over a relatively small stretch of cerebral terrain. At times Aiken seems to be writing quite deliberately (and reverently) under the influence of his friend Tom, but the intensity of Eliot is utterly missing here, and so is the sense, which one always has in Eliot, of the presence of a distinctive personality at the center of the poem. The speaker of the typical Aiken "symphony" comes across less as a flesh-and-blood individual than as a derivative, standard-issue Voice of Poetry.

In his prefaces to the "symphonies," Aiken describes his authorial intentions in the grandest possible terms. *Senlin*, he tells us, is about "the basic and possibly unanswerable question, *who and what am I*, how is it that I am I, Senlin, and not someone else?" The theme of *The Jig of Forslin* is "the process of vicarious wish-fulfillment by which civilized man enriches his circumscribed life and obtains emotional balance.... Forslin is not a man, but man." *The House of Dust* "is a symphonic poem about the city—ancient or modern, it makes no difference—and the crowd-man that inhabits it"; the poem considers that "in the evolution of man's consciousness...and in his dedication of himself to this supreme task, man possesses all that he could possibly require in the way of a religious credo." As for the eponymous hero of *The Pilgrimage of Festus*, he "is anybody or nobody. His pilgrimage is not real: it is imaginary. It is a cerebral adventure, of which the motive is a desire for knowledge"; although Festus conceives of himself "as a conqueror with nothing more to conquer," he has yet to conquer "the world of himself; and into this world he resolves to set forth anew." Yet these poems are neither as cerebral nor as adventurous as Aiken would have us believe, for he himself is never truly as exploratory as his oddly named protagonists; he consistently gives the impression of having gone into these poems already knowing what his protagonists were going to discover—namely, a host of Freudian, Jungian, and related concepts. That the poems' protagonists are essentially interchangeable is underscored in the preface to "Changing Mind," wherein Aiken notes that the poem's "wholly anonymous hero" takes up where Senlin left off and "carries the analysis a step farther."

Yet to describe what happens in these poems as "analysis" is misleading. By turns melancholy and ironic in tone, Aiken's "symphonies" read for the most part like an Edwardian poet's attempts to enter the Age of Eliot and Freud. Indeed, at times they read like attempts to *be* Eliot, to recast "The Love Song of J. Alfred Prufrock" (which Aiken had read, admired, and pushed on editors in manuscript) in less rigorous, more expansive language. *The Jig of Forslin* is especially rich in borrowings from Eliot's first great poem; unmistakably Prufrockian references to "Lazarus, raised from the dead," to drowning, to "seagirls," to the making of decisions ("You say, the time has come to make decisions,— / Question and vacillation must be ended") are plentiful; in place of Eliot's "yellow fog that rubs its back upon the windowpanes," Aiken gives us "yellow footlights blazing before my feet" and a "light winked out / Behind the yellow shades"; in the manner of Prufrock, who speaks of how his "hair is growing thin," Forslin says, "You see me: I am plain: and growing baldish." Eliot's "Let us" formulation (as in "Let us go then, you and I") gets a good workout: "Let us lounge in a bright cafe, and listen to music—"; "Let us drown, then, if to drown is but to change"; "Let us pull off our gloves: / Open the doors, and take the air a while"; "Let us go up among the pinewoods, / Let us go up the wind, it is cooler there; / Let us go slowly along hot yellow beaches." Aiken seems particularly eager to outdo Eliot in the matter of coffee and coffee-cups:

> Vermouth, then coffee… How much shall we tip the waiter?
> Here the fatigued mind wanders and forgets.
>
> .   .   .
>
> Isolda, leaning among her coffee-cups,
> Smiles at me.
> Helen of Sparta, bearing a silver tray,
> Laughs at me.
>
> .   .   .
>
> With the same coffee before me, and between my fingers

The same slow cigarette consuming in smoke;
And in my ears an echo of music lingers,
And the sound of a dying sentence that someone spoke.

Like Eliot in "Prufrock," Aiken in *The Jig of Forslin* sings the twentieth-century blues, while conveying—or attempting to convey—a sense of ennui, of despair, of the impossibility of enduring love in the modern world. Yet among the Eliotic chatter may be found lines and phrases more reminiscent of sentimental, crowd-pleasing Georgian verse than of High Modernism. "We blow in the air," Aiken writes, "like leaves our words are blown." (Leaves are ubiquitous in Aiken's fiction and poetry.) "And you do not hear the blood in my brain that cries, / 'I love you, I love you, I love you.'" (Aiken never says anything important just once.) "Time... Time... Time / And through the immortal silence we may hear / The choral stars like great clocks tick and chime." (The words *immortal* and *silence* are both favorites of Aiken's.) But it is not only in *Forslin* that Aiken indulges in such rhetoric. "Out of a vast sarcophagus of cloud," he writes in *The Pilgrimage of Festus*, "Pours the black death of rain." And death and rain make an equally sensational appearance in *Senlin*:

Hurry, spider, and spread your glistening web,
For death approaches!
Hurry, rose, and open your heart to the bee,
For death approaches!...
Death, huge in the star; small in the sand-grain;
Death himself in the rain,
Drawing the rain about him like a garment of jewels:
I hear the sound of his feet
On the stairs of the wind, in the sun,
In the forests of the sea...
Listen! the immortal footsteps beat!

To read one of these "symphonies" is to get the impression, eventually, that Aiken has almost nothing (or, at least, almost nothing original) to say, and that he is concerned mainly with working not-very-inventive changes on stock poetic formulas. It is, also, to note the stunning contrast between Aiken's and Eliot's poetic development. For while Eliot evolved dramatically from one major poem to the next, making extraordinary leaps in manner and perspective from "Prufrock" to *The Waste Land* to "The Hollow Men" to "Ash-Wednesday," Aiken's limp pentameter and banal treatment of his major themes—among them life and death, creation and consciousness, dreams and time, memory and desire—don't vary much from one "symphony" to another. The same handful of truisms—for instance, that life is a dream, that time is a dream, that life is delimited by time, that we all live in our own minds and can endure after death in the minds of others—is reiterated continually, and in the least imaginative of ways. Aiken even repeats words, phrases, and entire lines. His theoretical rationale for these repetitions is that in a real symphony the main theme is repeated and repeated again. But he seems to ignore the fact that classic symphonic form requires not merely repetition but variation and development. And the unfortunate truth is that there is simply not enough variation *or* development in Aiken's "symphonies." The critic J.G. Southwark makes a valid point when he says that Aiken fails to achieve the "significant form of a Haydn or Mozart symphony" and that he instead "gives us something more nearly akin to the diffuse symphonies of Bruckner or Mahler." But in their slackness, familiarity, and superficial prettiness Aiken's "symphonies" are less reminiscent of either Mozart or Mahler than of Mantovani.

Aiken's numerous non-symphonic poems and poetry collections—among them *Punch: The Immortal Liar* (1921), *The Coming Forth of Osiris Jones* (1942), *A Letter from Li Po and Other Poems* (1955)—take a remarkable variety of forms. There are sonnets and short free-verse poems; there are long monologues in blank verse and rhyming tetrameter; *Osiris Jones* looks like this most of the way through:

> *In a museum*
> visitors are requested not to touch the objects

> *In a concert hall*
> no admission after doors are closed

> *On an office door*
> Peter Jones

> *In a saloon*
> no treating allowed

Laundry-mark on linen
B69

Punch—which takes the form of an oral biography, as it were, of the fabled puppet (who is described by an acquaintance as "ugly and vile beyond all human knowledge")—is unexpectedly energetic and colloquial, and was, in its day, quite popular; today it seems little more than a curiosity, a period oddity. The relatively brief "Improvisations: Light and Snow," meanwhile, surprises one with its realistic touches and its controlled, unadorned language:

> On the day when my uncle and I drove to the cemetery,
> Rain rattled on the roof of the carriage;
> And talking constrainedly of this and that
> We refrained from looking at the child's coffin on the seat
>   before us.
> When we reached the cemetery
> We found that the thin snow on the grass
> Was already darkly transparent with rain;
> And boards had been lain upon it
> That we might walk without wetting our feet.

Aiken's best poems, indeed, are short ones, in which his ambitions seem more in line with the breadth and nature of his poetic gift. Some of his sonnets are very fine, and the most satisfying poetry in the "symphonies" may well be the uncharacteristically taut trimeter lines at the close of "Changing Mind," which can be read as a separate poem:

> My father which art in earth
> From whom I got my birth,
> What is it that I inherit?
> From the bones fallen apart
> And the deciphered heart,
> Body and spirit.
>
> My mother which art in tomb
> Who carriedst me in thy womb,
> What is it that I inherit?
> From the thought come to dust
> And the remembered lust,

Body and spirit.

Father and mother, who gave
Life, love, and now the grave,
What is it that I can be?
Nothing but what lies here,
The hand still, the brain sere,
Naught lives in thee

Nor ever will live, save
It have within this grave
Roots in the mingled heart,
In the damp ashes wound
Where the past, underground,
Falls, falls apart.

Yet, for the most part, the long poem remained Aiken's specialty until the end of his life. Perhaps the most celebrated of all Aiken's longer poems, "symphonies" or otherwise, are *Preludes for Memnon, or Preludes to Attitude* (1931) and its companion volume, *Time in the Rock, or Preludes to Definition* (1936). (Memnon, it will be remembered, was a nephew of Priam, slain by Achilles and wept for every morning thereafter by his mother, Eos, the dawn.) These two massive documents, each of which consists of several dozen largely self-contained sections of thirty or so lines apiece, aim unabashedly at the sort of stately profundity that Eliot would achieve in his *Four Quartets*. Aiken addresses his usual themes in an impressive variety of ways, casting different sections in the form of sonnets, odes, elegies, dramatic monologues, fables, verse anecdotes, and so forth. For all his formal wanderings, however, he never wanders far afield from his fundamental questions: What is the conscious mind? How do two conscious minds relate to each other? How can art—poetry in particular—movingly and meaningfully represent the nature of this communion? At their best, these poems manage to suggest the poignancy of the poet's quixotic search for answers, and to convey the magnitude of his frustration at the ultimate inefficacy of words to limn a world. Aiken writes affectingly, for instance, in section V of *Preludes for Memnon*:

Despair, that seeking for the ding-an-sich,
The feeling itself, the round bright dark emotion,

The color, the light, the depth, the feathery swiftness
Of you and the thought of you, I fall and fall
From precipice word to chasm word, and shatter
Heart, brain, and spirit on the maddening fact:
If poetry says it, it must speak with a symbol.

On the whole, however, *Preludes for Memnon* and its successor come across as pretentious and overupholstered. There is too much posing here, and too little sense of a poet truly grappling with an emotion or idea and trying to find the best words to express it; so frequently do certain locutions crop up that one begins to have the impression that the composition of the poems was less a matter of finding verbal equivalents to emotion than of fitting already selected words and phrases together into rhythmic sentences.

If I have dwelt at such length on Aiken's poetry, in spite of its manifold weaknesses, it is because Aiken is known mainly as a poet, because he identified himself mainly as a poet, and because Butscher, in his biography, places great importance on this self-identification. Yet it does not take long, after turning from Aiken's poetry to his longer fiction, to decide that he is considerably more successful as a novelist than as a poet. Or maybe it is more nearly correct to say that his novels, despite their shortcomings in overall design and in the development of character, have more than their share of absorbing, and even highly compelling, moments. It must be borne in mind, too, that Aiken's five contributions to the genre—*Blue Voyage* (1927), *Great Circle* (1933), *King Coffin* (1935), *A Heart for the Gods of Mexico* (1939), and *Conversation, or Pilgrims' Progress* (1940)—were hardly intended as conventional novels, with conventionally conceived plots and protagonists. On the contrary, they are extraordinarily idiosyncratic excursions—or, rather, incursions—which have been aptly described by R.P. Blackmur as "picaresque novels of the psyche." Opposite the first page of *Blue Voyage*, significantly, Aiken quotes Coleridge: "What is there in thee, Man, that can be known? / Dark fluxion, all unfixable by thought, / A phantom dim of past and future wrought, / Vain sister of the worm—." This is, one might say, Coleridge in his most Aikenesque mood, and the epigraph certainly captures the thematic thrust (and something of the spirit, too) not only of *Blue Voyage* but also of its four successors. For, whatever their ostensible settings, these novels, like Aiken's "symphonies," take place principally in the minds of their protagonists, and are concerned chiefly with the question of how well such minds—intelligent, ironic, inquisitive, and impossibly complex—can come to know themselves. Like *The Pilgrimage of Festus*, these novels are "cerebral adventure[s]"; like *Senlin*, they confront "the basic and possibly unanswerable question, *who and what am I*, how is it that I am I…and not someone else?" Yet the novels are not just "symphonies" in prose; in fact, they are a good deal more palatable than any of Aiken's longer poems, as fresh and lively as the "symphonies" are inert and derivative. Part of the reason for the difference, one imagines, is that outside of the realm of poetry Aiken may have felt less self-conscious, less compelled to adopt certain (inappropriate) forms or to assume a particular (pretentious) level of diction or to try to compete with anybody. At any rate, the elegant-but-unaffected language that makes so much of Aiken's poetry feel loose and prosy and Edwardian proves to be a positive asset in his novels; and whatever impulse drove him to infect his "symphonies" with so many false and melodramatic passages simply doesn't manifest itself in the novels.

This is not to suggest that Aiken's novels are plain and down-to-earth; it is only to state that the moments of intense contemplation which do figure prominently in these books are rendered in thoroughly believable form. It helps a great deal that Aiken takes the trouble to set a protagonist convincingly in motion, and to place him among other equally credible human beings, before getting down to the business of rendering at length that protagonist's deepest, most solemn thoughts. Yes, there is heightened rhetoric here by the bushel, as exemplified by this passage from *Blue Voyage*, in which Aiken memorably sets forth his view of the human individual as a universe unto himself:

> What was it he wanted? What was it that was driving him back? What was this singular mechanism in him that wanted so deliberately, so consciously, to break itself? A strange, a rich, a deep personality he had—it baffled and fascinated him. Everybody, of course, was like this,—depth beyond depth, a universe chorally singing, incalculable, obeying tremendous laws, chemical or divine, of which it was able to give its own consciousness not the faintest inkling…. He brushed the dark hair of this universe. He looked into its tranquil black-pooled eyes. Its mouth was humorous and bitter. And this universe would go out and talk inanely to

other universes—talking only with some strange minute fraction of its identity, like a vast sea leaving on the shore, for all mention of itself, a single white pebble, meaningless. A universe that contained everything—all things—yet said only one word: "*I.*" A music, an infinite symphony, beautifully and majestically conducting itself there in the darkness, but remaining forever unread and unheard.

Heightened or not, however, this excerpt works as prose—rhythmically, dynamically, dramatically—in a way that the comparable passages in the "symphonies" don't work as poetry. It is, for one thing, expressed with more vigor, more energy, than is common in Aiken's poems. The language feels natural, not forced. And—very importantly—the excerpt appears in a text which also contains realistic dialogue and precise descriptions of the physical world; these things give the protagonist's musings a context, a *raison d'être*. In the novels, that is, such a passage as the one I have quoted may be understood as representing the state of mind of a vividly evoked human being, and is therefore of human—and, potentially, dramatic—interest; in an Aiken "symphony," by contrast, the protagonist is invariably impossible to visualize or to believe in, and accordingly one finds oneself in the position of having to accept his often tiresome and hyperbolic meditations entirely on their own terms—as, that is, disembodied philosophical propositions—or to reject them *in toto*.

While Aiken's novels have their splendid moments, the finest of Aiken's many short stories are themselves splendid moments. Perhaps the saddest irony of Aiken's career is that while his ambition propelled him to expend the bulk of his creative energies on long, avant-garde forms—book-length "symphonic" poems, stream-of-consciousness novels—his talent seems to have been far better suited to short poems and (especially) to short stories of a more conventional nature. Certainly it is the case that in the longer forms Aiken tended to eschew traditional ideas about structure, while in the shorter forms he generally worked obediently—and often with remarkable effectiveness—within conventional boundaries. Why is this true? One has the impression that whereas Aiken, at book length, was incapable of sustaining interest in anyone's consciousness but his own, and consequently produced uneven novels and banal poetry which reeked of self-indulgence, he could (from time to time) escape the prison of this psyche for long enough to write a short story, and thus manages to render in that genre—with a powerful objectivity, and at times a great tenderness—people very different from himself, with ideas and tastes and fixations of their own. In one story after another, Aiken successfully translates into touching human terms his abiding preoccupations with the problematic nature of consciousness and the fragility of sanity, joy, beauty, and all good things. "Proximity to madness," Aiken writes in a story called "Gehenna," "is not a privilege of genius alone; it is the privilege and natural necessity of every consciousness, from the highest to the lowest." Nor, as Aiken's stories demonstrate time and again, is proximity to poverty or ugliness or imprisonment or death accorded only to some of us; even the healthiest, happiest, richest, and most beautiful of us stands a small step away from any of these fates.

"Mr. Arcularis," for instance, presents us with an old man who, after a successful operation, is released from the hospital (or is he?), and who thereupon goes on a cruise (or does he?); the story's stunningly abrupt and haunting conclusion, in which the truth of the matter becomes suddenly clear, underlines the fearsome closeness of reality and illusion, of dream life and waking life. Almost as effective is "Impulse," which dramatizes the proximity not of reality to illusion but of order to chaos. The story's protagonist is a good-natured and well-to-do young man named Michael Lowes, who commits an act of shoplifting on an inexplicable impulse and is immediately placed under arrest, deserted by his friends, and sued for divorce by his wife—thereby learning (like Sherman McCoy in Tom Wolfe's *The Bonfire of the Vanities*) how easily a contented, law-abiding life can turn into its hellish antithesis. "This was what life was," the astonished Lowes concludes once his fate has begun to take shape. "It was just as meaningless and ridiculous as this; a monstrous joke; a huge injustice." A similar motif is at the center of "A Pair of Vikings," wherein the middle-aged, small-town protagonist finds himself charmed by an exquisitely beautiful and vivacious young married couple, only twenty-two years old, both of them daredevils who regularly perform a remarkable—and exceedingly dangerous—stunt called the "Drome of Death" at a local fair. The young lady is less skilled than her husband, and it is obvious that her days are numbered; before the year is out, she dies in an accident, and when the protagonist runs into her widower some time later he finds the young man "faded and cheapened, and looking almost haggard—the beauty had gone out of him." Though he has defied death for years, only now does he really know the meaning of the word; only now does he recognize how close joy is to sorrow, beauty to ugliness, gay youth to the grave.

These are simple themes, and they are conveyed in a straightforward fashion. But the results are unusually affecting. The best of Aiken's stories have an easy, natural eloquence, an unerring sense of pace and of shape; consistently, Aiken holds back from interposing himself between the material and the reader. A story which is especially impressive for Aiken's expert handling of potentially mawkish material is "Hello, Tib." The story—barely an anecdote—could hardly be less complicated: a man waiting for his morning commuter train sees a friendly kitten gamboling toward him down the nearly empty platform. He is exhilarated by this sight, and by the pure affection he reads into it: "After all, that was what life was, wasn't it? Love, nothing but love!" Some children however, distract the kitten, calling "Hello, Tib!", and it goes over to them instead; when they tire of it, the kitten wanders away, jumps onto the track just before the train arrives, and is killed. No one sees this happen but the man himself, who is heartbroken by his failure to rescue the kitten from its fate. "For was he not the only person here, on this early-morning platform, who had really seen and loved this little cat, and foreseen her tragic destiny?" At the heart of his pain lies the fact that no one else witnessed the kitten's death: "It was as if nothing had happened…. He alone knew that she was dead. He alone could have saved her." It is an extraordinarily tender story, delicate in its perceptions and wonderfully controlled; Aiken considers the nature and meaning of the communion between man and kitten without ever falling into abstraction or sentimentality, without becoming too pretentious or inward or contrived. On the contrary, the story successfully translates Aiken's thematic preoccupations into the recognizable terms of everyday life; it renders his ideas in a form that enables one not only to understand them intellectually but to experience them emotionally. Such is the case not only in "Hello, Tib" but in several of Aiken's *Collected Stories*; this is one volume of Aiken's work, long out of circulation, that richly merits reprinting.

If Aiken's fiction is so obsessed with the proximity of a pleasant, orderly life to chaos and death and madness, it is doubtless because of the single great tragic event of his life, which plunged him, at the tender age of eleven, from an affluent, reasonably happy childhood into pure horror. Early one February morning in 1901, Aiken was lying in bed in his Savannah, Georgia, home when he heard, from his parents' bedroom across the hall, two gunshots and the sound of a body falling. "And so I got out of bed," Aiken explained in an interview sixty-seven years later,

> and went through the children's bedroom, where my sister and two brothers were in their cribs, and closed the folding doors between the nursery and my father's room, and stepped over my father's body... he'd sprung all the way across the room from the bed, and was lying on his face with his pistol still in his hand, and went to see if my mother was still alive—and of course she wasn't. Her mouth was wide open in the act of screaming.... So I closed the doors and got dressed. And told the children to stay in their beds and that the nurse would come up and take care of them, and went down to the maids' room in the basement, and woke them, and told them that there'd been a... a mishap, and that I was going for the police and would they go up and dress the children and bring them down, and keep them in the dining room. So I went to the police station which was only a block away from our house, and I told them about this.

The poet's father was William Aiken, a bright, ambitious, and well-to-do young physician with deep-seated insecurities; his uxoricide and suicide were the culmination of a long period during which he had grown increasingly anxious and paranoid, criticizing his wife, Anna, for her active social life and accusing her of infidelity. It was an event from which Aiken would never truly recover, and the family's way of dealing with the problems it engendered cannot be said to have facilitated his psychic adjustment. For one thing, the murder-suicide was never talked about in Aiken's presence, the boy never given an opportunity to come to terms with it. For another, Aiken and his siblings were split up, his sister and two brothers adopted by non-relatives and given new last names, while Aiken alone—the eldest—kept his name and was raised by relatives in Massachusetts, who sent him to an exclusive preparatory school and then to Harvard. Though as an adult he seems to have been more well adjusted than many people with less formidable traumas, Aiken did have his problems and peccadillos. Throughout his adult life (he died in 1973), he was both a heavy drinker and a compulsive adulterer; though over the decades he moved back and forth a number of times between the northeastern United States and England—the "mother country" which he identified, rather peculiarly, with his New England-born mother—he chose to spend his last years in Savannah, next door to the house in which his parents had died.

According to Aiken, the most important decision of his life—to become a writer—was made at an early age, before his parents' death. By his own account in *Ushant* (a book whose punning title—"you shan't"—would seem to be a response to the final word of *The Waste Land*, "shantih"), the young Aiken was first attracted to the idea of being a poet when he came across an epigraph in Thomas Hughes's *Tom Brown's School Days*: "I am the Poet of White Horse Vale, sir, with liberal notions under my cap." "[N]o doubt," Aiken writes in *Ushant*, "this had been the first occurrence of the magic, the all-precipitating word or at any rate the occasion for the first explanation of it: poets, there were such things as poets: they wrote poems!" In the years that followed, the boy lived under "the increasingly important and relevant shadow of the Poet of White Horse Vale." Thanks to the income provided by his inheritance (and, during his first marriage, by a legacy from the father of his wife, Jessie), Aiken would be able, for the most of his adult life, to devote himself full-time to the job of free-lance poet and fiction writer, and to the production of careful and intelligent literary reviews and essays for such publications as *The New Republic*, *Poetry*, and *The Atlantic Monthly*. (Many of these writings were brought together in 1958 in *A Reviewer's ABC*, which was reissued ten years later under the title *Collected Criticism*.) With this freedom came the opportunity to pursue literary friendships—with, among others, Amy Lowell, John Gould Fletcher, Rupert Brooke, Harriet Monroe, and of course Eliot—on both sides of the Atlantic. But the writer's vocation also carried certain powerful and solemn associations: since the writing of verse had been one of his father's many avocations, Aiken identified more and more with his late father as his interest in writing poetry burgeoned; in addition, because the word *liberal* appeared in Hughes's epigraph—bringing to the boy's mind his maternal grandfather, an extremely liberal Unitarian minister who had gone so far as to ban the Eucharist at his church—Aiken from an early age identified poetry with liberalism and with opposition to traditional religious practices. Unlike his friend Eliot, Aiken would always remain unenthralled by organized religion and the Christian God, venerating instead the twin deities of poetry and modern psychology.

It is Aiken's lifelong fascination with poetry and modern psychology, and the ways in which his childhood tragedy may have led to his yoking of the one with the other and inspired his intense dedication to both, that most interest Edward Butscher in his new biography of Aiken. At its best, the book does constitute an absorbing and perceptive account of the formation of a poet's mind. Butscher's interpretation of Aiken's life and work—an interpretation which is founded on the notion of his literary career as a "quest for the means to defuse the psychoanalytic time bomb ticking away inside his locker mind"—strikes one as highly defensible (if not always felicitously phrased). The biographer accepts—and there's no reason not to accept—the self-analysis of *Blue Voyage*, in which Aiken (or, rather, his autobiographical protagonist) characterizes his own reticence, impassivity, and restless inability to "lov[e] one person or place for more than a season" as the lingering ill effects of his father's crime. Furthermore, Butscher persuasively ascribes Aiken's relentless womanizing to his complex feelings toward a mother "who had to be simultaneously possessed and degraded, saved and punished, again and again"; and—in what seems to me a just and sensitive interpretation of the facts—he attributes Aiken's powerful literary drive to the "doubts of the self's very reality" that must have followed hard upon the sudden and dramatic loss of both parents. "In the vacuum left behind by William's and Anna's violent demise," Butscher suggests, "Conrad must have feared he was about to be sucked into their wake, snuffed out before he actually existed, though language and art alone might prevent this from happening."

These observations, one senses, have a great deal of validity. But even when he appears to be on the right track, Butscher is altogether too reliant upon—if not, indeed, madly in love with—psychiatric terms. Words like *gestalt*, *prepubic*, *experiential*, and *abreact* proliferate in his pages. Seemingly implicit in his prose style is the notion that the wisdom of any insight is directly proportional to the amount of psychological lingo that can be worked into one's explanation of it. By the second page Butscher is already knee-deep in the swamps of psychologist-talk, and loving every minute of it: "Certainly the form his [William Aiken's] delusional paranoia eventually assumed, a profound distrust of his wife, had environmental roots in his father's grim Puritan-ism and condescending distaste for the woman below his station he had married out of carnal weakness." At least once, moreover, Butscher is so wrapped up in his Psych 101 lecture that he leaves a sentence hanging in mid-air: "Sterility may ensue, budding careers be distorted or abridged, when this greenhouse environment, which tends to favor retreats into safe scholastic modes and infringes upon the tyro's free-dom to make silly mistakes, to take extreme risks in an art in which self must confront its secret visages." (Almost as noisome as Butscher's taste for jargon is his proclivity for highfalutin name-dropping; in a single half-page he manages to mention Socrates, Arnold, Marcus Aurelius, Spengler, Emerson, and Lacan, with no apparent purpose other than to impress and confuse.)

Before long, in fact, it is clear to the reader of *Conrad Aiken* that the methods and vocabulary of psychoanalysis serve more as a replace-ment for understanding, in this book, than as a means to it. Time and again, Butscher mistakes description for explanation, operating on the hypothesis that once one has attached a Freudian or Jungian or Adlerian tag to something, one has said all that one can about it. About Aiken's supposed identification of his mother and first wife with Amy Lowell, for instance, Butscher writes: "Mother, wife, Lowell—they were recur-rent forms of the ambiguous female archetype that he had to pursue and rebuff." But why, one must wonder, did Aiken fixate on Lowell and not someone else? This kind of analysis doesn't explain so much as it pigeonholes. The same is true of Butscher's discussion of Aiken's childhood tenderness toward helpless animals, in particular a kitten put out in the rain by a family maid. Butscher suggest that the boy's demonstrations of pity "were his sensibility's initial forays into the world beyond self, his compassion for the kitten a psychic expansion of the self-pity instilled by a father's erratic behavior and a mother's apparent defection." Yet Butscher fails to consider that another child, in the same circumstances, might have reacted by being especially cruel to animals. The question remains—what made Aiken "expand" his self-pity to include animals, rather than transfer to them his resentment and hostility toward his parents? To ignore this question is to fail to recognize what made Aiken a human being and not a case study in a psychology textbook. (It is also, of course, to analyze goodness out of existence.)

The overriding purpose of this biography is plain: Butscher wants to revive Aiken as a significant literary figure. But his argument for such a revival is based not on literary but on psychological grounds. "Aiken has to be considered a major force in the shaping of an American poetic tradition and intellectual focus," Butscher maintains, because "his awareness that Nietzsche's translation of philosophy into psychology was pivotal to an understanding of civilization and aesthetics" was "far more valid... than Eliot's conservative resurrection of abandoned pieties." In other words, Aiken is important because he knows that psychology matters more than philosophy or religion. It doesn't seem to cross Butscher's mind that some readers might not take this primacy for granted; consistently, he seems astonished by—and peeved at—those to whom psychology is not the queen of sciences. He ridicules the "metaphysical-minded philosophers" whose ideas about literary creativity and criticism held unfair sway (he says) until the advent of Aiken; and he endorses Aiken's sardonic put-down of "the aesthetic approach," whose partisans the poet assailed for regarding beauty as "something detached, independent, not to say absolute, something which would exist whether or not there also existed any creature to give it praise."

Butscher's understanding of a number of concepts borders on the simplistic. Implying an equation among literary modernism, political radicalism, atheism, and moral integrity, on the one hand, and among literary traditionalism, political reaction, the profession of religious faith, and moral corruption, on the other, he contrasts Aiken sharply with Eliot—an exercise from which the former, unsurprisingly, emerges as the clear victor. His argument, in sum, is that Eliot, by joining the Church of England, was "turn[ing] his back on the radical openness to experience implicit in his experimental aesthetic"; he was abandoning modernist rebellion and "returning to the fold, the privileged WASP Old Guard [that] Pound had never really abandoned." Aiken, by contrast, was a pillar of "intellectual integrity"; unable "to desert the 'liberal notions' associated in his mind with the germination and growth of his persona as the Poet of White Horse Vale,... he could not yield to the impulse to defy reason and wallow in a mystical revival." Needless to say, this analysis tells us less about Eliot and Aiken than about Butscher. To address only one or two of his points: first, Eliot cannot be said to have returned to the "WASP" fold with his conversion to Anglicanism, because he plainly never left it; when he wrote *The Waste Land*, after all, he was a London banker. And his embracing of religion, far from constituting a renunciation of some imagined modernist credo, seems quite consistent with the longing for faith implicit in *The Waste Land*.

His scorn for religion notwithstanding, Butscher's faith in the ability of Freud and company to explain absolutely anything smacks of the most obsessive religiosity. He appears to be constitutionally incapable of looking at life from any other perspective, of admitting the validity of any other system. His discussions of Aiken's work focus on its psychological aspect, and are thus inevitably repetitious and reductive; at times he behaves as if the poems are good to the degree that they lend themselves to such analysis. So absorbed is he in working out his analysis that it doesn't seem to occur to him how shocking, or funny, or both, some of his observations might sound to a lay reader:

> Attached to the sterile mask and obstinate pain was a permanent sexualization of his feelings into a satyr appetite for women as mere meat... including a penchant for cunnilingus—"our little peculiarities... canyon yodeling. Pearl diving. Muff barking."

Butscher is an eager teacher. But the most significant lesson this book teaches is that the talent of the psychoanalyst and the talent of the biographer are related but far from identical, and that Butscher would seem to have the former talent in greater proportion than he has the latter. When Butscher tells us, for example, that Aiken, soon after his first marriage, began to commit adultery, we're surprised; the newly married Aiken that he describes simply doesn't flow naturally out of the shy Harvard student we think we've come to know. Butscher thinks it's enough to show that the two different kinds of behavior are both explicable according to Aiken's background and psychological profile. But it's *not* enough, not for a biography. Butscher consistently seems not to recognize this. And the further he gets into the book the remoter Aiken seems, the less a person, the more a textbook case. To read this book, as a matter of fact, is to realize how wide a gulf there is between a human individual and the psychological terms that one may use to describe him; it is to realize that one might read such a treatise about one's closest friend and hardly recognize him. A single page of *Ushant* or of Aiken's *Selected Letters* gives one more of an idea of the kind of man Aiken was than does all of Butscher's book.

Ultimately, indeed, *Conrad Aiken* seems almost to have been an attempt to demonstrate the limitations of the psychoanalytical approach. A biography shouldn't be sensational, to be sure; but at the same time it shouldn't avoid the drama, the color, the flavor of a life. Aiken's life, judging by all the available materials, appears to have had more than its share of drama and flavor. But little of that drama or flavor has made it into Butscher's biography. There is no sense in this book of how Aiken structured his days, of how he spoke to his wife, of how he related to his children. We know everything about his neuroses, but next to nothing about his character—next to nothing, that is, about the form his neuroses took in human and literary terms. And neuroses without a human dimension are just entries in the *Merck Manual*.

Conrad Aiken looked upon life as a pilgrimage of the mind, a journey, a voyage to discovery. A resident in his childhood of two major seacoast towns—Savannah, Georgia, and New Bedford, Massachusetts—and a frequent passenger, in his adult years, on transatlantic liners between New York and London, Aiken made frequent use of the ocean voyage as a metaphor. The titles of several of his works—*The Pilgrimage of Festus*; *Blue Voyage*; *Conversation, or Pilgrims' Progress*; *The Divine Pilgrim*—reflect his preoccupation with such images. Yet Edward Butscher is unable to conceive of Aiken's life as anything other than a case study. The Conrad Aiken of this book, alas, is not a voyager on the sea of self-knowledge but an unfortunate patient-prisoner in some Bellevue of the mind. And the prime casualty of Butscher's method is, sadly, Aiken's art, which—though he discusses the poetry and fiction, and quotes from it quite frequently in the course of his psychoanalysis of the writer—does not receive much attention from him *as* art. And it is, after all, Aiken's art, more than anything else, that makes his life worth chronicling, his mind worth probing.

FEBRUARY 1989

I.A. RICHARDS: CRITIC AS SCIENTIST

For many of us with an interest in twentieth-century literary criticism, Ivor Armstrong Richards is at once a central and a problematic figure. He was, of course, one of the most influential critics of the modern age, if not *the* most influential. His emphasis on rigor, precision, and the poem-as-object earned him (from some) the impressive sobriquet "father of the New Criticism," while his preoccupation with theory and with the relativity of literary truth reflects more than coincidental—and less than delightful—affinities with the practitioners of deconstruction. As John Paul Russo observes in his exhaustive new study of Richards's life and work, Richards, for better *and* for worse, "led the age of analysis into literary criticism."[1]

Born in Cheshire, England, in 1893, the son of a chemical engineer, Richards was, for all his love of poetry, aware from a tender age of the centrality of science and technology to modern society; yet this centrality, in his view, was not properly reflected in the way literature was talked and written about. As a student at Magdalen College, Cambridge, around the time of the First World War (when recurrent tuberculosis kept him out of uniform), he looked upon the varieties of criticism then in vogue and found them—well, unscientific: in the wake of 1890s Aestheticism, literary critics tended toward post-Paterian impressionism, with its windy appreciation of "Beauty" and "The Grand Style," and toward biographical and historical readings. Richards, for his part, loathed biography and history: he was more interested in the future (and in the part he could play in it) than in the past, more interested in contemplating the forthcoming Age of Science than in examining the ways people had lived and thought in the days before Freud, Einstein, and *Gestalt*.

---

[1] *I.A. Richards: His Life and Work*, by John Paul Russo; John Hopkins University Press, 832 pages, $39.95.

So it was that, after devoting his freshman year to history courses, Richards turned his back on these studies and proceeded to concentrate on such rapidly advancing disciplines as physiology, chemistry, psychology, and modern philosophy. The influence of his courses in these disciplines—and of his extensive independent reading in related fields over the ensuing years—proved to be profound and lifelong. Though Richards would pass through several phases in his wide-ranging career as author and educator, his guiding article of faith throughout his life seems to have been that the constantly expanding body of scientific knowledge about the nature of man and his world must, of necessity, lead to an increased understanding of the nature of the experience of language and literature, and consequently to an improvement in man's understanding of himself. Like H.G. Wells, Richards was at once practical and idealistic, knowledgeable about science's accomplishments but encumbered by a misguided faith in its potential ability to unlock the mysteries of human character and feeling.

Nevertheless, Richards's contribution to literary criticism is extraordinary. It was he who introduced such terms as *tone* and *speaker* to the discussion of poetry, and who first named the two elements of a metaphor the tenor and the vehicle. He helped teach critics to approach a poem not as the direct expression of a poet's feeling (which, of course, it often is, but which it sometimes is not) but as a "dramatic" or a "semi-dramatic" utterance. In his most important books—*Principles of Literary Criticism* (1925), *Science and Poetry* (1926), and *Practical Criticism* (1929)—he raised fundamental but widely neglected questions about the nature of the literary experience, forcing professional and amateur readers alike to think long and hard about what actually happened when they read a piece of writing. At its best, Richards's work has wit, energy, and an impressive sense of conviction and purpose; if Ezra Pound reminded modern readers that poetry should be as well written as prose, Richards (like Eliot) reminded them that literary criticism should be as serious and disciplined as scientific discourse.

At its worst, however, Richards's work is deeply frustrating—by turns self-evident and incomprehensible, imprecise and tautological, pointless and pretentious. One might hesitate to speak so harshly about Richards's criticism, except that he was himself so thoroughly dismissive of the critics who had preceded him, and so outspoken about the unqualified superiority of his own approach. I quote from the celebrated opening pages of *Principles of Literary Criticism*:

The questions which the critic seeks to answer, intricate though they are, do not seem to be extraordinarily difficult. What gives the experience of reading a certain poem its value? How is this experience better than another?... But if we now turn to consider what are the results yielded by the best minds pondering these questions in the light of the eminently accessible experiences provided by the Arts, we discover an almost empty garner. A few conjectures, a supply of admonitions, many acute isolated observations, some brilliant guesses, much oratory and applied poetry, inexhaustible confusion, a sufficiency of dogma, no small stock of prejudices, whimsies and crotchets, a profusion of mysticism, a little genuine speculation, sundry stray inspirations, pregnant hints and random *aperçus*; of such as these, it may be said without exaggeration, is extant critical theory composed.

Richards proceeds to list famous slogans from Aristotle, Horace, Dryden, Carlyle, and other critics through the ages. For instance: "All men naturally receive pleasure from imitation." "The spontaneous overflow of powerful feeling." "A criticism of Life." "Significant form." Richards's comment on these snippets: "Such are the pinnacles, the *apices* of critical theory, the heights gained in the past by the best thinkers in their attempt to reach explanations of the value of the arts. Some of them, many of them indeed, are profitable starting points for reflection, but neither together, nor singly, nor in any combination do they give what is required."

The implication here, naturally, is that Richards *does* do what is required, that he does explain, once and for all, the value of the arts. Yet neither *Principles of Literary Criticism* nor any of its successors contains an explanation better than Wordsworth's or Arnold's. To read through his criticism is to gain the distinct impression that he specializes not in explanations of artistic value but in precise, categorical pronouncements about matters that simply do not lend themselves to precise categories. Indeed, generations of readers have legitimately questioned whether most of what Richards wrote can be classified as literary criticism at all. The majority of his writings—especially those of his middle and later years (he died in 1979)—are concerned less with literature than with language, and with the promulgation of hypotheses that are as applicable to laundry lists as to poetry. Discussions of specific literary works form a surprisingly tiny part of his *oeuvre*. As Russo notes, "Richards believed that theory is for books, and practical analysis of texts for the lecture hall." What is perhaps most remarkable about Richards's career is how small a part literature actually played in shaping his theories, and how deeply indebted he was, by contrast, to the teachers of his undergraduate science courses and to a few scientific journals. Scientific concepts, more than literary insights, lie at the core of his work; those concepts lend, as Russo observes, "an air of precision and objectivity to his proceedings."

All too often, however, that is all they do lend to Richards's work—an *air* of precision and objectivity. For although Richards readily admits that science "can tell us nothing about the nature of things in any *ultimate* sense," he nonetheless often behaves as if the introduction of scientific terms, graphs, charts, and analogies to discussions of literature automatically lends such discussions greater validity. He creates neat categories, for instance, where no one before him had ever thought in terms of categories. Among his inventions in this line are the three types of imagery ("typographical," "tied," and "free"), the three varieties of sentimentality, and the five (sometimes seven) kinds of work that language performs. (This way of thinking strongly influenced many of Richards's followers, most famously his student William Empson, who in 1930, at the tender age of twenty-three, published the classic *Seven Types of Ambiguity*.) From the physicist Niels Bohr, Richards borrowed the principle of "complementarity," which embodied Bohr's recognition that the results of scientific investigation are necessarily distorted by the properties of the investigative apparatus; Richards makes use of the word to describe the relativity of literature. "Speakers and readers," Russo explains, "are in a complementary situation with a text, and so are the words on the page with one another; the total context is always provoking new shades of meaning and definition."

Perhaps Richards's most well-known coinage is the word *pseudostatement*, which he defines as "a form of words which is justified entirely by its effect in releasing or organizing our impulses and attitudes (due regard being had for the better or worse organization of these *inter se*); a statement, on the other hand, is justified by its truth, *i.e.*, its correspondence, in a highly technical sense, with the fact to which it points." A work of non-fiction makes statements; a work of literature makes pseudo-statements. Thus Dante's Christianity, say, does not represent an actual expression of belief with which an agnostic reader must come to terms, but a "pseudo-belief" which should pose no problem at all.

For many readers, of course, the very idea of pseudo-statements and pseudo-beliefs poses a considerable problem. For though it is worthwhile to heed Richards's reminder that opinions, ideas, and beliefs enter a work of literature in a distinctly different manner than they do a work of non-fiction prose, the important thing is that they *do* enter, and that to appreciate the work of a writer (however great) whose beliefs strongly inform his work can be a very complex matter for a reader who does not share those beliefs. After all, to read a serious novel or poem is to confront, in some form and to some degree, another person's soul; if the fundamental assumptions of such a soul prove to be utterly different from one's own, a genuine assimilation of the work of art must necessarily become more difficult; a reader who does not find the process to be seriously complicated by such circumstances can only be failing to experience literature on a human level. And, in fact, one of the most unpleasant long-term consequences of Richards's critical theories (though one would hardly attribute this development entirely to Richards's influence) has been the proliferation of academic critics who plainly *don't* experience literature on a human level—who regard any sincere expression of strong emotion in literature as sentimentality and who consider true literature to be an entirely intellectual activity, a form of high-level wordplay.

And at times it seems as if wordplay is what Richards is all about. Just as he borrowed the word *complementarity* from Bohr, so Richards, dissatisfied by the vagueness of such words as *beauty* and *pleasure*, contrived a crude model of human aesthetic response based on C.S. Sherrington's 1906 study the *Integrative Action of the Nervous System*, and thereby redefined the abstractions of turn-of-the-century neurology. The model, to put it simply, enabled Richards to "explain" beauty and pleasure—and even such moral concepts as good and evil—as consequences of the effective organization of impulses. "For Richards," Russo writes, "the distinction between good and evil is the difference between 'free' and 'wasteful' organization, between 'fullness' and 'narrowness' of life." Thus, "by a good experience we mean one in which the impulses which make it are fulfilled and successful, adding as the necessary qualification that their exercise and satisfaction shall not interfere in any way with more important impulses."

Of course, to speak of an impulse as "fulfilled and successful" has no neurological meaning, and therefore such an "explanation" does not really explain anything; all it does is replace a relatively comprehensible abstraction with a relatively incomprehensible one. Perhaps such concepts as good and evil do all come down to neurology, in the end, but Richards's formulations are so scientifically primitive as to be worthless. To define "unfair or aggressive behavior," as he does, by saying that it leads "to a form of organisation which deprives the person so organised of whole ranges of important values" is to say nothing at all; at best it is meaningless, at worst misleading. As John Crowe Ransom observed in his 1941 essay "Criticism as Pure Speculation," Richards's "was an esoteric poetic...much too unrelated to the public sense of a poetic experience," which "very nearly severed the dependence of poetic effect upon any standard of objective knowledge or belief."

How is one to explain Richards's seeming compulsion to explain such things as aesthetic value and moral virtue in terms of neurological organization? Reading Richards's chief critical texts, one cannot help feeling that he was, quite simply, more comfortable with neurological mysteries than with moral and aesthetic ones. In any event, eager though he was to distinguish sharply between the ways that language works in science and in poetry, Richards patently felt that bringing the language and thought processes of science into literary criticism was essential in order to keep literature (especially poetry) and the serious discussion thereof vital and relevant in the twentieth century—in order to "bridge the chasm," as Russo puts it, "between science and art."

Yet surely the only hope of poetry in the modern age lies in leaving that chasm unbridged, in not confusing art with science and technology. This is not to deny that the careful internal analysis of a poem, in the manner of the New Critics, is the most sensible of all critical approaches to poetry; it is merely to deny that such analysis represents a bridging of the chasm between science and poetry, to deny that there is anything about the New Criticism that makes it especially suitable to an age of science, and to deny that there is a good reason for Richards to depend as heavily as he does upon scientific terminology. What is most urgently required of a first-rate literary critic is not an acquaintance with the argot of science, or with the latest issue of *Scientific American*, but a deep sensitivity to language and feeling, a mature understanding of human character, a sense of style, and (as Eliot said)

101

intelligence. And the fact, alas, is that more than a few of Richards's works betray surprising deficiencies in all but the last of these categories.

If Richards was inordinately fascinated by the latest achievements of science, and irresistibly tempted to incorporate them into his theory of criticism, it is because, as I have suggested, he was a believer—like Bernard Shaw, a prolific, iconoclastic, and sometimes rather starry-eyed believer—in the power of new ideas, during an age of science, to improve the lot of humankind. It was not only in the field of literary criticism that this quality of character manifested itself; another outgrowth of this tendency was his decades-long championing of Basic English, a simplified version of English which was invented by his friend and collaborator C.K. Ogden (*Foundations of Aesthetics, The Meaning of Meaning*) in the late 1920s to help in teaching English to foreigners, and which thrived between the two world wars. During his middle and later years, Richards spent an extraordinary amount of time (notably in China) teaching Basic English and propagandizing for its universal use. In the service of this cause he wrote *Basic English and Its Uses, Basic in Teaching*, and *How to Read a Page*; collaborated on books called *First Steps in Reading English* and *English through Pictures*; helped organized Basic English courses on three continents; and even translated Plato and Homer into Basic. Yet Basic—thanks, perhaps, to the widespread perception that it constituted an attempt to "dumb-down" the language— failed to have the staying power Richards hoped it would. (Which may have been for the best, for if the experience of education over the past few decades has taught us anything, it is that simplifying the material to be learned is not the best means of improving pedagogy in language, in literature, or in anything else.)

As innovative as Basic English was Richards's book *Practical Criticism*, the record of a notorious experiment in which he gave his Cambridge students the unsigned texts of various great and terrible poems and asked for their evaluations; the results were that such poets as Donne and Hopkins received a surprising amount of abuse while the work of various meretricious hacks was widely praised. (The book's title was taken from a phrase used in *Biographia Literaria* by Coleridge— whose critical theory, by the way, Richards treated at length in his 1935 study *Coleridge on Imagination*.) So impressed was Richards by the results of his experiment, by the insights they provided into the highly misguided assumptions and questionable standards of taste that guided his students' reading, and by the applicability of those insights to his teaching, that in later years he extended the method of *Practical Criticism* into other disciplines. (In a Cambridge course on "English Moralists," for instance, he asked his students to comment on unsigned passages from Hume, Mill, and Mussolini.) Though its reputation, in certain circles, is greatly out of proportion to its actual significance, *Practical Criticism* may well be Richards's most enduring achievement, a cleverly conceived, highly engaging, and truly useful application of his singular talents.

Like Shaw, Richards fiddled with typography, experimenting in his late books with capitalization, italics, and a set of quirky punctuation marks that he called (in an unfortunate employment of decon lingo) "meta-semantic markers." He was, in Russo's words, "dazzled by the media," seeing television as a potentially powerful tool for language education, a subject about which he wrote a book entitled *Design for Escape: World Education through Modern Media.* (He also used the word *media* in another—awful—book title, *Poetries: Their Media and Ends.*) In his later years, he published several volumes of unorthodox plays and of taut, eccentric, largely rhymed poetry (remarkably, he wrote his first poem at age fifty-nine), and collected these decidedly minor works in *Internal Colloquies* (1971); in his last book, *Beyond* (1974), which Richards identified as "my final thing, in any large way," the nearly eighty-year-old critic contrived a singular document which Russo describes as "a series of studies on the dialogues between human figures and their gods."

Though these products of Richards's declining years testify to the Shavian breadth of his creative interests—and though some of the poems earned the admiration of no less an authority than Robert Lowell—Richards's late books attracted surprisingly little attention at the time of their publication, and have failed in the intervening years to win an audience. The truth is that by the time Richards got around to writing verse and drama, his contribution to the world of letters was long since completed. A volume of memoirs would have been of interest, but Richards's antipathy toward biography prevented him from even contemplating such a book.

Which brings us to the paradox of sorts that is *I.A. Richards: His Life and Work.* What can one say about a more than eight-hundred-page biography of a critic who hated biography, and whose very fame rests in large part upon his vigorous objection to excessive critical probing into the lives of authors? Well, to begin with, Russo's book shares many of Richards's own virtues: it is extremely comprehensive and thoughtful, offering a remarkably thorough account of its subject's writing and ideas. There seems hardly to be a single essay in Richards's huge *oeuvre* that does not receive detailed treatment; indeed, Russo offers astonishingly full discussions not only of Richards's work but of many of Richards's undergraduate teachers, major intellectual contemporaries, and collaborators. Russo's attitude toward his subject, moreover, seems mostly fair and evenhanded.

There are times, though, when Russo, even as he acknowledges certain deficiencies in Richards's criticism, strains to make Richards's ideas sound more logical or attractive than they do in Richards's own language. In the manner of a script doctor seeking to improve an ailing Broadway play, for instance, Russo describes at one point how Richards's theory of value might be "rescued" from Richards's own incomplete and unclear presentation of it and "reconstituted" in more cogent fashion. Likewise, on another occasion he tries to make Richards's ideas about pseudo-belief sound more palatable:

> In a conversation in 1956 reported by Stephen Spender...
> Richards said that "what the poet believed inside his poetry, need have no—indeed must have no—authoritatively rational connection dictated by outside belief: 'The curious thing about poetry is that anything can happen inside its peculiar world without commitment to what goes on outside.'" This sounds like doctrinaire formalism.... But one notes in "authoritatively" a warning against authoritarian demands on a poet or poem. The fact that "anything can happen" in the test-chamber of poetry is a charter of freedom. The overall intensity of the experience requires the shutting down, for the moment, of external and internal pressures.

Perhaps the most surprising problem with this biography of Richards, however, is that it is not really a biography. Yes, it is chronologically organized and contains the essential personal data—place of birth, ancestry, education, marriage. But theses materials feel tacked on, as if Russo had first written a dissertation-style critical study and had then been persuaded by his editors to interpolate a few biographical facts so that the book could be marketed as a biography. On occasion, the matter-of-fact haste with which Russo gets the necessary biographical tidbits out of the way is well-nigh breathtaking:

> In the Welsh mountains, in 1917, Richards was introduced to his future wife, Dorothy Eleanor Pilley. She was born on 16 September 1894 in Camberwell, London, the eldest daughter of John James Pilley, a science lecturer and manufacturer of baby foods, and Annie Maria Young. She attended Queenswood, Eastbourne, and was sent to finishing schools in Paris and Hanover. When she met Richards, she was a budding journalist and had taken up rock-climbing. It is fitting that they should have met in the mountains, because it was their lifelong pastime. Pilley became one of the great sportswomen in the history of British mountaineering.

So much for Richards's spouse, to whom he would remain married for the rest of his life. While it is interesting to know where Mrs. Richards went to finishing school, Russo doesn't even touch on the more important questions about her. We never get a sense, for instance, of what Richards's marriage was like, of what influence (if any) his wife had on the development of his ideas or on the course of his career. Why should she be mentioned at all, in such a book, unless Russo can manage, by describing the mind and character of the woman with whom Richards chose to spend his life, to illuminate Richards's own mind and character?

So it goes. Whether Russo is writing about Richards's marriage or his friendships or his relations with colleagues, the human dimension seems missing, its place taken by a cut-and-dried influence study. While many of Russo's observations are undoubtedly valid, the question that a biographer must ask is why Richards allowed himself to be influenced, say, by this teacher and not that one, by one colleague and not another. The answers to such questions must be more complex and subjective ones than Russo typically provides; Russo, who is more interested in expostulating upon the nuts and bolts of literary theory than in probing the ambiguities of human character, seems not to understand this. Though he presents, then, a wealth of material about the critical and philosophical milieu in which Richards's ideas matured, he fails utterly to conjure up a vivid image of the young man who moved through this rich milieu and whose mind took shape in a singular way.

In his references to the New Critics, meanwhile, Russo is often somewhat condescending and sardonic, depicting Ransom, Tate, Brooks, Warren, and company as (to put it bluntly) a pack of ingrates who borrowed Richards's critical theories without proper acknowledgment, who applied those theories in their celebrated works of close analysis, and who then attacked Richards for those same theories. Russo reminds us, for instance, of Allen Tate's complaint that poetry "is not only quite different from science but in its essence is opposed to science"; and he recalls Cleanth Brooks's remarks about the "nonhuman order" and "simplification" of science, as well as Brooks's hopeful observation that "the growing self-doubt of science and the questioning of the belief in historical progress signaled a cultural situation more favorable to tragic complexities." In such expressions of difference with Richards, Russo discerns nothing less than filial betrayal: "Science had provided Richards with a large fund of ideas, many of which he transmuted and made useful for the New Critics. Now it was cast aside." The simple fact, of course, is that the New Critics, though practicing a type of literary analysis that owed much to Richards's critical theories, disagreed deeply—and, I feel, rightly—with his principal ideas about science and poetry; as critics, it was incumbent upon them to discuss these differences as straightforwardly as possible. What Russo sees as betrayal is nothing more, really, than a healthy and productive independence of mind.

Why does Russo prefer Richards to the New Critics? One reason is manifestly political. Russo contrasts Richards's politics favorably with those of Richards's contemporaries; Richards, he reminds us, "did not adopt the nostalgic agrarian conservatism or verbal mysticism of the American New Critics" or "retreat behind a reactionary orthodoxy like Eliot in the 1930s" or, "like Ezra Pound, embrace an organicist and totalitarian myth through the instruments of modern technology." Interestingly, one of Russo's few strongly stated criticisms of Richards is that "his social criticism lacks the well-defined categories, relentless logical consecutiveness, and Marxist bite of Adorno's and Horkheimer's." (Love that Marxist bite!) There are points in the book where Russo seems to be employing such Marxist critics as Adorno, Eagleton, and Raymond Williams as touchstones of excellence, remarking, for instance, that "any reappraisal of Richards on belief and sincerity should take into account Theodor Adorno's Hegelian-Marxist critique of inwardness and authenticity."

But Russo's tendency to give occasional free publicity to Marxist critics is hardly his book's most lamentable weakness. The main problem, I think, is that Russo is hampered by the same failing that most seriously marred Richards's criticism: namely, a certain inclination to reduce the richly, complexly, mysteriously human to the programmatic, the measurable, the scientific. Yet it would perhaps be unfair to dismiss Richards with such words. He does not, to be sure, stand up well to comparison with most of the New Critics, who refined his critical theories, cleansed them of their more egregious elements—in particular, the borrowings from neurology and the like—and, most importantly, put those theories into practice. (It is, indeed, the magnificent close readings by such critics as Cleanth Brooks and Robert Penn Warren that make their criticism feel vibrant and relevant today in a way that Richards's criticism, with its emphasis on pure theory and scientific analogy, does not.) But if one is cataloguing the differences between Richards and the New Critics, it is only fair to point out as well the dramatic and telling divergences between Richards and the deconstructionists. Whereas the deconstructionists tend to manifest a glib and expedient fealty to the notion of art's disconnection from life, Richards's work reflects a sincere and urgent sense of engagement with the question of art's relation to life; whereas the deconstructionists subscribe to the fashionable position that writing is ultimately meaningless, Richards testifies time and again to the innate significance of language; and whereas the deconstructionists seem to conceive of the critic as an academic speaking to academics, Richards sees himself, like Wordsworth, as a man speaking to men. In these ways, certainly, his is a legacy more than deserving of respect.

MARCH 1989

LOUISE BOGAN'S ANGRY SOLITUDE

W. H. Auden called her one of the four "important" American poets of her time (the other three were T.S. Eliot, Marianne Moore, and Laura Riding); both Auden and Edmund Wilson called her the best American critic of poetry; and when Robert Frost read her first book of poems he said, "that woman will be able to do anything." But Louise Bogan—who was born in 1897, flourished during the Twenties and Thirties, and died in 1970, more or less ignored by the literary world in which she had lived for half a century—seems to have been destined to remain, in the eyes of the multitudes, a minor figure on the landscape of modern literature. That Bogan published so little work, relatively speaking, certainly didn't help. Between 1923 and 1937 she produced only three slim volumes of formal lyric poetry, *Body of This Death*, *Dark Summer*, and *The Sleeping Fury*; her three later books, issued at even longer intervals—*Poems and New Poems* (1941), *Collected Poems 1923-1953* (1954), and *The Blue Estuaries: Poems 1923-1968* (1968)—were all essentially "collected" volumes, recapitulations of Bogan's poetic *oeuvre*, containing a minimal amount of new verse. And her criticism, consisting mostly of brief reviews from *The New Yorker* (she served as the magazine's poetry critic from 1931 to 1969), did not appear in book form until the publication in 1955 of her *Selected Criticism: Poetry and Prose*.

A more significant reason for Bogan's comparative obscurity, perhaps, is that her work was never of a sensational sort. Her poetry appeared during the heyday of modernism, but it did not introduce amazing new forms or ideas, or capture the rhythm of American speech, or "embody the spirit of the age." Rather, her lyrics were, for the most part, precise, carefully nuanced contemplations of the folly of passion and other timeless themes. The poems were taut, crabbed, firmly controlled, suggestive of considerable private anguish yet utterly unsentimental and objective in tone. Bogan was clearly a disciple of the Pre-Raphaelites and the French Symbolists, as well as of Yeats and Frost, and this was, in general, all to the good in the Age of Eliot. But, just as clearly, Bogan was no camp-follower, no trend-watcher, no knee-jerk modernist out to "make it new" at all costs. Many of her poems had a spare, exotic particularity that was reminiscent of H.D. (a less accomplished poet), but, unlike H.D., Bogan had no Pound-like publicist behind her, no taste for self-mythologizing, no interest in founding a movement or introducing new ways of seeing and saying. She was, her poems suggest, a serious, solitary literary artist, bent on going her own way—a woman manifestly tortured by life, but determined to sublimate her anguish into the exquisite order of art.

That Bogan was, indeed, among the most serious and solitary— and most profoundly tormented—literary figures of her time is one of the chief lessons of Elizabeth Frank's absorbing new biography,[1] in which she evokes the compelling inner drama of a life that was, on the surface at least, desolate, depressing, and without apparent direction. Frank convincingly traces the emotional torment that is implicit in Bogan's poetry—in particular, the poet's obsession with the notion that tragedy is inherent in human passion—back to her childhood. And a harrowing childhood it was. The poet's father, Daniel Bogan, was a "feisty, cocky" Irish mill clerk, her mother, Mary, a tall, beautiful, high-spirited woman who had married somewhat beneath herself—or at least felt that she had. Throughout Louise's early years the family shuttled from one New England mill town to another, Mary browbeating Daniel every step of the way for no particular reason and engaging in brief extramarital affairs that she barely bothered to conceal. It was not a pleasant family for a sensitive young girl to grow up in, and school provided little relief. There Louise was taught her place: the nuns at Mount Saint Mary Academy in New Hampshire blatantly favored the rich girls, and the authorities at Girls' Latin School in Boston insisted that, however talented the already lyrically inclined Louise might be, "*no Irish girl* could be editor of the school magazine."

Even in these early years, poetry was an escape hatch for Louise, a "life-saving process"—but not in any sense that Erica Jong would understand. Poetry was an opportunity not to confess her anguish, in all its miserable particularity, but, on the contrary, to flee the prosaic confusion of the specific for the hard, fine clarity of the abstract, and to find comfort in the awareness that her emotions were timeless and universal. From the beginning Louise perceived poetry in a purely clas-

---

[1] *Louis Bogan: A Portrait*, by Elizabeth Frank; Knopf, 460 pages, $24.95.

sical sense; the writing of verse was, accordingly, a serious vocation, a craft to be studied carefully and worked at assiduously. Bogan's first lyrics, composed at the age of fourteen, testify to the mature dedication with which she approached her chosen art. The poems are accomplished imitations of Swinburne, Morris, and the Rossettis, and demonstrate the precociousness with which Bogan learned how to handle alliteration and assonance and to achieve slow cadences. She was, as Frank points out, never to lose "the Pre-Raphaelite penchant for the filled-out line, in which every vowel, consonant, and syllable receives its complete, unhurried value...." What she loved above all, in true Pre-Raphaelite fashion, were authors who cultivated a rich, intricate style, who cared about *sound*. Thus at seventeen she read and was mesmerized by the symphonic prose of Pater, and resolved thereupon to burn with a "hard, gem-like flame"; at the same age she pored through Symons's *The Symbolist Movement in Literature*, discovered Rimbuad, Verlaine, and Mallarmé , and "adopted Symbolist aesthetics as [her] own." Thenceforth, as Frank notes, she "would always be engaged in transformations and correspondences, the two essential operations of the Symbolist mind."

Patently, poetry was a godsend to the teenaged Bogan, a bright spot in a rather gray life. Yet it did not, unfortunately, prevent her from developing into a highly insecure, unstable young woman. There were, Frank writes, "at least two Louises" during the poet's young adulthood: "one a tender, passionate, intensely sexual being, and the other a violent, cruel, and deeply suspicious fiend, who couldn't stand being loved...." Throughout this period, Bogan was continually wracked by hostility, fear, and resentment toward nearly everyone around her; she lived (in her own words) in "a burned and angry solitude," and had to enter psychiatric hospitals for treatment after suffering nervous breakdowns in 1931 and 1933.

Literary success provided no relief from her anguish; if anything, it contributed to it. That success, as it happens, came to her relatively early. By the age of twenty-four, in fact—having spent a year at Boston College, married a young German named Curt Alexander (a lieutenant in the United States Army), given birth to a daughter named Maidie, been widowed after four years of marriage, and moved to New York— Bogan was already a member of the literary crowd, publishing poems in such estimable venues as *The New Republic* and *Vanity Fair* and hobnobbing with the likes of Edmund Wilson, Morton Dauwen Zabel, Rolfe Humphries, and Léonie Adams (all of whom were to become close friends). In 1923, to cap it all off, Bogan fell in love with a rich, hand-some poet (lyric poet, of course) named Raymond Holden, and mar-ried him two years later. Her life was, at this juncture, everything she could have hoped for. But she was constitutionally incapable of enjoy-ing it. She was "repelled" by the comfort that Holden's family money provided, and found life on the literary circuit to be "menacing and corrupting." Having grown up in an atmosphere of marital browbeat-ing and betrayal, Bogan was pathologically suspicious of Holden and prone to hysterical fits of connubial violence—which he, to her confu-sion and irritation, insisted upon meeting with gentle words of love and reassurance. Holden was not the only target of Bogan's wrath. Apparently unable to forget that she had been despised as a schoolgirl for being poor, for being a "Mick," she directed a good portion of her hostility toward people whom she considered phony or supercilious. In particular, upper-class pretensions were anathema to her; she hated "'refined' manners, 'well-bred' accents, and 'nice' people; Ivy League attitudes; New York clubs." Though she had great affection for Wil-son—a lifelong friend—his Princetonian pomposities infuriated her; and John Dos Passos struck her as nothing more than "a Harvard fake." That merit counted for so little in the world, and social position for so much, never ceased to torment Bogan.

Perhaps the apotheosis of fakery, in Bogan's book, was the literary world—which, to her mind, was little more than a setting for intellec-tual one-upsmanship, reputation-brokerage, and logrolling. Though she deeply resented the failure of critics and public alike to give her poetry its due—as a rule, her books were respectfully but not promi-nently reviewed, and sold modestly—Bogan steadfastly refused to play the "literary game." Not till the mid-Thirties did she break her "public silence" and participate in a poetry reading. Such activities, to her way of thinking, were silly and self-aggrandizing, and had nothing at all to do with literature. She resented the indignity of having to "court" po-tential readers in such a manner. Couldn't her poetry speak for itself? It may be, of course, that she was simply unable to handle publicity, incapable of easily consolidating a public image with her private self. That, at least, appears to be the reason why she kept her daughter Maidie's existence a secret from her literary colleagues until her friend Margaret Mead happened to find out ("Louise," Mead berated her, "stop hiding your child!") and why, on the day she married Holden, she wrote a letter to Edmund Wilson without even mentioning the wedding.

It was during these confused, distressing years of her early adulthood that Bogan wrote the bulk of her mature lyrics. In these poems, the Pre-Raphaelite and Symbolist influences that characterized her juvenilia remained strong, but were tempered by the eloquent simplicity of Frost, the cold passion of Yeats, the precision of the Imagists, and the delicacy of her fellow priestesses of the lyric: Elinor Wylie, Sara Teasdale, Edna St. Vincent Millay, and Léonie Adams. The poems are, as a result, unusually rich in texture—at once morbid and vibrant, dry and luxuriant, obsessed with the tension between the heart's attraction to the pagan sacrament of passion and the mind's craving for solitude and chastity. There are few people in them, only extreme emotions presented by name ("rage," "passion," "love," "sorrow") and—to serve as symbols—natural objects (stones, fields) and elements (earth, air, fire, water). The language is compressed, baroque, sometimes antiquated; words like "indurate," "cedarn," and "infatuate" (used as an adjective) occur frequently, and allusions to "blood," "memory," and "hell" are common. The indomitability of time is a major theme ("The measured blood beats out the year's delay..."). But the main point is that romantic passion is difficult, destructive, demented—and unavoidable. So precarious, indeed, does Bogan consider passion be that its opposite, hatred, looks to her at times like a good thing; in a poem entitled "At a Party," she speaks of "enmity, that may save us all." To her mind, for a human soul to survive passion requires resolution and resilience beyond compare. In a poem, "Song," in *Body of This Death*, Bogan writes:

> Be strong, to look on my heart
> As others look on my face.
> Love me,—I tell you that it is a ravaged,
> Terrible place.

If one had a choice, she suggests in "Second Song" (from *Dark Summer*), one would renounce passion entirely:

> I said out of sleeping:
> Passion, farewell.
> Take from my keeping
> Bauble and shell,
>
> Black salt, black provender.

Tender your store
To a new pensioner,
To me no more.

But, as "The Alchemist" implies, passion cannot be renounced, any more than life can be denied:

I burned my life, that I might find
A passion wholly of the mind,
Thought divorced from eye and bone,
Ecstasy come to breath alone.
I broke my life, to seek relief
From the flawed light of love and grief.

With mounting beat the utter fire
Charred existence and desire.
It died low, ceased its sudden thresh.
I had found unmysterious flesh—
Not the mind's avid substance—still
Passionate beyond the will.

Many a Bogan lyric is, in a sense, a dialogue of self and soul—a rehearsal of the conflict between mind and heart. To Bogan, the heart and the mind are always at odds, for the passion to which the heart is drawn is categorically unwise. The love of women "is an eager meaninglessness / Too tense, or too lax." "What a marvel to be wise," she writes, "To love never in this manner!" One of Bogan's longer poems, "Exhortation" (from *The Sleeping Fury*), urges us to ignore the heart, and heed the counsel of the mind:

Give over seeking bastard joy
Nor cast for fortune's side-long look.
Indifference can be your toy;
The bitter heart can be your book.
(Its lesson torment never shook.)

In the cold heart, as on a page,
Spell out the gentle syllable
That puts short limit to your rage
And curdles the straight fire of hell,

Compassing all, so all is well.

Read how, though passion sets in storm
And grief's a comfort, and the young
Touch at the flint when it is warm,
It is the dead we live among,
The dead given motion, and a tongue.

The dead, long trained to cruel sport
And the crude gossip of the grave;
The dead, who pass in motley sort,
Whom sun nor sufferance can save.
Face them. They sneer. Do not be brave.

Know once for all; their snare is set
Even now; be sure their trap is laid;
And you will see your lifetime yet
Come to their terms, your plans unmade,—
And be belied, and be betrayed.

Yet the heart, to its bitter misfortune, will not be overruled by the mind:

The woman who has grown old
And knows desire must die,
Yet turns to love again,
Hears the crows cry.

For all its torturousness, though, life is wonderful and holy and worth struggling for: that this is her attitude is implicit in the very force and fervency of Bogan's lyrics. Elizabeth Frank is right when she locates Bogan "on the side of life" and describes her poetry as based upon a "passionate belief in the sacredness of life" and in "the tenderness and strength of the human heart."

Bogan's criticism is based on the same beliefs. She began contributing reviews to magazines in 1924, when Wilson, insistent that she train herself to write criticism—something she felt certain she was incapable of—"ordered her to sit down at her desk and begin." So well did she take instruction from Wilson that book reviews eventually became her livelihood. But, though Wilson taught her a great deal, she was no meek disciple of her formidable friend. Bogan the literary critic was, in fact, as independent a spirit as Bogan the poet, utterly uninterested, it would seem, in truckling to the trends of the day. One of these trends was New Criticism, a form of literary inquiry for which Bogan had little use. John Crowe Ransom, Allen Tate and company were, to her mind, "abstract, overingenious, and deliberately obscure mandarins, out to safeguard their academic and social prestige by demonstrating the need for a priestly class of explicators and interpreters." She resented their "assumption of intellectual superiority" to writers they analyzed, and in reviewing Ransom's *The New Criticism* in 1941, accused him of intellectual snobbery: "To think, and to express oneself in images," she wrote, "is becoming rather vulgar." When Ransom, in his response to the review, advised Bogan that there were many different and valid vocabularies in which to write literary criticism, she had an answer for him: "If one is to be a true critic of literature," she suggested, "beneath any vocabulary must exist a state of sensibility, an intuitive grasp, an open mind, and a generous and humble heart." Bogan didn't like the New Critics' poetry any better than she did their criticism. She described the verse in Tate's *Poems: 1928-1931* as "fakery," dominated by ideas and "completely lacking in intuitive flow." To Bogan, true poetry was built not upon ideas but upon images; mastering poetry, she felt, had less to do with being extremely intelligent than with being highly sensitive—sensitive not only to one's own feelings but to the exquisite and subtle nuances of human behavior and perception. It is perhaps better for the purposes of poetry-writing, she once said, "to be an ignorant one with insight than a wise, obtuse-to-delicate-veins-of-value one."

The most prominent critical trend of the 1930s, needless to say, was Marxist criticism. Several friends of Bogan's were adherents—Rolfe Humphries, for one, and of course Edmund Wilson. Given the pressure that Bogan endured to take a Marxist line in her own reviews, it is little short of remarkable that she managed to resist at all. But resist she did—entirely. That she did so is a tribute equally to her strength of character, the depth and seriousness of her love for literature, and her common sense. Marxism, apparently, held no attraction for her whatsoever. On the contrary, she was, as Elizabeth Frank writes, "contemptuous of any form of 'Social Realism' in either art or literature, and thought those who believed that the world had been born anew in the Soviet Union were fools." And they were not harmless fools, either;

they were, she felt, mindlessly endangering the humane Western culture that she treasured. Frank seems hardly to be exaggerating when she says that Bogan "f[ought] her way through the Thirties." "As the decade advanced," Frank says, "Bogan began to feel isolated in her love of what she called 'beautiful letters,'" standing nearly alone, it seems, against the hordes of "proletarian poets" who were, it seemed to her, out to rob poetry of everything that made it valuable, and against the leftist critics who excoriated Bogan, with her solid aesthetic criteria, as a vestige of the "obsolete twenties." (Bogan was, in the words of *The New Republic*'s Eda Lou Walton, "a dead leaf on a dead branch.") "I STILL THINK," she wrote Humphries in a letter, the upper-case letters indicating her desperation, "THAT POETRY HAS SOMETHING TO DO WITH THE IMAGINATION: I STILL THINK IT OUGHT TO BE WELL WRITTEN. I STILL THINK IT IS PRIVATE FEELING, NOT PUBLIC SPEECH."

What has happened is predictable enough. While the literary essays and reviews produced by most of Bogan's politically *au courant* contemporaries are, today, utterly worthless except as historical relics—cautionary reminders of the folly of political fanaticism—Bogan's literary criticism is timeless. Her reviews are solid and sensible, her standards consistent and beyond reproach. Though, admittedly, the reviews are woefully short on close analysis (these were, after all, brief notices for *The New Yorker*) and a little long on adjectives like "superb" and "delightful," they invariably provide thoughtful general descriptions of the works under consideration, and tally the strengths and weaknesses of those works with care, accuracy, and fairness. Bogan's style is smooth and elegant, her tone neutral to sardonic; she is so determined not to draw attention to herself that at times her prose is flatter and duller than it has to be. Once in a while, though, she gets off a memorable line. She describes *Three Guineas*, for instance, as an "exposé of upper-class Englishman's tyranny over upper-class Englishwoman," and at the end of her review acknowledges that, "Patently, being a lady is difficult, but artists have managed to make something of even worse situations and inheritances." (That she was thinking of herself here cannot be doubted.) Of Marianne Moore (one of her favorite modern poets), Bogan writes: "She relates the refreshing oddities of art to the shocking oddities of life." Reviewing Archibald MacLeish, on the other hand (who, to Bogan's mind, was more interested in "waken[ing] the population to 'Fascist' dangers" than in creating literature), Bogan finds even the title un-aesthetic: "*America Was Promises* is a sentence which even an untrained ear instinctively rejects; it sounds ugly. But it also sounds impressive, and 'public speech' is out to impress." And in a sensitive passage about Pound's *Cantos*, Bogan seems to speak not as critic to reader but as poet to poet:

> ...if Pound plans to make "plunges into Paradise," he must be able to put aside his hatred, as Dante managed to do. If one hates anything too long, one not only begins to resemble what is hated but one forgets, one becomes incapable even of imagining any longer, what it is that one could love. What Pound would do in a paradise unencumbered by old bills of lading and growls about usury, it is becoming difficult to think. Moral indignation is one thing; *l'amor*, which Dante said moved the sun and other stars, is something even more difficult.

The second half of Bogan's life was more solitary, more serene, and far less poetically productive than the first. After divorcing Holden in 1934, she never remarried, and had only a couple of affairs (one of them with the poet Theodore Roethke). Her capacity for both rage and love diminished following the treatment of her two nervous breakdowns in the early Thirties. Elizabeth Frank says that though "[s]he who had always felt everything felt little now, or controlled her feelings beyond reasonableness," Bogan was, nonetheless, "in every way a richer, more substantial person than she had been before her illness." While Bogan considered this newfound stability to be a personal blessing, it was also a professional curse: she recognized that the rage, bitterness and passion that had torn her apart in earlier times had kept her distanced, in a way, from the world, and had made possible an intense yet strangely impersonal poetry. Now that she was, in Frank's words, "no longer neurotically at a remove from life," the poems did not come to her so readily as they had before. Indeed, she could write poetry, she learned, "only when in a rage (of anger or of hatred), or in a state which I can only describe as malicious pity. And the emotion that writes tender and delicate poetry is so much akin to the emotion of love that it *is* love, to all intents and purposes." So mentally well balanced was Bogan that, for seven years during the 1940s, she did not compose a single poem.

Instead, she wrote prose—stories, "prose *capriccios*," journal entries. And, of course, reviews, though she grew more and more removed from the literary scene and increasingly disgusted with the crude confessional voices that shouted at her throughout the Fifties and Sixties. She broke her "public silence" to an impressive extent, becoming a visiting instructor of poetry-writing at various universities. She spent time with new friends like May Sarton; translated Goethe, Jünger, and Renard with Elizabeth Meyer and Elizabeth Roget; and, in her capacity as William Maxwell's unofficial editor and advisor, played a significant role in the shaping of his magnificent novel *The Folded Leaf*. But mostly she was alone with her thoughts and memories and occasional bursts of lyricism. What poems she did manage to complete during these lonely latter years were unmistakable products of the Bogan sensibility, but the style was often freer, the tone more relaxed, than in her earlier works. New influences found their way into her lines. Auden, as he developed from a young poet into an elderly master, became a favorite of Bogan's, and his witty conversational tone rubbed off on her. Rilke, whose poetry she discovered in 1935, became nothing less than an idol; what she treasured about his work was that "[h]e *looked* at things. He looked and looked and looked, and the poems are absolute and true.... My merciful God. I'm going to spend the rest of my life humbly looking."

In her enthusiasm, it must be said, Elizabeth Frank does overestimate Louise Bogan's contribution to literature, placing her alongside such great lyric poets as George Herbert and Gerard Manley Hopkins. But this is an enthusiasm that no one who loves poetry and takes its creation seriously can have trouble understanding. For—though she was, admittedly, a minor poet—Bogan was a poet's poet. She deserves to be remembered, with the greatest possible respect, not only for her highly accomplished poetry and criticism but for the consistent seriousness of purpose with which she approached her art. She was, as Frank's impressive book makes clear, the personification of literary commitment; in her biographer's words, she "revered art and lived for it as purely as Flaubert." In these peculiar days—when many a celebrated poet is distinguished only by his solipsism, and many a respected critic notable primarily for his ability to confuse—Louise Bogan is, more than ever, a literary figure whose memory is worth cherishing.

MAY 1985

OBSESSED WITH POETRY:
DELMORE SCHWARTZ AND RANDALL JARRELL

At first glance, the two most interesting American poet-critics of mid-century don't appear to have much in common. Delmore Schwartz, the New York Jewish intellectual, was turbulent, mad, brilliant, a destroyer of hotel rooms and imaginer of conspiracies. In his early poems he crossed Eliotic intellectuality with Yeatsian music and came up with a unique hybrid—an exuberant, fatalistic, teleologically compelling type of modernist poem that could be "about" anything from Orpheus to Caesar to the Romanovs' bounding ball; in his later years he dropped Eliot, found Whitman, and produced a series of bizarre, energetic, mesmeric post-Walt effusions about Seurat and Psyche and Marilyn Monroe. Randall Jarrell—to a casual observer—was quite a different sort. Serene, seemingly stable, far more comfortable in a sleepy Southern town than in a crude, dirty Northern city ("What a way to speak!" was his comment on New York accents), he was the author in his early years of quietly forceful poems about girls in libraries and dead soldiers; his later poems are pensive, wistful, sadhearted meditations about aging women and paper boys.

They would, then, seem to be worlds apart. Yet the closer one look at their lives and work, the more convinced one is that Schwartz and Jarrell were, in the ways that matter, two of a kind. Though known for their wit, humor, and capacity for enthusiasm, both were nonetheless profoundly terrified by life. "O Life is terror-full beyond belief," writes Schwartz. "How difficult it is to know and live." And Jarrell concurs: "It is terrible to be alive." Their poems hover about a handful of themes: love, loss, loneliness, insomnia, dreams. For them death was a constant presence. "Man is born in chains," writes Jarrell, "and everywhere we see him dead." "Each moment is dying," laments Schwartz. "We cannot stand still: time is dying, / We are dying: Time is farewell!" Their fear of mortality notwithstanding, at times they seem almost to have been half in love with easeful death. In at least one poem, Schwartz imagines death as an awakening from the nightmare of life: " *O what a metaphysical victory/The first day and night of death must be!*" And Jarrell (also italics-happy) agrees: "*In the end,*" he suggests, "*we wake from everything.*" The two poets felt alienated from their own bodies, Jarrell poeticizing about "his own flesh, set up outside him," and Schwartz bemoaning the existence of

> The heavy bear who goes with me
>
> .   .   .
>
> Moves where I move, distorting my gesture,
> A caricature, a swollen shadow,
> A stupid clown of the spirit's motive...

Both composed angry manifestos deploring the alienation of the poet in twentieth-century America. Jarrell argues in "The Obscurity of the Poet" that the contemporary poet "lives in a world whose newspapers and magazines and books and motion pictures and radio stations and television stations have destroyed, in a great many people, even the capacity for understanding real poetry." And Schwartz (in "The Vocation of the Poet in the Modern World") agrees: "As soon as the student leaves school, all the seductions of mass-culture and middlebrow culture, and in addition the whole way of life of our society, combine to make the reading of poetry a dangerous and quickly rejected luxury.... As soon as [the poet] departs from the pleasant confines of the university, he discovers that it is more and more true that less and less people read serious poetry."

Like their friends Robert Lowell and John Berryman—with whom they form a group of poets remarkable for the similarity of their upbringing, psychopathology, and poetic development—Jarrell and Schwartz were obsessed with poetry. Both, to be sure, were versatile writers: their literary criticism is sensitive and witty, and their fiction, at its best, is charming and original. They also had serious, non-literary intellectual interests. Schwartz took his undergraduate degree in philosophy, and Jarrell studied to be a clinical psychologist. (Both poets were—in their later years, at least—devout disciples of Freud.) They sought knowledge avidly, compulsively, self-destructively. "Knowledge and belief devour the mind of man," Schwartz observes; and Jarrell writes: "O knowledge ever harder to hold fast to,/O dream, O burden." If poetry overshadowed everything for them, it was because poetry was, to them, the ultimate form of knowledge—the *best* form, because it contained all the others: it was psychology, philosophy, physics, religion. To write poetry was to perform a physics experiment, to conduct a Freudian analysis, to hold High Mass. It was to plunge into the abyss, to make a solitary entrance into the unknown. Poetry was dangerous, harrowing—even as it renewed life, it threatened it. But neither Schwartz nor Jarrell questioned whether the enterprise was worth the risk. "Poetry should be worth a life," insists Jarrell. "Into the Destructive Element," declares Schwartz, "that is the way."

One might expect the collected letters of these two disturbed, self-dramatizing poets to enrich one's perception of the affinities between them. But the case is quite the opposite. What strikes one most forcefully, upon reading *Letters of Delmore Schwartz* and *Randall Jarrell's Letters*, is the same divergence of tone that characterizes the poems.[1] In his letters as in his verse, Schwartz nearly leaps off the page, exploding with ideas and opinions and *sui generis* turns of phrase; he is the very embodiment of agitation, artistic ambition, and *Angst*. Jarrell, on the other hand, is subdued and sensible, a gentle man with a lively but quiet wit. His letters—to speak only of the style and not the content—could be almost anybody's; Schwartz's are unique.

P artly for this reason—and partly because the story of his life describes a perfect three-act-drama bell curve—the more intriguing of these two books, hands down, is *Letters of Delmore Schwartz*. Robert Phillips (who has done an excellent job of editing and annotating) says justly in his introduction that "One of the pleasures of [Schwartz's] letters is his voice: he was a great conversationalist, and next to hearing his conversation, his letters come closest to capturing the raconteur." Schwartz's voice engages us from the start. His earliest letters date from the autumn of 1931, when he was a brand-new, seventeen-year-old, Eliot-mad freshman at the University of Wisconsin, desperately fixated on becoming a great writer and thrilled to be at an institution whose library "has files of the *Criterion, Dial, Bookman*—fourteen volumes of Pascal, and Pound, Eliot, H. Crane, Kenneth Burke, even." His correspondent is a high-school friend named Julian Sawyer, an aspiring homosexual Dadaist who (as James Atlas tells us in his compelling 1977

---

[1]*Letters of Delmore Schwartz*, edited by Robert Phillips; Ontario Review Press, 416 pages, $24.95; and *Randall Jarrell's Letters: An Autobiographical and Literary Selection*, edited by Mary Jarrell; Houghton Mifflin, 560 pages, $29.95.

biography, *Delmore Schwartz: The Life of an American Poet*) was "pathetic in his adoration of Delmore." When Julian writes him a *billet doux* in verse, Schwartz (who addresses Julian as "my jewel, my plague") responds by launching into Eliotic lit-crit: "Maybe I 'stir' the soul, the imagination—but everyone does, to the true sensibility." He is pretentious, patronizing, yet oddly touching, bragging to Julian that

> an intellectual group is around me, looks toward me.... [I] am the kind of influence... that I did not want to be: everyone (the nine or ten) is reading Spinoza. I purpose a cleavage, that I may entirely devote myself to the clouds (such forms, I mean), Georgia O'Keeffe, the Picasso black storms, and the Wordsworthian lake, and walks. (Such is the pomposity of my soul.)

Such indeed! He is the sort of student that professors think they want until they get one, refusing to write an examination on Stephen Vincent Benét and doing Valéry instead because "I could not permit my mind to be profaned by such intellectual whorishness." The plain style never had such an enemy. Instead of saying that he wants to see the sun rise, Schwartz (anticipating the manner of his mature poems and stories) says, "I desire to go out and walk East, and see the light translate the world to morning." Yet there is a sincerity, a seriousness here; the teenager of these letters has a genuine love of the true, the good, and the beautiful; he craves virtue. "Love God alone," he implores Julian, and is not kidding.

After his year at Wisconsin, Schwartz returned East, where he studied philosophy under Sidney Hook at NYU, and (over a weekend in July of 1935, when he was twenty years old) wrote a story called "In Dreams Begin Responsibilities." The story—published two years later, to great acclaim, in the first issue of the Rahv-Phillips *Partisan Review*—was Schwartz's *entrée* into New York literary circles. Before long he was appearing regularly in places like *The Southern Review* and *Poetry*, and was addressing his bossy, hectoring letters not to Julian Sawyer but to Allen Tate, Ezra Pound, and the like. "You seem," he tells Pound, "to have slowed up"—to have lost, that is, the feel for the literary scene; this is a shame, for "you used to ride the 'age'; if not for you, I would certainly have little notion of what it means to be caught up in a period of time, moved by it and attempting to move it." The audacity! But his last letter to Pound is truly admirable: having read the just-published, anti-Semitic *Guide to Kulchur*, Schwartz writes its author to "resign as one of your most studious and faithful admirers."

Schwartz's great year was 1938. He married a young woman named Gertrude Buckman, and New Directions published his first book, an engaging collection of poetry, fiction, verse, and drama entitled, after the story, *In Dreams Begin Responsibilities*. The reviews were mostly ecstatic—largely, it is clear in retrospect, because the book validated a certain conception of poetry. "What is in this book," wrote Mark Van Doren in *The Kenyon Review*, "is more important than anything personal could be." George Marion O'Donnell ventured in *Poetry* that "no first book of this decade in American poetry has been more authoritative or more significant than this one." Authoritative, impersonal: this was the closest thing to a new T.S. Eliot that the critics had seen in a dog's age. By the end of 1938, Schwartz was indisputably the leading poet of his generation.

But by the end of 1939, things had already begun to sour. The turning point was the publication of Schwartz's translation of Rimbaud's *A Season in Hell*. The critics savaged it, and sales were poor. Schwartz's next two books—his verse play *Shenandoah* (1941) and the awful first installment of his never-completed poetic magnum opus, *Genesis*, Book One (1943)—did not fare much better. All of this hurt Schwartz deeply, and it shows in the letters: if those written before *A Season in Hell* suggest an incomparably buoyant, busy, involved young man, those written afterward are the work of a writer increasingly despondent, alone, at loose ends. His self-assured pose disappears, to be replaced at times by a torturous self-doubt ("perhaps," he writes Robert Lowell after venturing an opinion on a story by Jean Stafford, "I am at fault as a reader"). Year by year, his enthusiasm for the literary life gives way to cynicism ("I received a kind of state visit from the Kazins. It was very literary....") and, finally, indifference. His letters begin to contain references to bouts of drinking, to spells of "nervous depression," and to "the moral chaos of my soul." "In my youth," he writes Blackmur, "I thought that Life was Shakespearean, but it becomes more and more obvious to me that it is Dostoyevskian." For months at a time he is unable to do any serious creative work at all. In a letter to Philip Rahv he explains that he has tried to write a book review for *The Partisan Review* but has been "unable to get through a page"; and he writes to Van Doren that "I still have no hope of any early return to being articulate." Helpless to do anything else, he pours his solitary despair into one letter after another. To Blackmur: "It is lonely, everyone is gone into the world of the night and I alone sit lingering here... " To Gertrude (who divorced him in 1944): "We all go into the dark." To Lowell: "'Tis bitter chill and I am sick at heart, for I feel as if I were one thousand years of age. I feel as ugly as yonder shoes. And yet as Lady Montagu said on her deathbed, 'It all has been most interesting.' But this does not belong in a letter."

And so it went. During the Forties and Fifties he taught at Harvard, worked for *Partisan Review*, published two books of mediocre stories and two volumes of poetry (including his Bollingen Prize-winning *Summer Knowledge: New and Selected Poems*), and married and divorced again. As he grew less and less productive, he became, in Atlas's words, an "impresario of journals and committees"—poetry editor for *The New Republic*, reader for New Directions, consultant to *Perspectives USA* and *Diogenes*. He was also (thanks largely, no doubt, to greater and greater doses of Dexedrine, Seconal, and alcohol) increasingly subject to the tortures of what Atlas calls "the manic-depressive roller coaster." From the time his second wife left him in 1957 to his death in 1966 he led an essentially nomadic and solitary life, teaching at UCLA one summer and at Syracuse University from 1962 to 1965, and residing the rest of the time in seedy New York hostelries; this was the decade of psychotic tantrums, broken furniture, and state hospitals.

The letters of the last fifteen or so years paint a fascinating, painfully human portrait of a gifted man at war with encroaching madness. "I've put off writing you repeatedly," he tells Meyer Schapiro in 1952, "because what I wanted to say was that I've been sunk for months in the worst part of the manic-depressive disorder which does not show much on the surface, but makes it an ordeal for me to see anyone.... During the last few days I've begun to break out of the longest depressed period I can remember." If the depressed periods immobilized Schwartz, the manic periods occasioned some peculiar samples of Delmorean wit. In 1954, for instance, he shares a very un-Eliotic literary judgment with Catherine Carver: "my impression, for what it's worth, is that Gaddis has real genius, but that his novel [*The Recognitions*] reads at times as if Ronald Firbank and Thomas Wolfe were Siamese twins who had written a novel to prove that Truman Capote and William Faulkner ought to become converted to Catholicism." A year later he lists some of "Schwartz's Paradoxes" for John Crowe Ransom: "There are more scapegoats than goats. There are more good book clubs than good books. There are more poems than trees. There are more poets than poems (and the converse is also true, at times). The world is a great success precisely because it is at once a prairie oyster, a white elephant, and a gift horse." One wonders what Ransom made of this.

Randall Jarrell's Letters is, by comparison, sedate. The first dozen letters—which take us, much too rapidly, through Jarrell's early and mid-twenties (he was born in May 1914, five months after Schwartz)—are all addressed to mentors like Robert Penn Warren and Allen Tate and are devoted largely to superficial and polite discussions of poems Jarrell would like to publish, books he wishes to review, teaching jobs he wants to secure. It isn't the most exciting of beginnings. One reads on, following Jarrell from Vanderbilt University, through teaching stints in Texas and Ohio and a hitch in the Air Force, to his final berth in the English department of the Women's College of Greensboro, North Carolina—and one realizes all too late that these letters are not going to be revealing in the way Schwartz's are. Jarrell is a member of the "How are you, I am fine" school of letter writing, so full of charming anecdotes about other people's children (like Schwartz, he never had any) and animals (like Schwartz, he doted on his pet cat), and so quick with his opinions about new books and old academics, that it takes a while to recognize that he is not really telling us much. Not only does he not pour out his heart: he seems never to have written a letter while angry, upset, or (except for the last year of his life) unusually depressed. To a reader unfamiliar with Jarrell's life and poetry, the man would undoubtedly come across as supremely well-balanced, a paragon of emotional stability. (And rather dull.) There is no sign, *none*, that a nervous breakdown is in the offing, a suicide waiting to happen.

Only when he is talking literature does Jarrell turn provocative. Most of his opinions—at least the most memorable—are negative ones. Writing from Princeton to his second wife, Mary, in 1952, he describes a lecture by Kenneth Burke as "so bad it was almost feeble-minded; so extravagantly mechanical and verbose and senseless and full of absolutely irrelevant free association that you felt a band of robbers had made up the speech and were *making* him deliver it, to his own disgrace, with a machine-gun trained on him." And in 1943 he writes his first wife, Mackie, that:

> Schwartz's *Genesis* is just awful: I wouldn't dare write a line
> about it anywhere, I'd be too embarrassed. He puts in a page

(of the history of a Jewish immigrant family) of prose so flat, abstract, and completely dull as to seem part of that old story with the numbered paragraphs in the *Kenyon*; then he has anonymous ghosts of the dead make long moral philosophical verse comments for two pages; then a page more of prose, two more of verse; and so on for 250 pages, with two volumes more to come. The great dead are, not enthusiastic but *enthused*, about the inane story flat as "The Loves of the Triangles," and act as if it were a perfect gospel, the ideal text for the final endless commentary. It's a sad affair; to read it through you need resolution, just resolution—more than even a soldier has, if I can call myself that.

"Give me a little précis of Delmore Schwartz in private life," he writes Lowell two years later. "That a person of his taste and intelligence should write the stories he does—half the sentences would serve as textbook models of banal and ingenuous vulgarity—is extraordinary, and must be symptomatic of some queer segmentation of his personal being into an objective part with taste and another part with nothing but adolescent self-absorption."

Mary Jarrell, the poet's second wife and editor of the letters, has placed commentaries—some brief, some over a page long—after most of the letters. In addition to identifying people, places, and literary works mentioned in the text, and filling in the chronological gaps between letters, these glosses contain a good deal of primary material—anecdotes about Jarrell and friends, quotations from critics' praise of his work, and the like. Indeed, the book is less a plain and simple collection of letters than it is an oddly structured memoir. Some of Mrs. Jarrell's offerings are not only useful but intriguing; she narrates in detail, for instance, a revealing, funny conversation in which a fogbound Robert Lowell plays my-family's-better-than-yours with her daughter (by a first marriage)—exactly the sort of thing one would never find in Jarrell's letters. But most of the time, Mrs. Jarrell simply overdoes it. She devotes most of a page to a discussion of B.H. Haggin's musical tastes, spends four rather long sentences telling us who Edmund Wilson is, tells us far more than we need to know about North Carolina campus politics and what the Warrens' house looked like and who wore a fur coat to the poetry festival. Her commentaries interrupt the flow of the letters, making it difficult to lose oneself in Jarrell's voice; also, they tend to give the book the feel of a family album. This is not a particularly bad thing, except that as a result one cannot help but wonder about its objectivity. That Mrs. Jarrell refers to herself throughout in the third person—as if the commentary had been written by some nameless scholar, or maybe a computer—only makes the format all the more disconcerting.

It is unfortunate, too, that just when Mrs. Jarrell might be able to shed some light, she fails to satisfy. I am speaking of her account of the last year of Jarrell's life. As she describes it, he turned fifty, suddenly got depressed (she carefully notes that the doctor found "no previous treatment for depression and no medical history of manic-depressive psychosis"), and was given a "mood-elevating drug." In her subsequent glosses she strongly implies—without ever saying so explicitly—that the failure of Jarrell's physician to cut back the dosage of this drug was the reason why Jarrell soon changed his personality, losing his sweet, gentle disposition and turning tense and mean. His behavior—as she describes it—brings Schwartz to mind: Jarrell became a "holy terror" to fellow teachers, held his students spellbound, tipped a waitress fifteen hundred dollars, and got up to introduce Hannah Arendt at a faculty gathering, and "with an ashen face, glittering eyes, and a look of haggard vivacity, talked for twenty minutes about meeting Johnny Unitas, the Colt quarterback."

Finally he was "admitted to Memorial Hospital in Chapel Hill for rest and observation." He stayed five months (during which he attempted suicide), was released, and four months later was struck and killed by a car on a highway near the Greensboro campus. Mrs. Jarrell spends a page arguing (not very convincingly) that it was not suicide. Nowhere in the pages covering this year-long debacle does she even attempt to answer the question uppermost in the reader's mind: *What happened?* Why in heaven's name did Jarrell, after a lifetime of putative sanity, all at once become a basket case? Mrs. Jarrell would have us believe it was purely a case of fiftieth-birthday blues plus an unfortunate pharmacological phenomenon—wrong drug, wrong dosage. But Jarrell's entire poetic *oeuvre* stands as evidence to the contrary. One cannot help but surmise that Jarrell had a well-oiled defense mechanism in place—by means of which he was able to keep the expression of his profound inner turmoil confined entirely to his poetry—and that, for some reason, it broke down. A letter written to Margaret Marshall years before the breakdown would seem to support this hypothesis. "I don't know whether you'd guess it," he writes her, "but I have an even, cheerful, and optimistic disposition: what I write is therapeutically the opposite, I guess." His refusal, moreover, to be of help during Lowell's manic periods—or to even visit Lowell in mental hospitals—also seems worth noting; this strange behavior suggests that Jarrell did not like to be reminded, by the sight of his friend's mind in chaos, of the precariousness of his own emotional stability.

What the world needs now, obviously, is a biography—an *objective* one—of Jarrell. In the past two or three years, almost every other gap in the biographical literature on this circle of poets has been filled in: aside from the letters of Schwartz and Jarrell, we've seen shoebox-sized lives of Lowell and Berryman, an elegant memoir by Eileen Simpson, and enlightening recollections in the autobiographical writings of William Barrett and other contemporaries. It may well be, of course, that these two volumes of correspondence simply mark the latest stage in the advance of yet another literary-circle personality cult—a cross, perhaps, between Bloomsbury and the Beats. Then again, the letters might actually encourage readers to take a first brave look at the best of their authors' work: the poems collected in Schwartz's *Summer Knowledge*; Jarrell's moving verse in *Little Friend, Little Friend* (1945) and *Losses* (1948); his agony-ridden (but exquisitely understated) lyrics in *The Woman at the Washington Zoo* (1960) and *The Lost World* (1965); his novel *Pictures from an Institution* (1954); and a number of critical essays by both writers. But the value of *Letters of Delmore Schwartz* and *Randall Jarrell's Letters* does not rest entirely in their potential ability to draw attention to their authors' poetry. Both books are of considerable worth in themselves, if only because they constitute the truest records we yet have of two remarkable lives that were consecrated to the art that Schwartz refers to (in a poem called "The Kingdom of Poetry") as "an everlasting Ark, / An omnibus containing, bearing and begetting all the mind's animals." Lives have been devoted to worse things.

DECEMBER 1989

THE ENIGMA OF RANDALL JARRELL

The ways we miss our lives are life.
—Randall Jarrell, "A Girl in a Library"

Who was Randall Jarrell? Doubtless his poetry has misled more than a few casual readers into thinking that it holds easy answers to this question. For if the generally elegant, well-bred manner of his most familiar poems seems closer to that of Elizabeth Bishop than to the emotional turbulence of so-called confessional poets like Sylvia Plath and Anne Sexton, the subject matter of much of Jarrell's verse seems, on first blush, to be frankly autobiographical. The first-person singular pronoun crops up frequently. A typical early poem, "A Camp in the Prussian Forest" (1946), begins: "I walk beside the prisoners to the road." The opening lines of a typical later poem, "The Player Piano" (1965), read: "I ate pancakes one night in a Pancake House / run by a lady my age." But the relation between the events presented in these poems and Jarrell's own life and personality proves to be far from straightforward. Though "A Camp in the Prussian Forest," like many of the poems from the collections *Little Friend, Little Friend* (1945) and *Losses* (1948), takes place in war-torn Europe, the fact is that Jarrell, who served in the Army Air Corps, never left the States during World War II and didn't visit Europe until two years after the poem's composition; as for "The Player Piano," its speaker—like those in many of the poems that Jarrell gathered in *The Woman at the Washington Zoo* (1960) and *The Lost World* (1965)—turns out to be female.

Jarrell's literary essays and reviews offer a similar illusion of intimacy. In them, he is quick to use the word *I*, quick to introduce personal anecdotes ("I was floating in a quarry with my chin on a log when I first discovered that I knew 'Provide, Provide'"), quick to refer to his own emotions (the first sentence of the first essay in his first collection of prose begins: "When I was asked to talk about the Obscurity of the Modern Poet I was delighted"). He presents himself as someone who, like Wordsworth, understands poetry as the expression of a "man speaking to men," and who responds to it as a man rather than as a disembodied Parnassian authority. His chummy, personal tone draws the reader to him, implies that the reader shares his wit and discernment, his superiority to crude and conventional ways of thinking about life and literature; one of the foremost achievements of Jarrell's essays, indeed, is that a typical reader, instead of being intimidated by his strict critical standards and by the blunt, even caustic way in which he often expresses his judgments, finds himself charmed by Jarrell's personality—his keenness, his rapture, his exasperation. The reader feels less as if he is perusing a literary essay than as if he is listening to a friend talking honestly and without inhibition about his latest reading. Here too, however, the appearance of intimacy is deceptive: one comes away from Jarrell's essays knowing very little, really, about the man behind them.

Yet the illusion of intimacy created by much of Jarrell's poetry and prose—and the poignant, tantalizingly brief glimpse of childhood that is afforded in his last collection of poems, *The Lost World*—serve only to make one more curious about Jarrell's life than one might otherwise be. As if to heighten this curiosity, recent years have seen a flood of revealing books about Jarrell's colorful fellow poets Robert Lowell, John Berryman, and Delmore Schwartz—all of which have underlined, by contrast, the degree to which the man behind Jarrell's *oeuvre* remains a mystery. Nor did the 1985 appearance of Jarrell's own letters satiate one's curiosity: energetic and friendly and opinionated as they were, Jarrell's letters (at least those chosen for inclusion by Mary von Schrader Jarrell, the poet's widow and editor of the *Letters*) were also quite superficial; one never had the feeling that one was seeing very far beneath Jarrell's surface. One came away from the letters, indeed, more certain than ever that a biography was needed—a biography that would augment the letters with ample testimony from other sources on Jarrell's life and personality. One was pleased to learn that William Pritchard, a professor at Amherst College and the author of *Frost: A Literary Life Reconsidered*, was at work on such a book, because the penetration and sensitivity of his literary criticism for *The Hudson Review* and other publications suggested that he would be a perfect match for Jarrell.

In many ways Pritchard has succeeded very impressively as Jarrell's biographer. His discussions of Jarrell's writings are perceptive, his critical judgments mostly impeccable. His prose style (despite several surprising grammatical slips) rather recalls that of Jarrell's best poetry. It is graceful, temperate, and lucid, with few outré words, never too much or too little punctuation, and (every so often) a word, phrase, or line repeated a few lines later for emphasis. It is (to use a word Pritchard applies to Jarrell's war poems) "unflashy."

But *Randall Jarrell: A Literary Life* is, in other ways, somewhat disappointing.[1] "My overriding purpose in this book," Pritchard explains, "is to give [Jarrell's] writings the detailed attention and quotation they deserve." Pritchard's main interest, in other words, is in Jarrell's writing, not in his life. There is nothing wrong with this, per se: one is hardly hungry for an excessively detailed biography along the lines of, say, Paul Mariani's voluminous *William Carlos Williams: A New World Naked* (1981), from which one emerges with the feeling that one has sat through every meal of the subject's life; nor does one want a book full of pointlessly sensational anecdotes, like Ted Morgan's *Literary Outlaw: The Life and Times of William S. Burroughs* (1988). It could, needless to say, be argued that there are too many literary biographies nowadays anyway. But Pritchard set out to do a biography, and there's little point to doing one in the first place if one is not determined to figure out what made one's subject tick. Pritchard not only seems to lack this determination; he seems overly discreet, reluctant to open any can of worms or peer into any family closets. His acknowledgments begin with the statement that his "foremost debt is to Mary Jarrell," and there is a feeling throughout almost of diffidence, of unwillingness to say things that might hurt the feelings of the poet's loved ones. This is, I suppose, admirable; but it hardly makes for revealing biography. Though Pritchard goes on in his acknowledgments, moreover, to thank many interview subjects, his biographical information comes almost entirely out of Jarrell's own letters. This is a significant failing: first, because no biography should rely so much upon the subject's own testimony (especially when there are scores of surviving students, friends, and relatives); second, because Jarrell's testimony is so unenlightening. (Nor has Mary Jarrell helped in this regard: though Pritchard thanks her for allowing him to read and quote from letters not included in *Randall Jarrell's Letters*, on at least one occasion in the biography it is clear that he has not been permitted to see everything.)

---

[1]*Randall Jarrell: A Literary Life*, by William H. Pritchard; Farrar, Straus and Giroux, 338 pages, $25.00. Pritchard also is the editor of Jarrell's newly published *Selected Poems* (Farrar, Straus and Giroux, 115 pages, $17.95).

Pritchard's treatment of Jarrell's death is representative of the problems with his approach. Soon after turning fifty in 1965, Jarrell (who had theretofore seemed, as twentieth-century American poets go, eminently stable) became depressed, then manic, giving a waitress a fifteen-hundred-dollar tip and introducing Hannah Arendt to a college audience with a twenty-minute disquisition on the quarterback Johnny Unitas; in short order, he slashed his wrist, was hospitalized and released, and (on October 14, 1965) stepped in front of a car and was killed. Most of those who knew Jarrell consider his death a suicide; the conspicuous exception is Mary Jarrell, who has always deemed it an accident. Pritchard is reluctant to side with the suicide faction, and is capable of waxing uncharacteristically sardonic about those who do, commenting that "the biographer Jeffrey Meyers has devoted much energy to proving conclusively that the death *must* have been a suicide." Pritchard is a far more sensitive and scrupulous critic than Meyers, but he seems, for his part, to have devoted an unusual amount of energy to challenging the case for suicide. He reviews the facts of the case in a manner that seems designed, at every turn, to cast doubt on the verdict of suicide, then concludes that "it is not only impossible but also unimportant to 'decide' about Jarrell's death by labeling it suicide or accident."

By refusing to "decide" about Jarrell's death, however, Pritchard refuses also to "decide" about the life that preceded it. For if Jarrell did kill himself, that act tells us something crucial about him—or, more specifically, confirms something that his letters and Pritchard's book lead us to suspect. For, though Jarrell doesn't come entirely into focus in the letters or biography, one impression emerges strongly from both books: that this was a man who was hiding an important part of himself from the world, and perhaps from himself as well. Yet Pritchard seems disinclined to uncover that hidden part, disinclined to push beyond the sunny surfaces of Jarrell's letters. On the contrary, he sometimes strikes one as being overly eager to protect Jarrell from the idea that he was emotionally more complex and troubled than he would have had people believe, and seems almost to approach the matter as if having well-developed defense mechanisms were a criminal charge and the biographer a defense attorney. Though Pritchard says in his introduction that, while working on the book, he has "become aware of just how strange a phenomenon [Jarrell] was," he nonetheless seems eager to paint Jarrell as an Essentially Normal Human Being who, in the last months of his life and for some unknown and unknowable reason, lost his emotional balance.

But Pritchard doesn't convince. He makes a point, for instance, of Jarrell's having had "deep" friendships; but the striking thing about this book is that, to judge by its account of what seem to have been Jarrell's most important friendships—with Robert Lowell, Peter Taylor, and Robert Penn Warren—none of them was at all close. Though Jarrell could converse brilliantly with his friends about literature and the arts, and offer superb critiques of their work, he was detached and inexpressive when it came to more personal matters. His letters, and the memorial essays collected by Lowell, Taylor, and Warren in *Randall Jarrell: 1914-1965*, reveal no outbursts of temper, no periods of emotional stress (before his last year), no occasion when he sat down with a friend and groused about his marriage or ruminated on the meaning of life. Even his best friends seem to have been completely surprised by his 1951 divorce from his first wife, Mackie; in a letter to Lowell, Jarrell mentions the divorce in a breathtakingly dispassionate and perfunctory tone, omits to inform Lowell of his affair with Mary (which had prompted the split), and attributes the break-up to the fact that he and Mackie have been "getting further and further apart" and that they "had almost none of the same interests."

At times, Jarrell comes across as one of those people who mistake tyranny for intimacy. If his friends were (as Pritchard writes) "either corrected, ignored or expected to loudly agree" with his opinions, the women in his life were expected to manifest "total immersion in his concerns." Pritchard describes Jarrell as being "interested in women rather than sex"; actually, one gets the impression that he was less interested in women than he was in their being interested in him. Complaining to Mary, during his year (1951-52) at Princeton, about the "sordid or faintly unpleasant or improper" conversation of "Princeton Intellectuals," he quipped: "Me for Queen Victoria, as far as Public Life is concerned." But he would seem to have been something of a Victorian even among friends. What emerges from Pritchard's book, in short, is a picture of an almost tragically remote individual. During his lifetime, some of Jarrell's fellow writers wondered why he was so happy in such a cultural backwater as the Women's College in Greensboro, North Carolina, where he taught from 1947 until his death; but one suspects that part of the reason he stayed there was that he felt more comfortable at Greensboro—where, as the faculty's sole *homme des lettres*, he could remain relatively aloof from the other professors—than he would have felt at, say, Harvard or Princeton, where he would doubtless have been forced into circumstances of fraternal intimacy (or some semblance thereof) with other highly intelligent poets and critics.

Friends also wondered at Jarrell's seemingly neurotic attachment to his pet cat, Kitten. His epistolary references to Kitten are numerous (as Pritchard notes, Kitten "is one of the principal characters in the index to Jarrell's letters") and by turns winsome and bizarre. Stationed in Texas during World War II, Jarrell wrote enthusiastically to Mackie about some photographs she'd sent: "I want some more of Kitten and some more of you." Years later, he listed the "precious objects" in his bedroom: "photographs of Donatello sculpture, photographs of Mary von Schrader, two of [his friend] Elisabeth [Eisler]'s drawings, a map of Salzburg on the door, and a big *big* picture of Kitten." Pritchard sees the Kitten complex as "a central instance of Jarrell's extravagance of spirit." But why did Jarrell get extravagant over a cat and not, say, over a series of teenage girls? One supposes it was because Kitten offered love and companionship without demanding openness, vulnerability, self-exposure.

Jarrell's favorite relationships seem to have been avuncular or teacher-student ones—relationships over which he could exercise a degree of control and in which he could keep a certain distance. Thus his extraordinary enthusiasm for other people's children (and his utter lack of interest in having children of his own) and for his students; it is as if he wanted to be close to others but was reluctant to let them become close to him. His relationship to his two stepdaughters (the offspring of Mary's first marriage) comes across as one-dimensionally affable and affectionate; the younger stepdaughter, Beatrice, has described him as a "ideal father," a characterization which occasions an astute comment from Pritchard: "The phrase is aptly dual in implication—in the sense not only of perfect but of unreal; he was not a 'real' father who made demands on, suffered through, and was thoroughly implicated in the life of his child." This is precisely the image one gets of Jarrell as a stepfather.

One might describe Jarrell as something of a bystander: at parties, he tended to sit off to the side, reading the host's books and commenting cleverly on them, or talking about the other guests. His only novel, the wonderfully witty *Pictures from an Institution* (1954), is an onlooker's book: its narrator, a smart, wisecracking teacher at a progressive women's college not unlike Sarah Lawrence (where Jarrell taught for a year before moving to Greensboro), observes the other characters, as it were, from the sidelines. As Pritchard notes, "the narrator 'is' Jarrell, to the extent that his qualities and characteristics are blatantly those of his animator." But those "qualities and characteristics" are wholly superficial; while he industriously catalogues the vices, hypocrisies, and vulnerabilities of everyone else on campus, Jarrell takes extraordinary care not to give us so much as a glimpse into the heart of his own alter ego. Part of the reason why Jarrell's personality doesn't come into focus in Pritchard's book, then, lies in the extremely private nature of that personality. But part also lies with Pritchard, who pays too little attention to most of his subject's extraliterary enthusiasms. For instance, Jarrell was passionately devoted to auto racing, of all things. But Pritchard doesn't scrutinize this interest at all; it takes on no more dimension or meaning than a hobby listed in a *Playboy* centerfold. Even more significant, perhaps, is Jarrell's rather disturbing post-World War II ardor for the German language. His 1950 poem "Deutsch Durch Freud" begins with the line: "I believe my favorite country's German." What, one wonders, brought on this curious passion—and in someone who had so recently been composing poems about concentration camps?

Perhaps Jarrell's biggest enthusiasm of all was childhood. Not only did he enjoy other people's children, compose a memorable long poem ("The Lost World") about his childhood, and write four highly regarded children's books; he was himself childlike in many ways—for example, in his frank displays of fervor and antipathy for people and poems alike, and in his public displays of affection for Kitten. (Lowell, in a sonnet, called him "Child Randall.") What was all this about? Notes Pritchard: "The man who, on the basis of his later poems, seems to have had a happy childhood was in fact deeply at odds with that childhood and with his parents' part—or lack of part—in it." The truth is that "The Lost World" draws only on a brief period of his childhood— namely, on the year when the twelve-year-old Jarrell lived with his grandparents (whom he called "Pop" and "Mama") and his great-grandmother in Hollywood, California. However much Jarrell romanticized this interval in later decades, it seems genuinely to have been the happiest time of his childhood. Certainly the rest of his childhood goes almost unmentioned in his work: his birth in Tennessee to Owen Jarrell (who came from poor rural stock) and Anna Campbell Jarrell (the daughter of a well-to-do Nashville business family); his early years in Los Angeles and Long Beach, where his father struggled along as a photographer's assistant and then as a photographer; his parents' separation, and his return, with his mother and younger brother, to Nashville, where Anna taught English at a secretarial school, and where (after his glorious year in Hollywood) Jarrell attended Hume-Fogg High School and Vanderbilt University.

Jarrell was a precocious boy, well-read and self-possessed and not above showing off his precocity. By his junior year at Hume-Fogg, he had already found his mature critical voice, scoffing wittily in the school paper at a Little Theatre production of *Hamlet* (the ghost, he remarked, had made him break into laughter) and lauding a production of *The Wild Duck*, which he called "one of the intellectual experiences of one's life." At Vanderbilt, he quickly became notorious for his ready sarcasm and classroom oratory: his teacher John Crowe Ransom remembered him as an "insistent and almost overbearing talker," an "*enfant terrible*"; Warren, also one of his teachers, found Jarrell so arrogant in class, and so patronizing toward his less-than-brilliant fellow students, that he had to speak to him about it.

Yet Ransom and Warren recognized Jarrell's intelligence and praised his solemn, grandiloquent verse. Within a couple of years, both men were publishing his poetry and reviews—Warren at *The Southern Review*, Ransom at the *Kenyon* (which was published, of course, at Ohio's Kenyon College, where Jarrell spent two years under Ransom as a graduate assistant and instructor). A third mentor was Allen Tate, though Tate's relations with Jarrell cooled considerably when the latter followed his own instincts, rather than Tate's directives, in putting together his first collection of poems, *Blood for a Stranger* (1942). Tate's resentment over this perceived betrayal lingered: after Jarrell's death, he would call him (in a letter to a friend) a "gifted, self-adulating little twerp." But one gathers that Jarrell's crime, in Tate's eyes, was not so much self-adulation as it was a stubborn native indifference to the unwritten rules of the academy: just as Ransom was put off by Jarrell's unacademic personal demeanor and by the immoderate, irreverent tone of his criticism, so Tate was angered by Jarrell's refusal to be a typical academic protégé—angered, in other words, by his independence of mind. (He wouldn't be the last.)

After receiving his M.A. from Kenyon, Jarrell taught for three years at the University of Texas, where his students' ignorance appalled him; in 1943 he entered the Army Air Corps, where his fellow soldiers proved to be even more ignorant than his students. "The conversation," he wrote Mackie (whom he had married in 1940) from a Texas base, "is on a level that makes you disbelieve even in the existence of, say, Proust.... In a lecture today we were twice told that we must obey orders 'promptly and willfully'; isn't that charming?" Pritchard comments that "Jarrell truly sounds charmed by [his fellow soldiers'] mistakes"; if so, it was in the way that tourists are charmed by animals in a zoo. Jarrell insisted in his letters—and Pritchard believes—that his fellow soldiers held him in high regard, and perhaps they did; but Pritchard shows no sign of having spoken to any of those soldiers, and offers no quotations from any of them on the matter. Nor is it clear, from Pritchard's discussion, whether Jarrell, in his letters, mentioned any fellow soldiers by name. No names, in any event, appear in the biography; and if Jarrell never did name any of them to Mackie it would seem to support one's sense that he related to them not as individuals but as types.

Certainly this conclusion seems to be supported by his war poems, whose collective weakness stems not, as some suggest, from Jarrell's utter lack of combat experience (as Pritchard points out, neither Whitman nor Melville, America's great Civil War poets, was a soldier) but from his supremely impersonal approach. Wilfred Owen remarked of his own war poems that "The Poetry is in the pity," and Pritchard perceptively suggests that Jarrell thought of his own war poems in much the same way; but James Dickey (in a 1955 review, quoted by Pritchard, of Jarrell's *Selected Poems*) gets to the heart of the poems' failure: "Did Jarrell never love any *person* in the service with him?" Dickey argues that Jarrell's war poems are populated by "types" and accuses him of a "monstrous, abstract, complacent, and inhuman Compassion." "Monstrous" may be going too far, but Dickey is otherwise right on the money: the graver his theme, the further back Jarrell tended to step from it, indulging in empty rhetoric, ponderous ironies, and a facile, generalized pity. His most famous poem, "The Death of the Ball Turret Gunner," is only one of many (and is certainly the best) whose speaker is dead, a casualty of war. In "The Metamorphoses," for instance, a sailor floats in a harbor "with gills in my sides," and notes that "the blood of the transports is red on the tide." In "Come to the Stone...," a child speaks from the grave: "The people are punish-

ing the people—why? / ... / *Come to the stone and tell me why I died."*
And in "The State," another child declares: "I'm dead, and I want to die."

Throughout these poems, Jarrell takes on potentially tragic themes and clutches at cheap pathos. During these early years, critics often chided him for echoing Auden, and that influence is certainly evident in his manifest longing to Say Something about the awfulness of war. But Jarrell had little gift for the poetry of vast pronouncements. His best military poems, indeed, tend to be quieter, smaller-scale ones, poems which could conceivably have been based on his own experience. Among these is "Absent with Official Leave," which enters the mind of a soldier lying in bed:

> The lights are beginning to go out in the barracks.
> They persist or return, as the wakeful hollow,
> But only for a moment; then the windows blacken
> For all the hours of the soldier's life.
>
> It is life into which he composes his body.
> He covers his ears with his pillow, and begins to drift
> (Like the plumes the barracks trail into the sky)
> Past the laughs, the quarrels, and the breath of others
>
> To the ignorant countries where civilians die
> Inefficiently, in their spare time, for nothing...
> The curved roads hopping through the aimless green
> Dismay him, and the cottages where people cry
>
> For themselves and, sometimes, for the absent soldier—
> Who inches through hedges where the hunters sprawl
> For birds, for birds; who turns in ecstasy
> Before the slow small fires the women light
>
> His charmed limbs, all endearing from the tub.
> He dozes, and the washed locks trail like flax
> Down the dark face; the unaccusing eyes
> That even the dream's eyes are averted from
>
> See the wind puff down the chimney, warm the hands
> White with the blossoms it pretends are snow...

He moans like a bear in his enchanted sleep,
And the grave mysterious beings of his years—

The causes who mourn above his agony like trees—
Are moved for their child, and bend across his limbs
The one face opening for his life, the eyes
That look without shame even into his.

And the man awakes, and sees around his life
The night that is never silent, broken with the sighs
And patient breathing of the dark companions
With whom he labors, sleeps, and dies.

This is just the right pitch for Jarrell. If his rhetoric generally got away from him when he tried to write about the more intense aspects of war and army life, this pensive, unhurried poem about a sleeping soldier finds him (for the most part) in control. The soldier here seems closer to a real human being than do the symbolically rendered servicemen, refugees, and *faux-naïf* children in most of Jarrell's other war poems. The best thing about "Absent with Official Leave," however, is that, unlike most of Jarrell's war poems, it does not throw off easy ironies or brazenly solicit pity: the tone is more one of commiseration than of condescension, more one of thoughtful resignation than of slick reproach. As Pritchard notes, the poem neither pities the soldier nor asks us to pity him: "If it is a pity things should be as they are, it is also the way in this world they must be."

In its gentle, prosy cadences, its rough approximation of iambic pentameter, and its wistful absorption in a single ordinary human life, "Absent with Official Leave" anticipates many of Jarrell's better postwar poems. One such poem is "A Girl in a Library" (1951), in which the speaker sees a homely, vacuous-looking student, a standard cow-college type, about to drift off to sleep "in this enclave [where] there are centuries / For you to waste." He regards her scornfully, even heartlessly: "One sees in your blurred eyes / The 'uneasy half-soul' Kipling saw in dogs." Yet his scorn is mixed with tenderness ("You are very human"), even empathy (for he realizes that he sees the same half-soul "in the glass, in one's own eyes"). As he imagines himself telling Tatyana Larina—the heroine of *Eugene Onegin*, who presumably represents, for

Jarrell, a realm as distant as possible from the girl's tacky little world of blind dates and such—she is missing out on life, on imagination, on all the precious things of the spirit, without even knowing it:

> Poor senseless Life:
> When, in the last light sleep of dawn, the messenger
> Comes with his message, you will not awake.
> He'll give his feathery whistle, shake you hard,
> You'll look with wide eyes at the dewy yard
> And dream, with calm slow factuality:
> "Today's Commencement. My bachelor's degree
> In Home Ec., my doctorate of philosophy
> In Phys. Ed.
> [Tanya, they won't even *scan*]
> Are waiting for me...."
> Oh, Tatyana,
> The Angel comes: better to squawk like a chicken
> Than to say with truth, "But I'm a good girl,"
> And Meet his Challenge with a last firm strange
> Uncomprehending smile; and—then, then!—see
> The blind date that has stood you up: your life.

As Pritchard notes, the poem mixes "mockery and love, satire and sympathy"—a paradox which is rehearsed in a very Jarrellian line toward the end of the poem: "I love you—and yet—and yet—I love you." It is not too much of an exaggeration, I think, to say that such combinations of satire and sympathy—wherein each takes the sting off the other, and the interplay helps generate a persona of plausible ambivalence—figure pivotally in many of Jarrell's better poems.

For many readers, to be sure, both the prosy style of "A Girl in a Library" and its concentration on a prosaic individual are far from salutary characteristics: to Dickey's mind, Jarrell's "romance with the ordinary" results in a poetry that is insufficiently "magical"; in Tate's view, Jarrell's lines were often too limp. Jarrell's reply to this charge was unequivocal: "I'd rather seem limp and prosaic than false or rhetorical, I want to be like speech." Indeed, in his mature poetry, Jarrell's ultimate criterion of excellence was authenticity; thus he berated Richard Wilbur for not being "real" enough, applauded Elizabeth Bishop for writing poems that "seem really about real life, and to have as much of what's nice and beautiful and loving about the world as the world lets them have," and preferred Philip Larkin to Dylan Thomas because the voice in Larkin's poetry was "like life." Though Jarrell claimed not to "put any real faith in abstractions," his poems are crowded with them, and life is at the top of the list; of the fifty poems in the *Selected Poems*, no fewer than five conclude with that very word. (Four of them, incidentally, end with the words *die*, *dies*, *dead*, and *death*.)

Yet life, in Jarrell's better postwar poems, is not at all an abstract thing. There may be mewling about life and death and fate, but it is likely to be done by a sympathetic, tangible speaker within the framework of an interior monologue. In place of the extreme, impersonal rhetoric of the war poems there are, in these poems, equally extreme assertions of personal despair; increasingly, as the years went by, Jarrell poured into his verse a profound anguish over the brevity of life, the passage of time, the horror of aging. In "The Face" (1950), a woman examines her countenance, no longer young and beautiful, and says "This isn't mine"; in "The Woman at the Washington Zoo" (1960), another woman roaming among the animals realizes that she is more truly caged than they, for she, unlike them, is trapped in the knowledge of aging and death; in "The Next Day" (1963), a third woman goes grocery shopping, her mind fixed on a friend's funeral the day before, "[c]onfused with my life, that is commonplace and solitary." And then there is "Aging" (1954):

I wake, but before I know it is done,
The day, I sleep. And of days like these the years,
A life is made. I nod, consenting to my life.
…But who can live in these quick-passing hours?
I need to find again, to make a life,
A child's Sunday afternoon, the Pleasure Drive
Where everything went by but Time; the Study Hour
Spent at a desk, with folded hands, in waiting.

In those I could make. Did I not make in them
Myself? The Grown One whose time shortens,
Breath quickens, heart beats faster, till at last
It catches, skips…. Yet those hours that seemed, were endless
Were still not long enough to have remade
My childish heart: the heart that must have, always,
To make anything of anything, not time,
Not time but—

but, alas! eternity.

With its forthright expression of melancholy about adult life and mortality, its ready exaltation of childhood and its institutions, and its prominent, exclamatory *alas*, "Aging" is precisely the sort of Jarrell poem that is widely scorned as sentimental. Alas indeed! These are not good times for the reputation of a poet like Jarrell; one suspects that, in today's literary environment, readers may dismiss all of these emotionally explicit later poems out of hand simply because their visible-feeling content exceeds current creative-writing-program recommendations. This is unfortunate, for "Aging," far from being emotionally self-indulgent, is actually very nicely controlled; and there are good things in many of the other poems of its ilk. Yet Dickey, in criticizing one of them, "The Lost Children," registers a valid complaint—namely, that Jarrell "does not search diligently enough for the thing that is his own beyond the thing that is owned both by him and by all those aging housewives." "Please do not understand me too quickly," wrote André Gide, and perhaps the major problem with these poems is that Jarrell populates them with characters who are rather too quickly understood, characters whose minds are a bit too easy for Jarrell's mind to encompass and comprehend. The problem with a poem like "Aging," in other words, is not that it is sentimental; it is that its speaker, while not quite a stereotype, lacks a certain dimension and ambiguity.

Yet there is something to be said for poems like "Aging," "The Next Day," and "The Woman at the Washington Zoo." The expression of despair in them is interestingly, peculiarly controlled; there is an alluring tension between form and content—between, that is to say, the inner torment of the speakers and the civilized regularity of the poems' quasi-pentameter lines. Lowell once described Jarrell's body as "a little ghostly in its immunity to soil, entanglements, and rebellion"; and the "body"—the form, the structure—of many a later Jarrell poem, for all its assertion of despair, likewise strikes one as being unnaturally aseptic and unentangled, possessed of an almost chilling false poise that cannot but make one think of the tranquil, imperturbable face that Jarrell himself showed to the world.

For despite the weighty existential agony that is communicated by these poems, Jarrell—if his friends, his family, and his own odd epistolary braggadocio are to be believed—went through life (until those troubled last months) with a smile on his face. Writing in 1945 to Margaret Marshall at *The Nation*, he explained that he had "an even, cheerful, and optimistic disposition: what I write is therapeutically the opposite, I guess." Pritchard comments: "My inclination is not to understand or 'accept' this split as an indication of a character at troubled odds with itself, but to take it rather as a measure of Jarrell's sanity. All of us, to one degree or another, look at life in these irreconcilable ways, even as, day by day, we entertain both of them and continue to function." Well, yes—most of us do experience both cheerfulness and anguish; but those of us who are emotionally healthy are able to face the anguish, to admit it to ourselves and others, and to work through it back to a more equable state. The disturbing thing about Jarrell is that he seems to have been as incapable of expressing despair outside of a poem as he was of introducing his cheerfulness convincingly into a poem. For this reason it is hard not to see his cheerfulness as, in large part, self-deceptive. Certainly his refusal to help in any way during Lowell's manic periods—or even to visit his friend in mental hospitals—suggests that he feared confronting in Lowell a reflection of what lay buried in himself.

More wholly satisfying than almost any of Jarrell's poems is his one novel, *Pictures from an Institution*; and Pritchard's discussion of it is among the most satisfying parts of his biography. Actually Jarrell himself called *Pictures* not a novel but a "comedy," and the distinction is worth keeping in mind, for this is not by any means a conventional novel; it is a book, Pritchard reminds us, "in which nothing happens except stylistically—within the sentences." As he shrewdly points out (and as its title suggests), Jarrell's comedy represents something of a mingling of genres: it has certain characteristics of both the dramatic poem and the essay; and its satirical depiction of the way art and culture are regarded in American colleges recalls both Jarrell's essay "The Obscurity of the Poet" and his poem "A Girl in a Library."

Pritchard is good on the book's intense, one-liner-heavy style, pointing out that its peculiarity "works against a sense of the book as real—as somehow about 'life'—in the way that *Anna Karenina* or even *The Groves of Academe* is real and about life"; and he is good, too, on the Jarrell-like narrator, whom Jarrell presents as "a clever, superior talent wanting also to insist that it wasn't *merely* clever, wasn't *really* superior in any exclusively elitist sense." Yet Pritchard's suggestion that *Pictures*, with its aversion to plot, be seen as a forerunner of the "anti-stories" of Robert Coover, John Barth, and Donald Barthelme is not persuasive: Jarrell was anti-plot not because he wanted to play lexical self-referentiality games but because he wanted his book's texture and rhythms and voices to more closely resemble those of real life, at least as he saw it. (Whether he succeeded fully in this regard—and whether we would have wanted him to—is another matter.)

Though *Pictures* continues to win him new admirers, Jarrell is best known to many readers as a literary critic, the author of *Poetry and the Age* (1953) and three other collections of prose. If there are two basic kinds of poetry criticism—positive and negative—Jarrell was notorious for writing the latter kind, and for doing it with remarkable verve and panache. He describes Karl Shapiro's *Trial of a Poet* as "a sort of bobby-soxer's *Mauberley*," calls Frederic Prokosch "a sort of decerebrate Auden," says that "some of [Joyce] Kilmer's poems are better than 'Trees,' but not enough better for it to matter," and reviews Archibald MacLeish's "America Was Promises" by pretending that it is "a brilliant and malicious parody of MacLeish's public-speaking period." Pritchard, who contributed an essay to *The New York Times Book Review* a while back about "nasty reviewing," seems to look upon the writing of negative reviews more as a psychological phenomenon (what *makes* Mr. X so nasty?) than as a necessary function of the serious critic. While giving some of Jarrell's funnier quips their due, he seems uncomfortable with Jarrell's negativeness; one gets the impression that, deep down, he looks upon a quickness to attack bad poetry as some sort of character flaw.

This is unfortunate, for Jarrell's unhesitating honesty in such matters is highly commendable. Implicit throughout his essays and correspondence is the idea that if poetry is genuinely important to you, and if you truly experience a poem with your whole self, then of course you'll be outraged by the publication of bad poetry, by the widespread neglect of good poetry, and by the inability of those around you to tell the difference. And if that is how you feel, then why pretend otherwise? What is the point of writing poetry criticism if not to communicate one's sincere response, and thereby to help separate the meritorious from the meretricious, and keep good work from drowning in a sea of mediocrity?

In this long, grim, theory-ridden twilight of what Jarrell called "The Age of Criticism," many literary critics would probably find Jarrell's view quaint, naïve; to their minds, writing criticism is simply what one does to get ahead—to get a teaching job, tenure, grant money— and writing nasty things about certain people might mean professional suicide. It wouldn't have occurred to Jarrell to think this way, for the need to speak his mind honestly about the art he loved clearly meant more to him than any such practical considerations. Nor would he have understood the complaints of many new-wave critics that critical standards are by definition elitist (and therefore evil), or the objections from many poets that since poetry is an endangered species, poets should write only nice things about each other. (As if a universal complimentary-reviews-only policy would draw people to poetry rather than drive them away from it!) Far from being a black mark against him, Jarrell's willingness to write negative reviews, whatever the consequences, is one of the things that make him most worth remembering and honoring.

Pritchard seems more at ease discussing Jarrell's positive poetry criticism, much of which he thinks splendid. And it is true that Jarrell was, as Pritchard reminds us, very good at selecting first-rate, previously neglected passages from the *oeuvres* of poets like Frost and Whitman. But Jarrell doesn't usually do much with those passages; instead, he says such things as the following: "In the last lines of this quotation Whitman has reached—as great writers always reach—a point at which criticism seems not only unnecessary but absurd: these lines are so good that even admiration feels like insolence, and one is ashamed of anything that one can find to say about them." The reader can identify with Jarrell's position here: doubtless every literary critic has written about authors who impress him so much that he feels ridiculously audacious even to voice his approbation in print. But, for heaven's sake, this is the critic's job; for Jarrell to eschew it seems something of a cop-out. To be sure, the essay in question, "Some Lines from Whitman," is famous for having helped establish Whitman's central position in American poetry; but it did so by quoting splendid neglected passages from *Leaves of Grass*, not by offering a convincing argument for the poet's greatness.

And what of Jarrell's position in American poetry? Though he was a wonderfully gifted writer, and though he wrote some of the most beautifully composed poems of his generation, he was far from a great poet. There is much in his *Selected Poems* that is deeply affecting and memorable. On the whole, however, one responds more enthusiastically to the idea of his poetry—his affection for the long, supple, meditative line, his preoccupation with the good and beautiful and innocent, and

his desire to make everything (as he put it) "a thing of human impor-
tance"—than one does to most of the poems themselves.

Pritchard (who, to his credit, makes no vast claims for Jarrell's
poetry) complains that Jarrell "learned almost nothing from his con-
temporaries"; a more magnanimous way to put this is to say that Jarrell
was independent-minded—that his poetry, unlike that of many who
work the assembly lines in today's creative-writing factories, was the
genuine expression of the man. Yet the fact that so much of that poetry
is ultimately rather disappointing would seem, ironically, to have more
than a little to do with the man's own lamentable insufficiency of genu-
ineness, his apparent reluctance—in poetry as well as in life—to con-
front and to grapple with whatever lay at the heart of his personal
darkness.

MAY 1990

DISPOSSESSION, DREAMS, DELUSIONS:
JOHN BERRYMAN

His real name was, of all things, John Smith, and he was born in 1914 in McAlester, Oklahoma, the elder son and namesake of a man who, after failing miserably both as a small-town banker in that state and as the proprietor of a modest Tampa, Florida, eatery, shuffled off this mortal coil in 1926 by means of a self-inflicted bullet wound. His death was followed hard upon—within ten weeks, in fact—by his canny widow's marriage to the family's landlord, a prosperous bond sales-man named John Angus McAlpin Berryman; and it was not long after-ward that the new Mrs. Berryman divested both her children, eleven-year-old John and six-year-old Robert Jefferson, of their father's last name and Catholic religion, changed her own name from Martha May to Jill Angel, and relocated the newly formed Berryman clan to New York. Three years later, the stock market crash devastated John Angus and forced Jill Angel to go to work; but her adored elder son, now named John Allyn McAlpin Berryman, continued to receive a first-rate education: after being graduated from the South Kent School, an Episcopal boarding academy in Connecticut, he proceeded to make a mark for himself as an up-and-coming poet and literary man at Co-lumbia College (where he studied under Mark Van Doren) and at Cam-bridge University (which he attended on a Kellett Fellowship).

Why a poet? The young man's intense, possessive mother—to whom he was tied by extraordinary bonds of mutual guilt, resentment, and love, and whose influence upon him, accordingly, was profound—had a special interest in literature. And Berryman seems to have needed *something* to put between himself and the ever-impinging thought of his father's suicide. For throughout his life, questions raged within him about that event's causes and aftermath. Had his father killed him-self out of despair over his business reversals, or because his wife had become involved with another man? What exactly *was* the extent of Jill Angel's responsibility for his death? Why had she remarried so quickly? And why had he (the poet) allowed her to change his name? Far from helping to set his mind at ease, moreover, Berryman's dominating, adoring, and expertly manipulative mother served only to make matters worse: as Eileen Simpson, his first wife and most perceptive biographer, writes in her memoir *Poets in Their Youth* (1982), Jill Angel told Berryman that his father was "a failure not only as a bread-winner but also as a lover," an indiscretion which (in Simpson's view) gave the poet "a damaging view of his father's manliness and, by extension, his own." One cannot, of course, make causal connections with absolute certitude, but the fact is that by his teens Berryman had developed a self-destructiveness as real as his father's: he attempted suicide at prep school, and threatened to kill himself at various times over the ensuing years. In Simpson's words, suicide was throughout his adult life "a kind of undertow, sucking at him, sometimes feebly, sometimes with terrifying strength."

And it was poetry, during Berryman's early adulthood, that provided him with the chief means of resisting that undertow. Amid the torment of muddled memories and turbulent reflections, poetry represented a principle of order, a means of curbing unstable tendencies. T.S. Eliot, of course, had explained it all years earlier. In "Tradition and the Individual Talent" (1919), Eliot had proclaimed that "[p]oetry is not a turning loose of emotion, but an escape from emotion; it is not the expression of personality, but an escape from personality." Eliot was, needless to say, the premier literary authority not only for Berryman but for his entire generation; but to the haunted and fervently Anglophilic young poet from McAlester, Oklahoma, the eminent London literary man who had managed to put the Eliots of St. Louis behind him and to transform himself magically into an Englishman must have made an especially powerful impression. Certainly Berryman brought to his art the high seriousness that Eliot demanded: as Simpson recalls, "[t]he important thing, the real thing, the *only* thing was to write poetry. All else was wasted time." And Berryman's early poetry makes it clear that he took Old Possum's famous pronouncements on poetry as gospel (and took them, it might be added, even more literally than did Eliot himself), dutifully heeding Eliot's directive, in "The Metaphysical Poets" (1921), to "be *difficult*," to "become more and more comprehensive, more allusive, more indirect." Published in *Five Young American Poets* (1940), *Poems* (1942), and *The Dispossessed* (1948), Berryman's early lyrics—almost all of which are formal and impersonal, elevated in diction and ambitious in range of reference, and preternaturally somber—patently reflect the earnest and arduous effort of a young man eager to be the most comprehensive, allusive, and indirect poet around. But these poems reflect other influences, too—notably those of W.H. Auden and William Butler Yeats (the latter of whom Berryman idolized). The most characteristic of Berryman's early poems, indeed, read like agglomerations of stylistic tics and pet phrases from all three of these elder poets, the poems' very titles alternately suggesting Eliot ("Rock-Study with Wanderer," "World-Telegram"), Yeats ("Ceremony and Vision," and "The Animal Trainer"), and Auden ("1 September 1939").

Yet to say that the young Berryman's stylistic and formal choices were heavily influenced by Yeats and Auden is not to say that he shared their ideas about poetry. The difference between, say, Berryman's "1 September 1939" and Auden's "September 1, 1939" (aside from the amusing fact that the Anglophile Berryman used the British system of date notation, and the English expatriate Auden followed American practice) is instructive: for all its concern with international events, Auden's poem represents a direct, colloquial, and personal response to the Nazi invasion of Poland, even beginning with the first-person pronoun:

> I sit in one of the dives
> On Fifty-Second Street
> Uncertain and afraid
> As the clever hopes expire
> Of a low dishonest decade:
> Waves of anger and fear
> Circulate over the bright
> And darkened lands of the earth,
> Obsessing our private lives;
> The unmentionable odour of death
> Offends the September night.

In the succeeding stanzas, Auden generalizes about man and history, drawing the conclusion that "We must love one another or die." Yet for all his talk of "Democracy" and "Collective Man," he doesn't lose sight of people themselves, the "dense commuters," the "helpless governors," and the "man-in-the-street" who share culpability for the day's tragedy; and he ends the poem where he began, with himself:

> May I, composed like them

Of Eros and of dust,
Beleaguered by the same
Negation and despair,
Show an affirming flame.

Berryman's poem, by contrast, begins by eliminating the human dimension of the events of September 1. Instead of people dropping bombs on people, we find

The first, scattering rain on Polish cities.
That afternoon a man squat' on the shore
Tearing a square of shining cellophane.
Some easily, some in evident torment tore,
Some for a time resisted, and then burst.
All this depended on fidelity...
One was blown out and borne off by the waters,
The man was tortured by the sound of rain.

The poem continues for two more stanzas in this allegorical vein, portraying the Soviet Union as a "Bear [that] crept under the Eagle's wing" and Nazi Germany as "the Eagle [that] soared and dropt." The differences between this poem and Auden's are striking: whereas Auden's reads like a profoundly felt response to the German attack, Berryman's reads like the work of an ambitious young poet who has self-consciously chosen a towering subject and is out to be as clever about it as he can. If Auden, in other words, draws straightforward connections between the invasion and real people in the real world, Berryman attempts to make ingenious metaphorical connections in the manner of the Metaphysical poets, representing bombs as rain, a continent as a piece of cellophane, two totalitarian states as a pair of animals. Yet one would hardly confuse this poem with anything by Donne; its imagery comes off not as fresh and witty but as pretentious and derivative—its title adapted from Auden, its eight-line stanza borrowed from Yeats, its rain metaphor and at least one turn of phrase ("His shadow / Lay on the sand before him") reminiscent of *The Waste Land*.

The impersonal route, then, wasn't very well suited to the tragic personal history and the idiosyncratic gifts with which fate had outfitted Berryman. There are, to be sure, several fine poems in these early collections; but the best tend to be those in which he rejects second-hand methods and grandiose themes and chooses not to escape emotion but to embrace it. One thinks particularly of "World's Fair" and "Fare Well," in both of which he allows himself to vent disturbing thoughts of his father: "Suddenly in torn images I trace / The inexhaustible ability of a man / Loved once, long lost, still to prevent my peace, / Still to suggest my dreams and starve horizon." In form as well as manner, both poems seem to anticipate *The Dream Songs,* which he began writing in 1955. Even more suggestive of Berryman's celebrated long poem is a sequence of three-stanza, eighteen-line poems called "The Nervous Songs," in which Berryman tries on a variety of whimsical, eccentric personas—a young Hawaiian, a demented priest, a tortured girl. The chattiness, the regular but flexible form, and the attempt at playfulness and irreverence all foreshadow *The Dream Songs;* but these early songs are just not very absorbing, perhaps because the characters and their stories were too removed from Berryman's own life to arouse in him the wit and pathos and urgency that characterize the finest of the *Dream Songs.*

All poetic careers that stretch out over decades undergo conspicuous modulations of some kind or another—changes in style, in tone, in subject matter. But the phases of Berryman's career are more distinct than most. His first major transition took place in 1947, when, over the course of a brief, intense extramarital affair, he composed a sequence of over a hundred sonnets that would not appear in print until twenty years later, under the title *Berryman's Sonnets.* In the newly published *Collected Poems,*[1] these poems are labeled *Sonnets to Chris,* marking the first time that the pseudonymous lover "Lise" of the 1967 book has been given her real name. These are odd poems: Berryman's tone swings from the elevated to the vernacular (and, not infrequently, the bawdy) and back again, all within the rigorously heeded constraints of the Petrarchan sonnet form. Read from a four-decades-later perspective, these poems strike one mainly as warm-ups for *The Dream Songs.* Yet their speaker—though plainly tormented by life and love in the same way as Berryman's *Dream Songs* alter ego, Henry—is a good deal more mindful than Henry of conventional literary etiquette; poetry remains, for him, something of a shield against the self-destructive impulse. At times, indeed, one has the feeling that the only thing stand-

---

[1] *Collected Poems 1937–1971,* by John Berryman; edited and introduced by Charles Thornbury; Farrar, Straus & Giroux, 348 pages, $25.

ing between Berryman and outright lunacy is his all-subsuming desire to finish off the sonnet at hand with a firm, coherent sestet.

It is clear, in any event, that Berryman the sonneteer was still mostly in thrall to the Eliotic idea of poetry. The sonnets are dense with exotic verbiage, with Metaphysical conceits, and with imitations and parodies of other poets (among them such masters of the form as Shakespeare, Wyatt, and Petrarch). They are dense, too, with highfalutin historical, cultural, and literary allusions, some of which seem thematically pertinent and some of which seem extraneous and mechanical. (The affair, he writes, began in "middle March"—an allusion to George Eliot that has no purpose other than to look clever.) Frequently the sonnets appear to be straining in two opposite directions: straining, that is, to sound cultivated and ingenious, and straining also to seem eccentric, funny, spontaneous, chockablock with personality. And there are times, alas, when the straining is all that one notices.

What's more, Berryman's apparent intentions notwithstanding, the sonnets rarely strike one as having much to do with love—unless, of course, one means a deeply neurotic self-love (which is balanced, as it were, by an equally deep and equally neurotic self-hatred). Too often, in these poems where the *I*s and *me*s typically outnumber the *you*s, Berryman comes off as glib, insincere, self-dramatizing, his putative devotion to Chris merely a handy excuse for reckless emotional excess and for the mass production of sonnets. And too often the inverted syntax that would become a familiar (and generally engaging) characteristic of *The Dream Songs* seems, in the sonnets, to be deployed largely for purposes of meter or rhyme:

> I lift—lift you five States away your glass,
> Wide of this bar you never graced, where none
> Ever I know came, where what work is done
> Even by these men I know not...

In sonnet 47, Berryman speaks of "[c]rumpling a syntax at a sudden need." This skill would figure importantly in his art. But at the time of the sonnets' composition it was a skill that he was still in the process of developing.

Berryman's only volume of poetry in the Fifties was *Homage to Mistress Bradstreet* (1956), a meticulously crafted, tightly packed poem of

456 lines that was five years in the writing, and that Edmund Wilson hailed upon its publication as "the most distinguished long poem by an American since *The Waste Land*." The poem consists mostly of a monologue by the colonial New England poet Anne Bradstreet, whom Berryman imagines himself summoning, as it were, from out of Spiritus Mundi: "Out of maize & air / your body's made, and moves. I summon, see, / from the centuries it." Cosmic communion having been established, Berryman's voice gives way in the fifth stanza to Bradstreet's, and she proceeds without further ado to describe her existence in the New World: the ruggedness of life on the edge of an alien wilderness, the joys and tribulations of marriage and motherhood, the succor of Christian belief ("God awaits us"), and the composition of poetry ("quaternion on quaternion, tireless I phrase / anything past, dead, far, / sacred, for a barbarous place"). At one point Berryman interrupts to engage her in a dialogue, wanly contesting her faith—"I cannot feel myself God waits.... Man is entirely alone / may be"—and declaring his love for her. It is he, too, whose voice closes the poem:

> O all your ages at the mercy of my loves
> together lie at once, forever or
> so long as I happen.
> In the rain of pain & departure, still
> Love has no body and presides the sun,
> and elfs from silence melody. I run.
> Hover, utter, still,
> a sourcing whom my lost candle like the firefly loves.

This stanza—which, like the fifty-six that precede it, strictly follows the intricate, exacting eight-line form that Berryman devised for the poem—is typical of *Homage*'s lyricism as well as of its frequent obscurity. The poem swarms with recondite words, with nouns and adjectives used as verbs ("One proud tug greens Heaven"), with trimmed-down adverbs ("Women sleep sound"), and with taut, sinewy, heavily punctuated, and syntactically contorted sentences. Berryman also incorporates snippets of Bradstreet's own poetry, though the voice in which she speaks is very much his own creation. It's a remarkable poem, impressively and beautifully crafted, and represents the closest that Berryman would ever come to the controlled passion of, say, Lowell's *Life Studies* or Jarrell's *The Woman at the Washington*

Zoo (to name books by two of Berryman's contemporaries and closest friends). But its control, unlike that in Lowell's and Jarrell's books, seems hard won; it *reads* like a poem that took five years to write, a poem that from the outset was intended to be nothing less than "the most distinguished long poem by an American since *The Waste Land*." It also reads, after Berryman's early lyrics and sonnets, like a last, monumental attempt to be a rigorously formal and impersonal poet. Berryman claimed to have fallen in love with Bradstreet while writing the poem, and the fact that lines from his sonnets reappear in *Homage* addressed to the Puritan poet makes one suspect that *Homage* was, in part, the product of an obstinate desire to find a more impersonal way of making poetry out of what Berryman must then have considered to be the overly personal materials of the sonnets. What is telling, however, is that Berryman could not help but inject himself into the poem, however briefly; and his fleeting declaration to Bradstreet of his love and despair seems to anticipate the tone and persona of *The Dream Songs* more surely than anything he had yet published.

It was at about the time of the publication of *Homage to Mistress Bradstreet* that Berryman began writing *The Dream Songs*. He would continue writing them for the rest of his life, much as Whitman kept revising *Song of Myself* and Pound kept adding to the *Cantos*. The comparison is fitting because, like those poems, *The Dream Songs* is a personal epic with a decidedly American personality; to read it on the heels of Berryman's earlier poems is to get the impression that the poet, after trying for so long to bring objective order to his verse, finally accepted—as did Pound in the *Cantos*—the fact that he could not "make it cohere." This is not to suggest, of course, that Berryman abandoned the idea of form. Though *The Dream Songs* as a whole can hardly be said to have a preordained shape, the individual songs themselves observe a form that, while making specific demands of the poet, is at the same time considerably more elastic than, say, an English sonnet. The typical song consists of three six-line stanzas, in each of which the first, second, fourth, and fifth lines usually approximate iambic pentameter, and the third and sixth lines tend to be shorter; there may by rhymes or slant rhymes within each stanza, though no particular scheme predominates.

The quality of the songs varies enormously. Too often, the humor shades into cuteness, the wit into easy flippancy, and the childlike candor into infantile display. At their best, however, the songs are singularly moving. Abounding in clever, seemingly effortless, and often nearly imperceptible patterns of rhyme, the most estimable of them reverberate with life and feeling, their splendidly supple style capable of conveying humor in one line and pathos in the next with what often seems the greatest of ease. It should be mentioned that while the songs are highly intimate, Berryman insisted that they were not about him at all; responding in a prefatory note to the second (and final) volume of songs, *His Toy, His Dream, His Rest* (1968), to some critics of the first volume, *77 Dream Songs* (1964), Berryman maintained that the poem "is essentially about an imaginary character (not the poet, not me) named Henry, a white American in early middle age sometimes in blackface, who has suffered an irreversible loss and talks about himself sometimes in the first person, sometimes in the third, sometimes even in the second; he has a friend, never named, who addresses him as Mr. Bones and variants thereof." But this is nonsense: as Joel Conarroe has written in his book-length study of Berryman, "anyone who reads the songs carefully will reject the assertion that they are about an imaginary character—some details, of course, are invented, but the sequence adheres closely to the facts of the poet's life and mind."

Why, then, did Berryman insist on Henry's separate identity? One reason may be that, as an impersonal poet of long standing, Berryman felt more comfortable hiding behind a persona, however transparent; the invention of Henry, in other words, may well have made it easier for him to be himself—to be, by turns, maudlin, obnoxious, charming, paranoid, poignant, and embarrassingly confessional, continually addressing us as "pal" or "friend," like a chummy, garrulous, dipsomaniacal stranger in a bar. (Indeed, the usual tone of Henry's monologues might fairly be described as a cross between drunk talk and baby talk.) The stranger can, at times, be wildly funny, whether he is parodying the halting oratory of President Eisenhower in "The Lay of Ike" ("Here's to the glory of the Great White—awk— / who has been running—er—er—things in recent—ech—") or making fun of the annual MLA convention (for which "[w]e are assembled here in the capital / city for Dull") or recounting his lust for a fellow diner at a restaurant, where

> only the fact of her husband & four other people
> kept me from springing on her
>
> or falling at her little feet and crying

'You are the hottest one for years of night
Henry's dazed eyes
have enjoyed, Brilliance.'

But he is mostly depressed, and the poem that he proffers, while volubly addressing such themes as love, fame, and God (and even, now and then, recording cherished moments of joy and tranquility), is predominantly a poem of loss, of mourning. Henry mourns his poet friends Delmore Schwartz, Randall Jarrell, and R.P. Blackmur; he mourns the literary masters Yeats and Frost and Eliot; and, as Conarroe writes, he's "in mourning for his own disorderly life." Then there is his late father, who is the object of both extraordinary rancor ("I spit upon this dreadful banker's grave / who shot his heart out in a Florida dawn / ... / When will indifference come, I moan & rave") and genuine compassion:

Also I love him: me he's done no wrong
for going on forty years—forgiveness time—
I touch now his despair...

I cannot read that wretched mind, so strong
& so undone. I've always tried. I—I'm
trying to forgive
whose frantic passage, when he could not live
an instant longer, in the summer dawn
left Henry to live on.

Aside from illustrating the striking degree to which Berryman bares his soul in *The Dream Songs*, this passage provides a good example of the poem's stylistic eccentricities. The seeming omission, in its closing sentence, of the one or two extra words that would make it sound like ordinary prose (i.e., "I'm trying to forgive *the man* whose frantic passage... ") is typical of *The Dream Songs*. Whether calculated or not, such shorthand locutions can be oddly expressive and touching; one thinks, for instance, of the fourth and eighth lines of a song lamenting the death of Delmore Schwartz:

Henry's mind grew blacker the more he thought.
He looked unto the world like the act of an aged whore.
Delmore, Delmore.

He flung to pieces and they hit the floor.
Nothing was true but what Marcus Aurelius taught,
'All that is foul smell & blood in a bag.'

He lookt on the world like the leavings of a hag.
Almost his love died from him, any more.
His mother & William
were vivid in the same mail Delmore died.
The world is lunatic. This is the last ride.
Delmore, Delmore.

Then there are the songs in which Berryman shifts tone with what can only be called mastery. For example, Dream Song 15, in which Henry reflects that women are emotionally stronger than men and offers, by way of support, an obscenely funny anecdote about a "haughtful & greasy" wench overheard in a bar, comes to an unexpectedly moving conclusion with two statements, the latter of which plainly refers to his father: "Some [men] hang heavy on the sauce, / some invest in the past, one hides in the land. / Henry was not his favourite." And there are songs that surprise one with their lyricism, with an unforgettable line or two: "Life, friends, is boring. We must not say so. / After all, the sky flashes, the great sea yearns, / we ourselves flash and yearn...."

Yet the songs can also be sloppy, slack, overly dependent on cheap shock value or on bad puns. (In one song, for instance, the bar-happy Henry speaks of himself as being "past puberty & into pub-erty.") And then there's what one may call the race question. Henry, in Berryman's own words, is "sometimes in blackface," which is to say that at times his chatter has a minstrel-show flavor. Why? Perhaps because, having made the Atlantic crossing with Anne Bradstreet and discovered himself to be not a pseudo-Englishman like Eliot but an American poet like Whitman and Pound, the ever-alienated Berryman found it appropriate, upon starting in on *The Dream Songs*, to identify his alter ego with the most isolated segment of American society,[2] namely the

---

[2]Certainly Berryman had a lifelong tendency to identify with minority groups: his most well-known short story, "The Imaginary Jew" (1945)—which was based on an actual incident that affected Berryman very strongly and that remained with him for the rest of his life—concerns a man who, on his way across a park in New York City, finds himself "accused" by several strangers of being a Jew.

black subculture. But *minstrel-show* talk? It is no surprise that Berryman has been accused by some critics of racial insensitivity, and one wouldn't want to have to defend him from the charge. But this insensitivity, if such it is, is only part of a larger problem with *The Dream Songs*: namely, that Berryman is almost invariably so engulfed in his own emotions that the feelings of other people—black or white, male or female, poet or non-poet—don't even enter into the picture. The songs teem with evidence to support the judgment of Allen Tate—one of the poet's closest friends—that Berryman "never grew up"; and anyone forced to read *The Dream Songs* from cover to cover can well understand Jeffrey Meyers's complaint in his book *Manic Power* that they "are simply paranoid projections of childhood manias and obsessions."

To put it somewhat more gently, if Berryman's early poems represented, for him, a means of resisting the "undertow" of suicide, by the time of *The Dream Songs* poetry had become rather a means of recording his struggle with it. "The older you get," he observes in Dream Song 185, "at once / the better death looks and / the more fearful & intolerable." "Can I go on?" he asks in Dream Song 159. "Maybe it's time / to throw in my own hand." But he has an answer to his own suggestion: "there are secrets, secrets, I may yet— / hidden in history & theology, hidden in rhyme— / come on to understand."

History and theology are, in fact, the twin quarries in which Berryman goes prospecting in *Love & Fame* (1970), the first book of his poetry to appear after the extraordinary success of *The Dream Songs*. Yet it's a messy, disorganized expedition: If *Homage to Mistress Bradstreet* had taken five years to write, the composition of the much longer *Love & Fame* is said to have occupied only five or six weeks' time, and after reading the book one can only wonder that it took that long. The first three of the book's four sections consist mostly of narrative poems about Berryman's life at Columbia, at Cambridge, and in later years, and virtually all of these poems are composed in appallingly slack, conversational free-verse quatrains. There is little artfulness in the selection of words or details; it is quite clear that these rambling and diaristic poems aspire, above all, not to an ideal of consummate artistry but to one of unmitigated honesty. Accordingly, some of them consist largely of pallid alumni-magazine reminiscences, studded with book titles and the names of friends, professors, intellectual heroes:

> I began the historical study of the Gospel
> indebted above all to Guignebert
> & Goguel & McNeile
> & Bultmann even & later Archbishop Carrington.
>
> The Miracles were a stumbling-block;
> until I read Karl Heim, trained in natural science;
> until I had sufficiently attended to
> The Transfiguration & The Ecstasy.

Other poems, meanwhile, contain gratuitous and vulgar locker-room anecdotes: Berryman tells how many women he slept with during his early manhood, tells about a college friend's meager genitalia, tells (in a flippant parenthesis) about his own illegitimate child. The general point of all this, when there seems to be one, is to underline the hopelessness of love, the futility of fame. (The book's title probably derives from the last line of Keats's poem "When I Have Fears": "Till love and fame to nothingness do sink.") But for the most part there doesn't seem to *be* a point to these poems: if in *The Dream Songs* there is the slightest vestige of an intention to make a universal statement about man and art, or life and death, Berryman manages in *Love & Fame* to write poems in which such a motive is well-nigh inconceivable.

Nor do these poems have a great deal to recommend them aesthetically. Passages from any given poem might easily be rearranged, deleted, moved to other poems, without any apparent loss. Nor, for all the sensational aspects, does the book itself even add up to a moderately compelling self-portrait in verse: for in abandoning the persona of Henry, Berryman also, alas, seems to have jettisoned much of the personality that went with it. When, in *The Dream Songs*, Berryman wants to emphasize the absurdity of hungering for fame, he does it in a rather charming fashion, remembering how he and Delmore Schwartz, in their youth, "were almost anonymous / waiting for fame to descend / with a scarlet mantle & tell us who we were." *Love & Fame* has little charm of this sort, less wit, and virtually no imagination. When Berryman is drinking, threatened with separation, and possessed by reflections on suicide and his father, all he can think of to say is—well—exactly that: "Reflexions on suicide, & on my father, possess me. / I drink too much. My wife threatens separation." As these lines suggest, this is a grim book, especially in Part Three—which concerns Berryman's post-Cambridge years, and whose poems have titles like "Damned," "Of Suicide," "Death Ballad," and "Purgatory"— and in Part Four, "Eleven Addresses to the Lord," in which the increasingly erratic Berryman, who claimed to have undergone "a sort of religious conversion" in the spring of 1970, offers his doubts and prayers up to God:

> If I say Thy name, art Thou there? It may be so.
> Thou art not absent-minded, as I am.
> I am so much so I had to give up driving.

Whatever Berryman's intention in these lines, their effect is both ludicrous and distressing. And in fact, as one reads through the post-*Dream Songs* collections, Berryman's poems seem less and less the spirited, imaginative record of a struggle against the undertow of suicidal impulses, and increasingly the stark whimpers and cries of a drowning man. The irony is sharp: *The Dream Songs* had won every major poetry award—a Pulitzer Prize, a National Book Award, a Bollingen— but once that work was past him, the now less-than-vigorous Berryman (who was hospitalized for alcoholism treatments several times between 1967 and 1970) appeared not to know what to do next. The posthumously published *Delusions etc of John Berryman* (1972) finds the poet still dwelling morbidly upon his earthly father's suicide, and still addressing his heavenly Father in a baffling and borderline delusionary way. The only thing that seems worth saying about the supposedly religious poems in this haphazard assortment—and, for that matter, about those in *Love & Fame*—is that they appear to be about God in precisely the same way that the *Sonnets to Chris* are about Chris. One hesitates to question the sincerity of anyone's religious ardor, but it must be said that Berryman, in his supposed enthusiasm for God, looks very much like a man grasping at a handy excuse to indulge himself in candid confession, in litanies of loss and longing, and in untempered, self-dramatizing apocalyptic rhetoric. Berryman's poems are at once too slipshod to be characterized, the way one would characterize the poems of Donne or Herbert, as beautiful objects created to the greater glory of God, and too flat and earthbound to be categorized as mystical or visionary.

The most provocative item in *Henry's Fate and Other Poems* (1977)— an assemblage of Berryman's previously uncollected poems and fragments—is less of literary than of biographical interest. It is a Dream Song that Berryman wrote on January 5, 1972, two days before leaping to his death from the Washington Avenue Bridge in Minneapolis:

> I didn't. And I didn't. Sharp the Spanish blade
> to gash my throat after I'd climbed across
> the high railing of the bridge
> to tilt out, with the knife in my right hand
> to slash me knocked or fainting till I'd fall
> unable to keep my skull down but fearless
>
> unless my wife wouldn't let me out of the house,
> unless the cops noticed me crossing the campus
> up to the bridge
> & clappt me in for observation, costing my job—
> I'd be now in a cell, costing my job—
> well, I missed that;
>
> but here's the terror of tomorrow's lectures
> bad in themselves, the students dropping the course,
> the Administration hearing
> & offering me either medical leave of absence
> or resignation—Kitticat, they can't fire me—

The undertow had gotten him at last.

It should not, of course, have surprised anyone. "The artist is extremely lucky," Berryman had once quipped in an interview, "who is presented with the worst possible ordeal which will not actually kill him." While there is some truth in this remark, it also bespeaks a neurotic compulsion, on Berryman's part, to abuse his brittle nerves, to make a fetish of intensity, to dive deep. (It would seem to have been the second great tragedy of Berryman's life—the first, naturally, being his father's suicide—that he inherited both his father's fragile nervous system and his temperamentally hardy mother's stubborn tendency to overburden it.) And while it could be argued that there was something truly heroic in Berryman's ability to create powerful imaginative works in staunch defiance of the urge to self-destruct, the tendency among many critics these days, alas, is to romanticize those self-destructive attitudes themselves.

I wouldn't necessarily describe Charles Thornbury, the editor of Berryman's *Collected Poems*, as such a critic, though his long, unconditionally worshipful introduction to the poems often hovers a bit too close to the frontiers of coherence, referring earnestly and without explanatory or critical comment to Berryman's "effort to turn suffering on itself," to the poet's desire "to replace his intensity of loss with an intensity of grace," and suchlike. Thornbury, an associate professor at St. John's University in Minnesota who (the dust jacket informs us) "is presently [*sic*] working on a full-scale critical biography of John Berryman," has given his subject the full scholarly treatment, providing the publication histories of all the poetry volumes whose contents have been included here and assiduously noting hundreds of variant renderings in the sundry typescripts, manuscripts, carbons, galleys, and page proofs that he has managed to track down.

What is particularly surprising, though, is what Thornbury does not include. He includes no previously unpublished or uncollected poems; he includes nothing from *Henry's Fate* (because, he explains, it was not selected and arranged by Berryman); and—though the title of the *Collected Poems* would seem to promise otherwise—he does not include *The Dream Songs*. (The rationale for this is that the combined edition of *77 Dream Songs* and *His Toy, His Dream, His Rest*, originally published in 1969, remains in print as a separate volume.) Nor has he sifted through Berryman's published poems and separated the wheat from the chaff. What he has done, quite simply, is to publish the complete contents of each of the collections of short poems that Berryman assembled during his lifetime, plus *Homage to Mistress Bradstreet*. It's a handsome volume, I suppose, and I'm sure we should all be glad that Thornbury has regularized Berryman's quotation marks, worked out the proper spacing for his ellipses, and so forth, but somehow all this apparatus looks like needless clutter, like some sort of grotesque academic make-work project. Who, one wonders, came to the decision that such an edition was called for? Why should the name of an associate professor at St. John's University in Minnesota be on the cover of John Berryman's collected poems? And why, if it was felt that the time had come for a collected Berryman, wasn't someone engaged to winnow out the worst of Berryman's truly bad poems? One can only hope that the next major assemblage of a contemporary poet's *oeuvre* will bear a somewhat closer resemblance to, say, Elizabeth Bishop's simple and elegant *Complete Poems* (1983) than to this formidable-looking scholarly document from whose dust jacket the bearded face of John Berryman stares out so dolefully.

DECEMBER 1989

DYLAN THOMAS IN HIS LETTERS

The first thing that may occur to one, upon learning of the imminent appearance of a nearly thousand-page edition of the complete available letters of Dylan Thomas, is that there is hardly an aching need for such a compilation. Who, after all, in this world full of good books that most of us will never get around to reading, is really clamoring for an exhaustive account of the life and times of this archetypal postwar "celebrity" poet? Hasn't the story of his bibulous Anglo-American misadventures already become too stale and ubiquitous a legend? Isn't it about time that his verse stopped taking a back seat to his turbulent personality? Shouldn't we be beginning, at last, to attempt to make a sensible judgment as to the real value of his contribution to poetry in our time?

Well, yes. But to commence reading *The Collected Letters of Dylan Thomas*[1] is, nonetheless, to become hopelessly hooked. From the outset, the reader of this impressive volume—whose editor, Paul Ferris, has written the finest extant biography, *Dylan Thomas* (1977)—is in the intimate company of a fascinating human being, unmistakably the Dylan Thomas of legend, but at the same time a man far more mesmerizing, exasperating, amusing, and touching than the buffoonish, bigger-than-life media-darling we have all come to think we know. The Dylan Thomas of these letters is vulgar, guileful, manic, terminally immature, eternally obsessed with sex, death, words, and himself, and contemptuous of English professors, women, other poets, and other Welshmen; to indulge in a bit of Dylanesque alliteration, he's hyperbolic, high-strung, hierophantic, borderline hysterical. In the book's third letter, written to his friend Trevor Hughes at age seventeen, he confesses: "I can't concentrate. My mind leaps from thought to thought like a wombat.... I've got a head like a windmill." And

---

[1] *The Collected Letters of Dylan Thomas*, edited by Paul Ferris, Macmillan; 1024 pages, $39.95.

throughout the book it continues to spin, spin, spin almost without let-up. So vivid and colorful a portrait does this assemblage give of Thomas in action, in fact, that it reads at times nearly like an exuberant epistolary novel by some twentieth-century Samuel Richardson—a novel that is wonderfully absorbing, full of humor and pathos, rich in revealing detail, dramatic reversals, and (ultimately) tragic irony.

Thomas was born in Swansea, Wales, in 1914, the son of David John Thomas, a schoolmaster (whom the poet revered), and Florence Thomas (whom he despised). D. J. Thomas, as a young man, had wanted to write, and, though the couple had a daughter, Nancy, eight years older than Dylan, "it was on his son," writes Ferris in a prefatory note, "that D. J. lavished the attention of a disappointed man." Dylan was brought up on poetry and began to write it at a very early age; indeed, the very first letter in *The Collected Letters*, written to Nancy in his childhood, contains a few brief childish verses, presumably of his composition. Interestingly, these routine pieces of doggerel reflect some of the quintessential characteristics of Thomas's mature poetry: the preoccupation with death, the infatuation with the sea, the tendency to indulge in wordplay.

From the very beginning, then, the principal subject of these letters is poetry and literary creation. The subject never ceased to enthrall him. Nowhere in his correspondence, though, is he more elaborately revealing, and more amusingly and outrageously dogmatic, about his ideas on this subject than he is in his earliest letters—specifically, the ones he wrote, in 1932 and 1933, to Trevor Hughes, and, in 1933 and 1934, to Pamela Hansford Johnson, both of whom were ambitious young writers like himself. In one letter, for instance, the eighteen-year-old Thomas advises the twenty-nine-year-old Hughes, who he feels is in danger of becoming a commercial writer of stories about "pasteboard characters," to

> Write, write, write, out of your guts, out of the sweat on your forehead and the blood in your veins. Do not think about Mr. Potter's guide to the salesmanship of short stories produced, apparently, on the lines of the Ford works. Do not bother your head about the length of the stuff you are writing.... Write a story (if you must write stories) about yourself searching for your soul amid the horrors of corruption and disease, about your passionate strivings after

something you don't know and can't express. (This is one
of the few ways [of] knowing it and expressing it.)

He tells Hughes to "delve deep, deep into yourself until you find your
soul, and until you know yourself.... [U]ntil you reach that little red
hot core, you are not alive. The number of dead men who walk, breathe,
and talk is amazing.... Into the sea of yourself like a young dog, and
bring out a pearl." (This last image, incidentally, may explain Thomas's
title *A Portrait of the Artist as a Young Dog* better than anything else.)
"There is only one object: the removing of veils from your soul & scabs
from your body."

Clearly, by the age of eighteen Thomas was already certain of the
type of poet he was. The writers he holds up to his friends as examples
are for the most part visionary mystics and *symbolistes* like Poe,
Baudelaire, Verlaine, Rilke, Yeats, Francis Thompson, and Gérard de
Nerval; Thomas describes himself as following "in the path of Blake,
but so far behind him that only the wings on his heels are in sight." He
seems to identify strongly with D. H. Lawrence, with whose *oeuvre* he
has something of a love-hate relationship; but he despises Walt
Whitman (whom he would later come to admire), Robert Frost, Will-
iam Carlos Williams, Virginia Woolf, and such late Victorians as Arnold,
Kipling, and Ernest Dowson. Above all he despises the English Ro-
mantics, especially Wordsworth, whom he characterizes as "a human
nannygoat with a pantheistic obsession," a "tea-time bore, the great
Frost of literature, the verbose, the humourless, the platiudinary re-
porter of Nature in her dullest moods.... He writes about mysticism
but he is not a msytic; he describes what mystics have been known to
feel, but he himself doesn't feel anything, not even a pain in the neck.
He could well have written his Ode in the form of a treatise: 'Mysti-
cism and its Relations to the Juvenile Mind.'"

The foregoing excerpt, as it happens, is part of a page-long anti-
Wordsworthian tirade in one of Thomas's letters to Pamela Hansford
Johnson. These letters—which number about thirty—are, all in all, the
meatiest, most enthralling ones in the book. Johnson, obviously, was
the perfect foil for Thomas—a "tea-time" poetess, more or less, refined,
mannerly, and tamely romantic (though capable of writing poems that
remind Thomas of Christina Rossetti, "the best Pre-Raphaelite of the
whole bunch")—and she came along at the perfect time, when Tho-

mas was beginning to publish poems and was hungry for someone to show them to and discuss them with. Just two years older than Thomas, she initiated their long-distance friendship when she wrote to congratulate him on a poem he'd had in the *Sunday Referee*, a newspaper to which she too contributed. (She would later abandon poetry and become a well-known writer of fiction and the wife of C. P. Snow.) Johnson's side of the correspondence does not appear here, of course, but one never feels the need for it; Thomas's long, fervid responses to her letters, and his blistering critiques of the poems she sent him, tell us much of what we need to know about her—and a great deal of what we need to know about him. In his first extant letter to her, the nineteen-year-old Thomas comes across as a precociously sophisticated literary critic, a self-consciously outrageous propagandist for "the cosmic significance of the human anatomy," and an irredeemably crude and cocksure enemy of "arty" poetry, sentimental poetry, and poetry that seeks to record "the chaos of to-day." ("So much new verse," he writes her, "can be summarised into, 'Well, there's been a hell of a war; it's left us in a mess, what the hell are we going to do about it?'") He complains that a poem she has sent him contains "[t]oo many adjectives, too much sugar. And the fifth and sixth lines are pure cliché. 'I write from the heart,' said a character in some novel I've forgotten. 'You write,' was the reply, 'from the bowels as after a strong emetic.' Not that I apply that rude remark to 'Prothalamium'; I'm quoting not because of it but for the sake of it." (As her diary reveals, Johnson found this letter—which was actually the second she had received from him—"Charming & very, very modern, not to say rude.")

In his letters to Johnson, as in those to Hughes, Thomas speaks up continually for his own sort of poetry, the poetry of the "guts," which apparently, at its gutsiest, offended Johnson's delicate sensibilities. "What you call ugly in my poetry," Thomas argues, "is, in reality, nothing but the strong stressing of the physical." Why, he asks, should some aspects of the physical be regarded as more offensive than others? "Only by association is the refuse of the body more to be abhorred than the body itself.... it was chance that decided [Adam and Eve] to hide their genital organs, and not, say, their armpits or throats." "I fail," his *apologia* continues,

> to see how the emphasizing of the body can, in any way, be regarded as hideous. The body, its appearance, death, and diseases, is a fact, sure as the fact of a tree. The greatest de-

scription I know of our own "earthiness" is to be found in
John Donne's Devotions, where he describes man as earth
of the earth, his body earth, his hair a wild shrub growing
out of the land. All thoughts and actions emanate from the
body. Therefore the description of a thought or action—how-
ever abstruse it may be—can be beaten home by bringing it
onto a physical level. Every idea, intuitive or intellectual,
can be imaged or translated in terms of the body, its flesh,
skin, blood, sinews, veins, glands, organs, cells, or senses.

If, he says, his physicality seems too obsessive, that's because there's
no middle ground. The young writer "must class himself under one of
two headings: under the philosophy (for want of a better word) which
declares the body to be all and the intellect nothing, and which would
limit the desires of life, the perceptions and the creation of life, within
the walls of the flesh; or under the philosophy which, declaring the
intellect and the reason and the intelligence to be *all*, denies the warmth
of the blood and the body's promise." He is honest enough to admit
that his partiality toward the "poetry of the flesh" may have some-
thing to do with his own physical exiguity. "It is typical of the physi-
cally weak to emphasise the strength of life (Nietzsche); of the appre-
hensive and complex-ridden to emphasise its naiveté and dark whole-
someness (D. H. Lawrence); of the naked-nerved and blood-timid to
emphasise its brutality and horror (Me!)." Indeed, it becomes increas-
ingly obvious in these letters to Johnson that beneath the arrogant sen-
suality hides a highly insecure young man. Even in that first extant
letter to her he fibs, compulsively it seems, about his age and publica-
tion credits; in later years he habitually makes ironic references to the
less-than-heroic dimensions of his own body (he was about five foot
six), calling himself "a short, ambiguous person" and saying that "the
more despondent I become the littler and weaker I feel." He is inse-
cure not only about his height but about his background, which he
puts down constantly. He speaks of Swansea as "the worst of provin-
cial towns" and of "little colliers, diseased in mind and body as only
the Welsh can be." "It's impossible to tell you," he writes, "how much
I want to get out of it all, out of its narrowness and dirtiness, out of the
eternal ugliness of the Welsh people, and all that belongs to them, out
of the pettiness of a mother I don't care for and the giggling batch of
relatives." He shares his innermost torments with Johnson, apprising

her of his fears, his frustrations, his humiliation in a local bar by a group of young toughs; he informs her (a schizoid fiction based on his neurotic mother's contention that he had "weak lungs") that he is dying of tuberculosis, and has only a few years left; in a hysterical, partly unpunctuated letter, he "confesses" a liaison (probably invénted) with a young lady of the neighborhood; he tells Johnson that she is his "only friend"; and he interpolates the following lines in an otherwise seemingly normal (for him) letter:

> Very Serious Question?
> Am I mad?

Was he? Ferris, in his absorbing introduction, is equivocal, describing Thomas's extremist persona as utterly manufactured, the manifestation of "a conscious determination to be taken for a poet," while acknowledging that this conscious determination may have been "underpinned by a deeper response to demons that pursued him in adolescence and thereafter." But with Thomas, as with Hamlet, the question of whether he "put an antic disposition on" or was truly disturbed seems, in the end, to be immaterial: for to put an antic disposition on is, after all, in itself the act of a disordered mind. One might say that like Hamlet (as described by J. Dover Wilson), Thomas "assume[d] madness because he [could not] help it." Or, to put it somewhat differently: being unable to shake off his mental instability, he did all he could to make it interesting—to be mad, as it were, with a theatrical flair. (It is perhaps worth noting, in this connection, Thomas's participation in Swansea's Little Theater during his teenage years.) That at times he was patently putting on an act by no means mitigates the genuineness and profundity of his desperate emotional infirmity.

Certainly it cannot be denied that Thomas's obsession with poetry was authentic. And along with that uncontrived and unchangeable obsession went an equally obsessive awareness of mortality; if he was mad, perhaps it was essentially in this obsessive awareness that his madness resided. Virtually all his poems are founded upon an intense consciousness of the nexus among sex and birth and death—a recognition that to have intercourse is to make possible the conception of a baby, and that to be born, in turn, is to begin to die. The centrality of this nexus is more explicit in some poems than others; take, for instance, the uncharacteristically direct poem, "Written for a Personal Epitaph":

Feeding the worm
Who do I blame
Because laid down
At last by time,
Here under the earth with girl and thief,
Who do I blame?
Mother I blame
Whose loving crime
Moulded my form
Within her womb,
Who gave me life and then the grave,
Mother I blame.
Here is her labour's end,
Dead limb and mind,
All love and sweat
Gone now to rot.
I am man's reply to every question,
His aim and destination.

Man's "aim and destination" are, indeed, Thomas's theme in one poem after another. "Their Faces Shone Under Some Radiance," for example, presents a couple making love in a cemetery, surrounded by graves and illuminated by the moon's radiance, both of them unaware that "radiance came and passed"—that time and nubility, in other words, are transient. In "We Who Are Young Are Old," a voice cries,

"We who are young are old. It is the oldest cry.
Age sours before youth's tasted in the mouth
And any sweetness that it has
Is sucked away."

The most beautiful of Thomas's poems, "Fern Hill," likewise concerns itself with the fact that even the youngest (their youth symbolized, as in all of Thomas's poetry, by the color green) are in some sense time's laughingstocks:

Nothing I cared, in the lamb white days, that time would take me
Up to the swallow thronged loft by the shadow of my hand,
   In the moon that is always rising,
     Nor that riding to sleep
  I should hear him fly with the high fields
And wake to the farm forever fled from the childless land.
Oh as I was young and easy in the mercy of his means,
    Time held me green and dying
   Though I sang in my chains like the sea.

It is, of course, because of his preoccupation with the inevitable con-
nection between birth and death that Thomas frequently brings to-
gether wombs and tombs, cauls and shrouds, describing a womb, for
instance (in "The Woman Speaks"), as spitting forth "a baby's corpse,"
and depicting his own birth (in "Twenty-four Years") as follows:

In the groin of the natural doorway I crouched like a tailor
Sewing a shroud for a journey
By the light of the meat-eating sun.

In a number of poems, however—among them some of his best—
he attempts to interpret the way of all flesh so as to emerge from his
contemplations with sense of victory. This is the case with "And Death
Shall Have No Dominion":

And death shall have no dominion.
Dead men naked they shall be one
With the man in the wind and the west moon;
When their bones are picked clean and the clean bones gone,
They shall have stars at elbow and foot;
Though they go mad they shall be sane,
Though they sink through the sea they shall rise again;
Though lovers be lost love shall not;
And death shall have no dominion.

The poem derives its sense of consolation (or its illusion thereof) from
a recognition of (or insistence upon) the unity of all life. One is re-
minded of Hardy's poem "Transformations," in which buried corpses
"are not underground, / But as nerves and veins abound / In the

growths of upper air." Thomas's poem "A Refusal to Mourn the Death, By Fire, of a Child in London" takes a similar perspective: "After the first death," it concludes, "there is no other." Mortality, in short, is a horror we all share; there are no new tragedies under the sun.

One of the things that distinguish Thomas's poetry is that, though it deals with such morbid matters, it is generally exuberant in tone—though perhaps *manic* would be a more accurate term. The poems' images are chiefly of the human body and of other natural phenomena; the four elements, earth, air, fire, and water, are ubiquitous. Thomas habitually creates mixed natural images—"the whinnying light," "your grave in my breast," "a desolate boy who… sheds dry leaves"—the aim of which is to suggest nature's interconnectedness (and which has often caused him to be described as a Surrealist). His frequent half rhymes and internal rhymes serve the same purpose, as does his recurrent use of synesthesia (exemplified by such titles as "The Colour of Saying" and "When All My Five and Country Senses See"). In his concentration upon natural and physical imagery, more than in any other respect, Thomas was, it should be recognized, carrying out a rebellion against the most celebrated English poets of his youth, the Oxford poets—W. H. Auden, Stephen Spender, C. Day Lewis, and Louis MacNeice—whose most fashionable poems excluded human beings and the natural world almost entirely in their relentless piling up of "modern" images: pistons, pylons, submarines, and the like. Sex, in particular, was rarely mentioned explicitly in their poems.

By contrast, sex is omnipresent not only in Thomas's poems but—unsurprisingly—throughout *The Collected Letters*. The poet's ideas about the subject were far from conventional. "From the first months of puberty," he writes Johnson (who, after they met in February of 1934, became his girlfriend for a brief period), "girls & boys should be allowed to know their bodies… their sexual expression should be encouraged." This apparent openmindedness, however, does not seem to have extended to homosexuality. In one of many curious references to homosexuals, he writes:

> Have you remarked upon the terrible young men of this generation, the willing-buttocked, celluloid-trousered, degenerates who are gradually taking the place of the bright young things of even five years ago? Or is the degeneracy,

the almost unbelievable effeminacy, the product of the Welsh slums alone?

He proceeds to describe, in considerable detail, a young man he observed at a hotel the night before, "the most perfect example I've ever seen, the sort of thing one hears of in coarse stories but rarely encounters in the flesh.... It's the only vice, I think, that revolts me and makes me misanthropic." In another letter to Johnson he facetiously suggests that she is "turning male," unfortunately for him, because "I'm sure I don't like little boys in That Way." Images of buggery occur often in his letters, as they do in many of his poems and stories (the village of "Llareggub" in *Under Milk Wood*, for example, is "bugger all" spelled backward). The abundance and hostility of such references cannot but make one think, after a while, that he doth protest too much. And sure enough, it develops that after Thomas moved to London in November of 1934 (an event that helped end his friendship with Johnson, who soon learned that Thomas was harder to take in person than by mail), he had brief affairs with a couple of young men, to one of whom he wrote three surprising pseudo-love letters, each more nauseatingly coy than the next.

His ability to shift gears sexually seems to have carried over to politics as well. During his Swansea years he was capable of turning out fanatical-sounding left-wing harangues about "mass production," "economic despotism," "the composition of the classes," and "the death of the West." A couple of these jargon-packed tirades are addressed to the editor of the *Swansea and West Wales Guardian*, and two or three— including the following passage—appear in letters to Johnson:

> The hope of Revolution, even though all of us will not admit it, is uppermost in all our minds. If there were not that revolutionary spark within us, that faith in a new faith, and that belief in our power to squash the chaos surrounding us like a belt of weeds, we would turn on the tap water and drown ourselves in its gases.
>
> *Everything* is wrong that forbids the freedom of the individual. The governments are wrong, because they are the committees of prohibitors; the presses are wrong, because they feed us what they desire to feed us, and not what we desire to eat; the churches are wrong, because they standardize our gods, because they label our morals, because....

And so on. Ferris informs us that these spurts of political zealotry were the result of Thomas's association with A.E. ("Bert") Trick, a passionately left-wing Swansea grocer whose parlor was the local center of literary and political discussion. Considering the heat of Thomas's rhetoric in such letters, it is remarkable that virtually none of his poems—most of which were written in the politically preoccupied 1930s—is even slightly political. For all his youthful left-wing zealotry, he had a strong antipathy for literature that sought to make statements about the "class struggle." "I shall never, I hope," he wrote Trick from London, after meeting some of the leading young Communist intellectuals of the day, "be mixed up in any political ramifications of literary, or pseudo literary London; honest writing does *not* mix with it; you can't be true to party *and* poetry; one must suffer, and, historically, poetry is the social and economic creed that endures." Clearly, his devotion to poetry ran far deeper than his devotion to any political idea.

Indeed, Thomas's interest in left-wing politics faded rapidly once he found himself, in London, part of a rather more interesting literary crowd than the one that met in Trick's salon. Beginning at this point, Thomas's correspondence consists primarily of businesslike dispatches to agents and editors and chummy notes to literary figures like Geoffrey Grigson, Rayner Heppenstall, Frederic Prokosch, Edith Sitwell, T. S. Eliot, Vernon Watkins, and Julian Symons, several of whom became his friends and supporters. Thomas was on his way. His first book, *Eighteen Poems*, published in 1934 by the relatively small-time *Sunday Referee*, was succeeded in 1936 by *Twenty-five Poems*, published by the distinguished London firm of J. M. Dent. Meanwhile, his poems and stories were appearing in major literary periodicals; he was beginning to be recognized as a young writer of conspicuous gifts. He also, alas, was beginning to acquire a reputation as a slothful, heavy-drinking panhandler. Unable to support himself by writing, he had early fallen into the habit of soliciting money from relatives, friends, and admirers. The "begging letters" to his friends are generally amiably blunt. "Are you rich temporarily?" he asks Vernon Watkins in 1936. "Would you like to lend me some money, a pound or, at the very most, two pounds?" (Watkins came through generously, and would continue to do so over the years.) A year later, aware that his sister and her husband disapprove of his plans to marry an Irish girl named Caitlin Macnamara, he hits them up for a wedding gift: "As a gesture, Christian, gentlemanly, ladylike, sisterly, in-law-brotherly, friendly, & (in face of your obvious distrust of what could be, & has, by father, been called

'this lunatic course of action') congratulatorily from a married couple
of some years' standing to two younger persons about to embark on
the voyage of legal matrimony, would you like to slip me a couple of
quid?"

Perhaps the most interesting begging letters are the shamelessly
sycophantic ones, many of them sent to such estimable literary acquain-
tances as T.S. Eliot and some of them addressed to complete strangers
like the literary patrons Sir Edward Marsh and Lord Howard de
Walden. Invariably, Thomas depicts himself in these letters as a sto-
ically suffering young man on the brink of financial ruin who has con-
secrated his life to his art and who simply wants to feed himself and
his family (he and Caitlin had three children in all, the first of whom
was born in 1939) and to pursue his sacred vocation. In 1938, for in-
stance, when James Laughlin of New Directions wrote with an offer to
become Thomas's American publisher, Thomas responded with an
appeal for funds:

> I must say, straight away, that I *must* have some money,
> and have it immediately. I live entirely by my writing; it can
> be printed only in a small number of advanced periodicals,
> and they pay next to nothing, usually nothing. I was mar-
> ried recently—against all sense, but with all happiness,
> which is obviously more sensible—and we are completely
> penniless. I do not mean that we just live poorly; I mean
> that we go without food, without proper clothes, have shel-
> ter on charity, and very very soon will not have even that
> shelter. I have now less than a shilling; there is no more to
> come; we have nothing to sell, nothing to fall back upon. If
> I can be tided over for a little time, I think I will be able to
> work hard enough to produce poems and stories that will
> provide some kind of food and shelter. If not, there is no
> hope at all.... Can you, at once, give me money for which,
> in return, I promise you all the work I have done and will
> do?

Thomas was, it would seem, eternally on the lookout for a wealthy
mark. Shortly after moving in 1938 to the Welsh coastal town of
Laugharne (where he and Caitlin would make their home, off and on,
for the rest of their peripatetic life), Thomas wrote John Davenport
that "Thirty bloody pounds would settle everything. If you know any

rich chap fond of a jingle, who knows his Peters & Quennells, do let me know at once. Otherwise it'll be traipsing again, no stability at all, no hope, and certainly no work. Try to think of some sap, some saint." When Davenport informed him that Alec Waugh, though supporting Thomas's application for a grant, had recommended that he "write more stories and fewer letters," Thomas was irked. "When I want advice from Alec Waugh," he replied sarcastically, "I'll go to his brother." Those who took pity on Thomas often lived to regret it. Lorna Wilmott, one of many people who lent the poet a house or apartment, returned to her London flat in April of 1940 to discover that he had pawned a fur coat, a typewriter, a gramophone, some cutlery, and the family silver. In an "attempt to cover his tracks," as Ferris puts it, Thomas sent Wilmott a deliberately misdated letter indicating that he had left the apartment months earlier.

As the years went by, Thomas's income rose. His books did well, especially those published by Laughlin in the United States: *The World I Breathe* (1939), *New Poems* (1943), *Selected Writings* (1946), *In Country Sleep* (1952), and *Collected Poems* (1953). Beginning in 1941, he earned a good deal of money by writing film, radio, and television scripts, and his reading tours of America in the early 1950s yielded impressive sums. But neither he nor Caitlin (whose improvidence appears to have equaled his own) was able to hold onto money for very long. Much of it, apparently, went to buy drinks, not only for Dylan and Caitlin but for friends and for strangers they met in pubs. The poet and his wife were, in this respect, a sort of Welsh version of Scott and Zelda Fitzgerald, a pair of childish, self-destructive romantic egoists. A famous manifestation of Thomas's Fitzgeraldian irresponsibility was his gift for missing appointments; several of his letters contain apologies for broken dates, complete with dubious explanations for his failure to appear. In 1934, for example, he writes Trevor Hughes to explain that he had shown up at the Fitzroy on Wednesday, only to discover, upon returning home, that *"Tuesday was the night."* In 1944, having missed Vernon Watkins's wedding—at which he was supposed to have served as best man—he proffers an elaborate and extremely fishy story involving a missed train, a wartime priority phone call, and an inability to recall the name of the church. Perhaps the most honest explanation of this sort is the one that he gives Eric Walter White. Whenever he comes into London, Thomas writes, "bang go my plans in a horrid alcoholic explosion that scatters all my good intentions like bits of limbs and clothes over the doorsteps and into the saloon bars of the tawdriest pubs in London."

So self-centered was Thomas that when war broke out with Germany, his only thought (to judge by his letters) was to keep it from interrupting the progress of his literary career and, if possible, to benefit from it financially. On the first of September, 1939, he writes to his editor to ask, "This bloody war won't stop Dent's monthly allowance, will it?" Ten days later, he confides to Glyn Jones: "I want to get something out of the war, & put very little in (certainly not my one & only body)." Never for a moment, it seems, did the twenty-five-year-old poet consider joining the service. Later in September he writes Desmond Hawkins for advice on obtaining conscientious-objector status, insisting: "I'm Mr. Humanity and can't kill or be killed (with my approval)." His dormant Leftism seems, opportunely enough, to have resurfaced: "What have we got to fight for or against? To prevent Fascism coming here? It's come. To stop shit by throwing it? To protect our incomes, bank balances, property, national reputations? I feel sick. All this flogged hate again." In a letter to Trick (wherein, incidentally, he deploys one of his buggery images), he declares: "I don't know how you feel about all this, but I can't raise up any feeling about this war at all and the demon Hitlerism can go up its own bottom: I refuse to help it with a bayonet." Though he seems, to a degree, to remain Trick's disciple ("Write soon and tell me about the War: I've only my feelings to guide me"), he is determined, in his awesomely egocentric way, not to allow his precious time and energy to be wasted on a war against people "with whom I have no quarrel": "There's a need now for some life to go on, strenuously & patiently, outside the dictated hates & pettinesses of War, & that life I, for my own part, shall continue to support by my writing and thinking & by living as coolly, hotly, & as well as I know how." In April of 1940 he writes Laughlin that "the Germans are not my enemies, I do not want to die or kill, freedom's only a word and I'm a thinking body." In 1941 he is still singing the same tune. "What a lot of trouble it would have saved," he tells Vernon Watkins, "if We had sunk the Hood and They the Bismarck."

As the Forties wore on, Thomas's Muse seems to have begun to fizzle out. Gradually, he stopped writing poetry. In 1933, his most productive year, he had turned out forty-four poems; in 1934 the number had fallen to fifteen, and thereafter, through 1945, the per-year average hovered at around six. In 1947, 1949, and 1950, he wrote one poem per year; in 1946, 1948, 1952, and 1953 he wrote no poems at all. Some of his late verses, of course, were among his greatest. "Poem in October" was composed in 1944, "A Refusal to Mourn," "Fern Hill," and "In My Craft and Sullen Art" in 1945, "Lament," "Do Not Go Gentle Into That Good Night," and "Poem on His Birthday" in 1951; the sole 1947 poem was "In Country Sleep," the sole 1949 poem "Over Sir John's Hill," the sole 1950 poem "In the White Giant's Thigh." Even as his productivity declined, then, the poems themselves grew in clarity and strength. It was during the late Forties and early Fifties, too, that Thomas wrote his play *Under Milk Wood*.

But these last years were, on the whole, the darkest of his life. Thomas was confused, despondent, convinced that his poetic powers were failing, desperate for some place or somebody to escape to. And in May of 1949 the opportunity came. John Malcolm Brinnin, the new director of the Poetry Center at the 92nd Street YMHA in New York, invited Thomas to read at the Center, and offered to line up other readings in the United States. Thomas, to whom America was less a real country than a symbol of wealth and of withdrawal from cruel reality, had been hoping for years to receive such an invitation. In 1945 he had tried to arrange an American trip, writing to Laughlin: "I should like to come over to the States after the war for a few months. Any chance of getting a job to keep me while over there? Reading, talking?" Later that year he had corresponded with the American anthologist Oscar Williams: "I'd love a little ladleful from the gravy pots over there.... How could I earn a living? I can read aloud, through sonorous asthma, with pomp; I can lecture on The Trend of Y, or X at the Crossroads, or Z: Whither? with an assurance whose shiftiness can be seen only from the front row...." But the plans had come to nothing. Now he answered Brinnin's letter eagerly, and his subsequent letters to Brinnin, and to others, are full of enthusiasm for the journey.

But when he got to America, the enthusiasm seems almost to have given way to hysteria, to a terminal case of overload. From a midtown hotel room in New York, Thomas writes to Caitlin about

> the *noise* all day & night: without some drug, I couldn't sleep
> at all. The hugest, heaviest lorries, police-cars, firebrigades,
> ambulances, all with their banshee sirens wailing & scream-

ing, seem never to stop. Manhattan is built on rock, a lot of demolition work is going on to take up yet another super Skyscraper, & so there is almost continuous dynamite blasting. Aeroplanes just skim the tips of the great glimmering skyscraper, some beautiful, some hellish. And I have no idea what on earth I am doing here in the very loud, mad middle of the last mad Empire on earth....

Though he speaks admiringly of many American people and places, and refers to San Francisco as "the best city on earth," a place of sunlight and hills and ocean, words like *hell* and *mad* and *nightmare* recur throughout the hyperkinetic letters he sent Caitlin. From Washington, for instance, he writes that the room he's in is

hell on earth. Oh why, why, *didn't* we arrange it *somehow* that we came out together to this devastating, insane, demonaically [*sic*] loud, roaring continent.... Oh, Cat, my beautiful, my love, what am I doing here? I am no globetrotter, no cosmopolitan, I have no desire to hurl across the American nightmare like one of their damned motorcars. I want to live quietly, with you & Colum, & noisily with Aeronwy, & I want to see Llewelyn, & I want to sit in my hut and write, & I want to eat your stews, and I want to touch your breasts and cunt, and I want every night to lie, in love & peace, close, close, close, close, close, to you, closer than the marrow of your soul. I LOVE YOU.

But he could no more live quietly than he could fly. Thomas was a born addict, and America was to him the ultimate vicious intoxicant that he could neither resist nor take in moderation. And most intoxicating of all was New York, which he described, in a letter to his parents, as "this titanic dream world, soaring Babylon...."

The reading tour was, of course, wildly successful. Virtually overnight, Dylan Thomas became famous—as much for his drunken carousing as for his spellbinding recitations. Much in demand, he returned to America for extensive reading tours in 1952 and twice in 1953, during which time he made many American friends, was a habitué of the White Horse Tavern in Greenwich Village, and had affairs with a number of American women. But as his fame grew by leaps and bounds, his ego collapsed with equal rapidity. Writing to Charles Fry, a London editor, about the 1952 trip, he explained that as a result of endlessly "ranting poems to enthusiastic audiences," he

> gradually... began to feel nervous about the job in front of me, the job of writing, making things in words, by myself, again. The more I used words, the more frightened I became of using them in my own work once more. Endless booming of poems didn't sour or stale words for me, but made me more conscious of my obsessive interest in them and my horror that I would never again be innocent enough to touch and use them. I came home fearful and jangled. There was my hut on a cliff, full of pencil and paper, things to stare at, room to breathe and feel and think. But I couldn't write a word. I tried then to write a poem, dreading it beforehand, a few obscure lines every dumb day, and the printed result shook and battered me in any faith in myself and workman's pride left to me. I couldn't write a word after that. These are the most words I have written for a year.

And so it went. In the fall of 1953, Thomas was in New York on his fourth American visit. On October 29, he made his last public appearance at City College. During the next few days he drank heavily and took Benzedrine at the White Horse Tavern, wept in his Chelsea Hotel room in the company of his mistress Elizabeth Reitell, and spoke to John Malcolm Brinnin about suicide. On November 5, he was given a morphine injection "to relieve the symptoms caused by alcohol" and slipped into a coma; on November 9, he died at St. Vincent's Hospital. The death was an accident—its official cause was alcoholism and pneumonia—but then Thomas had, all his "naked-nerved and blood-timid" life, been an accident waiting to happen.

As the whole world knows, death was kinder to Thomas than life had been. His boisterous personality, at the podium and in the barroom, and the mysterious and controversial manner of his demise combined to make him, after his passing, far more of a hot item than he had been for most of his life. Before long, his books (which had sold well enough, during his lifetime, for poetry books, but had hardly made him rich) were selling like romance novels. Like Sylvia Plath, he had become a posthumous cult hero, his personal tragedy ironically translated into an absurd romantic legend, his coarse egocentrism worshipped by armies of impressionable young people who thought that they were honoring the spirit of poetry. If *The Collected Letters* establishes anything, though, it is that Dylan Thomas the man was, to say the least, most unsuitable hero material. He was vain, unreliable, self-centered, obnoxious, a man who used people in every way possible. He wasted too much of his time sitting at bars and trying to impress people who were not worth trying to impress. Yet it is a mistake to dismiss his poetry on this account, to write him off as a fluke, a flake, a celebrity poet who owes his fame solely to an outrageous manner and an untimely death. Certainly what is important, in the end, is not the way he lived but the poetry he wrote; and the fact is that more than a few of his poems are undeniably, unequivocally magnificent. Whether his misbegotten legend endures or not, Dylan Thomas is a poet of exquisite gifts whose finest work most assuredly deserves to survive. And *The Collected Letters*, by virtue of the unprecedented view that it offers of the inner life from which those often obscure poems sprang, can only help make them more accessible.

APRIL 1986

GENIUSES ALL THE TIME

What was the Beat Generation all about, anyway? Here's Jack Kerouac's answer, as quoted by fellow beatnik John Clellon Holmes: "It's a kind of furtiveness... Like we were a generation of furtives. You know, with an inner knowledge there's no use flaunting on that level, the level of the 'public,' a kind of beatness—I mean, being right down to it, to ourselves, because we all *really* know where we are—and a weariness with all the forms, all the conventions of the world.... So I guess you might say we're a *beat* generation."

Got that? For further illumination, there's this from Gregory Corso:

> What we are witnessing is a delicate shift of total conscious-ness in America—It won't be done through publicity or pro-paganda, articles or any form of—brainwashing persua-sion—it will occur as response to altered history scene.... The shift and new recognition can only be incarnated and commenced through great works of Art (as Whitman rightly demanded from poets to come)—Art to stand beacon like Statue naked and courageous, individual statement of pri-vate actual, uncensored individual perception.... Therefore a new art whose objectivity will be the accuracy of its intro-spection—the bringing forth of heretofore hidden materi-als, lusts, spiritual ambitions, experiences—in the new forms in which they will necessarily arrive—rather than the cring-ing self-consciousness of the psyche whose individuality has been so thwarted—that it masks itself and deceives others—under a guise of a received system of thought, of a system of thought at all, a received mode of feeling (which is never received but constantly occurs on its own) (when true) (when at all) or measure, stanzaic or structural, as far as its poesy is concerned. O fear of the fury of subjective revolution, death and new beat insight!—

And here, for good measure, is Michael McClure on the same subject:

> We were locked in the Cold War and the first Asian debacle—
> the Korean War.... We hated the war and the inhumanity
> and the coldness. The country had the feeling of martial law.
> An undeclared military state had leapt out of Daddy
> Warbucks' tanks and sprawled over the landscape. As art-
> ists we were oppressed and indeed the people of the nation
> were oppressed.... We knew we were poets and we had to
> speak out as poets. We saw that the art of poetry was essen-
> tially dead—killed by war, by academies, by neglect, by lack
> of love, and by disinterest [sic]. We knew we could bring it
> back to life.... We wanted to make it new and we wanted to
> invent it and the process of it as we went into it. We wanted
> voice and we wanted vision.

When Allen Ginsberg introduced the world to "Howl" at a now-fabled 1955 reading in San Francisco's Six Gallery, everyone present knew "at the deepest level," declares McClure, "that a barrier had been broken, that a human voice and body had been hurled against the harsh wall of America and its supporting armies and navies and academies and institutions and ownership systems and power-support bases."

Reading such slovenly, overheated prose in *The Portable Beat Reader*, edited by Ann Charters, one hardly knows which is more astonishing: that these men and their cohorts could ever have acquired significant literary reputations in the first place, or that, more than thirty years later, when many of their far more gifted contemporaries are virtually forgotten, every last member of the Beat fraternity who ever picked up a pencil (or, in the case of Neal Cassady, stole a typewriter) has been accorded an honored place in the history of American letters.[1] Few have played so industrious a part in this enterprise as Charters, who has for three decades been what one must, I suppose, call a "Beat scholar"; the biographer of Kerouac and editor of a two-volume ency-clopedia entitled *The Beats: Literary Bohemians in Postwar America*, Char-ters functions in the present *Reader* as an utterly uncritical tour guide, a literary version of the cordial, discreet lady from the P.R. office who shows you around corporate headquarters. Moreover, if in one sense

---

[1]*The Portable Beat Reader*, edited by Ann Charters; Viking, 642 pages, $25.

Charters is the literary antithesis of the Beats—her prose as orthodox of syntax and as wearisomely academic in tone as theirs is frenzied and ungrammatical—in another sense she is their true compeer, for her writing evinces a thoroughly Beat-like ungainliness. "As a facet of our country's cultural history," reads a typical sentence in her introduction, "clusters [i.e., literary cliques] have been an outstanding feature of our literature.... The discovery of the word 'beat' was essential to the formation of a sense of self-definition among the earliest writers making up the cluster that would later call itself members of a 'Beat Generation.'" By the time one has reached the end of the introduction (in which she identifies one of Burroughs's favorite books as "Spengler's *Decline and Fall of the West*"), one knows better than to expect from Charters anything resembling literary taste or critical intelligence.

Indeed, she toes the entire Beat line, celebrating the writers' "attack on such cherished institutions as capitalism, consumerism, the military-industrial complex, racism, and ecological destruction" and explaining that while "[e]arlier modernist poets like Ezra Pound or Lost Generation writers like Ernest Hemingway had attacked the system from the safeguard of their life abroad as expatriates,... the Beat Generation writers protested their country's excesses on the front lines." The front lines! To speak in this way of the likes of Ginsberg and Kerouac is to insult anyone who ever engaged in selfless, perilous struggle against a perceived wrong. The Beats didn't know what it meant to commit oneself, heart and soul, to real political action (nor, McClure to the contrary, did they have a clue how it might feel to be oppressed or to live under martial law); what Charters chooses to deem their "protest" consisted, in the years before they became famous, of hanging out, taking drugs, having indiscriminate sex, and living off money stolen from acquaintances or cadged from friends and family. Once they'd achieved celebrity status, moreover, they were too busy making the front pages to put themselves on any front line; far from hurling "Howl" against a harsh wall, Ginsberg lobbed it into the appreciative arms of newspaper reporters and magazine editors who were eager for some sign of sensational dissent in America—and into the arms, as well, of a growing population of young people in search of an image to suit their notion that they were a special generation.

For the Beats came along at a time when hardly anyone in America was rebelling (and when, for a middle-class white American man, there was hardly any reason *to* rebel); indeed, an early *Life* magazine article on the Beats was entitled "The Only Rebellion Around." (One of the more amusing ironies of Beat history is that while *Time* and *Life* were among the Beat writers' favorite targets, those trend-happy periodicals played a big part in making them famous.) For America, it was a time of peace and freedom and unparalleled affluence; but it was also a time when many Americans were buying simpleminded self-help books that told them how to win friends and influence people, how to improve their lives through positive thinking, and so forth. The Beats appealed to the underside of this trend: what they peddled to young people, essentially, was a look, an attitude, a strategy for self-redefinition. It was every bit as crude a strategy as those peddled by Dale Carnegie and Norman Vincent Peale; the difference, of course, was that the aim was not to become a more happy and successful member of American society but to become a misfit. If, like Carnegie and Peale, the Beats and their *Weltanschauung* hit it big, the ultimate reason, ironically, lay in the tolerance and prosperity of 1950s America: youngsters became beatniks, in other words, only because they knew that the society they lived in was tolerant enough to let them get away with it and that their parents were affluent and indulgent enough to bankroll them.

The Beats were hardly, then, true stormers of barricades. (To be sure, in later years Ginsberg and others were happy to associate their names with various movements, including those for black and gay rights, but those causes owed nothing to the Beats, who were patently vexed less by the shortcomings of American society than by the inherent burdens, limitations, and responsibilities of adult life itself, and who were, in this regard, precursors of the Sixties at their most juvenile.) Indeed, their notions of sex roles were as traditional as those of any Rotarian. Charters doesn't face up to this; she even manages to blame the Beats' adherence to the double standard on "the sexism of the times," without explaining how this jibes with their supposedly wholesale rejection of "the times." Why doesn't the fact that the Beats conformed perfectly, in this regard, to middle-class practices communicate something to Charters about the shallowness of their so-called revolt?

This shallowness is in evidence from the opening pages of *The Portable Beat Reader*, the first of whose six parts, entitled "The Best Minds of a Generation," begins with the principal texts of the movement: fifty-odd pages apiece by Kerouac (mostly from *On the Road*, whose first chapter is reprinted *in toto*), Ginsberg (mostly "Howl" and "Kaddish," both presented in their entirety), and Burroughs (roughly equal-length bits from *Junky*, *The Yage Letters*, *Naked Lunch*, and "Deposition: Testimony Concerning a Sickness"). These are followed by a brief passage from John Clellon Holmes's novel *Go* (in which the Kerouac character borrows some money, saying "My mother gets paid on Friday, so we can get it back to you by then") and a few short poems by Gregory Corso, as well as works by two Beat figures whom one does not ordinarily think of as writers: Herbert Huncke, the thug who turned Burroughs on to heroin and introduced the Beats to the word "beat," is represented by a couple of clumsy vignettes that might well be the work of an eighth grader; Carl Solomon, the mental patient to whom Ginsberg dedicated "Howl," weighs in with three scraps, part memoir and part musing, from his collection *Mishaps, Perhaps*. (If Charters's motive, in including Huncke and Solomon, was to make the selections by the big names look stronger by comparison, she has succeeded: Huncke and Solomon prove that prose *can* be more dopey and disjointed than in Kerouac and Burroughs.)

What is left to say about the Beat movement's chief monuments? To reread *On the Road* is to be reminded why its romanticism and energy appeal to many high-school and college students. For all its repetitiousness (and, ultimately, tedium), there are moments of dizzy lyricism in this book, and Kerouac does capture something of the restlessness that motivates his characters to ramble back and forth across the United States; he evokes something, too, of the rural highways and mean streets, and of the pathetic desperation with which his overgrown adolescents watch time—and their youth—passing them by. But the book's first chapter doesn't stand up very well on its own; and from the perspective of 1992, the whole thing feels terribly dated—it's a fading relic, not an enduring artwork. Of the other Kerouac excerpts, the five choruses culled from "Mexico City Blues" read like old TV-sitcom parodies of beatnik verse (sample: "All the endless conception of living beings / Gnashing everywhere in Consciousness / Throughout the ten directions of space"); the two-page list of "Essentials of Spontaneous Prose," which was presented to this critic in graduate school as a key document in the history of American literature, is staggeringly vapid; and even sillier is "Belief & Technique for Modern Prose," which consists of a numbered "List of Essentials" for the modern prose writer. These "essentials" range from relatively lucid fortune-cookie mandates ("Accept loss forever"; "Be in love with yr life") to bemusing and/or dubious vatic assertions ("Visionary tics shivering in the chest"; "You're a Genius all the time"). The recurring idea is that insanity is a literary asset: "Be crazy dumbsaint of the mind"; "Composing wild, undisciplined, pure, coming in from under, crazier the better."

As for Ginsberg's "Howl," it seems more heavyhanded and fraudulent than ever. Ginsberg has so often endorsed the "crazier the better" philosophy ("I'm so lucky to be nutty," he wrote in "Bop Lyrics") that his implied anguish over the destruction by madness of "the best minds of his generation" seems unconvincing—as, of course, does the idea that the people he's writing about could be the best minds on the block, let alone of their generation. In "America," his Stalin-era sarcasm about his countrymen's posture toward "them bad Russians" strikes a Yeltsin-era reader as particularly repugnant; and one finds oneself more irked than ever by his self-dramatization ("America I'm putting my queer shoulder to the wheel"). At least the Burroughs selections are evocative and of documentary interest: in the pages from *Junky*, for instance, he takes the reader on an expedition into the lower depths of wartime Manhattan and explains the difference between "tea heads" and "junkies."

But one can't pretend to be very impressed by any of these Beat artifacts. On the contrary, one waits in vain for a clever or felicitous turn of phrase or a single coherently expressed idea. Bad as the Beat corpus is, moreover, it is at a special disadvantage when read in excerpts. These writers, to the extent that they shine at all, don't shine sentence by sentence or even page by page; the strength, if one can call it that, of a Kerouac or Burroughs lies not in a knack for the beautifully shaped vignette but in an ability to capture, over a long stretch, and with all the clunkiness, if you will, of a modern (if lesser) Melville or Dreiser, the mood and rhythm and moral vacuity of a certain kind of bohemian life. In fact, the very notion of an anthology would appear to contradict Kerouac's credos about "Deep Form," "undisturbed flow," "the holy contour of life," etc.: a true Beat acolyte, one should think, would no more read Beatlit piecemeal than a jazz aficionado would buy an album consisting of thirty-second cuts of Charlie Parker.

To one's surprise, Part One proves to be the most substantial section of the *Reader*; almost everything that follows feels like filler, marginalia, afterthoughts. Part Two is taken up entirely by letters between Kerouac and Neal Cassady (the prototype of *On the Road*'s Dean

Moriarty) and by excerpts from Cassady's autobiography and from Kerouac's second book about him, *Visions of Cody*. In a typical missive, Cassady recounts in painfully illiterate prose how he met a virgin on a bus ride from St. Louis to Kansas City and

> decided to... seduce her, from 10:30 AM to 2:30 PM I talked. When I was done, she (confused, her entire life upset, meta-physically amazed at me, passionate in her immaturity) called her folks in Kansas City, & went with me to a park (it was just getting dark) & I banged her; I screwed as never before; all my pent up emotion finding release in this young virgin (& she was) who is, by the by, a *school teacher*!

All the excerpts in this section have manifestly been chosen for their elucidation of the temperament and life style of Cassady, who for his fellow Beats personified the Beat ethos. Yet readers may be excused for being loath to slog through these slipshod accounts of his grubby life.

In Part Three, Charters surveys eight poets of the "San Francisco Renaissance," among them Kenneth Rexroth, Philip Whalen, Gary Snyder, and Lawrence Ferlinghetti. Whalen, Charters tells us, "broke free from his obsession with imagist poetry and the formal academic poetry of T.S. Eliot and Wallace Stevens after taking peyote in 1955: 'all my dopey theories and hangups and things about writing... suddenly disappeared.'"(Yes, that would do it, wouldn't it?) As for Rexroth, his longest contribution here is his notorious poem "Thou Shalt Not Kill," which is dedicated to Dylan Thomas and which, as he explains in an author's note, "was written in one sitting, a few hours after a phone call came from New York with the news that Dylan had died." The poem is a standard Beat harangue about America, capitalism, the System. "They are murdering all the young men," Rexroth insists, and goes on to compare Thomas's death to the stoning of Stephen. After naming many dead and broken poets—the ragtag roster includes Edwin Arlington Robinson, Hart Crane, and Sara Teasdale—Rexroth focuses again on "the sparrow of Cardiff," blaming his demise on "[Robert] Oppenheimer the Million-Killer," "Einstein the Grey Eminence," and, in effect, every other true-blue American, including the reader of the poem:

Who killed him?

GENIUSES ALL THE TIME

Who killed the bright-headed bird?
You did, you son of a bitch.
You drowned him in your cocktail brain.
He fell down and died in your synthetic heart.

He was found dead at a liberal weekly luncheon.
He was found dead on the cutting room floor.
He was found dead at a Time policy conference.
Henry Luce killed him with a telegram to the Pope.
Mademoiselle strangled him with a padded brassiere.
Old Possum sprinkled him with a tea ball.
After the wolves were done, the vaticides
Crawled off with his bowels to their classrooms and quarterlies.

I want to run into the street,
Shouting, "Remember Vanzetti!"
...And all the birds of the deep sea rise up
Over the luxury liners and scream,
"You killed him! You killed him.
In your God damned Brooks Brothers suit,
You son of a bitch!"

Its lack of literary merit aside, what, one wonders, does any of this have to do with Dylan Thomas, who died of alcoholism, pneumonia, and a collapsed ego after living a "naked-nerved and blood timid" life mostly in Wales and London? Far from constituting a tribute to Thomas, this poem, with its inane attempts to attribute the Welshman's death to *Time* magazine, to various elements of the military-industrial complex, and to patrons of Brooks Brothers, represents an insult to the poet's memory; Thomas serves as a cudgel with which Rexroth clubs his own enemies for his own reasons. If there is anything resembling a clear motive here, it is not righteous indignation but a powerful resentment with which the poet seems not to have come to terms—resentment not only toward the sort of people who can afford to shop at Brooks Brothers but also toward a recently deceased foreign poet whose verses had, if the truth be told, received far more attention on these shores than Rexroth's.

From Rexroth and friends we proceed to Part Four, a grab-bag of work by thirteen "Other Fellow Travelers" who might be described as marginal Beats at best. These range from Bob Dylan (Charters actually includes the lyrics to "Blowin' in the Wind" and "The Times They Are A-Changin'") to Tuli Kupferberg (who is represented by an excerpt from his college-humor-magazine-style inventory of *1001 Ways to Beat the Draft*) to Peter Orlovsky (a high-school dropout whose chief claim to fame is his unenviable thirty-year stint as Ginsberg's significant other). Charters dutifully reproduces Orlovsky's witless description of his method of "spontaneous prose": "Just follow the mind out like this, when you have a hunch working in your mind or see a picture that has already expressed its self in the mind, then let that come out and not some other fast thought or idea that just jumped into the main one—but just write out what you feel the most at one moment and you can't go wrong for you can just write out forever—the pen knows its job—." The section also includes the longtime anthology standbys "In Memory of Radio" by Amiri Baraka and "The Day Lady Died" by Frank O'Hara, neither of whom one would classify as a Beat poet—though both at least provide the book with some desperately needed variety in style and theme.

One thing that the *Reader*'s first four sections underscore is that the great majority of Beat writing, whether prose or verse, is highly autobiographical, drawn directly from the real-life adventures of the Beats and their womenfolk. (In an excerpt from Kerouac's novel *The Dharma Bums*, Charters even puts the characters' "real" names in brackets, as if to acknowledge that this stuff is meant to be read not as literature but as gossip.) Over and over, one encounters the same historical tidbits—first in Charters's introduction, then in the biographical notes that precede the selections, and then in the selections themselves. For this reason, it is hard not to turn to Part Five, "Tales of Beatnik Glory: Memoirs and Posthumous Tributes," without feeling that one has already had quite enough of memoirs and tributes. The curious thing about these pieces—whose authors include Kerouac's wife, Jan; Cassady's wife, Carolyn; and Burroughs's son, William, Jr.—is that they evince remarkably little variation in manner and sensibility; after a while, the anecdotes all blend together into a single sad story from which nobody involved seems to have learned a thing. That includes Charters, whose title for this section would appear not to be ironic: to her, one gathers, the story of the Beats *is* a tale of glory.

It was also—to the Beats themselves, if not to many discriminating readers—a tale of holiness. As Charters explains, to Kerouac "the linguistic root of the word 'beat' also carried the connotations of beatitude or beatific." Throughout the *Reader*, sprinkled about like so much salt or pepper, one finds words suggestive of the sacred. In a postscript to "Poet of the Streets," Jack Michelene notes that the poem was "written on First Avenue off the Bowery in an alley of great souls." Philip Lamantia writes that "In the silence of holy darkness I'm eating a tomato" and finds "everywhere immanence of the presence of God." Ginsberg speaks of Huncke's "holy Creephood in New York," and in "America" asks: "America how can I write a holy litany in your silly mood?" Then, of course, there is his "Footnote to Howl," whose first line consists of the word "holy" repeated fifteen times, and whose next few lines make up a would-be Whitmanian catalogue: "The world is holy! The soul is holy! The skin is holy! The nose is holy! The tongue and cock and hand and asshole holy!" If this litany is less than convincing, it's because one finds here no sense of awe or wonder in the presence of the things of this world and not the slightest hint of humility before the idea of Godhead. For all the renown of "Howl" and "Footnote to Howl," it seems to this reader that only in a spiritually destitute era could so many intelligent people accept the idea that an Allen Ginsberg understands the first thing about what it means to be holy.

But then such is the Beat mystique, which will, alas, doubtless be with us as long as we live in an age that prizes personality over character, display over discipline, superficial vigor and provocativeness over intellectual and emotional depth, and sensational self-indulgence over unspectacular self-sacrifice. For a generation, people who pride themselves on not falling for a television ad for Dow Chemical or Archer Daniels Midland have allowed themselves to be taken in by the Beats' slickly marketed corporate image; people who recognize a cynical act by a mainstream politician at a hundred paces have chosen not to notice the calculatedness with which the Beats have manipulated the news media and the literary world to their own ends; and people who sneer at the conceit of movie stars have preferred to overlook the appalling narcissism with which Ginsberg, on many a public occasion, has attracted notice by disrobing. (Well, it's easier than writing a good poem.)

If readers have refused to see the Beats for what they are, however, so, it would appear, have the Beats. For all their blanket maledictions, Kerouac, Ginsberg and company could never be faulted for being excessively humble or self-critical (Charters notes that Ginsberg was so irate at Holmes for his less than reverential rendering of him in *Go* that

"The publisher withheld the paperback, fearing legal action"); they have rarely exhibited any irony or sense of humor about themselves; and though they vilify society for exploiting them in every conceivable (and, for that matter, inconceivable) way, there is nothing in their *oeuvres* to suggest that any of them has ever felt remorse over the very real ways in which they have used others—e.g., Ginsberg's sexual exploitation of minors, Kerouac's scrounging off his mother, and Burroughs's trolling of his fourteen-year-old son past his ephebophile drinking buddies in Tangier. Reaching the end of this disgraceful volume—which closes with a section of post-Fifties work by Ginsberg and others and an appendix that includes Norman Mailer's essay "The White Negro"—one cannot help feeling that Charters would have rendered American letters a far more valuable service had she dropped this project and instead done a study of Beat self-promotion, complete with reprints of the Sunday-supplement profiles and newsmagazine features that brought the Beats fame and, eventually, transformed them into legends; for it is in the realm of publicity, and none other, that the Beats have demonstrated their much-vaunted genius.

APRIL 1992

THE PHENOMENON OF ALLEN GINSBERG

I'm so lucky to be nutty.
—Allen Ginsberg, "Bop Lyrics" (1949)

The very first poem in Allen Ginsberg's *Collected Poems 1947-1980*[1] seems, in a way, to prophesy Ginsberg's entire career. It is titled "In Society," and it dates from 1947, when the poet was twenty-one years old. The poem records a dream: Ginsberg is at a high-society cocktail party, is more or less ignored, and is told by a woman, "I don't like you." He screams at her:

> ..."What!"
> in outrage. "Why you shit-faced fool!"
> This got everybody's attention.
> "Why you narcissistic bitch! How
> can you decide when you don't even
> , know me," I continued in a violent
> and messianic voice, inspired at last,
> dominating the whole room.

Could Ginsberg have known, at that tender age, that he would spend much of his adult life dominating rooms in this manic, "messianic" manner—indeed, that his attention-getting tactics at poetry readings, political conventions, sit-ins, be-ins, protest marches, and Yippie Life Festivals would be a crucial catalyst in his rise to fame? Even Richard Howard, who in his no-nonsense survey of contemporary American poetry, *Alone with America*, begins forty of forty-one essays with a businesslike disquisition upon the poetic career at hand ("In 1960, Howard Moss selected an appropriate showing of poems from his first three

---

[1] *Collected Poems 1947-1980*, by Allen Ginsberg; Harper & Row, 837 pages, $27.50.

volumes..."), makes an exception in the case of Allen Ginsberg. The long opening paragraph of Howard's essay on Ginsberg is devoted not to *explication de texte* but to an anecdote. The gist of it is that once, at a poetry conference attended by Howard, an elderly poet just back from Nigeria was "extol[ling] the rare privilege of moving among a race of women proudly nude," whereupon the bard of the Beat Generation rose from his seat, "stepped up onto the dais and without a word, without a smile, without a single deprecating gesture, Allen Ginsberg took off all his clothes."

You could fill a book with Ginsberg anecdotes of this sort. (The stories about him removing his clothing at one public gathering or another would by themselves make up a long chapter.) What is remarkable is not that Ginsberg has advertised himself with such arrogance and audacity, but that it has worked like a charm; thanks to such shameless scene-stealing antics, he has attained a measure of fame that he could never have secured by his poetry alone. He is, unarguably, the only poet in America who is not just a member of the august American Academy of Arts and Letters but a bona fide celebrity, the sort who appears on network talk shows. He is idolized by English professors as well as rock stars, and associates comfortably with both groups. He is truly famous.

The *Collected Poems 1947-1980* is the ultimate testimony to this fame. Two inches thick, clad in a bright, firetruck-red wrapper, this imposing tome, like its author, stands out big and brash among its fellows, demanding to be recognized. Its message could not be more obvious: that this poet, whose verse has heretofore been packed into numerous shoddy little small-press volumes, henceforth belongs to the ages. What's more, the *Collected Poems* is only the first step in what amounts to the mainstream press's canonization of Allen Ginsberg. In the words of the publicity flyer accompanying the review copy, Harper & Row will, in the fullness of time, "make available [Ginsberg's] journals, letters, literary essays, and lectures on American literature, as well as a new collection of poems scheduled to coincide with his sixtieth birthday in 1986." What poet, living or dead, has been treated so reverently by Publishers' Row? There can be no denying it hereafter: Allen Ginsberg, who rose to renown as the outspoken enemy of the Establishment, and the most prominent feature of whose poetry has always been its hostility to the order of things in the United States of America, is now the Republic's premier Establishment poet.

Ginsberg's parents, at least, would have been happy. And if there is anything in America that Allen Ginsberg has not rebelled against in his three decades as the amazingly tireless (and drearily tiresome) Poet of Protest, it is his parents. Ginsberg's father, Louis, was a poet—a premodernist rhymester, to be sure, but a poet; his mother, Naomi, was a Communist agitator whose paranoid psychosis (as any reader of "Kaddish" knows) eventually necessitated her commitment to a mental institution. Poetry, paranoia, protest; this was the mixed legacy of Ginsberg's parents, and it is a legacy to which Ginsberg—who has dedicated his *Collected Poems* to their memory—has been eternally and entirely faithful. When, at age sixteen, he left their Paterson, New Jersey, home to attend Columbia University, Ginsberg took up studies in literature, his father's field; and, just as loyally, he rejected the opportunity that Columbia offered to breathe sane air for the first time in his life. Rather—in a clear attempt to cultivate a Naomi Ginsberg-like rebelliousness—Ginsberg took up with the Beats.

Or, more precisely, the as-yet-unknown Beats-to-be. At first, in addition to Ginsberg, there were three of them: Jack Kerouac (a middle-class boy who lived with his mother in Ozone Park, Queens), William Burroughs (an heir to the gigantic corporation of the same name), and Lucien Carr (a slim, handsome student at Columbia). Though they looked harmless enough, Kerouac, Burroughs, and Carr had the same problem Ginsberg did: they craved chaos. They looked down upon the society in which they lived, for no other reason than that, like any other nonanarchic society, it had laws, a government, a way of life; they considered the classical, intellectually oriented education offered at Columbia to be pointless and stifling; and they romanticized poverty, criminality, and rootlessness in a way that only naïve, sheltered young men could do. They felt themselves to be geniuses—literary geniuses, to be precise—and disdained the "well-made" piece of writing as much as they did the well-ordered mind. Truly great minds, they insisted, were not sane and stable and logical, and did not express themselves in lucid, beautifully balanced sentences; instead, such minds soared above the surface of the earth, touched the stars, whirled and shook and spun erratically in the upper air. The great, in short, were always a little mad. Thus it was with genuine pride that the Beats asserted—at first to one another, and then, later, to an increasingly attentive world—their own madness.

The Beats have been spoken of as populist writers, as celebrators

of the democratic spirit. But the truth is that they were confirmed elit-
ists. Their collective self-image was nothing short of messianic; in their
judgment, they were, by virtue of their self-proclaimed mental insta-
bility, incomparably superior to the civilization into which they had
been born, to the professors who had been designated to instruct them,
to the great authors that everybody read. The appeal of this anti-logic
to the young Ginsberg, in particular, is obvious: what could bring more
comfort to a sensitive young man who loved his mother than the idea
that her mental illness, far from being a family tragedy, was, on the
contrary, something to be proud of? It was this anti-logic, at any rate,
that persuaded Ginsberg, when he was not yet twenty years old, to
reject Lionel Trilling and the other too-sane "squares" of the Columbia
English department as being utterly incapable of giving him a real edu-
cation, and to allow the loosely bound Burroughs (who was twelve
years older than he was) and the wacky Kerouac (four years his se-
nior) to be his literary mentors. The Beats used the same anti-logic to
determine which outsiders would be allowed to join their fraternity.
Thus Herbert Huncke, a psychopathic burglar and drug addict who
was known to New York police as "the Creep" (and whom Ginsberg
once described as "the only sophisticated man in New York"), was
heartily welcomed into the fold. (Huncke would make an enduring, if
unwitting, contribution to American literature: he introduced his cro-
nies to the word "beat," meaning worn-out, jaded; it was Kerouac who,
in a deliberate echo of Gertrude Stein's "lost generation" remark, bor-
rowed Huncke's word and coined the appellation "the Beat Genera-
tion.") And Neal Cassady, a dashing railway brakeman from Denver
who arrived on the scene in 1946, was such an excellent specimen of
the obsessive-compulsive type that the Beats not only let him into their
charmed circle but, endlessly fascinated by his hyperkinetic hedonism,
made a literary hero out of him. Kerouac would immortalize him as
Dean Moriarty in *On the Road* (1956) and other novels, and Ginsberg
(who fell in love with Cassady) would write numerous poems about
him over the ensuing decades, one of the first being "Dakar Doldrums"
(1947). The initial stanza of this poem not only demonstrates the inten-
sity of Ginsberg's unrequited passion (Cassady had thrown him over
for a woman, and a despondent Ginsberg had signed onto a freighter
bound for Senegal) but provides a good illustration of his extremely
imitative, pseudo-Elizabethan early style (the first of many extremely
imitative Ginsberg styles):

Most dear, and dearest at this moment most,
Since this my love for thee is thus more free
Than that I cherished more dear and lost;
Most near, now nearest where I fly from thee:
Thy love most consummated is in absence,
Half for the trust I have for thee in mind,
Half for the pleasures of thee in remembrance—
Thou art most full and fair of all thy kind.

Amid all the *non compos mentis* carryings-on, then, there *was* some writing going on among the Beats. But, all in all, the history of Ginsberg's first years with his subterranean compeers bears less resemblance to a literary chronicle than it does to a textbook of case histories in schizophrenia. Two incidents stand out. The first, which took place in 1944, was the murder by Lucien Carr of a young man named David Kammerer, who according to Carr, had made a pass at him. Since the crime was therefore an "honor slaying," Carr was let off with a relatively brief term in an Elmira, New York, reformatory. His fellow Beats, for their part, appear to have gotten a Norman Mailerish thrill out of the affair; the murder, one gathers from the many narratives that have touched on the crime, confirmed their image of themselves as a dangerous band of underground rebels. Then, in 1948 (the year he was finally graduated from Columbia), Ginsberg had his first brush with fame. He was implicated in one of Huncke's burglaries, got his picture on the cover of the *Daily News* as a result, and was sent to the Columbia Psychiatric Institute instead of prison. There he met and befriended Carl Solomon, a well-read maniac who (one gets the impression) made the Beats look like the Sitwells; upon release from the Institute, Solomon immediately assumed the role of the group's so-called "lunatic saint." (He would also, in time, become the raving mad junkie-protagonist of Ginsberg's most famous poem, "Howl.") Solomon was, in the words of Beat historian John Tytell, something of a Platonic ideal of "the artist as outrage"—and therefore, obviously, a model of sorts for the outrageous public persona that Ginsberg was eventually to assume.[2]

Besides being the year that Ginsberg joined Carr in the pantheon of hipster hoods, 1948 was also the year of two supposedly epiphanic

------

[2]Tytell's book is *Naked Angels: The Lives and Literature of the Beat Generation* (McGraw-Hill, 1976).

events in the life of the aspiring poet. The first involved William Blake. One day, Ginsberg was alone in his apartment, having just read "Ah! Sun-Flower" (a poem in *Songs of Experience*), when suddenly he heard a voice—that of Blake himself, he figured—reading the verses aloud. Over the next few weeks, the voice returned and read other Blake poems to him. The Ginsberg groupies have made much of this incident; Paul Portugés devotes a whole book (*The Visionary Poetics of Allen Ginsberg*) to an interpretation of Ginsberg's entire corpus in light of it, insisting that the auditory hallucination "revolutionized [Ginsberg's] ideas about poetry, his concept of self, and his perception of the quotidian world." Ginsberg himself (as quoted in Jane Kramer's book *Allen Ginsberg in America*) puts it this way:

> The thing I felt was that there was this big god over all, who was completely aware and completely conscious of everything, and at the same time completely the same as everybody, and that the whole purpose of being born was to wake up to Him.... I felt everything vibrating in one harmony— all past efforts and desire, all present realizations.... And I felt that even *my* previous ponderings had been harmoniously flower-petaled toward this final understanding of what it was all about and that all my poetic musings about supreme reality were prophetic, really, and just the sweet, well-intentioned strivings of a poor mind to reach what was already there.[3]

What it comes down to is that this "visitation" (which occurred, by the way, after Ginsberg had been smoking marijuana and inhaling Benzedrine regularly for several years) gave Ginsberg an abrupt push in the direction of the cosmic. It made him more of a transcendental poet than he had been before—the sort of poet, that is, who does not think of a poem as an object, a "made thing," but rather as the effusion of a poetic self that sees all, knows all, encompasses all. This was, then, the beginning of the end of whatever interest the twenty-two-year-old Ginsberg might have had in developing his poetic technique.

---

[3]*Allen Ginsberg in America*, by Jane Kramer (Random House, 1969), pages 72-73. Jane Kramer, a *New Yorker* writer, plays Boswell to Ginsberg's Johnson, reverently recording every "yeah," "like," "wow," and "om" that the poet uttered over a period of several months in 1967.

The second epiphanic event of 1948 was somewhat more down-to-earth. Ginsberg went to hear his fellow Patersonian, William Carlos Williams, read at the Museum of Modern Art, and when the older poet recited his poem "The Clouds," which at its end trails off in mid-sentence, the device struck Ginsberg with the force of a revelation: you could write the way you talk! Up to this point he had been, in his own words, "hung up on cats like Wyatt, Surrey, and Donne," and had churned out reams of pseudo-Elizabethan poems (and would continue to do so for a couple more years, finally abandoning the iamb—for a while, anyway—after "Ode: My Twenty-Fourth Year" in 1950-1951). Now, hung up on a cat named Williams, he began dividing entries from his prose journals into lines and calling them poems:

> I walked into the cocktail party
> room and found three or four queers
> talking together in queertalk.
> I tried to be friendly but heard
> myself talking to one in hiptalk.
> "I'm glad to see you," he said, and
> looked away. "Hmn," I mused. The room
> was small and had a double-decker
> bed in it, and cooking apparatus:
> icebox, cabinet, toasters, stove;
> the hosts seemed to live with room
> enough only for cooking and sleeping.

Now, *that* was the way to write a poem—no muss, no fuss! Williams, whom Ginsberg soon came to know quite well (and whom he would refer to in later years as his "guru"), was flattered by these imitative (if utterly unimaginative) verses and provided an introduction for the book in which Ginsberg planned to publish them.

That book, however—*Empty Mirror* was its title—would not find a publisher till 1961; so Williams obligingly contributed a second introduction to what became Ginsberg's debut volume, *Howl & Other Poems* (1956). Between the writing of *Empty Mirror* and of *Howl*, though, Williams's influence waned. There were (aside from the obvious incompatibility of Williams's "no-ideas-but-in-things" approach and Ginsberg's Blake-born neo-Platonism) several reasons for this decline in influence. One of them was Kerouac's new "theory" of spontaneous writing, to which Ginsberg subscribed enthusiastically upon its introduction in 1951. The idea, as set forth in Kerouac's essay "Essentials of Spontaneous Prose" (and applied in the fast-as-lightning composition of *On the Road*), was that, when one is writing, the first words to enter one's head are always the best ones for the purpose; revision is a deceitful process because it involves *thinking*, that dreaded enemy of honest feeling and consequently of true art. "First thought, best thought": it was a ridiculous concept, but one perfectly suited to the Beats, who were impatient, impulsive, and incomparably conceited, who hated order, and who didn't really want to spend all that much time writing anyway. (If they did, there wouldn't be any time left to be "hip.") Ginsberg, for one, would never be the same after "Essentials of Spontaneous Prose"; Kerouac, he was later to say (in one of the most dubious compliments in the history of American literature), "taught me everything I knew about writing."

But Kerouac was not the only member of the Beat Generation who was making discoveries. Sometime between the writing of *Empty Mirror* and of *Howl* Ginsberg made a big one: Walt Whitman. Here, he realized, was the perfect model for the spontaneous, transcendental poet he wanted to be. Ginsberg's Open Road was to be different from Whitman's, though; his journey down the "long brown path" of Whitmanian fame was not to be a lyrical, lighthearted hike but a bumpy, buffoonish protest march. "Paterson" (1949), his first poem in imitation of the Bard of Paumanok, not only made it clear that he had shamelessly appropriated the entire arsenal of Whitmanian devices—the vatic tone, the long lines, the comprehensive lists, the names of American places, the programmatic egocentrism, the rampant sensuality, the practice of beginning a series of lines with the same words or phrases, and the obsession with the past, present, and future of America—but established the distinctly un-Whitmanian uses to which he would put them. At the beginning of "Paterson," Ginsberg bluntly declares his hostility toward the American way of life: "What do I want in these rooms papered with visions of money?" He despises the idea of participating in an economic system governed by "the slobs and dumbbells of the ego with money and power / to hire and fire and make and break and fart and justify their reality of wrath / and rumor of wrath to wrath-weary man." What sort of life would Ginsberg prefer? A demented, disordered one, of course:

> I would rather go mad, gone down the dark road to Mexico, heroin
> dripping in my veins,

eyes and ears full of marijuana,
eating the god Peyote on the floor of a mudhut on the border
or laying in a hotel room over the body of some suffering man
    or woman;
rather jar my body down the road, crying by a diner in the Western
    sun;
rather crawl on my naked belly over the tincans of Cincinnati;
rather drag a rotten railroad tie to a Golgotha in the Rockies;
rather, crowned with thorns in Galveston, nailed hand and foot in
    Los Angeles, raised up to die in Denver,
pierced in the side in Chicago, perished and tombed in New Orleans
    and resurrected in 1958 somewhere on Garrett Mountain,
come down roaring in a blaze of hot cars and garbage,
streetcorner Evangel in front of City Hall, surrounded by statues of
    agonized lions,
with a mouthful of shit, and the hair rising on my scalp,
screaming and dancing in praise of Eternity annihilating the
    sidewalk, annihilating reality,
screaming and dancing against the orchestra in the
    destructible ballroom of the world,
blood streaming from my belly and shoulders
flooding the city with its hideous ecstasy, rolling over the pavements
    and highways
by the bayoux and forests and derricks leaving my flesh and my bones
    hanging on the trees.

With "Paterson," then, Ginsberg set the course he would follow for the rest of his life: that of the self-proclaimed martyr and madman, the Hyde to Whitman's Jekyll, the prophet-poet turned enemy of the system.

Ginsberg made other significant "discoveries" besides Whitman, of course. From around 1952, the poet, in his own words, "experimented with poetic effect of psychedelic drugs." What this means is that he wrote "Howl" on peyote, "Wales Visitation" on LSD, "I Hate America" on heroin, "On Neal's Ashes" on morphine or marijuana, "Denver Doldrums" on Benzedrine, "Kaddish" on methadrine, "A Ghost May Come" on marijuana, "Death to Van Gogh's Ear!" on codeine. He composed a series of poems that take their titles from the name of the drug on which they were written: "Mescaline," "Laughing Gas," "Lysergic Acid." He went all the way to Peru just to bring back a hallucinogenic vine called *ayahuasca*. Portugés's book contains an interview in which Ginsberg discusses in depth the various effects of these substances on his work. "All mellow poems seem to emerge out of heroin. Endless metaphysical-political ravings in my journal and other stuff you've seen were written on morphine and heroin." He speaks of poems like "Marijuana Notation" and "Psalm I" as having a "grass-like clarity." He says of laughing gas: "It gives the appearance of enlarging perception to a point where the totality of the universe invades the individual entity and dissolves the individual entity into the blackness of space." These were not, of course, private "experiments"; Ginsberg, like his friend and fellow chemist Timothy Leary, proselytized long and hard for the use of psychedelic drugs, travelling from campus to campus reciting poems like "Aether," in which he asserts that "you can see / God by sniffing the / gas in a cotton...."

Ginsberg also discovered Eastern religion. His full-dress involvement with it dates back to the early Sixties, when he went to Asia and found himself intrigued by Hinduism and Buddhism. What appealed to him most about these religions was their emphasis on the self-determination of the individual and their understanding of morality as a subjective consideration. Life was not a matter of objective right and wrong, it was a matter of being true to one's own karmic sense of things. No philosophy of life could have pleased Ginsberg more. His exploration of Eastern religions has continued ever since; in the autobiographical notes to his *Poems All Over the Place, Mostly Seventies* (1978), Ginsberg indicated that he was spending a good deal of his time practicing both "mantra-heart meditation" (with one Swami Muktananda) and Tibetan Buddhist meditation. The influence of Hinduism, Hare Krishna, and the various species of Buddhism on his work has been largely semantic; in his poems and journals, for instance, he habitually (and gratuitously) describes relationships in terms of karmas and yogas. This is not to suggest, of course, that the babas, swamis, gurus, and lamas have not had a substantial impact upon the way Ginsberg lives and writes; like his psychedelic drugs, they have helped him fight off the desire for intellectual order that exists in some corner of every conscious mind and to give even freer rein to his id. Ginsberg, in typical fashion, prefers to describe this process as the "holy divine yoga of losing ego."

Ginsberg's id, of course, was unusually healthy even without the help of the gods of the East. It was, in fact, years before he signed his soul over to them that Ginsberg and his id became famous. The setting for this historic occasion was a place called the Six Gallery in San Francisco; the poem—in which Ginsberg brought the mad-anarchist persona of "Paterson" into full bloom—was, needless to say, "Howl." Ginsberg had moved to the Bay City two years earlier, establishing connections with such local poets as Gary Snyder, Philip Whalen, Kenneth Rexroth, Philip Lamantia, Michael McClure, and Lawrence Ferlinghetti, and finding himself a twenty-year-old lover named Peter Orlovsky, who was (in Orlovsky's own words) "crazy as a wildflower" and who has lived with Ginsberg, on and off, ever since. (Like Ginsberg, Orlovsky had had a visionary epiphany: he had been walking down the street one day and the trees had bowed down to him.)

That evening in the Six Gallery all of the above were present—as were Kerouac and Cassady—as Ginsberg introduced "Howl" to the world in his best artist -as-outrage manner. The poem created a sensation, one that a brave reader (aware, perhaps, that Ginsberg had earned a living for a time as a "marketing research consultant") might ascribe not so much to its literary merits as to Ginsberg's truly impressive job of packaging—to his projection, both in print and in person, of a sharply defined, attention-getting persona. "Howl"—which, as Norman Podhoretz was to write soon afterward, "got the San Francisco renaissance off to a screaming start"—succeeded even better than "Paterson" in conveying the Beat movement's hatred of bourgeois life, its rejection of every known type of order (whether psychological, social, or aesthetic), and its conviction that America's best and brightest were to be found wherever the disturbed and the delinquent congregated. The extremity of the poem's point of view, the singular way in which Ginsberg delivered it, and the obscenity trial that followed its publication by City Lights Books fixed Ginsberg in the literary firmament in a way that a less outrageous piece of writing (however magnificent it might be) could never have done.

Ginsberg learned his lesson. Since "Howl," he has published (and read from a thousand platforms) over a dozen books of poetry, and the recipe has remained pretty much the same throughout: take one part anti-Establishment rhetoric, one part sexual indelicacy, one part scatology and general grubbiness, and mix rather sloppily. *Voilà*—a book of poetry. And a Guggenheim, a National Book Award, a membership in the American Academy of Arts and Letters, a *Collected Poems* issued by Harper & Row. Ginsberg is thought of as a radical poet, but in a sense he is anything but; like the most uncreative contributor to *Reader's Digest* or *Time* (the two magazines he most frequently maligns in his verse), he has always known his audience and has always given it exactly what it wanted. The one thing that can never be found in his poetry is the unexpected. He has, for instance, been carrying on about Americans and their money for decades, and the subtlety of his observations and the eloquence of his expression have failed to develop beyond the monotonous Moloch-chant of "Howl" ("Moloch! Moloch! Nightmare of Moloch! Moloch the loveless! Mental Moloch! Moloch the heavy judger of men!", etc.) or the sloppy superficiality of his 1957 poem, "Death to Van Gogh's Ear!":

> Money! Money! Money! shrieking mad celestial money of
>   illusion! Money made of nothing, starvation, suicide! Money of
>   failure! Money of death!
> Money against Eternity! and eternity's strong mills grind out vast
>   paper of Illusion!

Money, he howls, "has reckoned the soul of America." Money has put

> millions of agitated fanatics in the bughouse for the sake of the
>   screaming soprano of industry
> Money-chant of soapers—toothpaste apes in television sets—
>   deodorizers on hypnotic chairs—
> petroleum mongers in Texas—jet plane streaks among the clouds—
> sky writers liars in the face of Divinity—fanged butchers of hats and
>   shoes, all Owners! Owners! Owners! with obsession on prop-
>   erty and vanishing Selfhood!

For awkwardness and lack of originality, the poem is hard to beat; but Ginsberg has valiantly spent the rest of his career trying. In a 1970 poem called "Friday the Thirteenth," he is still singing the same unmelodic, rhythmically ragged tune:

> Slaves of Plastic! Leather-shoe chino-pants prisoners! Haircut
>   junkies! Dacron-sniffers!
> Striped tie addicts! short hair monkeys on their backs! Whiskey freaks
>   bombed out on 530 billion cigarettes a year
> twenty Billion dollar advertising Dealers! lipstick skin-poppers &
>   syndicate Garbage telex-Heads!

Star-striped scoundrelesque flag-dopers! Car-smog hookers
    Fiendish on superhighways!
Growth rate trippers hallucinating Everglade real estate! Steak
    swallowers zonked on Television!
Old ladies on Stockmarket habits—old Wall Street paper
    Money-pushers!

Yes, it certainly does sound like the literary equivalent of a *Pravda* cartoon, but for the past few decades there has been a substantial segment of the American literary public eager to applaud such brassy banalities. This is not to suggest that Wall Street and Madison Avenue are not excellent targets for satire. They are. But these collocations of anti-capitalist clichés are not satire. Satire requires wit, and these witless lines attest only to the extremity of Ginsberg's attitude toward America. Ginsberg cannot stand the fact that Americans purchase homes, buy clothing, eat well and regularly, use cars to get places. The orderliness of it all enrages him. That Americans do other things in the course of a day besides buy stock, wear synthetics, and watch television does not seem to occur to him; the only emotional depth or sensitivity of which he appears to be aware is his own and that of his cronies. These poems attack the supposed monomaniacal consumerism of the typical American, but it is Ginsberg who is the monomaniac: he cannot look at middle-class America without seeing a race of faceless, heartless, mass-consuming, polluting, war-mongering, credit-card-using, *Reader's Digest*-reading robots. That he himself watches television, buys property (a good deal of it, too), and eats well does not deter him in the least from waxing hysterical about the fact that others do. He knows *he's* okay—he sweats, drools, performs all the other bodily functions, and describes it all in graphic detail every chance he gets. And he knows his friends and lovers are okay, too. It's the rest of the country in whose loving, feeling, laughing, crying, thinking, breathing reality he is incapable of believing. It's as if you have to drag yourself through the Negro streets at dawn looking for an angry fix, bite detectives in the neck and shriek with delight in police cars, and howl on your knees in the subway in order to be recognized by Ginsberg as having feelings.

One of Ginsberg's favorite themes is the FBI-CIA-Mafia-Pentagon-White House-Chase Manhattan-Standard Oil-ITT-NBC-ABC-CBS-*New York Times-Reader's Digest* cabal. In "Television Was a Baby Crawling Toward That Deathchamber" (1961), Ginsberg describes "the Presidential mike & all its starry bunting" as a "front for some mad BILLION-AIRES / who own United Fruits & Standard Oil and Hearst The Press and Texas NBC and someone owns the Radios owns vast Spheres of Air...." He suggests secret and sinister connections among a multitude of American corporations, the Mutual Network and the *Reader's Digest*, and maintains that

> Six billionaires that control America are playing Scrabble with
> antique Tarot—they've just unearthed another Pyramid—in the
> bombproof Cellar at Fort Knox
> Not even the FBI knows who—They give orders to J.E. Hoover
> thru the metal phonegirl at the Robot Transmitter on top of
> RCA....

And on and on it goes, in "'Have You Seen This Movie?'" (1970):

> ... What Mafia runs N.J.? What Mafia knew J. Edgar FBI?
> What's Schenley's Whiskey trader Fleishmann's Hoover Institute?
> What opium's passed thru CIA Agents' airplane's luggage in Saigon,
> Bangkok, Athens, Washington?
> What narcotic agent's not dependent on Shit for a living?
> What Bank's money created ex nihil serves orphan, widow,
> monk, philosopher?
> or what Bank's money serves real Estate Asphalt over widow's
> garden? Serves old Nick in the Pentagon?

—and in "Anti-Vietnam War Peace Mobilization" (1970), wherein Ginsberg describes the White House as

> ...filled with mustached Germans
> & police buttons, army telephones, CIA Buzzers, FBI bugs
> Secret Service walkie-talkies, Intercom squawkers to Narco
> Fuzz & Florida Mafia Real Estate Speculators.

—and in "Thoughts on a Breath" (1974), a meditation upon

> Police state, Students, Poetry open tongue, anger and fear of Cops,
> Oil cops, Rockefeller Cops, Oswald Cops, Johnson Cops Nixon
> Cops president Cops
> SMU cops Trustee Cops CIA Cops FBI Cops Goon Squads of Dope

—and in "Hadda Be Playing on the Jukebox" (1975):

> Hadda be Central Intelligence The Family "Our Thing" the Agency
>   Mafia Organized Crime FBI Dope Cops & Multinational
>   Corporations
> one big set of Criminal gangs working together in Cahoots
>
> .   .   .
>
> Secret Police embraced for decades, NKVD & CIA keep eachother's
>   secrets, OGPU & DIA never hit their own, KGB & FBI one mind—
>   brute force

—and in "Birdbrain!" (1980):

> Birdbrain runs the World!
> Birdbrain is the ultimate product of Capitalism
> Birdbrain chief bureaucrat of Russia, yawning
> Birdbrain ran FBI 30 years appointed by F.D. Roosevelt and never
>   chased Cosa Nostra!
>
> .   .   .
>
> Birdbrain runs the Pentagon his brother runs the CIA, Fatass Bucks!
> Birdbrain writes and edits *Time Newsweek Wall Street Journal Pravda
>   Izvestia*....

Does Ginsberg believe in the literal truth of all these accusations of conspiracy? Certainly not. He is showing us what runaway paranoia looks like. But to what purpose? Apparently, this is not meant to discredit *him*, to make him look ridiculous, but is intended rather as an eloquent condemnation of the American economic and political system. And critics and readers buy it in droves. It is as if Ginsberg's absurd, anarchistic paranoia is itself, to some people's way of thinking, evidence against "The System." Nor do Ginsberg's fans seem to be disturbed by the indiscriminateness of his put-downs. "In America it's Attica in Russia it's Lubianka Wall," he writes in "Capitol Air" (1980). Television and Nazi gas chambers, the mass media and Stalin's gulags: to Ginsberg, as far as one can tell, they are all equally horrible. He makes no distinctions at all—he is just *against, against, against*—and this is a significant failing, for perceptive, sensitive distinctions are the basis of all intelligent discourse and all worthwhile art. Such catalogue poems as "Capitol Air" and "Yes and It's Hopeless" and "Birdbrain!" lump the unpleasant in with the evil, link various phenomena of American popular culture with some of the more hateful manifestations of Soviet totalitarianism. Ginsberg's point is identical throughout: "The System the System in Russia & China the same." What he hates, patently, is the very idea of a *system*; and he sees absolutely no difference between a system that is essentially democratic and one that is out-and-out totalitarian.

To read such poems as these back-to-back in the *Collected Poems* is to be stunned by the oversimplification, the repetition, the self-indulgence, the egocentrism, the utter inability to develop a theme. Doesn't he ever, one wonders, get sick of reiterating these banalities? Doesn't he ever yearn to get beyond the surface cliché, to develop a more sophisticated view of the world, and to express it in more memorable and meticulously chosen words? How can he stand to keep drawing the same distorted picture of a psychedelic universe in which everyone conspires against Allen Ginsberg, rather than exploring and attempting to understand the complexities that make the actual world interesting and frustrating and *real*? Reading these poetically and intellectually vapid verses one after the other, one is constantly reminded that they were written not to be read in privacy but to be declaimed to an audience—an audience that is supposed to cheer, not think; to applaud opinions it already shares with Ginsberg, not to mull over unfamiliar ideas or admire a finely turned phrase.

Ginsberg's most famous subject, of course, is the Vietnam War. Now that his anti-war poems have been published in chronological sequence with the rest of his poetry in the *Collected Poems*, it is more obvious than ever that, to a substantial degree, the war was less a cause for Ginsberg than an opportunity. The peace movement provided him with an occasion, a focus, and a wider audience than ever for the anti-American anarchism that he had been peddling for a decade. Ginsberg's attitude toward Vietnam, as expressed in his poetry, was never that American military involvement in that part of the world was a bad idea, and that it would be in the best interests of the United States and of the ultimate cause of democracy to withdraw. No; to Ginsberg, the war was just another miserable manifestation—like television and *Time* magazine—of a system he despised. In "Returning North of Vortex" (1967), Ginsberg makes his position clear. "I hope we lose this war," he writes. "Let the Viet Cong win over the American Army!" Perhaps the most revealing lines are the following: "And if it were my wish, we'd lose & our will / be broken / & our armies scattered as we've scattered the airy guerrillas of our own yellow imagination." Scattered armies, broken wills: is this the dream of a man who wants genuine peace— that is, order, stability, tranquillity—or of a connoisseur of chaos?

The answer seems obvious. And yet the literary critics of this country, in their infinite wisdom, have elevated Ginsberg to an unequaled stature among his poetry-writing contemporaries. What makes this situation all the more paradoxical is that surprisingly few of the critics who have celebrated Ginsberg in print seem honestly convinced that his poetry has any literary value at all. One critic after another, in fact, has gone out of his way to avoid remarking at any length upon the manifest mediocrity of most of Ginsberg's verse; repeatedly, one finds Ginsberg's partisans walking rhetorical tightropes, praising the poet while managing to avoid judging the poetry (or, at the very most, acknowledging its inadequacy as literature, but ingeniously discovering some nonliterary reason for admiring it). Oddest of all, many of the critics are in the habit of suggesting that it is just plain *wrong* to judge Ginsberg's poetry *qua* poetry. Richard Howard, for instance, writes in a recent issue of the *Boston Review* that the *Collected Poems* "may not be poetry at all, [but] it is always testimony, a kind of processional martyrology—in that martyrs are witnesses to the truth." John Malcolm Brinnin said much the same thing a decade ago in reviewing a book of Ginsberg's lectures and talks called *Allen Verbatim*: "As John Middleton Murry said of D.H. Lawrence, 'To charge him with a lack of form... is to be guilty of irrelevance. Art was not his aim.'" Gerrit Henry, writing in *Poetry* in 1974, observes admiringly that "the poems in *The Fall of America* aren't much as poems, but there's one whale of a *mensch* behind them." Is there any other American poet who gets reviews like this?

Not only does Ginsberg win Brownie points from his critics for being a *mensch* and a "martyr" (a martyr to what? fame? wealth? honors?); he actually gets credit for his courage. What courage? Why, the courage—believe it or not—to print such rubbish and call it poetry. Indeed, as Gerrit Henry sees it, Ginsberg's gutsiness on this account makes him nothing less than a "culture hero." "There's no doubt," Henry writes, "that Ginsberg takes an enormous risk in gathering the effect of that slapdash, patchwork sort of journalism-of-the-soul that he goes in for and calling it poetry, laying himself bare to all sorts of criticism and, indeed, mockery...." Ginsberg, says Henry (in a repudiation of critical responsibility that is surprisingly common among

Ginsberg's apologists), acts on a "messianic" impulse "which no critic of poetry is really empowered to judge." So there.

One of the more celebrated writers who prefer to discuss Ginsberg as messiah, rather than as poet, is Saul Bellow. In his recent story "Him with His Foot in His Mouth,"[4] Bellow, speaking through his protagonist, delivers a tribute to Ginsberg which is based entirely upon the image the poet has cultivated of himself as the twentieth century's answer to Whitman. America needs a transcendental poet, Bellow's speaker insists, and "the only authentic living representative of American Transcendentalism is that fat-breasted, bald, bearded homosexual in smeared goggles, innocent in his uncleanness." Ginsberg, the speaker suggests, "takes a stand for true tenderness and full candor. Real candor means excremental and genital literalness." (Does this mean that Euripides, Shakespeare, Dante, Goethe did not write with "real candor"? Conversely, is "excremental and genital literalness" all that "real candor" requires?) Bellow's speaker goes on:

> What Ginsberg opts for is the warmth of a freely copulating, manly, womanly, comradely, "open road" humanity which doesn't neglect to pray and to meditate. He speaks with horror of our "plastic culture," which he connects somewhat [!] obsessively with the CIA.... This psychopathic vision, so touching because there is, realistically, so much to be afraid of, and also because of the hunger for goodness reflected in it, a screwball defense of beauty, I value [highly].... He is a faithful faggot Buddhist in America, the land of his birth. The petrochemical capitalist enemy (an enemy that needs sexual and religious redemption) is right here at home. Who could help loving such a comedian!

"The petrochemical capitalist enemy... such a comedian": what sort of logic is at work here? If the speaker is serious about capitalism being the enemy, what does being a comedian have to do with it? Or *is* he serious? One thing, at least, is clear about this bizarre passage: Ginsberg's poetry is not mentioned once. Bellow's speaker praises Ginsberg not because he is a fine poet but because he is a "comedian," because he holds the "correct" political views (that is, he is obsessive

---

[4]The story appears in the recent collection, *Him With His Foot in His Mouth and Other Stories*, by Saul Bellow: Harper & Row, 294 pages, $15.95.

about the hazards of American capitalism and oblivious to the out-rages of Soviet Communism), and (incredibly) because he is "psycho-pathic," a "screwball." At the end of this tribute, Bellow's speaker (al-though by this point it is clearly Bellow speaking and no one else) pays Ginsberg the most peculiar compliment of all:

> I... refuse to overvalue the erotic life. I do not believe that the path of truth must pass through all the zones of mastur-bation and buggery. [Ginsberg] is consistent; to his credit, he goes all the way, which can't be said of me. Of the two of us, he is the more American.

This from the author of *The Adventures of Augie March*![5]

This seems to be the way to handle Ginsberg these days—call him the Atomic Age Whitman, but sidestep, as much as possible, the ques-tion of whether his poetry makes the grade. James Atlas, in his review of the *Collected Poems* for *The Atlantic*, obviously finds the poems, on the whole, offensive and mediocre, but, rather than letting the chips fall where they may, comes up with an assortment of excuses for them. Yes, he admits, some of the poems are nothing more than pornographic records of Ginsberg's pederastic revels—but, "lurid as they are, they belong to the convention of the horny old poet celebrating the tran-sient beauty of youth." Yes, a lot of the poetry is "stoned babble" and "there aren't many memorable lines in even the best" of it—but at least "it's never dull. Crammed with gossip, anecdotes, and confessions of sexual miscreancy, his garrulous, untidy narratives read like a good novel." Yes, "these poems are uneven, to say the least"—but so are Williams's *Paterson*, Olson's *Maximus Poems*, Lowell's *Notebook*. Amid all these clever rationalizations, Atlas manages to describe Ginsberg as the "heir of Whitman" and to allude to the poet's "Whitmanesque lines"—and, of course, to title the piece "A Modern Whitman."

Then there is Francis X. Clines (who is—fittingly, somehow—the *Times*'s White House correspondent), the author of a profile of Ginsberg published recently in *The New York Times Magazine*. Clines makes a

---

[5] Interestingly enough, Louis Simpson—whose poetry, like Bellow's novels, has helped memorably to define the character of late twentieth-century America—says much the same thing at the end of the chapter on Ginsberg in *A Revolution in Taste* (Macmillian, 1978): "With his beard, bald head and intent brown eyes [Ginsberg] is definitely a personality, as American as apple pie and the flag."

point of saying that Ginsberg "carefully claims no large place in American literature"; but he adds that "his labor and style alone, *regardless of the esthetic judgments of later generations* [my emphasis], currently put him [*sic*] as a major working writer in the nonclassical tradition of Walt Whitman and William Carlos Williams." What in the world does *this* mean? What it means, I think, is this: "Look, *you* know his poetry's terrible, and *I* know his poetry's terrible, but, heck, everybody knows that he's the modern Whitman, and who am I to buck the crowd?"

Such are the ways of personality cults. One of the many ironies of the Ginsberg cult is that this particular poet has profited hugely by his lack of originality. He began his career as a blatant imitator of Elizabethan poets, went on to become a rather faint xerox copy of William Carlos Williams, and finally settled on being a fourth-rate pseudo-Whitman. He has never learned selectively from his masters in the way most poets do—has never, that is, developed his own personal style by borrowing, in various subtle ways, from a number of poets; instead, he has simply copied styles wholesale. And, of course, to make the imitation worth the trouble, the former marketing research consultant has promoted himself more ingeniously than any American poet in history. By drawing attention to his combative, outrageous public personality and to his connections with Whitman, Williams, Blake, and other poets, Ginsberg has subtly steered the critics away from writing about his poetry as a literary phenomenon and has beguiled them into discussing him as a social force, a symbol, an heir to a tradition. Clines, for example, describes Ginsberg as "the celebrity poet who once piped a flood of hippie humanity into Golden Gate Park in the 1960's on the strength of 'flower power,'" as "the poet of resistance who once could rile authorities with the single syllable 'om,' his mantra chant against the Vietnam War sounding through the Chicago tear gas of '68," and as "the symbol of social iconoclasm and doctored mind expansion, one of the first to sing brazenly beyond the closet of homosexuality." Ginsberg has created such a myth about his person, in fact, that many of the people who write about him seem shocked, and a bit disappointed, that he lives pretty much the way the rest of us do. Clines describes Ginsberg and Orlovsky looking pensively over their financial accounts, and says, "It is startling to witness this mundane anxiety in two of the surviving souls of the beats, the artists who were so refreshing in thumbing their nose [*sic*] at the materialist preoccupation of post-war America." Jane Kramer suffered a similar rude surprise: "I'm not sure what, exactly, I had expected of Ginsberg, but I remember coming home from our first day together astounded by the fact that he had gone to the bank to deposit a check and then slipped into a local diner for some bacon and eggs." Imagine—Ginsberg with a bank account! Ginsberg handling *money*!

How can one explain the eagerness of such reputable members of the literary establishment to embrace the Ginsberg myth? Clearly, these writers and critics (not to mention the people who give out Guggenheims and major book awards) don't despise America; in some sense they *are* America, or at least its cultural representatives. But for some reason they are nonetheless comforted by the fact that somewhere in these states there is an Allen Ginsberg who *does* despise America— who has, in fact, spent most of his life thumbing his nose at everything they represent. One suspects that by admiring Ginsberg, many of these Establishment writers and critics are simply playing mind games with themselves. They know that they are bourgeois, and they know that being bourgeois is very unhip; applauding the revolutionary ravings of an Allen Ginsberg is one easy way to remove that bad old bourgeois stigma—for a brief interval, anyway—and to feel a bit like a madman oneself. What this amounts to, in other words, is radical politics as a form of entertainment—dissent-as-diversion. Those apologists for Ginsberg who are not attracted to the poet as a sort of polemical performance artist are, one supposes, simply living up to their notion of liberalism; for among many members of the intellectual and artistic classes in postmodern America, it is considered a sign of true enlightenment not only to tolerate but to celebrate the writer-as-radical—however bad his writing, however inane and irresponsible his radicalism. Few Americans have benefited more from such naïve, nonsensical "everybody-loves-a-radical" ways of thinking than Allen Ginsberg. What makes it all especially despicable is that although these writers and critics glorify Ginsberg for his supposed "candor" and "honesty," they cannot even be honest with themselves; for the only reason they are willing to cheer Ginsberg on is that they know very well that however much he propagandizes for the overthrow of the status quo, he will never achieve it. Applauding Ginsberg, in short, costs them nothing.

This is not to suggest, of course, that Ginsberg is harmless. Thanks to the support he has received from the literary establishment, he has been in a position to do—and *has* done—considerable damage to both American society and American literary culture. Besides being largely responsible for making drug use fashionable among this country's edu-cated young (the tragic results of which hardly need to be explained here), Ginsberg has helped to promulgate the ridiculous notion, now regarded as dogma by all too many young people in the United States, that a poem is whatever you pour, unedited, onto a page. He has been the model for countless aspiring writers to whom the distinctive char-acteristics of a good contemporary poet are his disdain for literary tra-dition, his refusal (and often inability) to write in conventional forms, his lack of attention to matters of craft, his vulgar exhibitionism, and his preoccupation with knee-jerk political dissent. Ginsberg is, in short, the father of a generation of Americans to whom "culture" is a word most often used immediately following the word "drug"—a genera-tion to whom poetry is something marked not by intelligence, sensi-tivity, and an imaginatively expressed apperception of natural order, but by incoherent egoism, fashionable anarchistic platitudes, and put-on paranoia. This is the legacy of Allen Ginsberg, the legacy to which Harper & Row has chosen to raise a substantial monument in the form of the *Collected Poems 1947-1980*. With all due respect to that venerable publishing firm, it is not a legacy to celebrate.

FEBRUARY 1985

SYLVIA PLATH AND THE POETRY OF CONFESSION

Back when America was careening from the Eisenhower era—the "tranquillized Fifties," as Robert Lowell called them—toward the Age of Aquarius, American poetry was undergoing a dramatic shift as well. A period of highly controlled, formal, and impersonal poetry, dominated by the likes of Richard Wilbur and Anthony Hecht, gave way with surprising rapidity to one of unrestrained, exceedingly personal free verse, often about extreme emotional states, by people like John Berryman, Anne Sexton, and W.D. Snodgrass. So revolutionary did these effusions seem at the time that the critic M.L. Rosenthal found it necessary, in a review of Lowell's 1959 volume *Life Studies*, to coin a new name for them: confessional poetry. To be sure, although the confessionalists tended to be more explicit about their divorces, orgasms, and such than poets of earlier generations, there was nothing fundamentally new about verse that took the poet's private life and feelings for its material; accordingly, though Rosenthal's term gained widespread currency, there were from the beginning those who objected to it as unnecessary and even denigrating, and who maintained that to label a poem in this fashion was to draw inordinate attention to its often sensational subject matter and thereby to slight its literary merit.

Of course, the literary merit of confessional poetry varied widely; and perhaps the most unfortunate effect of the term's broad acceptance was that, in the years after *Life Studies*, many a poet and critic began thinking of confessionalism as something that aspired not to aesthetic excellence so much as to the total honesty of the psychiatrist's couch or—well—the church confessional, and that should therefore be judged by the degree not of its artistry but of its candor. What was lost sight of, by many, was that for such poetry to be of literary importance it must, through a concentration not on universals but on intimate particulars, awaken in all sorts of readers (whose lives might, needless to say, be extremely different from the poet's in those intimate particulars) a sense of common humanity, a mature recognition that the essentials of one life are the essentials of all. If bad confessional poetry, in other words, appeals to a reader superficially, soliciting his attention and empathy on the basis of shared background or politics or neuroses or sexual tastes—or, alternatively, taking him out of himself in much the same way as a lurid, gossipy supermarket tabloid—the best confessional poetry introduces him to individuals with whose social lives and ideas he might not identify at all, but whose personal testimony nonetheless manages somehow to draw him inward. Like the poetry of Wilbur and Hecht, moreover, the best confessional poetry is marked by balance, control, a sense of form and rhythm, and even a degree of detachment.

Though, of all the confessional poets, Robert Lowell earned the most substantial literary reputation, it was Sylvia Plath who, in the years following the posthumous publication of her second poetry collection, *Ariel* (1965), became the movement's chief icon. Yet while Lowell's fame needs no more explanation than the aesthetic merit of his work, Plath's quick rise to near-legendary status owes much to other factors. For one thing, Plath's image of herself as a victim of two domineering men—her father, who died when she was a child, and her husband, the poet Ted Hughes, from whom she was separated at the time of her suicide in London in 1963--made her extremely useful to the women's movement. (Perhaps no one has more memorably expressed the feminist position on Plath than Robin Morgan, who in a poem entitled "Arraignment" accuses Hughes of Plath's murder and envisions a group of women entering his home, "disarm[ing] him of that weapon with which he tortured us, / stuff[ing] it into his mouth, sew[ing] up his poetasting lips around it, / and blow[ing] out his brains.") Meanwhile, Plath's proudly flaunted self-destructiveness, and her romantic image of herself as a sensitive genius in a brutal and indifferent world, made her a natural idol for many a young person in the throes of adolescent torment. (What, after all, could be more irresistible to a saturnine, self-romanticizing teenager than a passage like this, from Plath's college journal: "nothing is real, past or future, when you are alone in your room with the clock ticking loudly into the false cheerful brilliance of the electric light. And if you have no past or future, which, after all, is all that the present is made of, why then you may as well dispose of the empty shell of present and commit suicide.") I think it is safe to say that these two groups account for the majority of Plath's devotees, and I think it is also safe to say that neither group cherishes her work chiefly for its literary merit.

For such readers, patently, the real interest lies not in Plath's art but in her life. And her life—from her childhood in Jamaica Plain, Winthrop, and Wellesley, Massachusetts, through her undergraduate career at Smith and two Fulbright years at Cambridge, to marriage, mother-hood in Devon and London, the beginnings of literary prominence, marital estrangement, and self-slaughter at thirty—*is* fascinating, though not on the superficial level that such readers tend to focus upon. It is fascinating, rather, as a study in the nexus among art, ambition, and abnormal psychology, and, more specifically, in the formation of an author whose most anguished poems, composed only weeks be-fore her suicide, are widely considered to be the quintessence of con-fessional poetry. The story of this formation must begin with Plath's parents, Otto Emil Plath, an authoritarian, German-born entomology professor, and his submissive wife, Aurelia, a second-generation Aus-trian-American. Both parents shared a belief in discipline, a disincli-nation to make (or to allow their children to make) close friends, and—in the words of Anne Stevenson, author of the impressive recent biog-rapher *Bitter Fame: A Life of Sylvia Plath* (1989)—a "veneration for work";[1] together, they raised an obedient, overachieving daughter who found security (or, at least, a semblance thereof) in the structures and schedules of the classroom and whose sense of self-definition appears to have depended from an early age upon her ability not only to meet but to exceed the expectations of her parents and teachers. Otto's death when Sylvia was eight years old (she insisted, the next day, on going to school) led to a lifetime of rage at him, both for being a tyrant—which he may or may not have been, depending upon how one de-fines the word—and for abandoning her, and led also to a lifetime of tireless effort to surpass the goals set for her by the authority figures she erected in his place.

To be sure, as long as she was a student, Sylvia functioned splen-didly—or seemed to. At twenty, invoking an image that later provided the title for her autobiographical novel, she would write to a friend

---

[1]*Bitter Fame* is published by Houghton Mifflin at $19.95. The other biographies of Sylvia Plath mentioned in this piece are available in paperback: Edward Butscher's from Pocket Books at $9.95, and Linda Wagner-Martin's from St. Martin's at $12.95.

that "I've gone around for most of my life as in the rarefied atmosphere under a bell-jar, all according to schedule, four college years neatly quartered out in seasons." But the daughter of Otto Plath needed that bell-jar, needed the structure provided by school and college, needed her mother and teachers to set goals for her. If, as she admitted, she suffered from a "terrifying fear of mediocrity," it was because anything less than first-rate work might shatter her fragile sense of self; and if, furthermore, she referred to a college boyfriend as her "major man," one suspects that it was because she was unable to understand anything in life—whether it was dating, marriage, or the making of a literary career—except by analogy with schoolwork, choosing friends as if they were honors courses and competing for beaux as if they were class prizes.

Peter Davison, who met Plath when she was a star undergraduate at Smith, wrote later that she was "always trying to create an effect, to make an impression," and that she talked about her own life "as though she were describing a stranger to herself, a highly trained circus horse." Which, in a way, she was: for she would jump through almost any hoop to please those in authority. The images established by others formed the cornerstone of her identity: she embraced the role of All-Around Coed, for instance, with an inane fervor astonishing in one so intelligent ("I still can't believe I'm a SMITH GIRL!" she wrote her mother soon after entering college). She would stop at little to win academic distinction: friends complained of her manipulativeness, of how she used people to get ahead and discarded them callously when they were no longer needed.

Even in literature, image ruled. Plath writes her mother about course possibilities at Smith: "Imagine saying, 'Oh, yes, I studied writing under Auden!'...Honestly, Mum, I could just cry with happiness." If many a bard before and since has longed to forge the uncreated conscience of his race, Plath, in journal entries about her poetic aspirations, takes the tone of a high-school climber angling for a graduation medal, noting that "I must get philosophy in [i.e., into her poetry]. Until I do so I shall lag behind A[drienne] C[ecile] R[ich]." Her willingness to bow to both literary and subliterary totems is exemplified by her habit (as noted by Stevenson) "of talking of Wallace Stevens in one breath and *Mademoiselle* in the next." Just as she deliberately wrote insipid stories at Smith to win approval from the editors of *Seventeen*, in later years she was equally desperate for the approbation of *The New Yorker*, whose first acceptance of a Plath poem occasioned an almost frighteningly rhapsodic journal entry.

Writing was always important to Plath. Her father had been an author—of, among other things, a textbook on bumblebees—and had used the family supper table as a writing desk. Stevenson, who has a sensitivity to the motives behind Plath's writing that seems to have eluded earlier biographers, highlights a memory of Mrs. Plath's. During Sylvia's early childhood, at times when her mother was attending to Sylvia's infant brother, Warren, and wanted to prevent her daughter from trying to draw attention away from the boy, she encouraged the little girl to read letters in newspapers. Stevenson's savvy comment: "even at two and a half her daughter was being urged to treat negative emotion (jealousy of her brother) with words." This was something that Plath would do throughout her life. For her, writing became a way of asserting herself, of combating her deficient sense of identity. "Haunted by a fear of her own disintegration," Stevenson notes, Plath "kept herself together by defining herself, writing constantly about herself, so that everyone could see her there, fighting and conquering an outside world that forever threatened her frail being." No wonder, then, that, as Edward Butscher observes in his 1976 biography *Sylvia Plath: Method and Madness*, "getting published was not merely important [for Sylvia], it was everything": for her, seeing one's name in print was the ultimate proof not merely of acceptance but of existence.

The literary life, however, proved to differ so drastically from life at home, school, and college that Sylvia's first excursion from familiar territory into the *terra incognita* of publishing was almost her last. During the summer of 1953, she went to New York as an undergraduate editorial intern for *Mademoiselle*—an experience that exposed her for the first time to a chaotic, equivocal adult world in which the first thing authority figures demanded of her was simply that she be herself. And being herself, alas, was one thing that Sylvia was not good at. Butscher quotes Plath's editor at *Mademoiselle* as saying that she had "never found anyone so unspontaneous so consistently….[Sylvia was] all façade, too polite, too well-brought-up and well-disciplined." In any event, removed from the closed system of accomplishment and approval within which she had operated for so long, Plath became unstrung. Soon after returning home, she attempted suicide, and spent the next several months undergoing psychiatric treatment at McLean Hospital, which over the years would gain fame as the treatment center of choice for

Plath's fellow confessionalists Robert Lowell and Anne Sexton. (The whole experience, of course, is retold in fictional form in her 1963 novel *The Bell Jar*.)

What is one to make of this suicide attempt? Though they differ considerably in tone and emphasis, the interpretations of Plath's biographers are not as inconsistent as one might expect. Butscher's centers on the notion that Sylvia

> was three persons, three Sylvias in constant struggle with one another for domination: Sylvia the modest, bright, dutiful, hard-working, terribly efficient child of middle-class parents and strict Calvinist values who was grateful for the smallest favor; Sylvia the poet, the golden girl on campus who was destined for great things in the arts and glittered when she walked and talked; and Sylvia the bitch goddess, aching to go on a rampage of destruction against all those who possessed what she did not and who made her cater to their whims.

To complicate matters, Butscher speaks of additional, if secondary-level, Sylvias, whom he describes as "fitful shadows of the three main configurations." One was "Sylvia the sad little girl still hurting from the profound wound of her father's rejection and abandonment of her and wanting to crawl back into her mother's cave-safe womb"; another was "Sylvia the ordinary teenager who yearned for a kind husband, children, and a house like her grandmother's by the seashore."

Stevenson, for her part, settles for two Sylvias—a false outer self and a real inner self—and argues that the poet's self-destructiveness sprang from the yearning of her real self to kill her false self "so that her real one might burn free of it." This picture seems much simpler than Butscher's, but Stevenson also chooses to complicate things a bit by maintaining that

> Sylvia had long been confusing two very different battles within herself. One was with an artificial Sylvia, modeled on her mother, driven by ambitions she believed Aurelia harbored for her and ideas she thought Aurelia projected. This battle was occurring on a comparatively superficial level. Beneath it, so to speak, raged an altogether more serious war, where the "real" Sylvia—violent, subversive, moon-

struck, terribly angry—fought for her existence against a nice, bright, gifted American girl. This "real" self may have been created, and gone underground, at the time of her father's death in November 1940. It had emerged in August 1953, before her suicide attempt, and it remained in charge during the months of her slow recovery at McLean. It would be too simple to say that the nice girl wanted to live while the vengeful, deserted daughter wanted to die. But it was probably the case that Sylvia's powerful buried self was deadly in its determination to emerge at any cost.

To a considerable extent, of course, there is no need to choose between Butscher's and Stevenson's formulations: they are largely two ways of looking at the same thing. Stevenson's "'real' self," for instance, despite the drastic difference in tone, is essentially equivalent to Butscher's "bitch goddess."

At McLean, Plath underwent shock treatments and was told by her doctor that it was all right (a) to hate her parents and (b) to have sex. She claimed to have found all this liberating, and returned to Smith supposedly cured. (Certainly her success-oriented approach to literature returned, strong as ever. "Must get out SNAKE PIT," she confided to her journal in 1959, referring to Mary Jane Ward's bestseller. "There is an increasing market for mental hospital stuff. I am a fool if I don't relive it, recreate it.") But Butscher and Stevenson both believe that McLean did her more harm than good. Butscher's view is that Plath's doctor "resurrected the mask [i.e., her good-girl façade] and gave it "a firmer fit by letting Sylvia participate in the unearthing of the classic Electra complex." Stevenson focuses her attack not on the psychoanalysis but on the shock treatments, arguing that they critically weakened Plath's façade (which she, unlike Butscher, sees as protective and necessary). "It may be that she never really recovered" from the shock treatments, writes Stevenson, suggesting that they

> changed her personality permanently, stripping her of a psychological "skin" she could ill afford to lose. Attributable to her ECT is the unseen menace that haunts nearly everything she wrote, her conviction that the world, however benign in appearance, conceals dangerous animosity, directed particularly toward herself. Sylvia's psychotherapy almost certainly opened up the dimensions of her Freudian

psychodrama, revealing the figure of her lost, "drowned" father...whose death she could neither forgive nor allow herself to forget; psychotherapy also intensified the presence of her much-loved yet ultimately resented mother, whose double she had to be, for reasons of guilt or ego weakness, and to whom she was tied by a psychic umbilicus too nourishing to sever.

Though the "Freudian psychodrama" is at the center of both interpretations, Butscher places more emphasis on Otto Plath, stating on his first page that Sylvia's "central obsession from the beginning to the end of her life and career was her father," and interpreting that life in terms of a "frustrated will to power." Stevenson, by contrast, insists that "[i]t is not clear how much of Sylvia Plath's existential anxiety can be traced to her social isolation as a girl and how much to her father's death." But it seems to me that both factors are important: if Plath hadn't been sequestered from other children, her father might not have been such a god to her and his death might therefore not have affected her so catastrophically.

Though their interpretations can be seen as largely consistent in their essentials, Plath's biographers differ dramatically in style, method, and perspective. Butscher's book is a mixed—and rather overstuffed—bag. Though he offers a number of perceptive observations and sensitive close readings, he includes countless extraneous details (providing, among much else, the dates on which the Bradford High School honor roll was released). As he demonstrated in his recent biography of Conrad Aiken, moreover, Butscher has an inordinate faith in the ultimate power of psychiatric nomenclature to illuminate anything and everything in the realm of human behavior; to his mind, one gathers, understanding an individual is almost entirely a matter of attaching labels like "neurotic" and "schizophrenic" to that individual's behavior. Butscher assigns these labels with an alarming alacrity and a well-nigh palpable relish, and, quite often, on what would appear to be the slightest of evidence. (A sentence about the mother of one of Plath's boyfriends begins: "Sylvia's dislike of Mrs. Willard, which she of course repressed...." And: "Sylvia's attitude toward Davison himself remained distant, perhaps because of repressed guilt.") One comes away from Butscher's book thinking that there should be a psychological label to describe someone overly devoted to psychological labels. Linda Wagner-Martin, in *Sylvia Plath: A Biography* (1987), has the opposite problem: she performs too little analysis, whether literary or psychological. She treats Plath's suicidal depression almost as if it were a phenomenon unrelated to the poet's day-to-day psychology, and occasionally leaves the impression that she considers Plath to have been, most of the time, as sound of mind as anyone else—at least, that is, until Ted Hughes entered the picture in February 1956, barely more than two years after her suicide attempt.

It was Plath, then an exchange student in Cambridge, who engineered their meeting: one day she read some of his poems in a magazine—poems as intense and dark as she wanted hers to be, and *real* in a way hers were not—and decided immediately that she had to meet him. That same night, she introduced herself to him at a party, where (as she wrote in her journal) the tall, brooding, Lawrentian young Yorkshireman "kissed me bang smash on the mouth and ripped my hairband....And when he kissed my neck I bit him long and hard on the cheek, and when we came out of the room, blood was running down his face." And so they were married. Hughes was the first man Plath had ever known to whom she could imagine subordinating herself without difficulty—as both poet *and* woman—in the way that her mother had subordinated herself to her father. Months later, she would write that Hughes "fills somehow that huge, sad hole I felt in having no father"; for the meantime, however, in letters divulging her new love to her kith and kin, Plath described him as "a violent Adam," "the only man in the world who is my match," "the strongest man in the world...with a voice like the thunder of God," "a breaker of things and of people." What more could a girl want?

It was after her marriage to Hughes that Plath began to write the poems that eventually appeared in her first collection, *The Colossus and Other Poems* (1960). In their intellectual and stylistic sophistication, they represent a significant advance over the unremarkable verse of earlier years (fifty examples of which are relegated to the appendix of her 1981 *Collected Poems*). Like their predecessors, however, all but a few of these *Colossus* poems read like descriptive exercises—and with good reason, for many of them *were* exercises, written to order for Hughes, who when Plath could not come up with anything to write about, would arbitrarily select some object, animal, or location that was near at hand and assign her the task of composing a poem about it. Plath did her job competently, employing all the resources about which she had learned during her years of study. The metaphors and similes in these poems are often quite vivid (the cadavers in a dissecting room are "black as burnt turkey"), and her language frequently betrays the influence of some of the major poets of the day, notably Dylan Thomas. ("No doubt now in dream-propertied fall some moon-eyed, / Star-lucky sleight-of-hand man watched / My jilting lady squander coin, gold leaf stock ditches, / And the opulent air go studded with seed.") And an especially important influence is that of the early poems of Hughes himself, whose lean, grave, and austerely symbolic evocations of nature red in tooth and claw were in turn influenced both by his moor country upbringing and by his extensive reading in anthropology. To be sure, many of the natural phenomena Plath observed in Devon and described in the *Colossus* poems did apparently move her deeply; Hughes, in an essay published after her death, notes that "[h]er reactions to hurts in other people and animals, and even tiny desecrations of plant-life, were extremely violent."

As a rule, however, Plath's *Colossus* poems seem more skillful than inspired. They are, as Anne Sexton commented, "all in a cage (and not even her own cage at that)." Though Hughes presumably tried to suggest topics that would tap Plath's profoundest emotions, almost everything in these verses strikes one as forced, from the intensifying adjectives and adverbs to the patterns of alliteration and assonance. Stevenson notes that as a student Plath, copying words from a thesaurus onto flash cards, had built poems "word by word, like novel, intricate structures"; reading the *Colossus* poems one can almost see her poring over her Roget's. The irony, of course, is that while the bleak, often violent depictions of nature in many of these poems sincerely reflect Plath's own brittle sense of security in a brutal world—and though some of them plainly seek to draw on her complex, powerful emotions about her father's death—almost all of them have a labored quality, a manufactured intensity, their savage images striking one as overwrought and self-conscious, their rage and loathing coming across as false. Unlike Hughes's poems, moreover, the *Colossus* poems almost invariably fail to convey a personality, a point of view, let alone a passionate attachment to or understanding of the people, places, and things that they take as their subjects. Time and again, one feels that Plath is attempting to force greater significance upon scenes and situations than they really hold for her—to force it upon them, that is, rather than to discover it within them. While these poems, then, contain vivid images, striking lines, and pleasing configurations of sound, the poems don't work *qua* poems.

Not until 1960 did Plath begin to write the poems that would appear in *Ariel* (1965). The contrast with the most typical *Colossus* poems is remarkable: Plath's new poems are colloquial, muscular, unafraid of repeated words or odd line lengths or the first person singular pronoun. In the best of them, such as "Tulips," she breathes some life into her descriptive skills, and yokes wit to feeling. The poems that are almost universally acknowledged as Plath's strongest, however, and that more faithfully represent the characteristic style and tone of the book, are those like "Lady Lazarus" and "Daddy," in which, rather than trying to turn homely objects and settings into objective correlatives for her emotions, she embraces wholeheartedly the idea of poem as subjective (and often highly surrealistic) effusion. So frequently praised and ubiquitously quoted are these two poems that it almost seems at times as if Plath's entire reputation rests upon them. There is, to be sure, good reason why these two perverse and passionate poems should receive special attention, because nowhere else in her verse does Plath more bluntly address her most fundamental psychological conflicts. In both poems, Otto Plath and Hughes figure prominently, as does Plath's suicide attempt at twenty. The speaker of "Lady Lazarus," indeed, brags darkly about her prowess at such attempts ("I do it so it feels real"), marvels at her survival of her attempt at age twenty (and of a near-fatal "accident" a decade earlier), and addresses an unnamed tormentor as "Herr Doktor" and "Herr Enemy." She compares herself to an extermination-camp inmate, suggests that her victory over death makes her a "sort of walking miracle, my skin / Bright as a Nazi lampshade," and perceives that victory as securing for her a grotesque vengeance upon the opposite sex: "Beware / Beware. / Out of the ash / I rise with my red hair / And I eat men like air." Manifestly, we are meant to understand here that the speaker's experience with men (or with a certain man or men) was responsible in some way for her suicide attempt, and that her survival of it represents a miraculous triumph over them. "Daddy" draws on the same preoccupations and takes the same tone. Here the speaker refers to her father as a "black shoe" in which she has lived for thirty years and attributes her suicide attempt at twenty to a desire to "get back, back, back" to him. Spared death, she "made a model" of her father, a man with "a love of the rack and the screw," said "I do, I do," and lived with him for some time; but now she's murdered one man, in some sense, and by so doing has killed both: "Daddy, daddy, you bastard, I'm through."

These poems, along with the other most ferocious and famous poems in *Ariel*, flowed from Plath's pen in October and November of 1962, sometimes at the rate of more than one a day, soon after Hughes became involved with one Assia Wevill (who would become his second wife) and separated from Sylvia. Anne Sexton referred to these as "hate poems," and that they most certainly are, expressing time and again, in very similar terms, the most extreme and blatant of emotions, invariably aimed in the same direction. "Lady Lazarus" and "Daddy" are the most arresting of Plath's verses, and it is their hate, really, that makes them so—a hate communicated, often quite effectively, by way of natural language and rhythms, manically insistent repetitions and multiple rhymes, and sensational, often surrealistic images, all of which are designed to grab the attention of the most impassive reader. And grab the reader they do—on the first reading, anyway. In fact, this ability to capture the attention of readers—and even, at times, to shock them—helps explain why the *Ariel* poems, nearly three decades after Plath's death, remain a force to be reckoned with. And yet what ultimately makes the poems memorable is less the hate that they express, or the blunt language that they employ, or even the inexcusable, hyperbolic metaphors that equate the poet's suffering with that of prisoners in Nazi concentration camps, than it is the fact that all these elements combine to convey, with vigor and directness, the extreme emotional state of a highly unbalanced, self-destructive woman.

It might be argued that there is a degree of aesthetic value in such an accomplishment. But the more one reads these poems, the more one realizes that beneath the thoroughly convincing representation of profound psychological disturbance—behind, that is, Plath's shrill, deranged voice—there is precious little human dimension. It has been argued that the *Ariel* poems are saved by their irony, but Plath's irony is facile and, moreover, always directed at others—never at the poet herself. She is capable of quipping sardonically, in "Lady Lazarus," "Do not think I underestimate your great concern"; but it doesn't occur to her, in her utter self-absorption, that her own dearth of concern for others might itself be a worthwhile target for irony. It is hardly an exaggeration, I think, to say that the chief problem with these poems is their constricting, claustrophobic solipsism. Compared to Plath, even

Lowell—himself no tower of sanity or selflessness—seems quite actively involved with mankind, what with his numerous *Life Studies* poems about relatives, fellow poets, Czar Lepke, and the like; alongside Plath, even Berryman, with his often puerile attitude toward romantic relationships, comes off in the *The Dream Songs* as painting a nuanced, mature picture of love, sex, and marriage, and as providing, in his Henry persona, a model of proper authorial distance.

This is not to say that poems of self-scrunity, as such, are necessarily bad, but rather to say that in the *Ariel* poems the self is so absorbed in itself that there appears to be little possibility of enlightenment, of discovery; to read them is to feel that their goal is not self-knowledge but self-display, a morbid absorption in and superficial celebration of the poet's own sensitivity and imagined victimhood. Throughout the poems, the world beyond the poet is seen consistently as despotic, destructive; yet she seems not to realize to what degree she is in fact her own destroyer, her own victim. The biographies of Plath make it clear that these poems are the work of a psychologically complicated and fascinating woman; but the poems themselves are, by comparison to the woman, woefully simple and—after the first reading—progressively less interesting.

In virtually every regard, then—in range of theme and invention, in complexity of feeling and structure, and in sophistication of style and technique—the *Ariel* poems are less impressive than the best so-called confessional poems of Lowell and Berryman. Certainly they are smaller in vision. Butscher quotes Irving Howe as complaining that "in none of the essays devoted to praising Sylvia Plath have I found a coherent statement as to the nature, let alone the value, of her vision." Butscher's reply is that "Sylvia did indeed have a vision: it was to plunge into the depths of self, the dark side of the mind's moon, and hope to touch the bottom of degradation and sorrow." Putting aside for the moment Butscher's mixed metaphor, what can one say about this defense? It can hardly be denied, of course, that the *Ariel* poems take such a plunge as Butscher describes. But is it correct, really, to say that they evince a "vision," in the sense that Howe plainly means? Yes, poems like "Daddy" and "Lady Lazarus" pierce the poet's surface as sharply as a surgeon's knife; but the incisions are narrow, the innards unilluminated, the result (for the reader) not a laying bare of the intricate workings of a self and soul but a raw, lurid exhibition of private agony and bloodletting. To put it a bit differently, the *Ariel* poems provide a startlingly naked glimpse into the mind of a deeply disturbed woman; but a glimpse, however naked, is not necessarily the same as an insight, nor revelation necessarily the same as art.

Wagner-Martin would have us believe that the *Ariel* poems were a triumphant apotheosis—the inevitable consequence of Plath's rejection of Hughes's artificial little assignments and of her "com[ing] into her own as a woman"—and that Plath's suicide, which came soon after the completion of the poems, was essentially the result of Hughes's betrayal and withdrawal from her life. There is, however, nothing triumphant about the *Ariel* poems; far from reflecting a newly proud and independent womanhood, these poems, with their mad, unbridled hostility, plainly express the poet's sudden helplessness at the withdrawal of the protective canopy underneath which she had erected her entire life as wife, mother, and author. In Hughes, Plath had found a father-substitute, and his departure from her life served to release, after decades of suppression, an eight-year-old's exorbitant fear and fury at her father's death. Plath's sudden outpouring of thoroughly unfettered *Ariel* poems, in other words, represents less a breakthrough than a breakdown; for the poems show little sign of control over or understanding of her rage, let alone mature insight into the human complexities that produced it.

Nor can one blame Plath's suicide on Hughes. Her original attraction to him, after all, had much to do with his status as a "breaker of things and of people"; plainly, the self-destructive part of her had craved such a consort, and if he had never existed, she would have had to invent him. While in some sense, moreover, Hughes may indeed have failed Plath, in her mind the failure was doubtless her own: their marriage was, so to speak, the big postgraduate honors course that she could not pass. For just as she had aimed for excellence in school and college, she had also set herself the goal of being an A-plus wife and mother; what she could not accept was that one cannot conduct one's personal life as if they gave prizes for it, any more than one can write serious fiction or poetry while aiming, above all, to please some editor, whether at *Mademoiselle* or *The New Yorker*.

If Wagner-Martin renders Plath's marriage as something of a feminist domestic tragedy—with Hughes as the villain—Stevenson seems eager to prove that, in W.S. Merwin's words, "there was something in Sylvia of a cat suspended over water, but it was not Ted who had put her there or kept her there." The sharp contrast between the views of

Wagner-Martin and Stevenson in this matter is reflected in their respective prefaces: whereas Wagner-Martin claims, in her preface, that her unwillingness to alter her manuscript in accordance with demands by Olwyn Hughes (Ted Hughes's sister and Plath's literary executor) led to a denial of permission to quote at length from Plath's works, Stevenson thanks both Ted and Olwyn for all sorts of assistance (and, by the way, quotes extensively from the poems). Stevenson appears to go out of her way to catalogue Plath's offenses, especially against her husband (for instance, her rudeness to his humble Yorkshire mother), and to point out the various ways in which she considers him to have been a positive force in Plath's life. Some of the latter observations— for example, the argument that Hughes made the *Ariel* poems possible by persuading Plath "to be true to her gift rather than to her ambition"—seem eminently valid. But Stevenson's tone is too often prosecutorial, and sometimes one feels as if she is copying out a list of the Hughes camp's long-nursed grievances. Plath's *Ariel* poems, we are reminded, have caused great pain "to the innocent victims of her pen"; after Plath's separation from Hughes, her frequent reference to her lawyer's instructions "helped to make negotiations...difficult." To hear Stevenson tell it, Plath was always the one making things "difficult": time and again, the biographer leaves the impression that Hughes was a perfectly balanced and responsible man dealing as honorably as he could with a demented woman. Perhaps most astonishing of all is Stevenson's implication that the attraction between Hughes and Assia might never have developed into an affair had Plath reacted less hysterically upon noticing it—that, in short, Plath, not Hughes, was responsible for his adultery. All this is most unfortunate, for, such matters aside, Stevenson's is by far the most perceptive and well-written of the Plath biographies; until Hughes steps onstage, Stevenson's picture of Plath rings truer, on the whole, than anyone else's.

What did the poet herself make of *Ariel*? It is interesting to note that Plath—presumably sensing that the *Ariel* poems' crude, superficial confessionalism was a deficiency, while not knowing precisely how to mitigate it in presenting her verses to an audience—described "Daddy" and "Lady Lazarus" to A.A. Alvarez as "some light verse." Likewise, in an apparent attempt to put over the idea that the voice in these poems was not hers but rather that of an imaginary persona, she told an interviewer that "Daddy" had as its speaker a girl whose father was actually a Nazi and whose mother "very possibly [was] part Jewish." Such addenda, of course, if seriously accepted by a reader, rob a poem like "Daddy" of what force it has, a force that derives precisely from the speaker's mad, unreasoning hate; yet the fact that Plath felt compelled to describe the poem in this fashion suggests that, even though she was incapable of eliminating the poem's weakness, she was astute enough to recognize where that weakness lay. It is only to be hoped that, in the next century, such astuteness in regard to Plath's work will be less rare than it is today among poetry readers, and that future generations will be less inclined to confuse questions of aesthetic significance with those of political serviceability or personal idolatry.

FEBRUARY 1991

RICHARD WILBUR'S DIFFICULT BALANCE

Some people were born to be poets; Richard Wilbur was born to be a Poet Laureate. Forget, if you wish, his distinguished good looks, his genteel manner in television interviews, the mellifluous yet authoritative voice in which he recites his work at poetry readings, and the tasteful tie and blazer he sports on the dust-jacket photograph of his recently published *New and Collected Poems*.[1] He is, leaving all such things aside, the outstanding contemporary American instance of the type of poet who writes in strict forms about traditional themes, and whose poems—making, as they do, frequent, appropriate, and instructive use of meter, rhyme, imagery, alliteration, assonance, and even the occasional classical allusion—could serve as models in a textbook of prosody. (Poetry, Wilbur has written, "should include every resource which can be made to work.") If one wanted to compile a résumé for such a figure, one could not do better than Wilbur's: service in the European theater during world War II, a B.A. from Amherst, an M.A. from Harvard, faculty positions at Harvard, Wellesley, Wesleyan, and Smith, regular appearances in *The New Yorker*, a Bollingen, a Pulitzer, a Prix de Rome, a National Book Award, and—yes—a term as Poet Laureate.

If Allen Ginsberg represents one end of the postwar American poetry spectrum, Wilbur represents the other. While Ginsberg sees chaos and conspiracy in the world around him, Wilbur sees beauty and order; while Ginsberg conceives of poetry as an opportunity to vent defiant, anarchic, and often apocalyptic passions, Wilbur sees it as a means of articulating, with great poise and restraint, a sanguinary devotion to the enduring forms of nature and civilization. Wilbur's poetry is as self-effacing and mannerly as Ginsberg's is conceited and coarse; if Ginsberg may be described as wildly uneven, Wilbur is extraordinar-

---

[1] *New and Collected Poems*, by Richard Wilbur; Harcourt Brace Jovanovich, $27.95.

ily—well—*even*, a creator of poems that, while not uniformly arrest-
ing, have, since his widely hailed debut at age twenty-six with *The
Beautiful Changes* (1947), evinced a remarkable consistency in thematic
concerns, in general tonal and stylistic features, and in aesthetic profi-
ciency. (Astonished though one is to learn that Wilbur eliminated noth-
ing from his *oeuvre* in compiling his *New and Collected Poems*, one is
even more astonished to discover, upon reading the book, that there
are no poems in it that cry out to be eliminated.) If Ginsberg's diction
is colloquial and frequently lewd, Wilbur's ranges from the elegantly
plain to the ornately esoteric ("The walls / Are battlemented still....
Now all this proud royaume / Is Veniced"), and his lines are often
crowded with the sort of sophisticated wordplay ("Lambs are con-
strained to bound"; "habitude, if not pure / Hebetude") in which
Ginsberg would never indulge. While Ginsberg, moreover, has spent
his career raucously attacking the American political and corporate
establishment, Wilbur (while acknowledging what he has called "the
full discordancy of modern life and consciousness") has written po-
ems celebrating such bourgeois achievements as the construction of a
new railway station in Rome. It should not come as a surprise, then,
that critics who have applauded Ginsberg for the recklessness of his
life and art have chided Wilbur for "playing it safe."

For all his prominence, however, Wilbur seems nearly marginal.
We do not, after all, live in the Age of Wilbur. He began his career as
one of his generation's two most celebrated American poets, along with
his fellow formalist Robert Lowell (who was four years his senior); but
while Lowell transformed himself into a confessional poet—helping,
at the same time, to transform American poetry as well—Wilbur con-
tinued to write the sort of formal verse (though his lines did become
slightly plainer and simpler over the years) that came to seem old hat.
Many poets who have studied in creative-writing programs in recent
decades have learned to regard meter and rhyme as ways of strait-
jacketing the soul; self-styled political poets, for their part, tend to re-
gard them as tools of the System. Of the post-World War II American
poets, the one whose name is most familiar to high school students
today is not Wilbur or even Ginsberg but probably Sylvia Plath, whose
angry, intense poems, in the nearly three decades since her death, have
helped to convince countless young people that it is not a poet's rea-
son, wit, or equipoise that matters, but his willingness to serve up raw,
rude personal testimony. During Wilbur's middle age, indeed, the ca-

reers of Plath, Lowell, and their fellow confessional poets—among them John Berryman and Anne Sexton—constituted, for many romantic-minded readers, a veritable guidebook to the ways *real* poets thought and wrote and conducted their lives; to these readers, such a poet as Wilbur could only be considered out of step.

No one is more conscious of this state of affairs than Wilbur himself. Or such, at least, is the conclusion one comes to after reading Wilbur's poem "Cottage Street, 1953," in which he draws quite neatly the contrast between his own approach to poetry and that symbolized by Plath. The poem recalls a meeting between the two poets under the auspices of Wilbur's mother-in-law, Edna Ward. With ironic matter-of-factness, Wilbur recalls that he was present "to exemplify / The published poet in his happiness, / Thus cheering Sylvia, who has wished to die." Realizing that he was in a hopeless position, however, he compares himself to a "stupid life-guard" and Plath to "a girl / Who, far from shore, has been immensely drowned."

> How large is her refusal; and how slight
> The genteel chat whereby we recommend
> Life, of a summer afternoon, despite
> The brewing dusk which hints that it may end.

The poem's development offers a top-notch example of Wilbur's characteristic rhetorical shrewdness. For he faces a tremendous strategic problem: how to refute the prevalent romantic view of Plath and of her manic confessionalism without seeming insensitive or self-aggrandizing. Wilbur resolves the problem beautifully. Having disparaged himself for his own purported stupidity and for the slightness of his conversation (thus allowing us to see that he doesn't share Plath's notorious egocentrism), and having appeared, in his use of such words as *immensely* and *large*, almost to echo the admirers of Plath who would magnify her art by citing the magnitude of psychological difficulties, he deftly, and in thoroughly un-Plathlike fashion, steps offstage and proceeds to contrast Plath not with himself but—surprise!—with their elderly, unrenowned hostess:

> And Edna Ward shall die in fifteen years,
> After her eight-and-eighty summers of
> Such grace and courage as permit no tears,

The thin hand reaching out, the last word *love*,

Outliving Sylvia who, condemned to die,
Shall study for a decade, as she must,
To state at last her brilliant negative
In poems free and helpless and unjust.

"Grace," "courage," "love": these are among Wilbur's chief values, and by noting gently that Edna Ward exhibited all of them he reminds us that Plath, despite her brilliance, was not famous for exhibiting any of them. While Wilbur acknowledges that brilliance, and admits Plath's constitutional incapacity to employ it otherwise than in the way she did—that is, in poems whose form is "free" and substance "negative"—he nonetheless, in his poem's perfectly chosen last word, makes clear his conviction that her work is morally objectionable, not just because it wronged her loved ones but because it undervalues life. Implicit in Wilbur's tacit criticism of Plath's egoism and negativity, of course, is a reminder of how modest and affirmative his own poetry is. Yet the important thing is that this reminder is implicit; if "Cottage Street, 1953" makes it point effectively—and, to my mind, it most assuredly does—it is largely because Wilbur has the good sense to realize that his mother-in-law belongs in the poem and that references to the qualities of his own poetry do not. A reader who recalls Plath's famously fierce "Daddy," in which she equates her father with a Nazi, can only admire Wilbur's ability, in this poem, to submit a devastating indictment of Plath even as he maintains a seemingly compassionate tone toward her.

This poem's indulgence in personal recollection—and, especially, its naming of identifiable individuals other than the poet—makes it a rarity for Wilbur. Far more common, in his *oeuvre*, are poems of decorous, dexterous, and thoroughly detached observation. Wilbur has a wonderful gift for seeing familiar sights afresh. Consider his landscape description in "Winter Spring": "A script of trees before the hill / Spells cold, with laden serifs." Or his rendering of midday in "Sunlight Is Imagination": "Now swings / The sky to noon, and mysteries run / To cover." Or, from "Marginalia," this analogy of losing consciousness to plunging downward in an elevator: "Descending into sleep (as when the night-lift / Falls past a brilliant floor), we glimpse a sublime / Décor and hear, perhaps, a complete music."

Yet some sights in Wilbur's poetry become a bit *too* familiar; it is easy to imagine that a reader of the *New and Collected Poems*—especially of Wilbur's earlier poems—might come to lose his appetite for yet another poem about leaves, however dazzlingly conceived, or for yet another poem that elaborately personifies the wind and sea. Invariably, Wilbur's poems on such themes are carefully observed and brilliantly evocative; but when read one after the other, rather than encountered individually in magazines, they can become almost monotonous. Likewise, in such works as his verse definition of "Shame" ("a cramped little state with no foreign policy, / Save to be thought inoffensive..."), his meditations on such things as the ampersand ("perhaps a lyre / Or a clef wrung wry in tuning untunable tunes, / Or a knot..."), and the letter "O" ("The idle dayseye, the laborious wheel..."), his translations of ancient riddles, and his ballade composed in whimsical response to a fifteenth-century contest sponsored by the Duke of Orléans, Wilbur seems a bit too eager to impress the reader with his cleverness and virtuosity. Reading these poems, one does not long for more recklessness on Wilbur's part; but one does find oneself thinking that a major poet should be more urgent and passionate, more patently *inspired*, than this.

One wishes especially, when reading such poems, that they had more human beings in them. Even when people do crop up in Wilbur's verse, they often seem, in some way, to be subordinated to nature. The speaker in "Looking into History," for instance, tries to feel some sense of connection with five Civil War soldiers in a Matthew Brady photograph, but fails because their appearance is dated (they "[s]how but the postures men affected then / And the hermit faces of a finished year"); it is only when he recognizes some background trees as sycamores that the picture comes alive for him. "Superiorities," meanwhile, contends that men who brave an ocean storm on an open deck are "far superior" to those "[h]uddled below with wives and buddies, / Comforting, caring, sharing pills, / Prayers and other proper studies." And in the lovely poem "Boy at the Window," a boy weeps to see his snowman "standing all alone / In dusk and cold," while the snowman, wiser and stronger of spirit, weeps not for himself but "[f]or the child at the bright pane surrounded by / Such warmth, such light, such love, and so much fear." Reading these poems, one finds oneself troubled by the suspicion that the poet harbors a readier sympathy for the natural world than for humankind, and regards nature as purer, finer, somehow more authentic than man.

Too often, moreover, when Wilbur does write ostensibly intimate poems, he unsettles and disappoints by abandoning personal particulars in favor of grandiloquent rhetoric. In "Pardon," for example, the speaker remembers the death of his pet dog when he was ten years old, and one has the impression at first that Wilbur is genuinely purging a deep-seated, decades-old trauma. Yet the poem shifts abruptly from its unpretentiously rendered childhood anecdote to grown-up oratory: "I dreamt the past was never past redeeming: / But whether this was false or honest dreaming / I beg death's pardon now." Though beautifully accomplished, the poem ultimately seems less a sincere purgation than a calculated mining of the poet's past for material, a dredging up and manipulation of memory toward a premeditated conclusion. Randall Jarrell makes a similar observation about Wilbur's poem "Death of a Toad," commenting that when one reads the description of the toad, whose leg has been severed by a power mower, one feels at first that the toad "is real, all right."

> But when you read on, when Mr. Wilbur says that the toad "dies / Toward some deep monotone, / Toward misted and ebullient seas / And cooling shores, toward lost Amphibia's emperies," you think with a surge of irritation and dismay, "So it was all only an excuse for some poetry."

Considerably more admirable are those poems in which Wilbur puts his faculties at the service of a recognizable human emotion or idea. "Potato," for instance, opens with several strong lines of description: "Cut open raw, it looses a cool clean stench, / Mineral acid seeping from pores of prest meal; / It is like breathing a strangely refreshing tomb." Yet Wilbur goes beyond this description to observe how the potato—"simple as soil," "blind and a common brown"—meant for many, in wartime, the difference between life and death: "'It was potatoes saved us, they kept us alive.' / Then they had something to say akin to praise / For the mean earth-apples, too common to cherish or steal." In the end, then, "Potato" is not merely an exercise in description but a poignant meditation upon the fact that something as plain and disesteemed as a potato could, in the time of adversity, save people's lives and come to be treasured. In similar fashion, "First Snow in Alsace" begins by describing a snowfall: "The snow came down last night like moths / Burned on the moon." Yet the poem, set at an army post, is not simply about snow but about how snow can conceal the scars of combat, prompt moments of human communion ("the new air white and fine" causing people to "[t]rade glances quick with shared surprise"), and, for a time, restore even a soldier's childhood innocence: "The night guard coming from his post / Ten first-snows back in thought, walks slow / And warms him with a boyish boast: / He was the first to see the snow." In both "Potato" and "First Snow in Alsace," people who have been engaged in killing each other, destroying property, and blasting craters in fields are reminded of the restorative powers of even the homeliest natural phenomena.

I have cited these poems, both from *The Beautiful Changes*, because they are relatively uncomplicated early examples of Wilbur's ability to turn his descriptive talents to the production not just of competent landscape studies or still lives but of sensitive reflections on the moral and metaphysical dimensions of man's relation to the universe. A more substantial instance of this ability is the striking poem "Love Calls Us to the Things of this World" (the title is from Saint Augustine), wherein the speaker, awakening to see laundry fluttering on a clothesline outside his bedroom window and imagining that the bed sheets and blouses are inhabited by angels, "rising together in calm swells / Of halcyon feeling," finds himself momentarily shrinking from the thought of the day ahead. He thinks: "Oh, let there be nothing on earth but laundry, / Nothing but rosy hands in the rising steam / And clear dances done in the sight of heaven." Yet at the end of the poem he accepts life's imperfection, the soul having descended, so to speak, into his waking body and decreed that the clothes be brought down "from their ruddy gallows" and placed on "the backs of thieves": "Let lovers go fresh and sweet to be undone, / And the heaviest nuns walk in a pure floating / Of dark habits, / keeping their difficult balance."

Part of the strength of this poem derives from the freshness and seeming spontaneity of its conceit (no artful reworking of conventional images here), and part stems from the vigor of Wilbur's language, which is looser and simpler than in many of his poems. But the most important thing about the poem is the speaker's ultimate rejection of the impulse to spurn or subordinate the human. To be sure, the poem begins with an attraction, on the part of the speaker, to the idea of clothes that are immaculate and that will never be worn by people (an attraction that might, the reader reflects, be shared by the speaker of "Looking into History" or "Superiorities"); but the poem moves beyond this momentary enchantment to a desire for human contact and an awareness that, in order to live and love in the world, one must face the daily accretion of soil and stain, both literal and figurative, and must remain stable and stouthearted in the face of madness, misfortune, and iniquity. The poem is exquisite, and one of its more remarkable qualities is the difficult balance that Wilbur manages to sustain between the temporal and the spiritual, between impetuousness and design, between a natural-seeming expression of feeling, which never deviates into sentimentality, and an unaffected contemplativeness, which never strays into a confining, impersonal pseudo-intellectuality.

It might be said, then, that Wilbur's finest poems are those in which his extraordinary craft is animated by a touch of enthusiasm or awe in the presence of what Wilbur, in the title of his third collection, refers to as "the things of this world," and in which he addresses what he has called "the proper relation between the tangible world and the intuitions of the spirit." What is amazing about his poems is that, earthbound as they can seem when he is proffering a meticulous description of a tree or an eggplant, Wilbur is capable of raising such images to a Platonic plane with what appears to be the greatest of ease. He speaks in one poem of "the mystery of things that are," and this mystery is one with which his best work communicates a lively fascination. He realizes, too, that in order to keep alive one's appreciation of this mystery, it helps to get a new slant on the familiar. He underlines the importance of fresh perspectives in a winsome poem called "Digging for China," whose speaker remembers a childhood attempt to reach China—"a place where nothing was the same"—by digging a backyard hole. Naturally, he fails—and yet he succeeds as well, for, having finally grown tired of hanging upside down into the hole and "looking into darkness,"

> I stood up in a place I had forgotten,
> Blinking and staggering while the earth went round
> And showed me silver barns, the fields dozing
> In palls of brightness, patens growing and gone
> In the tides of leaves, and the whole sky china blue.
> Until I got my balance back again
> All that I saw was China, China, China.

An even lovelier poem, the sonnet "Praise in Summer" (written when Wilbur was in his twenties), likewise contemplates the need to turn the world upside down, as it were, in order to recognize its wonders:

> Obscurely yet most surely called to praise,

As sometimes summer calls us all, I said
The hills are heavens full of branching ways
Where star-nosed moles fly overhead the dead;
I said the trees are mines in air, I said
See how the sparrow burrows in the sky!
And then I wondered why this mad *instead*
Perverts our praise to uncreation, why
Such savor's in this wrenching things awry.
Does sense so stale that it must needs derange
The world to know it? to a praiseful eye
Should it not be enough of fresh and strange
That trees grow green, and moles can course in clay,
And sparrows sweep the ceiling of our day?

The answer, of course, is that it *should* be enough that trees grow green and moles can course in clay, but it isn't. Human nature is such that what we marvel at one day, we take for granted the next. And this, to Wilbur's mind, is why we need poets: to wrench things awry for us a bit, to "derange" the world time and again so that we may know and marvel at it anew. And also so that we may join him in praise: for Wilbur is a Christian poet who finds holiness not only in the ordinary world but (as his respectful references to Edna Ward might suggest) in the life humbly and patiently lived, and in work steadily and conscientiously performed. "A Plain Song for Comadre" pays tribute to a woman who, "[f]or love and in all weather," has for seventeen years "kept the church / Of San Ysidro," sweeping and scrubbing and polishing, "[a]nd seen no visions but the thing done right / From the clay porch / To the white altar." Yet sometimes "the early sun / Shines as she flings the scrubwater out, with a crash / Of grimy rainbows, and the stained suds flash / Like angel-feathers." If Wilbur's poems are so consistently well made, it is largely, one gathers, a consequence of his devotion to the ideal of honest, diligent labor represented by the woman in this poem. A corollary to this devotion is Wilbur's antipathy toward shoddy merchandise, the manufacture of which he characterizes as nothing less than a dishonorable act. In the poem "Junk," for instance, the speaker sees a badly made axe in his neighbor's ashcan, and pronounces it "hell's handiwork" "The heart winces / For junk and gimcrack," Wilbur writes, "for jerrybuilt things / And the men who make them / for a little money, Bartering pride / like the bought boxer / Who pulls his punches, / or the paid-off jockey / Who in the home stretch / holds in his horse."

Like many of Wilbur's poems, "Junk" can be read, of course, as a commentary upon the writing of poetry. One is reminded of Wallace Stevens, who continually wrote about poetry by writing about other things, and whose preoccupation with reality and imagination Wilbur shares. If Wilbur is a smaller figure than Stevens, it is partly because he puts his ample expertise at the service of a smaller vision, rejecting the temptation to write long, cerebral, coldly passionate poems in the manner of Stevens's "The Idea of Order at Key West"—in which one can practically feel the intellect groping its way, from insight to insight, toward a fuller understanding of itself and its context—and preferring instead to create less ambitious, smaller-scale lyrics that are impeccably shaped objects, rich in echo and epigram. Wilbur's attitude toward reality and imagination is, furthermore, different from that of Stevens. Convinced of the non-existence of God, Stevens envisions the poet as a substitute deity, a maker of supreme fictions; as he writes in "The Man with the Blue Guitar," "Poetry / Exceeding music must take the place / Of empty heaven and its hymns, / Ourselves in poetry must take their place." Many of Wilbur's poems, like Stevens's, make witty comparisons between divine and literary creation. But to Wilbur it is the deity who is the supreme maker; the poet, in his view, is a lesser creator, charged with the task of awakening his readers' appreciation of the world in which they find themselves, reminding them of the need to live with the sometimes dispiriting facts of life while never losing sight of its rewards. If Stevens, at his strongest and most characteristic, is grandly remote and oracular, Wilbur, for all his commanding wit, radiates, at his best, a quietly appealing humility. Yet his most exceptional poems are enriching in a way that is very rare in our time; surely there are few living American poets whom one would place before him.

SPRING 1991

"AVEC UN ÉLÉGANCE GRAVE ET LENTE": THE POETRY OF DONALD JUSTICE

On the American poetry scene these days, the only thing rarer than a fine poem is a negative review. Yet reviewers of Donald Justice—who has written some of the finest poems of our time—have often been not only negative but surprisingly hostile. Calvin Bedient, assessing Justice's 1979 *Selected Poems* in the *Sewanee Review*, described him as "an uncertain talent that has not been turned to much account." Wrote Gerald Burns: "*Selected Poems* reads like a very thin Tennessee Williams—little poems about obscure Florida people and architecture.... As a *career* his, though honest, does not quite make the ascent to poet from racket." And Alan Hollinghurst, appraising the same volume for *The New Statesman*, complained that Justice's poems lacked "vitality... urgency... colour and surprise," that they suffered from "lassitude," "a weary passivity," and "a habit of elegance which cushions meaning," and that the poems, "formal but *fatigués*,... create the impression of getting great job-satisfaction without actually doing much work."

What has Justice done to deserve such attacks? Well, he was imprudent enough to begin writing poetry at a time when the Beats were at the height of their popularity and when many readers were unable to see, in his low-decibel traditional verses, anything but an absence of the "vitality and urgency" that they admired in the Beats and in the recognized non-Beat camps of the day: the Black Mountain poets, the New York poets, the confessionalists. Nor did Justice necessarily appeal to the academic admirers of his fellow traditionalists Richard Wilbur and Anthony Hecht; for it was, and is, in the nature of a certain kind of postwar academic critic to feel very much at home with the poems of a Wilbur or a Hecht—many of which seem, by their intricacy and impersonality, to solicit critical attention—while feeling uncomfortable with a plainer and more personal poet such as Justice, to whose sublime and delicate music such a critic may well be deaf and to whose conspicuous and compassionate interest in people's lives and feelings he may be constitutionally incapable of responding except by reflexively and defensively dismissing the poet as sentimental.

Nor has Justice gone out of his way to endear himself to the poetry world. While many poets of his generation have distributed enthusiastic blurbs like Halloween candy, Justice has committed the grave error of saying what he really thinks about his contemporaries. In the interviews collected in *Platonic Scripts,* he scorns the vapid, glibly romantic *idées reçues*—"*Nature is good… government is bad….* [poetry is] *good for the soul*"—that form the contemporary Poets' Code; in a time when poets pay more attention to politics than to aesthetics, Justice declares that poems should not be didactic; in a time when one of the major prerequisites for an American poet seems to be an endless capacity for self-righteousness about his vocation, Justice observes stingingly that poets today "act as if they believe there were something almost sacred in the name of *poet.*" While other poets hesitate to step on toes, he refers bluntly to the "so-called poetry of the Beats," dismisses terms like Olson's "organic form" as so much pretentious blather, and is "appalled" by poets who brag about moving young people to tears, saying that such things are "morally wrong" and that poems should properly be "objects of contemplation." Ultimately, the dismissive reviews of Justice's *Selected Poems* are a reflection not of any failing in the work itself but of the manifold moral and cultural failures of an age in which it has been Justice's peculiar honor to be the apotheosis of the unfashionable poet.

Justice's poetry is, it must be said, understated. (He once agreed with an interviewer who remarked that "understatement is to you, practically, a religious principle.") But it does not lack vitality and urgency. What it lacks, rather, are the vulgarity, hysteria, conceit, anarchism, and morbid fixation on madness, drug abuse, grubby sex, and the like that characterize the most extreme Beat and confessional verses and that some readers, alas, equate with vitality and urgency. The urgency of Justice's finest verse is of a thoroughly different order. It is the urgency of deeply controlled feeling about loss and mortality, about the inevitable passing of time and the irrevocable pastness of the past. And while a table of contents that includes such titles as "Sonnet to My Father" and "Tales from a Family Album" and "On the Death of Friends in Childhood" might well strike many a critic as a firm guarantee of a poet's sentimental leanings, Justice's poems are delivered from sentimentality by honest feeling, careful observation, and fresh expression—and by a seemingly stoical resistance to grief. In an age of emotional exhibitionism, Justice rises, time and again, beyond his particular circumstances toward the level of tragic myth. To be sure, many a line from a Justice poem might sound maudlin in other contexts, such as the closing line of one poem: "But already the silent world is lost forever." Yet such a line is maudlin only if it strikes one as false and easy, as having been forced onto a poem rather than having grown out of it. Such is not the case here. On the contrary, the poem positions the reader perfectly for the line, so that it seems true and heartfelt, the inevitable terminus of a very real emotional journey; the poem, in other words, captures with extraordinary precision the tenor of a mind and the rhythms of its thought, and the concluding line comes as the natural reflection on all that has gone before.

It is, to be sure, misleading to speak of Justice's poetry as if it were all of an ilk. His first book, *The Summer Anniversaries* (1960), established the intelligent, composed, and pensive voice with which it is most frequently identified—and established, too, his independence from the accepted poetic modes of the day. For many of his contemporaries, notably his teacher Robert Lowell (whose pivotal *Life Studies* had appeared a year earlier), the breakthrough to using autobiographical material in poetry was coupled with a break with form, a rejection of virtuosity as the ultimate poetic value in favor of sincerity; but though many of the poems of *The Summer Anniversaries* patently concern people and places that are of great personal significance for the poet, none of the poems is in free verse; Justice refuses to join Lowell, Snodgrass, et al., in emphasizing sincerity at the expense of formal artistry ("Now that is simply not the kind of poetry I write," he once told an interviewer apropos of Snodgrass). Justice distinguishes between writing about himself, which he tries not to do ("I've always felt it was an author's privilege to leave himself out if he chose," he has said, citing with approval Eliot's now-unfashionable theory of the impersonality of the poet), and writing about people and places that have been important to him. Indeed, though his family and friends proliferate in *The Summer Anniversaries*, Justice attempts to restrict himself to the role of observer and chronicler; and when he *is* present (or, more accurately, when there is an *I* in the poem that one tends to identify with the poet), he does his best to objectify his experience, to place mythic elements in the foreground and to exclude the irrelevantly personal.

Justice has said that poems, at their best, transform a subjective experience into an object not unlike a treasured family photograph, an object that preserves a precious moment for readers of present and future generations as well as for the later refreshment of one's own memory, and he has expressed the hope that "some of the poems I've tried to write were treasurable in the sense that I *know* a photograph can be treasurable. Treasured." ("I like it," he has said of his poem "First Death," "because it records something otherwise lost.") Rather than write subjective, anti-literary, free-verse effusions in the manner of the Beats or the confessional poets, then, he seeks to create timeless, unapologetically literary objects—*made* objects ("I think of poetry as making things")—that preserve selected encounters, observations, and reflections. More than one interviewer has seemed bemused by Justice's traditional bent, by his habit of constant revision and his devotion to established forms; one interlocutor even asked if he ever felt the need to "free yourself from this restraint or control?" Justice's reply: "I don't think I feel the need to let go. Nowadays people may think of that as a flaw. I don't." Critics routinely praise the "courage" of an Allen Ginsberg; but there is more pluck in Justice's firm "I don't" than in all of Ginsberg's *Collected Poems*.

Formal though they are, though, Justice's poems do not recall what he has called the "hard, thuddy iambic pentameter line" of Lowell's dense, formal verses in *Lord Weary's Castle* any more than they recall the more relaxed free-verse rhythms of *Life Studies* and after. Rather, his poems exhibit a limpid lyricism, a gracefully flowing music; trained in his early years as a pianist, Justice himself makes reference to the musicality of his poems, prefacing his volume *The Sunset Maker* with several tempo markings from major modern composers: "Sec et musclé" (Milhaud), "Avec un élégance grave et lente" (Debussy), "broadly singing" (Carl Ruggles). Justice's most representative poems do tend to display these characteristics: they are dry, muscular, elegant, grave, and slow (one might mark them *piano* and *andante*), with a fine, smooth, and austere melodic line, as it were, reminiscent of many a modern French composer.

Justice is, moreover, a poet who, even as he pays tribute to the radiant possibilities of human experience and the natural world, associates unalloyed wonder and joy at these things with the innocence of childhood, characterizing life, in "To a Ten-Months' Child," as a state that one enters from a "remote... kingdom" and, in "Song," describing a glorious dawn with awe and saying that "all that day / Was a fairy tale / Told once in a while / To a good child." To Justice, growing up is a matter of recognizing that life is not the perfectly sublime affair that one may have believed it to be in one's early years: in "The Snowfall," he refers to the "terrible whispers of our elders / Falling softly about our ears / In childhood, never believed till now." The innocence of joy and the terror of knowledge are also themes of the memorable "Sonnet," in which the innocents are not children but Adam and Eve:

> The walls surrounding them they never saw;
> The angels, often. Angels were as common
> As birds or butterflies, but looked more human.
> As long as the wings were furled, they felt no awe.
> Beasts, too, were friendly. They could find no flaw
> In all of Eden: this was the first omen.
> The second was the dream which woke the woman:
> She dreamed she saw the lion sharpen his claw.
> As for the fruit, it had no taste at all.
> They had been warned of what was bound to happen;
> They had been told of something called the world;
> They had been told and told about the wall.
> They saw it now; the gate was standing open.
> As they advanced, the giant wings unfurled.

Both in its vision of man and his world and in its means of imparting that vision, this poem is vintage Justice. With one stunning final image—an image that is all the more effective for the quiet simplicity with which it is presented and for the omission of any reference to Adam and Eve's reaction to it—Justice makes one feel the terror of the knowledge that comes to all of us when we move beyond the complacent bliss of childhood: the knowledge of our mortality, of the world's imperfection, and of our separation from the awful, winged majesty of God and His angels. The irony here, a familiar one in Justice's poetry, is that though the happiness of a child, or of Adam and Eve in Eden, is untainted by the adult's bitter knowledge, it is only in that state of knowledge, born of loss, that the irreclaimable joys of creation can be fully appreciated.

A reader of "Sonnet"—and of the numerous poems in which Justice refers to saints and angels and heaven—might be excused for concluding that he is a religious man. Yet though he was raised as a Southern Baptist, Justice has said that he lost his faith as a young man. "I don't believe in the spiritual," he declared flatly in a 1975 interview. "You know, there is a power in the obvious. That which is hidden I can't see." Yet in these secular times, Justice has a remarkable sense of what one cannot describe as anything other than the sanctity of the quotidian (he writes in "Unflushed Urinals" of "The acceptingness of the washbowls in which we absolve ourselves!"); to him, sin and grace manifestly remain vital concepts, and life, for all its deficiencies, has its moments of sublime radiance.

His second and third collections find Justice in territory that one doesn't necessarily think of as his own. These are books of experiment, in which Justice wanders afield from the disciplined forms and elegant musicality of his debut volume to try his hand at blank verse, syllabic verse, and free verse. Both books also contain a number of verses inspired not by personal experience but by the work of other poets; since such poems as "The Telephone of the Muse" suggest that Justice felt abandoned by the Muse, one presumes that imitation and experiment were his way of keeping busy at his craft during her supposed absence. And indeed, though they are far from unaccomplished, the poems of *Night Light* (1967, revised 1981) and *Departures* (1973) represent something of a loosening, a thinning out, a descent into the fine but familiar from the serene and singular music of *The Summer Anniversaries*.

The models for the poems in these two volumes come from all over the map. There is a group of "American Sketches" written in imitation of William Carlos Williams (to whom they are dedicated); there is a poem entitled "After a Phrase Abandoned by Wallace Stevens"; and there are several elliptical, portentous poems, with wildly different line lengths and short, clipped sentences, in imitation of Lorca and Vallejo. These poems, surreal and often deliberately disjointed and fragmentary, are quite admirable of their kind, but they strike one as being very much against the grain of Justice's own native music, which typically casts its spell by means of clear and coherent imagery, elegant and supple language, and delicate variations on the iambic line. Justice's Lorcaesque poems, by contrast, tend to be metrically varied, too expressionistic, and too loosely conversational in tone and rhythm to satisfy fully a lover of Justice's best work; conversely, there may well be too much in these poems of Justice to satisfy fully an ardent admirer of Vallejo or Lorca. The bottom line is that Justice's gently responsive sensibility and strong sense of control don't really lend themselves to the jagged rhythm and erratic thought patterns of a Lorca-type poem; to read Justice's Lorcaesque poems, in fact, is a bit like hearing an opera singer do *Showboat*: it's not great opera and it's not great Kern. Nonetheless, both books show a side of Justice that one cannot but admire: namely, Justice the astute and sensitive student of his art, who has never lost the essential humility, and the willingness to learn, of the earnest young painter copying an Old Master canvas in a museum.

In the new poems included in the Pulitzer Prize-winning *Selected Poems* (1979), Justice leaves Lorca and company behind and writes in what might be described as a sharper, more seasoned version of his *Summer Anniversaries* voice. Indeed, one of the finest poems in *Selected Poems* is "Summer Anniversaries," a heavily revised version of "Anniversaries," the opening poem in his debut volume. The poem charts the speaker's growth from a ten-year-old who, though wheelchair-bound, gloried in the bounties of the earth—

> I thought it absurd
> For anyone to have quarreled
> Ever with such a world—
> O brave new planet!—
> And with such music in it.

—to a twenty-one-year-old who sees a balloon "veer crazily off" and compares it to himself, "All sense of direction gone"; to a thirty-year-old who watches

> Through the window beside my desk
> Boys deep in the summer dusk
> Of Iowa, at catch,
> Toss, back and forth, their ball.
> Shadows begin to fall.
> The colors of the day
> Resolve into one dull,
> Unremarkable gray,
> And I watch them go in from their play,
> Small figures of some myth
> Now, vanishing up the path.

With extraordinary concision and effectiveness, the poem captures in turn the child's naive enthusiasm about life, the adolescent's confusion and romantic self-pity, and the adult's preoccupation with the prosaic business of existence, which, when he notices young people at all, causes him to think of them—and of his own younger self—as if they were part of some half-remembered legend. The poem is a splendid example, too, of Justice's genius for distancing: as much as any sonnet of Donne, it represents not an indulgence of personality but an escape from personality's restrictions; the specifics take on a symbolic weight, and one does not find oneself wondering (as one does with much confessional verse) about the poem's degree of autobiographical accuracy. (The poem is reminiscent, in particular, of Donne's "A Valediction: Of Weeping," in which three round objects—a ball, a tear, and the earth—are connected imagistically; here, similarly, Justice connects three round objects—a wheelchair wheel, a balloon, a ball—all emblems of the cycle of life.)

The Sunset Maker (1987) displays the music of Justice's poetry at its most elevated and austerely beautiful. In this volume, which contains not only twenty-four poems but two stories and a prose memoir, Justice is more than ever a poet of things past and passing, lamenting his incalculable losses and tendering his most cherished memories—mostly of his parents and of his childhood piano teachers—in language replete with allusions to the fragile beauty of music, to the ever-shifting light and shadow of nature ("The sun seems not to move at all, / Till it has moved on"), and to the tenets and typology of Christianity, with its assurance of an eternal and omnipresent deity (after rain, Justice writes in "Mule Team and Poster," the sun returns, "Invisible, but everywhere present, / and of a special brightness, like God"). The echoes of Stevens are more multitudinous than ever: if a line like "Mordancies of the armchair!" (in "Tremayne") brings to mind "Sunday Morning," a reference to "the last shade perhaps in all of Alabama" (in "Mule Team and Poster") recalls "Anecdote of the Jar." As in earlier volumes, Justice takes somber note of the contrast between the real world and childhood's fanciful view of it, noting that the world a child dreams "is the world we run to from the world."

For the Justice of *The Sunset Maker*, the chief function of art is to preserve what little it can of life. Perhaps the book's two most idiosyncratic items are the poem "The Sunset Maker" and its pendant, a story entitled "Little Elegy for Cello and Piano"; both works concern the speaker's friendship with a recently deceased and largely forgotten composer named Eugene Bestor, who survives only in a six-note phrase remembered by the speaker:

> The hard early years of study, those still,
> Sequestered mornings in the studio,

The perfect ear, the technique, the great gift
All have come down to this one ghostly phrase.
And soon nobody will recall the sound
These six notes made once or that there were six.

It is to be hoped—not only for his sake, but for that of American po-
etry—that Justice's work will be more widely remembered than that
of the fictional Bestor. Certainly there is more than one phrase in
Justice's verse—plain, unaffected, and gently apocalyptic—that haunts
the memory: "Darkness they rise from, darkness they sink back to-
wards." "It is the lurch and slur the world makes, turning." "To shine
is to be surrounded by the dark." Justice is the poet of a world in which
loss is ubiquitous, sorrow inevitable, and adult joy always bittersweet;
a world in which the genuinely heroic act, for a literary artist, is not to
thrash about uncontrollably, raising a manic and ugly din, but to fash-
ion a body of work whose beauty and poise and gravity in the face of
life's abominations may, one trusts, help it to endure.

WINTER/SPRING 1992

HELEN VENDLER, POETRY CRITIC

Helen Vendler is the colossus of contemporary American poetry criticism. In an age when the audience for poetry has dwindled down to a precious few, and when only a handful of general magazines even bother to publish poetry criticism at all, Vendler looms hugely over the ever-shrinking landscape. No one in America today has more power to create or to damage a poetic reputation. Even T.S. Eliot, in his time, did not exercise so considerable an influence upon American poetry as Vendler does at present. Simply to list her credits is to describe a degree of visibility, in relation to her peers, that no other critic of poetry has ever enjoyed in America. She is, first of all, the poetry critic—not simply *a* poetry critic, but *the* poetry critic—for the two most prominent journals in this country that feature poetry criticism, *The New Yorker* and *The New York Review of Books*. (She has also reviewed poetry frequently for *The New York Times Book Review*.) She is the William R. Kenan Professor of English and American Literature and Language at Harvard University, and is the centerpiece of the American poetry criticism list of that university's highly prestigious press. Not only does Harvard publish her books of criticism, furthermore—among them *On Extended Wings: Wallace Stevens's Longer Poems* (1969) and *Part of Nature, Part of Us* (1980)—but when it came time to compile the *Harvard Book of Contemporary Poetry* (1985), it was Vendler who was signed up as editor. Likewise, when the producers of the Public Broadcasting System's recent "Voices and Visions" series about American poetry wanted a series consultant, it was Vendler whom they hired.

In short, Helen Vendler has assumed a singular, and a truly remarkable, place in the criticism of our time: she is that individual to whom a disproportionate number of the most influential editors, publishers, and producers automatically turn when the subject is poetry. In some of the most august editorial chambers in the country, to think of poetry criticism is to think of Helen Vendler. How, one may wonder, has this peculiar state of affairs come to pass? The answer is, I think, an involved, interesting, and instructive one. To begin with, it seems to me that Vendler's prominence is directly related to the unprominent position of the art in which she specializes. Let me explain. A generation ago, it was a frequent complaint among poets that the typical educated American was ignorant of and uncomfortable with poetry; nowadays, alas, even the typical professional literary person—whether writer, editor, or publisher—is rather ignorant of and uncomfortable with it. And even those relative few who retain a lively interest in and affection for the poetry they learned in school don't know much about the poetry that is being written today. Yet, every so often, such people must make decisions relating to contemporary poetry—decisions about review assignments, editing assignments, consulting assignments. In such an atmosphere, name recognition is all-important. An editor who knows little about contemporary poetry is unlikely to know much about those who do know something about it. He will tend, therefore, to go with a known quantity. What this means is that he will be likely to go for established poets and for big-name English professors at major universities.

But how many poets or academics of this description are actually capable of writing for a general audience about poetry these days? Not many. In growing numbers, the academics are irredeemable ideologues, straitjacketed by perverse conceptions of the nature of literary art (not to mention incapable, by and large, of producing readable prose). How about the poets? After all, since the Renaissance it has been poets who have made the most estimable contributions to poetry criticism. One thinks, for instance, of Sidney's "Apologie for Poetry," Dryden's "Essay of Dramatic Poesie," Wordsworth's "Preface to *Lyrical Ballads*," Coleridge's *Biographia Literaria*, Arnold's *The Function of Criticism*, and Eliot's "Tradition and the Individual Talent." As recently as a generation or two ago, the major American poetry critics—such people as Randall Jarrell, Delmore Schwartz, and Louise Bogan—were also distinguished poets. But things have changed dramatically. In our time, most American poets seem largely incapable of thinking critically or of writing competent, intelligent prose about their art; when they do want to say something, whether about their poetry or someone else's, or indeed about the art of poetry in general, they tend to do so in interviews or published "conversations." And what they have to say often proves to be astonishingly banal.

That leaves a relatively small number of suitable candidates for the role of American poetry critic to the multitudes—among them Helen

Vendler. One factor in her favor is that she is not an ideological critic but, by her own description, an "aesthetic critic." Quite admirably, she believes that a poem should be judged according to its value as a work of art and not according to its fealty to one or another set of extraliterary principles; she has little affection for poststructuralsim, and even less for Marxist and feminist criticism. What's more, she writes (for an academic) a relatively lucid prose, relatively free of jargon. All this make her more welcome in the pages of a general-audience magazine like *The New Yorker* than many a member of the Derrida-era professoriat would be. Beyond these factors, however, the fact that Vendler, rather than some other, similarly qualified individual, came to be the most known of known quantities in her field is doubtless largely a matter of chance. What is certainly undeniable is that for some time now, the main factor in Vendler's rising visibility has been the snowball effect; every time an editor, producer, or publisher taps her for another high-visibility assignment, the known quantity becomes even more of a known quantity. The problem of whom to retain for the occasional poetry assignment no longer exists. Thus does Vendler's fame feed both upon itself and upon the very obscurity of the art she criticizes.

As I have suggested, Vendler's role is doubly unprecedented. Not only is she the first American poetry critic to occupy so prominent a position in relation to her fellow American poetry critics; she is also the first non-poet to ascend to the first rank of those American critics who focus primarily on poetry. To my mind, the fact that Vendler does not write poetry (or, at least, does not publish it) is of considerable significance. For while such arts as music, painting, and architecture have often drawn their finest critics from the ranks of non-practitioners (e.g., Ruskin on art, Shaw on music), poetry is different. Poetry shares a medium—the written word—with criticism. Accordingly it is a good deal easier to imagine, say, a person attracted to the writing of art criticism but not to the practice of painting, than it is to imagine a person who is at once (a) drawn by his talents and his passions to the vocation of a writer and (b) genuinely and deeply responsive to the music of poetry but who (c) has no gift for, or attraction to, the composition of poetry. Indeed, it is here, I believe, that Vendler's principal deficiency as a poetry critic lies. For, deeply responsive though she may think herself to be to the music of poetry, the simple fact is that she lacks the one thing a critic of poetry cannot do without: a good ear. She has no taste. She is as likely to praise a bad poet as a good one, as likely to quote with admiration an awful stanza as an exquisite one.

The poets whom she has attempted to add to the contemporary canon—notably Michael Blumenthal, Louise Glück, Jorie Graham, Charles Wright—are conspicuously and uniformly bad. Vendler claims to be an admirer of Wallace Stevens, but the positively awful taste she has displayed in regard to poets who are her age or younger suggests that if Stevens were Vendler's exact contemporary, and had started publishing his poetry about the same time she started reviewing, she would never have paid any attention to him.

To be sure, Vendler has her virtues as a critic. Above all, she is good at taking poems apart and putting them back together again. Her explications of specific poems can be thoughtful and intelligent; she has a fine analytical mind, and can discuss with conviction and authority everything from a poem's sound patterns to its structure of meaning. I share her desire, moreover, that students be familiar with "a hoard of poems in the mother tongue, known so intimately that they become nature, not art," and her worry that "the classical and English canon may be slipping out of our grasp, to be replaced by a modern canon of unrhymed and translated pieces." (Yet who has done more than Vendler herself to canonize contemporary poets with no gift for form?) I think she's right to be uncomfortable when she sees a critic (Robert Hass) who can't read Polish writing about a poet (Czeslaw Milosz) whose work is written in Polish. (Yet Vendler herself, who is equally unfamiliar with Polish, has herself written an essay about Milosz.) She is correct, too, in criticizing Dave Smith for the inconsistent tone of his essays, which are by turns chatty, hortatory, and academic—and yet she seems incapable of recognizing that much of Smith's poetry, which she purports to admire, shares this same lack of tonal control. Which brings us back to her bad ear. Manifestly, Vendler's failure to perceive the deficiencies of Dave Smith's work is a vivid illustration of her inability to *hear* poems—and in an age when most other academic critics can't hear them either, and when otherwise thoughtful and sensitive editors feel too intimidated by and unfamiliar with the subject of contemporary poetry to question her critical judgments, Vendler (to speak bluntly) manages to get away with this cardinal failing. Her power is such, moreover, that whereas there is probably no one else whose name stirs up so much heated negative comment when poets and poetry readers come together, virtually nobody has ever dared to air his misgivings about her in print. More than one poet-critic known to gripe loudly about Vendler at literary gatherings has been known, upon being assigned a book of hers for review, to turn around and praise her fulsomely.

That Vendler's ear for poetry has not improved in recent years is made painfully manifest in her newest book of critical essays, *The Music of What Happens: Poems, Poets, Critics.*[1] Reprinted not only from *The New Yorker, The New York Review of Books,* and *The New York Times Book Review,* but also from the *Times Literary Supplement, The New Republic, Salmagundi, Poetry, Critical Inquiry,* the *Bulletin of the American Academy of Arts and Sciences,* and two academic anthologies entitled *What Is a Poet* and *Textual Analysis: Some Readers Reading,* the thirty-six essays collected in this volume are concerned with the work of some thirty or so poets (from Wordsworth and Keats to Ashbery and Ginsberg), with a handful of critics (e.g., Bloom, Barthes, Robert Hass), and with—to quote the title of the opening essay—"The Function of Criticism." It is while reading this very first essay that one begins to entertain grave doubts about the nature of Vendler's responsiveness to poetry. For throughout much of this essay, Vendler's emphasis is not upon the question of the value and purpose of literary criticism (which is, of course, an ancient and valid area of inquiry) but upon the question of the critic's reason for writing criticism—the "motives for criticism," as she puts it. The best Vendler can offer, by way of an answer to this question, is a frightening list of possible "motives" which she herself describes as "discreditable (if entirely human) ones… envy, competition, defensive reaction-formation, poem-seeking, and spiritual parricide."

Not a word does Vendler breathe about what, to my way of thinking, should be the foremost motive of any true poetry critic: a love of poetry so strong that one feels compelled to voice one's reverence for the art's most gifted practitioners, compelled to separate the wheat from the chaff, compelled to express one's outrage whenever mediocrity is celebrated and beauty ignored, compelled to understand as well as possible what it is, in a given poem or body of work, that stirs one's soul. Vendler's failure even to give this motive a place on her list seems to me a mark of the thoroughly academic nature of her sensibility: to Vendler, plainly, criticism is not a calling but a profession. That this is indeed the case would seem to be supported by the revelation, in her

---

[1] *The Music of What Happens: Poems, Poets, Critics,* by Helen Vendler; Harvard University Press, $29.50.

1980 collection *Part of Nature, Part of Us,* that her career as the nation's number-one poetry reviewer began as the result of "a lucky chance": "*The Massachusetts Review* annually commissioned someone to consider the year's work in poetry, and in 1966, when I was teaching at Smith, I was asked to take it on." Before that assignment, Vendler's writing had been of the most routine professorial sort: she had published a few academic essays and a scholarly book entitled *Yeats's Vision and the Later Plays* (which, by the way, she does not include in the dust jacket list of her "major books"). Her turn to poetry reviewing seems quite clearly to have been less a case of a woman following her heart than of a professor making a savvy career decision.

Vendler is, indeed, an academic through and through. One often gets the impression that poetry is unimaginable, for her, outside the English department. Certainly it doesn't occur to her that someone other than a university professor might read or write about poetry. ("[A] greater problem for those of us writing commentary on poetry," she maintains in one essay, "is the American compulsion to 'communicate,' intensified by our profession as teachers.") Her sensibility is essentially that of an academic clubbist. Though not a practitioner of literary theory, she nonetheless speaks of herself—and of everyone who writes criticism—as having "been put on notice, by the salutary sternness of literary theory, that our terms are likely to be interrogated." Likewise, though she disagrees strongly with the assumptions of feminist criticism, she quite blithely accepts the feminists' politicization of literature and their affirmative-action approach to the making of canons and reading lists as part of the academic status quo. ("As Sexton passes into the anthologies," she writes, "the more obviously 'feminist' poems will no doubt be chosen, and there is no reason not to represent them.")

Like a true academic, moreover, Vendler writes as if poetry without criticism is as valueless as an LP without a record player. The first chapter of *The Music of What Happens* concludes with the assertion that "[n]o art work describes itself," that "[o]nly by repeated casts of the critical imagination is the world around us, including the world of literature, finally described and thereby made known, familiar, and integral." (To be sure, the book's introduction ends with the seemingly more modest observation that "the art of poetry is far larger than any single description of its powers"—yet would it even occur to a truly modest critic to make such a self-evident pronouncement?) Likewise, citing some lines in which Ashbery "asks for a new criticism, deriving from the actual current practice of poetry," Vendler comments: "it is as though poetry were incompetent to see its own image until reflected in the discursive analysis of criticism. And it may be so." One gets the impression, in fact, that what Vendler admires so much about the work of Ashbery is that it cries out for a critic to explain it; implicit in her feverish analyses of Ashbery's poems is the notion that it is the very need for elaborate analysis that makes them deserving of attention. Vendler is strangely indifferent to the question of their actual merit, writing that "[n]o line, or… passage, or… inception or conclusion from Ashbery [can] be isolated as good or bad." When she wants to give an Ashbery poem, "Songs without Words," the ultimate accolade, she doesn't say that it's a great poem; rather—in a sentence that speaks volumes about the academic mentality—she writes, "Surely this poem will be anthologized."

Yet the fact is that Vendler has a much better understanding of how anthologies are put together than of how poems are put together. Whenever she tries to think like a poet, she comes off as surprisingly obtuse. Quoting four lines from a Seamus Heaney poem ("They were two-faced and accommodating. / And seed, breed and generation still / they are holding on, every bit / as pious and exacting and demeaned."), she comments that "[t]he five adjectives and the four nouns in this passage… cannot be budged (as anyone can discover by trying to put 'two-faced' in the place of 'demeaned,' or 'generation' in the place of 'seed')." Isn't this true, however, of any good poem—that to rearrange the words would be to weaken it? Indeed, the very concept is a cliché; but one has the feeling that for Vendler it's a fresh insight. She reveals this same obtuseness in an essay on Milosz, writing that the "linguistic versatility" demonstrated by Milosz and other poets—"combining words that have never been combined before, but doing it with a sublime justice and propriety, so that the effect is not a jolt but a confirmation of rightness—gives perhaps the highest pleasure that poetry exists to confer." Then there's a review of Amy Clampitt, wherein Vendler observes that "it is not just visual 'rendering' (by whatever analogies) that makes visual poetry 'work.' Poetic diction has its own laws that must be satisfied along with the requirements of the eye. Poetic diction demands that words be linked one to the other so that it will seem that they 'grew' there by natural affinity." Well, yes, and yes again. But don't we know these things already? Isn't Vendler restating, in these sentences, the very definition of poetry: a sublimely pleasing, truly original, but thoroughly right-sounding combination of words? For Vendler to make such observations as if they were provocative and recherché, and not central to the practice of any first-rate poetry critic, is surpassingly odd—but, alas, entirely characteristic of her.

Even when she turns from poetry to life, Vendler makes remarks that seem astonishingly fatuous. Reviewing Stephen Spender's journals, she suggests that his interest in politics may be "a result of his partly Jewish descent on his mother's side" (where does that leave Auden and C. Day Lewis?) and comments that "Spender always remains a neophyte in life, capable of being hurt, shocked, surprised; when David Hockney tells him in 1983 about someone who had died of AIDS, he writes, 'All this seems inexplicable, baffling, terrifying'— adjectives we associate more with adolescence than with the eighth decade of life." Vendler's implication here is that fear, confusion, and terror are things we leave behind when we become adults; on the contrary, one suspects that it is the rare person in the eighth decade of life who is not at least as familiar with these emotions as the average adolescent. In adolescence, after all, we think ourselves immortal, and it is only as we age that we begin to grow wary and fearful of death; if we appear more serene than adolescents, it is not because we have shaken off fear, confusion, and terror, but because we have learned how to behave in public. In any event, it seems to me that a writer (of whatever age) who is no longer capable of being hurt, shocked, and surprised isn't going to be writing much of value. Vendler exhibits this same distrust of emotion when she complains about Robert Hass's poetry criticism that he is "sometimes, to my tastes, sentimental... too fond of coercive words: *terrible, painful, wonderful, terrifying, agonizing, mysterious, shocking, raw, seductive.* Such words not only say 'Admire with me'; they are shopworn."

As a rule, Vendler's own professions of enthusiasm don't convince. When she speaks, for instance, of "[Ted] Hughes's remarkable adjectival gift," or of "Ginsberg's exuberant comedy," her praise seems *pro forma*; when she says that Merrill's rhymes "are the cleverest the language has seen since Byron," it sounds hyperbolic. Her characterization of various poems as "shocking" rings especially false, if only because shock, for whatever reason, is one of the few types of emotional response to literature with which academic criticism seems wholly comfortable. Vendler refers, for example, to the "shock" with which one reads Sylvia Plath's comparison of worms to "sticky pearls," and says of a line in a pallid Ashbery poem that "[a] middle-aged American reads 'Hardly anything grows here' with immediate recognition, a shock not possible any longer from the mention in a contemporary poem of 'stubble plains' or 'the barrenness / Of the fertile thing that can attain no more.'" Vendler indulges, too, in what may be called the "no one else" formula:

> [A]t his best [Michael Blumenthal] sounds like no one else. I cannot think of anyone in America just now who might write as Blumenthal does about looking down on one's house after death.

> There has not been for a long time a poem that sees us so helplessly in love with the rhythms of victimage and brutality, societal, sexual, and religious [as does Amy Clampitt's "Easter Morning"].

> [Ammons is] the first poet to have the conceptual equipment... to think this way. [That is, to reject anthropomorphism.]

Writing about Clampitt, Vendler says: "If Iowa has not had a poet before, it has one now"; in her essay on Ammons, she observes similarly that "[b]ecause of his coming, the literary map has changed, and as we have the New York of Whitman, and the Pennsylvania of Stevens, and the Massachusetts of Lowell, we now have the North Carolina of Ammons. There are states, many of them, still without a genius of the place. In celebrating the sixtieth birthday of A.R. Ammons, one celebrates as well the birth of North Carolina in his poems."

What Vendler values most in poetry is that which she describes, in "The Function of Criticism," as "the beautiful bizarre, not the beautiful familiar." To her, a given poet's most characteristic work—that is, his quirkiest, goofiest, most "original" work—is by definition his best. It follows from this that the quirkier a poet is, the better—and that when Vendler calls Merrill, for instance, "firmly idiosyncratic," she means it as the highest of praise. At the beginning of *On Extended Wings*, Vendler announces that her "touchstone has been the best Stevens could do—those poems in which he seems most himself, most original." Not surprisingly, this aesthetic criterion makes for some peculiar critical judgments: Vendler claims to prefer Stevens's "The Auroras of Autumn" to "Sunday Morning," and states that "the poem characteristic of Ginsberg, the one he writes over and over, is seen in its purest form in the faultless 'American Change.'" In "Looking for Poetry in America," she argues that "[e]very perception, without exception, does indeed, in poetry, need to be rendered strikingly." One would be more comfortable with this formulation if it had made use of a different adverb: *eloquently*, perhaps, or *beautifully*. Though it can serve as a synonym for either of these words, *strikingly* also connotes shock value, noticeably for its own sake. (And we've already seen, of course, how prominently the word *shock* figures in Vendler's criticism.)

In the first paragraph of a piece on Stevens, Vendler makes it clear that, to her mind, greatness and conservatism are antithetical: "Was Stevens good? great? original? or reactionary? conservative? derivative?" Later in the same essay, speaking of Milton Bates's book *Wallace Stevens: A Mythology of Self*, she expresses the hope

> that a new generation of readers, brought up on this book, will recognize that the naïve canards about Stevens—that he was a heartless hedonist, an ivory-tower poet insensitive to social distress, a cold, over-cerebral aesthete, a poetic conservative, and so on—are all untrue. Bates's book rightly describes Stevens as a poet constantly enlarging the self...aware of social unrest, passionately concerned with the accurate way of conceiving the artist's role in the social order, evaluating the claims of Marx, Freud, and Nietzsche long before most members of his generation....

Patently, Vendler is eager here to rescue Stevens from the charge of being a conservative, formalist intellectual, and to help create an image of him as a "socially concerned" individual who was, by the standards of the American academy in the 1980s, politically correct. Vendler seems utterly unaware that it is Stevens's intellectuality, his rigid aesthetic, and his powerful sense of form—not his politics, whatever they may have been—that make him a great poet.

A corollary of Vendler's love of the idiosyncratic is that she likes poets whose poems run away from them, and dislikes poets who know what they want to say and how they want to say it. Taking note of a description of clouds in a poem by Charles Wright, Vendler comments admiringly that whereas "in another poet visual accuracy would be uppermost, in Wright the *symbolic arbitrariness of the mind's play* [my emphasis] is at least as visible in such passages as any putative appearance of the clouds." She is equally impressed by Dave Smith, whose poems she finds "torrential, impatient, exasperated," and whose language is "theatrical, even melodramatic." She is less happy with Adrienne Rich and Philip Levine, whose poems aren't as "wayward" as Vendler would like: "They [Rich and Levine] are stern, even grim, ringmasters to their poems, and the hoops, once aligned at the beginning, remain in place in the poem for all subsequent jumps. One longs, reading Rich's *A Wild Patience Has Taken Me This Far* (1981), for the poem to take an unexpected byway, to reverse itself, to mock itself, to question its own premises, to allow itself, in short, some aesthetic independence." It is, needless to say, a most questionable notion that a poem should be "aesthetically independent" of its author; but this sort of idea is typical of Vendler.

Vendler doesn't like poems that *say* something—or, more accurately, she's very strict about the ways in which she thinks it is proper for a poem to say something. She draws a rigid distinction between art (as exemplified by painting and music) and discourse (philosophy, history, etc.), and finds it highly problematic that writing straddles both categories. Though at least once, in *The Music of What Happens*, she describes poetry as partaking of each of these tendencies ("The reflective and discursive verse of paradox represents one extreme of lyric; the opposite extreme is song. Song and reflection are the two sources of lyric, and poems move along a continuum between them"), she seems more often to see true poetry as "action," not "discourse"—as belonging, that is, only in the category of art. The more predominant the rhetorical or intellectual content of a poem, then, the less Vendler is likely to think of it as a true poem. She dismisses "This Dust Was Once the Man," for instance, as the work of Whitman "the orator-eulogist," not of Whitman the poet. What's more, in order to feel comfortable praising a poem widely thought to contain ideas, she finds it necessary to underplay, or even to deny, the presence of those ideas in the poem. Thus she ridicules Lionel Trilling's reading of Wordsworth's "Immortality" ode as a statement of certain ideas about life. Time and again in Vendler's essays, language-as-action wins the day. Though she admires "When Lilacs Last in the Dooryard Bloom'd," for instance, Vendler finds the poem flawed insofar as it does not approach the "vigor of language which we find in 'Song of Myself' or 'As I Ebb'd with the Ocean of Life'"; to the extent that the poem is "stately," imprisoned in "the fetters of a formal occasion and a formal genre," it deviates from Vendler's ideal of the "purely lyric" poem. It is in accordance with this conception of poetry that she distinguishes sharply between words and ideas, saying that "a writer who loves words—all words, single words—for their materiality and for their image-inspiring power is at the furthest remove from someone who loves 'ideas.'" A real poetic mind, in her view, "thinks in images." (Where does that leave Alexander Pope?)

One of Vendler's favorite words of approbation is *fluid*—a lexical choice that seems to follow from an envisioning of discourse as solid, art as liquid. Thus she speaks of Ashbery's "fluid syntax," says that "Louise Glück's sense of myth, while as firm as Ashbery's, is less fluid," and notes that A.R. Ammons "is sure that the number of fluid inner states is infinite... and the only mediating instrument between the liquid currents of mind and the mountains and deserts of matter is language." Often her distinctions between the fluid and the not-so-fluid are, to say the least, rather murky: "Ashbery's fluidity put us in the *res cogitans* as it carries on its marvelous observations and retoolings; Glück's sterness reminds us that we have also a precipitate, a residue, from life's fluidity—that which we recite by heart, the immutable, the unadorned, the skeletal, the known."

As some of these quotations may suggest, Vendler would seem to spend much of her time trying to figure out what to say about a given poet or poem, in the manner of one to whom the act of criticism doesn't come at all naturally. The questions about the purpose of poetry criticism which she raises in "The Function of Criticism" never seem to be put to rest. She begins a piece on the criticism of Dave Smith, Robert Hass, and Robert von Hallberg by asking "What is there to say about a poem? about poetry? about a national poetry? about a poetry and the culture from which it issues?" On the first page of a piece about Harold Bloom, she says: "there has been a good deal of difficulty in knowing what it is proper to say about a lyric poem beyond what can be said about human imaginative expression in general." To be sure, the purpose of poetry criticism is certainly a valid subject for discussion, but Vendler returns to this question so often that you get the feeling she really *doesn't* know why she's reading verse and writing about it, aside from the fact that *The New Yorker* pays well and that it's good for her career. At times one feels like yelling at her: "For heaven's sake, if you really don't know why you're writing about poetry, then why don't you just keep quiet?"

And the fact is that time and again Vendler gives evidence that she really doesn't know what to say about a poem. Like many academics, she sometimes seems to think that it is the job of the critic to discover (or pretend to discover) in a work of literature a controlling theme or structural principle that no one has ever noticed before. Implicit in criticism of this kind is the conceit that everyone who has previously read the work under discussion has misunderstood it; the paradox of such criticism is that any work capable of being so ubiquitously misunderstood could hardly be regarded as effectively constructed in the first place, and thus could hardly be considered deserving of such close critical attention. Sensible but kind English teachers euphemistically call interpretations of this kind "ingenious": while they show a certain inventiveness, they have relatively little to do with the actual work of literature supposedly under consideration. Much of Vendler's criticism has been of this sort; her book on Keats, for instance, centers upon a dubious interpretation of the odes as a coherent sequence. Equally dubious readings occur in the present book. The essay "Reading Walt Whitman" offers an interpretation of "When Lilacs Last in the Dooryard Bloom'd" which is based on the notion that the poem represents a radical reworking of certain passages from earlier poems; Vendler argues that an awareness of these borrowings is essential to a full appreciation of the poem's pathos. While there are indeed similarities between parts of "Lilacs" and some of these earlier passages, Vendler describes the composition of "Lilacs" in a way that, it seems to me, would sound utterly foreign to anyone who had ever actually written a poem. And she engages in rather too much mind-reading: "Other fragments pressed forward in Whitman's mind as he composed.... It was in 'Lilacs' that Whitman sought to find a middle ground between triumph and 'the mournful voices of the dirges pour'd around the coffin'.... He wished to find, in the language of perception, an equivalent for transcendence." The lamentable consequence of such an approach is to make Whitman sound less like Whitman than like Helen Vendler. It is one thing for a critic to write about poems in the language of a critic; it is another for a critic to write about poets as if they thought like critics. Whatever genuine insights Vendler may have into a poem's form and meaning are rendered considerably less valuable by her thorough inability to understand the way a real poetic mind actually goes about creating form and meaning.

And yet Vendler has many of her readers convinced that she not only understands poetry, but also has a special insight into the nature of American poetry. Indeed, though she's written books about English classics—among them *The Odes of John Keats* (1983) and *The Poetry of George Herbert* (1975)—Vendler is best known as a critic of American poetry. She has some very firm, and questionable, ideas about the subject. Like many critics, she recognizes certain qualities as being more prevalent in American poems than in their English or continental counterparts; but she goes further than this, arguing that the very presence of these qualities in American poems makes the poems more American than poems without these qualities, and consequently makes them better. If she admires Ashbery so much, it is largely because "Ashbery is an American poet, always putting into his poems our parades and contests and shaded streets. He sometimes sounds like Charles Ives in his irrepressible Americana." Indeed, "Ashbery's gift for American plainness is his strongest weapon." Yes, Ashbery's poetry is full of clichés—but this is perfectly fine with Vendler, who claims that "Ashbery's deep literary dependencies escape cliché by the pure Americanness of his diction." What Vendler is trying to say in this characteristically clumsy sentence, I think, is that the clichés in Ashbery's poetry are *American* clichés—that he writes the way we really talk here in America—and that his work therefore can't be faulted as poetry. On the contrary, Vendler would have us believe that those American clichés give Ashbery's work much of its strength. Ashbery, she writes, "insists[s], by his manner, that everything that is 'in English' has to be written over 'in American'"; to Vendler, this is precisely what an American poet should insist upon. She proffers an example of the contrast between British English and the "American language" of Ashbery's poetry:

If Keats's sonnet reads,

When I have fears that I may cease to be
Before my pen has glean'd my teeming brain,
Before high-piled books, in charact'ry,

> Hold like rich garners the full-ripen'd grain;

then Ashbery will write,

> I think a lot about it,
> Think quite a lot about it—
> The omnipresent possibility of being interrupted
> While what I stand for is still only a bare canvas:
> A few traceries, that may be fibers, perhaps
> Not even these but shadows, hallucinations…

> …The "educated" reader thinks that "poetry" must sound
> Keatsian, rhythmic, and noble. But our American language
> cannot speak in those "noble accents / And lucid inescap-
> able rhythms" (Stevens) without modification. "I think a lot
> about it" *is* how we say "When I have fears."

To Vendler, in short, British English is "noble," American English colloquial. But surely every language has its high and low levels of diction. Vendler's implication here seems to be that in England, in Keats's time, common people actually talked in the elevated language of Keats's poetry, and that this alone made it proper for him to use such language in his work. Nonsense. In the same way, she appears to be saying that what validates Ashbery's poetry is that it represents the way we actually talk in America nowadays. But though the first two lines quoted from Ashbery seem colloquial enough, the rest of the quotation—beginning with "The omnipresent possibility of being interrupted"—doesn't sound any more colloquial than Keats. The main difference between the language of these lines and that of Keats's poetry is not that one is "noble" and the other colloquial, or that one is English and the other American, but that Keats's words are beautiful and expressive and Ashbery's are banal and unattractive. Vendler acknowledges Ashbery's prosiness; indeed, she praises the poem for its "flat American beginning." To her, clearly, a flat, prosaic American poem is a distinctly American poem—and the more distinctly American an American poem is, of course, the greater a poem it is. When Vendler wants to praise a poet who does not fit into this formula, such as James Merrill, she feels compelled to apologize for, or explain away, his artfulness: "Merrill's diction, though it can be fully literary [ugh!], is also colloquial and topical [huzza!], and in that way, though he generally writes in meter [alas!], he writes in the current language of America [yippee!]."

Vendler is uninhibited in her praise of Ashbery for his "comic" and "eclectic" use of the American language. Lines containing the expressions "show through" and "run out of" inspire her to rejoice in our native idioms: "when did 'to run out of something' become our normal way of saying that the supply was exhausted?" Look it up in your *OED*, Mrs. Vendler: the first citation of "run out of" dates back to 1713, to an English writer; in fact, it's not a uniquely American idiom at all. Nor is "show through," both of whose *OED* citations are of nineteenth-century English writers. In short, these aren't exclusively American idioms at all. But what does this matter, anyway? What does the provenance of these expressions have to do with the aesthetic value of poems in which they happen to appear? The fact is that while Ashbery does make frequent use of such idioms—which are really more distinctively colloquial than they are distinctively American—he rarely does anything interesting with them; if Vendler sincerely wants to see clever and funny uses of genuine colloquial American English, she'd be better off looking at the lyrics of Lorenz Hart, Ira Gerswhin, and Johnny Mercer, say, than at the poetry of John Ashbery.

Throughout *The Music of What Happens*, "Americanness" serves as a well-nigh inflexible criterion of poetic excellence. If Vendler is less enthusiastic than one would like her to be about Elizabeth Bishop, it is largely because Bishop "resists the label 'American poet': there is in her work no self-conscious rebellion against English genres, or even English attitudes, of the sort we find in our poetry from Whitman and Dickinson on." It is largely on this account that Vendler compares Bishop unfavorably with Ashbery; on similar grounds, she compares Robert Frost unfavorably with A.R. Ammons. However much one may admire Ammons, one cannot but be embarrassed for Vendler when she remarks disparagingly that "when we read Ammons... we see how distant Frost is from his rural characters, even when they are adapted from his own experience."

Patently, Vendler has extraordinary ideas about the distinctions between American and non-American sensibilities. For instance, she writes in a review of Robert von Hallberg's *American Poetry and Cul-*

ture, 1945-1980 that

> The reasons why the general public [in America] does not
> read poetry are probably neither political ("Read those out-
> laws? those fascists? never!") nor psychological ("I never
> could figure out that difficult stuff"). Rather, the reasons for
> the marginal status of lyric poetry tend, I would guess, to
> be largely historical and institutional. Poetry is not system-
> atically and intensively taught in America as it is in Europe;
> since most world poetry does not reflect American history
> or culture, it has been thought irrelevant to our nation. Each
> European nation cherishes its poetry (and the classical po-
> etry born on the same soil from which it grew) as part of the
> deposit of patriotism, and therefore institutionalizes it in
> the schools. There are no such reasons for America to insti-
> tutionalize Virgil or Milton. A critic's demonstration that
> poetry is really about your life and mine and can be under-
> stood without difficulty cannot institutionalize poetry in
> America if a large social commitment to it as a patriotic value
> did not exist.

Well! All this American can say, in response to these observations, is
that he, for one, read a good deal of poetry in the New York public
schools he attended as a child. The main problem with poetry in
America is not that people don't read it in school but that they don't
read it once they get out of school. (But then Vendler wouldn't recog-
nize such a problem, because poetry is, to her, an academic phenom-
enon; sometimes you get the feeling that if she weren't being paid to
do so, she wouldn't be reading poetry either.) Likewise, in an essay on
Roland Barthes, Vendler writes that "[t]he intellectual formation of a
French child attracted to literature is hardly imaginable to Americans.
We are unfamiliar with those sacred French institutions the *cahier* (the
notebook in which never a blot can appear), the *dictée* (the oral dicta-
tion in which faults of spelling and punctuation are subsequently mer-
cilessly reproved), the *manuel littéraire* (a potted version of literary his-
tory)—all the furniture of the school and the *lycée*." Sorry to break it to
you, Mrs. Vendler, but many of us who attended school in America
can identify well enough with such things—we had our notebooks
checked for neatness, punctuation and spelling, and even had our
equivalents of the *manuel littéraire*. The same ridiculous sort of con-

trast appears in a piece on Yale critic Geoffrey Hartman and his book *Criticism in the Wilderness*. Vendler readily accepts Hartman's notion that American students are congenitally less competent readers of poetry because (in her words) "they haven't the cultural equipment to read it," not having "grown up in that architectural and civic context which surrounds Europeans and reminds them that art always issues from a historical, religious, and philosophical ground." This is absurd. Vendler speaks as if "cultural equipment" were something that Europeans are issued at birth; as if culture were something that one absorbed from buildings, like ground radiation, rather than from learning.

Similarly, in her article on Milosz, Vendler writes that "[t]here are no direct lessons that American poets can learn from Milosz. Those who have never seen modern war on their own soil cannot adopt his tone; the sights that scarred his eyes cannot be seen by the children of a young provincial empire. A thousand years of history do not exist in American bones, and a culture secular from birth cannot feel the dissolution of the European religious synthesis, on which Milosz dwelt in *The Witness of Poetry*, his Charles Eliot Norton lectures at Harvard." Where does one begin to argue with this? First of all, the ghosts of John Winthrop, Roger Williams, Anne Bradstreet, Edward Taylor, and their fellow New England colonists would be surprised to hear that America has been "secular from birth." Vendler writes about Americans, furthermore, as if we sprang up day before yesterday from the Virginia soil, with no churches, no forebears, no libraries, no awareness of world history, no consciousness of a heritage beyond these shores. Certainly a thoughtful and imaginative American is as capable of feeling "a thousand years of history" in his bones as well as any European; for the fact is that people exist not merely as pieces of a culture but as individuals. And it is as individuals, furthermore, that they read poetry and experience the emotions that it communicates. Too often Vendler, in her eagerness to promulgate sweeping definitions of America, its people, and its culture, ignores this simple fact.[2]

---

[2]Besides, it might be convincingly argued that since it is much more common in America than in Europe for an individual to claim descent from several different Old World national groups, the typical American individual has a more natural "feel" for European history, in Vendler's sense, than the typical European. But of course it is silly to make such comparisons in the first place.

And too often she ignores such things as grace and clarity of style. For a writer whose job it is, in large part, to make delicately nuanced judgments about other writers' use of language, Vendler has perpetrated more than a few breathtakingly awful sentences. Some are disfigured by ugly jargon: "Keats declares that art requires a social cooperation between the encoder-artist and the solitary decoder-beholder.... In the sonnet 'When I have fears that I may cease to be,' Keats summons up a rich gestalt." (Would anyone who honestly responded to the music of Keats willingly sign her name to such sentences?) She can be sloppy about sentence logic ("Such passages alternate with a more relaxed mood") and diction (she refers to Seamus Heaney's colorful life as "an extreme sequence"); and sometimes she simply churns out the same sort of phony, fuzzy, fatuous prose that one may find under the bylines of a thousand overworked, underinspired professors on the publish-or-perish treadmill: "[Barthes] exemplifies his own definition of the human person—a consciousness constituted by the available languages of its social and historical era." Or: "Wordsworth is following, in his ode, the classic proportions of elegy." Or: "[Spender] takes upon himself the full consciousness of happenings in countries other than his own." Or: "Leithauser's search for perfection has, I think, been insufficiently noticed." Interestingly, the pieces in this book that were originally published in *The New Yorker* are considerably more well written than the others; indeed, one can tell from the first paragraph whether an essay is from that magazine or not. This may be a reflection of the famous extent and expertise of *New Yorker* editing, or it may simply indicate that Vendler puts more effort into her contributions to her flagship magazine than into her work for other publications.

Vendler herself has described her style as "Francophone and rhapsodic," and while I don't think that rhapsodic is quite the correct word, there are altogether too many sentences in *The Music of What Happens* in which Vendler's reach exceeds her grasp. She writes of Whitman's perceptions, for instance, that they "diffuse into the oceanic or the impalpable, as they draw further away from the senses and closer to the pure rhythmic utterance of words forming in air." (How's that again?) Similarly, she comments about a Seamus Heaney poem that "[t]he aesthetic claim made by a poem like this is that the passage of life can indeed be tallied in a narrative, and that the physical processes of life exquisitely resemble the mental ones, with a fluid sliding of import between them." She writes that Louise Glück's "struggle to find a fluent that is not false is the shadow-twin of her claim that there is a fixed that is not marred." (This sentence is a little clearer in context, but no more graceful.)

Pretentious diction abounds in Vendler's essays. Though she pretty much avoids poststructuralist argot (e.g., *metataxis*, *paralogical*, *intertextuality*), she delights in words like *appetitive*, *cotemporal*, and *methodized*, uses *instance* as a verb, speaks of "transcultural philosophic universals" and "linguistic economies," and refers (in various essays) to Whitman's "perceiving apparatus," A.R. Ammons's "conceptual equipment," and Charles Wright's "descriptive equipment." The word *enable* is a favorite (Vendler tells us that folk tales "enabled [Sexton] as a satirist" and that a certain realization "enables the song of the bird" in "When Lilacs Last in the Dooryard Bloom'd"). So is *enact*. She explains how poets resist the pressure to be political "by enacting an aesthetic which embraces social reality in an algebraic way"; how "[a]rt, in its social function,…enacts for us the paradox of our orderly symbolic capacity as it exists within the disorder it symbolizes"; how two poems by Heaney and Milosz "enact [the poem's]…necessary connection with social reality"; and how "stiff resolve and chagrined change of heart are enacted in separate [Davie] poems." In some essays she seems especially to favor pairs of esoteric nouns or adjectives, speaking, for example, of the "phrasal and atomistic" nature of perception, of Spender's "continuities and disruptions," of Hughes's "predatory and avian" poetry in *Crow*, of the way Heaney "aggrandized and consecrated his infant world," of the "trenchant and pugnacious self visible in Donald Davie's prose," of the "prophecy and peccancy" of Davie's verse, of the way a certain Davie poem "ends in temporariness and temporizing," of the "stinting and bare" quality of a second Davie poem, and of the "processional and epigrammatic" syntax of a third. (Vendler's characterization of her own style as "Francophone and rhapsodic," of course, also belongs in this category.)

There are many other things about Vendler's criticism that one could choose to elaborate upon. One might mention, for instance, the extremely narrow range of writers to whom Vendler is in the habit of making passing references; throughout *The Music of What Happens*, she continually cites either Keats, Stevens, or Ashbery (or all three) for purposes of comparison, even though in most cases none of these names seems remotely relevant to the discussion. But enough. It is not my intention here to enumerate every last flaw of Vendler's critical method. Nor do I mean to suggest that there are not less competent people than Vendler writing about poetry these days; on the contrary, America certainly has its share of critics (not to mention celebrated contemporary poets) who, notwithstanding their intelligence, knowledge, and analytical skills, are crippled by perverse aesthetic criteria and by a tin ear. Far be it from me to suggest, then, that Vendler's deficiencies as a critic are in any way unparalleled. What is exceedingly disturbing, however, is that these deficiencies have never been written about prominently and at length, and that this altogether pragmatic public silence which her fellow critics have maintained in regard to her shortcomings has enabled her to accrue power and influence out of all proportion to her deserts. While Helen Vendler, in short, is not a thoroughly bad critic, it is without question a thoroughly bad thing that she wields such unparalleled influence upon the direction of American poetry in our time.

WINTER 1989

"VOICES AND VISIONS" ON PBS

Thirty-five years have passed since Randall Jarrell complained, in the lead essay of his book *Poetry and the Age*, about the indifference of the American public toward the American poet, and it is safe, I think, to say that the situation has not changed appreciably since. Indeed, for all the poetry workshops and little magazines that have proliferated in the intervening decades, Americans have, if anything, grown steadily more uninterested in poetry. This lack of interest is particularly discernible on the part of college students. To be sure, many of these students are eager to *write* poetry—which to them typically means pouring their passions, resentments, and idle thoughts onto the page in whatever words happen to pop into their minds—but few of them have much interest in reading the stuff. And why should they? Outside of the classroom, they've never seen a poem, never seen anybody read one, never heard anybody discuss one. They've grown up in an age all too many of whose cultural arbiters and institutions categorically refuse to distinguish between high art and pop culture, and so it has never been made clear to them that by ignoring poetry they might be causing themselves to miss something important. For many of them, as it happens, the art form of choice is the music video, which requires nothing of them beyond the willingness to set their minds on neutral and gaze passively at a series of diverting images for three or four minutes at a stretch.

So it is that the college teacher of poetry has his work cut out for him. Poetry, after all, demands many attributes to whose development a habitual indulgence in music videos and the like is patently inimical: patience, discipline, a sense of form, an ability to detect subtle nuances of thought and feeling, a sensitivity to language. The only way for a teacher to help such students to understand poetry is, simply enough, to have them read poetry—and read it again, and again, and talk about it, and memorize a great deal of it. A teacher must make it clear to his students that poetry exists in an utterly different sphere from rock music and TV shows, that poetry is generally much harder to "get" than rock music and TV shows, that one must approach poetry through a different (and perhaps previously underused) part of the mind than that with which one approaches these entertainments, and that the cultivation of an appreciation for poetry can take a considerable amount of time.

Certainly the last thing that one would want to bring into a poetry class is a television set. To introduce a television set into a room full of college students—students for whom one is trying to make extended concentration upon literary texts an easier and more natural activity—would be rather like bringing a six-pack to an Alcoholics Anonymous meeting. Yet that, figuratively speaking, is precisely what the Public Broadcasting System is eager for America's college English teachers to do. For the network has put together a thirteen-part television series on American poetry which—though the rest of us are more than welcome to watch—has patently been manufactured with a huge, captive college-student audience in mind.

Indeed, *Voices and Visions*—for such is the title of the series, each of whose episodes covers the career of a different American poet, from Whitman to Sylvia Plath—is described throughout its reams of publicity materials as "a PBS television series and college credit course." The packagers have not missed an angle. To begin with, there is the series itself, which in addition to being aired around the country in thirteen weekly one-hour installments beginning in late January, can be ordered on tape from an outfit called "The Annenberg/CBS Project" for $29.95 per program, $350 the lot. Accompanying the series, moreover, is a large hardcover essay collection, *Voices and Visions: The Poet in America*, edited by Helen Vendler, published by Random House, and "recommended for advanced students."[1] Written by such big-name academic critics as Hugh Kenner, Marjorie Perloff, and Richard Poirier, the essays number thirteen in all, one for each poet covered by the series: Walt Whitman, Emily Dickinson, Robert Frost, Wallace Stevens, William Carlos Williams, Ezra Pound, Marianne Moore, T.S. Eliot, Hart Crane, Langston Hughes, Elizabeth Bishop, Robert Lowell, and Sylvia Plath. Also issued by Random House is a "text/anthology" entitled *Modern American Poets: Their Voices and Visions*, which contains "all the published poems featured in the programs" and is edited by Robert

---

[1]*Voices and Visions: The Poet in America*, edited by Helen Vendler; Random House, 528 pages, $29.95.

DiYanni. Then there's a "viewer's guide," published by the American Library Association, and a "student study guide," published by Kendall/Hunt Publishing Company. Finally, there's a toll-free number (1-800-LEARNER) designed to help us sort these various items out.

What it all adds up to is an elaborate package of come-ons, tie-ins, and handouts that any corporate sales division would envy. (One can only wonder why they're not putting out a set of *Voices and Visions* poet-dolls: a nine-inch-tall Marianne Moore, say, in a broad-brimmed hat, a William Carlos Williams in doctor whites with a tiny little stethoscope, and so on. Collect them all!) The credits are perhaps the most Byzantine that this writer has seen anywhere. The series as a whole is "produced by the New York Center for Visual History and presented by the South Carolina ETV Network." Its executive producer is Lawrence Pitkethly, a longtime journalist and filmmaker with the BBC—he was born in Northern Ireland—and a co-founder of the aforementioned Center, which the series' publicity materials describe as "a non-profit media center that produces innovative material on American culture." (Apparently, Mr. Pitkethly is himself the very first person to receive an "education" in American poetry from *Voices and Visions*; in an interview with *The New York Times*, he is quoted as saying that when he began work on the series, "I didn't know that much about American poetry…. I feel as though I got a $7.5 million education in American poetry—on a scholarship, at that.")

The series adviser is Helen Vendler, the Kenan Professor of English at Harvard University and poetry critic of *The New Yorker*, who has probably had a greater influence (or, at least, a more inimical influence) on critical thinking about contemporary American poetry than anyone else. Major funding for the series derives from the Annenberg/CPB Project (which offers "a variety of high quality educational programs for lifelong learning and for college credit") and the National Endowment for the Humanities; other funding derives from a variety of sources, including the National Endowment for the Arts, Great Britain's Channel Four, and a number of private foundations, corporations, and state cultural commissions. In addition, each episode has its own director, writer, and program consultant as well as its own sources of "special funding." "Langston Hughes: The Dream Keeper," for instance, was funded in part by Soft Sheen Products, Inc., and by the Ohio Humanities Council. (Similarly, "Robert Frost" was funded in part by the Vermont Council on the Humanities and Public Issues; New Jersey kicked in for favorite sons Whitman and Williams; and Ohio helped pay not only for the program on Hughes but for the episode devoted to his fellow Ohioan, Hart Crane.)

If I have gone into detail about such esoteric matters as credits and funding, it is partly because I find it remarkable that so many individuals and organizations have gone to such effort and expense to produce so misguided a series. Misguided, because the whole enterprise seems to me to be founded upon a gross misapprehension (on the part of some participants) and a willful disregard (on the part of others) of the nature of the poetic experience. What, after all, one must ask, is the purpose of *Voices and Visions*? If one telephones 1-800-LEARNER to find out, one's call will be answered by a tape recording on which a chillingly flat, dehumanized voice explains that one has reached the offices of the Annenberg/CPB Project, whose *Voices and Visions* series

> chronicles the collective achievements of American poets and their contributions to American poetry. The programs make poetry a visual experience by capturing the poets' ideas in striking images and photography. They create an appreciation of an important cultural heritage by bringing poetry to life as a dynamic art form. *Voices and Visions* illustrates poetry as an expression of common experiences and feelings. The programs enable the viewer to recognize how poems work, what poems mean, and how an individual poem relates to the larger literary tradition.

What sort of thinking is at work here? What sort of mentality takes for granted the wisdom of "capturing [a] poet's ideas in striking images and photography" and of "mak[ing] poetry a visual experience"? Was poetry not already alive, already "a dynamic art form," before Lawrence Pitkethly and company got their hands on it?

One hesitates to attribute major importance to a taped telephone message, but then this message is one of the only places in which those responsible for the series state explicitly what its purpose might be. The series itself never satisfies one's curiosity on this point: nor does Professor Vendler's "companion" book. The series' publicity materials, however, do (fleetingly) address this question. Somewhere in the pile of *Voices and Visions* publicity releases one finds these sentences: "The poetry [in *Voices and Visions*] is seen as well as heard through the television medium. On-screen text and animated words give the poems spirit and immediacy. Drama, dance, musical performance, interview segments, voice-over recitation, documentary, archival and location footage, and recordings of the poets reading their own work where possible are used to engage the viewer." Plainly, the same mentality is at work in this publicity release as in the Annenberg/CPB Project recording: poetry is something that needs the magic of television to give it "spirit and immediacy" and to make it "engage" an audience. To think this way about poetry, it seems to me, is to reduce a great poem to the status of a libretto, as it were, to an electronic operetta; if an audience is indeed "engaged" by such tampering, is that audience truly experiencing the poem or is it merely being entertained by a degraded high-tech adaptation?

Unquestionably, the answer is the latter. For though *Voices and Visions* is indeed occasionally informative and even diverting, the experience of watching it bears little resemblance to the experience of reading poetry. As a matter of fact, to watch the typical episode of this series—in which half a dozen or so poems (or excerpts) by a given poet are "presented," and his career summarized, his influences catalogued, and his themes and style discussed by various narrators, critics, and fellow poets—is rather like watching several hours' worth of MTV. The only difference is that instead of music videos we are offered "poetry videos." Like music videos, these take several forms. In some of them, a poem is dramatized; in others, a voice-over reading of a poem is accompanied by a series of atmospheric, often surrealistic, visual effects. Sometimes the words of the poem appear onscreen, sometimes not. The results of both approaches are generally little better than disastrous.

Take, for instance, the episode on Robert Frost, in which the poem "Home Burial," a dialogue between a husband and wife who have just buried their child, is presented as a brief drama, complete with background music. It begins as follows: a pensive young man enters his house, pauses at the foot of a staircase, looks up to see his wife on the upstairs landing, starts heavily up the stairs (*terrible* overacting, by the way), and finally, in a dreadfully flat voice (rather like that of the recording at Annenberg/CPB), delivers his first line: "What is it you see / From up there always—for I want to know." She doesn't reply. "What is it you see," he repeats. "I will find out now—you must tell me, dear." Finally he realizes what his wife is looking at:

"The wonder is I didn't see at once.
I never noticed it from here before.

I must be wonted to it—that's the reason.
The little graveyard where my people are!
So small the window frames the whole of it.
Not so much larger than a bedroom, it is?
There are three stones of slate and one of marble,
Broad-shouldered little slabs there in the sunlight
On the sidehill. We haven't to mind *those*.
But I understand: it is not the stones,
But the child's mound—"

What a beautiful poem! And what a terrible idea to have these lousy actors turn it into a soap opera! The dramatization achieves the impossible: it makes "Home Burial" ludicrous. Why wasn't there anyone on hand to tell Lawrence Pitkethly the obvious—that this poem was never meant to be *acted*, that Frost's words sound awkward and unnatural coming out of the mouths of actors, that lyric poetry and drama (whether composed in prose or verse) are two drastically different things?

Such grotesquely inappropriate presentations of poems are more the rule than the exception in *Voices and Visions*. The poetry video for T.S. Eliot's "Preludes," for instance, shows a slatternly, half-undressed grisette sitting wordlessly on the edge of a bed in a grubby little flat and removing her stockings, while a barechested, unshaven young lout hovers over her; it might just as easily be the video for a new Cyndi Lauper song. Like "Home Burial," part of the "Game of Chess" section of *The Waste Land* is dramatized: two middle-aged women sit in a pub, one of them chattering away in the words of the poem ("When Lil's husband got demobbed, I said— / I didn't mince my words, I said to her myself, / ... / Now Albert's coming back, make yourself a bit smart"), the other one listening, while the barkeeper periodically breaks in to say, "HURRY UP PLEASE ITS TIME." By contrast, the first section of the poem, "The Burial of the Dead," serves as the voice-over accompaniment to a rapid-fire sequence of surrealistic images—for example, of natives performing obscure desert rituals, of rain falling in the desert, of a hotel in the Alps, of people skating and sledding, of a woman weeping on a bed, and so forth. It is an arresting montage—quite as arresting as some of the more artsy, Dali-esque perfume commercials they're making these days—but it serves only to distract the viewer from the poem. And the poem, heaven knows, is difficult enough to take in without such distractions.

The fact is, indeed, that the great majority of these poetry videos are not only distracting but distorting. Part of the purpose of any poem, after all, is to conjure up images in the reader's mind; a filmmaker who provides ready-made images as an accompaniment to a poem is thus not helping the poem to communicate its message but is, on the contrary, working against the poem, overwhelming the poet's images with his own. This happens continually in *Voices and Visions*. In one episode after another, the creators of the series appear unwilling to let poems simply be *poems*. Pitkethly has obtained films of Eliot, Frost, and several other poets reading their own work, but rarely in these thirteen hours do we see any of these poets recite an entire poem from beginning to end without interruption or adornment; time and again, the producers assume that a few seconds of Frost or Eliot onscreen (or Robert Lowell, or Marianne Moore) are quite enough—we've got to keep the images *moving*, you see—and so generally we're accorded only brief glimpses of the poets, sandwiched between thick slices of "striking images and photography," while the poets read in voice-over. The shameful truth about *Voices and Visions*, then, is that, for all the pious words about the art of poetry that fill their publicity materials, the series' creators seem to work from a single fundamental hypothesis: that poetry, by itself, cannot possibly be expected to capture and to retain the interest of a television audience for two or three minutes at a time, let alone for an entire hour, and that every time a poem is presented on one of the shows, it had better be accompanied by as many visual fireworks as possible.

Some of the poems, to be sure, are more effectively presented than others. Invariably the effectiveness is directly proportional to the simplicity of the accompanying visual images. Elizabeth Bishop's "The Shampoo," for example, is presented with a refreshing lack of distraction: while the poem is read, its words appear in white letters on a black screen, with the gentle sound of running water in the background. (One worries throughout the poem, alas, that at any moment the producers will cut to a shot of Mary Martin washing Ezio Pinza out of her hair.) Other Bishop poems are accompanied by equally simple and elegant visual images: a moon over the ocean, a beach at night. Even the dramatization of Bishop's poem "In the Waiting Room" is tolerable. The actress Blythe Danner (one of several celebrities who provide the series with voice-overs) offers a sensitive reading of the poem, in which

Bishop recalls a momentous realization that came to her one day in her childhood, while she sat in a dentist's waiting room quietly reading the February, 1918, issue of *National Geographic*. This dramatization works because it is almost completely static: we are shown a little girl in period dress, sitting in just such a waiting room, reading that very issue of *National Geographic*, and not doing much at all except changing expression occasionally (and convincingly too: she's a much better actor than the husband and wife in "Home Burial"). It is because of the Bishop episode's refusal to overwhelm its subject's poetry that it is probably the most successful hour of the thirteen. (One must also admit that it is rather nice to look at the beautifully photographed scenes of the Brazilian town of Santarém while listening to Bishop's poem of that name, and to see the other exotic South American settings in which Bishop lived and from which she drew inspiration for her elaborately descriptive poems of nature.)

A particularly noisome aspect of these programs is that whenever any but the briefest of poems is read in its entirety, the director cuts away *in medias res*—in many cases not only once but several times—generally to one or more poets, critics, or poet-critics (e.g., Joseph Brodsky, Octavio Paz, Richard Wilbur, Derek Walcott, Grace Schulman, Alfred Kazin) who proceed to offer an instant analysis of what we've heard so far. It's as if the viewer can't be expected to concentrate on a whole poem, as if Pitkethly is afraid to risk losing viewers by presenting a poem in a single unbroken stretch. For instance, the recording of Lowell reading his "Quaker Graveyard in Nantucket"—which is accompanied by views of the sea and of fishermen working on ship decks—is interrupted for remarks by the critic Robert Hass; Moore's reading of "Marriage" is interrupted for a reminiscence by her friend Monroe Wheeler (and when the poem resumes it is being read not by Moore but by an actress). This is like breaking into Beethoven's Ninth for a dog-food commercial.

A great deal of time on these programs, in fact, is given over to brief snippets of interviews with authorities of various kinds—not only critics and poets but archivists, literary historians, biographers, and assorted relatives and friends of the subjects. Among the more interesting such interviews are those with people who knew the subjects intimately: Ezra Pound's mistress Olga Rudge and his daughter, Mary de Rachewiltz; Robert Lowell's second wife, Elizabeth Hardwick; Sylvia Plath's mother, Aurelia (who speaks candidly about Sylvia's first suicide attempt and her reaction to her father's death), Plath's friend A.

Alvarez (who admits that "her friends, me included, abandoned her—she was very difficult"); and Marianne Moore's housekeeper of thirty-six years (who remembers how fond Moore was of T.S. Eliot and how hard she took it when he married). Though on the whole the poets interviewed in the series—most of whom are not, shall we say, world-class experts on the subjects at hand—tend to be vaguely reverent in their remarks, some of the series' more perceptive and affecting obser-vations are in fact made by poets, especially by those who were ac-quainted with the subjects. The late Howard Moss, for instance, offers some quietly insightful comments about the work of his friend Eliza-beth Bishop, and John Thompson's discussion of the work of his friend Robert Lowell is equally valuable. It is particularly refreshing, by the way, to watch Thompson, after he has begun to read a Lowell poem aloud, react with undisguised joy to the beauty of the first line; in the Stevens program, James Merrill's enthusiasm for "Final Soliloquy" is similarly heartening.

Alas, there is altogether too little of this sort of enthusiasm in the series, especially on the part of Vendler and her fellow academics, most of whom make the reading of poetry look just about as exciting as the practice of dentistry. If I were a college student unfamiliar with poetry, it would take little more than a glance at the humorless, bored, self-important countenances of Vendler, Marjorie Perloff, and Harold Bloom—to name the three critical heavyweights who appear more fre-quently than anyone else in these shows (or maybe it just seems that way)—to make me switch over to *Cheers*. Of course, there are admi-rable moments: A. Walton Litz is good on Stevens's attempt "to under-stand the relation between words and physical reality," as is Vendler on Stevens's affinities to his favorite painters, Klee and Cézanne. (The most memorable remarks about Stevens, however, are those made by Merrill, who eloquently addresses the question of Stevens's obscurity.) But too often the critics on *Voices and Visions* make poetry seem little more than a pretext for highfalutin theorizing. What, for instance, can the creators of the series possibly have expected the average college student to make of the irritable-looking Sandra Gilbert, who in the Plath program pours out paragraphs of nonsensical, automatic-pilot academese about Plath's "enclos[ure] in patriarchal history" and about how in Plath's poems "the father metamorphoses into a kind of figure with tremendous mythological reference"? (Joyce Carol Oates likewise carries on about patriarchy during the program on Dickinson.) All too often, I'm afraid, Pitkethly lets academic jargon and ideology get the upper hand; at such times one feels as if one is not in an introductory poetry class but—horrors!—at an MLA convention.

This being the case, it should not be surprising that many of the programs evince an unseemly preoccupation with the subjects' sexual psychology and sex lives. Nor do the series' creators permit the fact that some of the poets *had* no sex lives—or, at any rate, that they left no record thereof—to inhibit their curiosity about this topic. So what if Marianne Moore was a prudish spinster who, while an editor at *The Dial*, reportedly "turned down a lot of first-rate literature" because it struck her as naughty? The program manages to find someone (Kenneth Burke) who is willing to testify that "I never saw a more sexual woman." In the Eliot program, meanwhile, Joseph Chiari discusses the poet's "sexual inhibition." On the Hart Crane program, the ever-reliable Malcolm Cowley offers the opinion that "Hart was in love with me." And the Ezra Pound program, while ignoring many important chapters of Pound's life, does not fail to cover his "ménage à trois" with his wife and mistress.

Most notable of all, in this regard, is the Whitman episode, which carries on interminably about Whitman's love of physicality while showing us several minutes' worth of bizarre turn-of-the-century films of naked men exercising. Of all the issues that this episode might have focused on, moreover, it chooses to occupy itself with the question of whether Whitman ever actually slept with a man. Three "authorities"— Harold Bloom, Galway Kinnell, and Allen Ginsberg (who, incidentally, is talked about in this episode, by himself and others, as if he were the good gray poet's One True Heir)—give their solemn opinions on this matter, and in support offer quotations from *Leaves of Grass*. As if this were not enough, Ginsberg, apropos of nothing at all, apprises us gleefully of the possibility that "there was some genital directness" between himself and Whitman, since he (Ginsberg) slept with Neal Cassady, who had slept with one Gavin Arthur, who had in turn slept with Edward Carpenter, who claimed to have slept with his friend Walt Whitman. (Will this be on the test?)

But then we should be grateful, I suppose, that Ginsberg is not one of the poets featured in *Voices and Visions*. Indeed, though most readers of American poetry would doubtless select a somewhat different Top Thirteen, the list that Pitkethly and company have put together is essentially unobjectionable. Yet one would have liked to see, at some point, an explanation of how these thirteen came to be chosen. One would have preferred, too, a somewhat less cozy and claustrophobic approach to the subject—for the writers of the various programs and companion-book essays appear to have been encouraged to discuss their poets' relationships to other poets covered in the series, but discouraged from elaborating upon their poets' connections to colleagues *not* covered by the series. (The name of Louise Bogan, for example—to name just one poet who is at least as important as some of those featured in *Voices and Visions*—doesn't appear once in the entire Vendler book.)

Then there is the matter of sequence. The strikingly unchronological order in which the episodes are scheduled to be aired—with Frost batting first, and the nineteenth-century poets Whitman and Dickinson buried in the middle of the line-up—only serves to destroy any possibility of conveying a sense of historical development. If viewed in chronological sequence, after all, *Voices and Visions* would come across not just as a survey of American poetry but as a history of the development of modern poetry. Patently, Vendler doesn't *want* the series to have this emphasis: she doesn't want students to regard these poets, with their remarkable innovations in style, theme, and structure, primarily as examples of a historical movement known as modernism; rather, she wants students to think of them as *American poets*, and—as her introduction to *Voices and Visions: The Poet in America* makes clear—wants students in turn to recognize American poetry as something that is by nature "particularly willing to be surprising, unsettling, and fresh in its intuitions. It is that freshness and originality that we have wanted to show in each of our poets." Originality, rebelliousness, Americanness: these are three different qualities, but throughout the series—as well as in the Vendler book—one finds them being subtly equated. The misapprehensions that are likely to result from this distortion are not inconsiderable.

This is not to suggest that Vendler's companion book is completely unworthy. On the contrary, once one has gotten past her meandering introduction, the book is a great deal less dismaying than the series itself. The authors of the essays, Vendler informs us, were asked to consider "what [the poets] inherited, what they were fostered by, where they found their language, what they created in the way of forms." The results are extremely mixed. Richard B. Sewall, the biographer of Emily Dickinson, contributes a very fine prolegomenon to her poetry; Frank Kermode, for his part, provides a truly splendid essay on Eliot, containing a wonderfully sensible discussion of *The Waste Land* and as satisfying an account of "Tradition and the Individual Talent" as I have ever read. Some of the other essays, unfortunately, suffer from the usual academic failings. Take Calvin Bedient, for example, who tries too hard to match Whitman's energy and ends up combining unappetizing academic jargon (he speaks of Emerson's "paratactic brilliance") with equally unappetizing slang, and perpetrates an astonishing number of sentences that are either incomprehensible or ugly or both:

> Democratic enumeration of all things as equal-in-the-Whole would create, was creating, out of the God's plenty before it, its own bushel-barrel aesthetic of the concrete discursive manifold and its own log-rolling aesthetic of vigorous, uncheckable cadence and syntax.

> [Whitman] needed a verse-style that was cut to the same X-tra large size as the nationalistic Personality.

> He strikes the note of *personal* reality as the joyfullest definiteness against the elusive resolution of everything, and the note of *external* and *universal* reality as a rapturous release from the twangy, hard "I."

> Everything Whitman wrote is sharply interesting, except where he wrote it better before.

Bedient speaks of Whitman's verse-style as being "aphoristically fisted," characterizes a certain Whitman line as "moving in its triumphantly willed but reluctant darts and escapes" (with *darts* and *escapes*, that is, both serving as nouns), and twice describes Whitman's long, smooth descriptive lines as "cornucopia pours" (with *pours* serving as a noun). Here's his attempt to capture the effect of the Frederick Church painting *Niagara* upon a viewer: "The whole immediate spread of the infinitely varied motion of the waters becomes an extended agitation amidst serenity in the viewer's breast."

To read this wildly uneven book is to wonder who, exactly, are those "advanced students" for whom it has been compiled. Though essentially introductory in content, most of the essays read as if they were written for people who are way past the introductory stage: the essays, that is, aside from lapsing into jargon, contain numerous offhand references to writers, events, and movements with which even a very bright and well-read college freshman would probably not be familiar. In some of the essays, moreover—particularly Marjorie Perloff's piece on Williams—the critics appear to be doing nothing so much as talking to themselves, repeating tired academic formulas, asserting strong enthusiasms and convictions in which it is difficult for a reader to believe.

But even such a book is infinitely preferable, as an academic tool, to the television series it accompanies. For the fact remains that, however much money one spends on such a series, television can do little to help students accustom their minds to the modalities of poetry. Quite simply, the two media are incompatible; in trying continually to turn poems into something else—namely, into background music for stunning visual images—Pitkethly and company have implicitly acknowledged this cardinal truth. It is largely because of the series' wholesale degradation of poetry in this manner—and because of the vigorous manner in which the whole package is being marketed—that one worries profoundly about the possibility that the $350 videotape edition of *Voices and Visions*, along with the various companion books, will become a staple of high-school and college literature instruction, and that it will therefore drive many of the more worthwhile texts and anthologies off the market. For let there be no mistake: notwithstanding the occasional pleasures of *Voices and Visions*, to use it to introduce American poetry to anyone—whether high-school student, collegian, or "lifelong learner"—would be an act of genuine irresponsibility.

MARCH 1988

DAVE SMITH'S "CREATIVE WRITING"

We live in an era when the poetic act—in America, at least—is increasingly performed on assignment and negotiated in committee under the auspices of a bureaucracy. I am speaking, of course, of that unique contemporary phenomenon known as the university creative-writing program. A bizarre institution, it has, in the manner of a black hole, grown more ominous and powerful with every poet, big and small, that it has swallowed up. It is a venue in which poetry is viewed, above all, as a career—a venue in which, all too frequently, the quality of the verse that a contemporary poet has written seems a far less reliable index of his relative importance than the grants and fellowships he has received, the writing colonies he has attended, the universities at which he has studied, taught, or given readings, and the number of books he has published. A poem is, after all, a fragile thing, and its intrinsic worth, or lack thereof, is a frighteningly subjective consideration; but fellowships, grants, degrees, appointments, and publication credits are objective facts. They are quantifiable; they can be listed on a résumé. Like any bureaucracy, the university creative-writing program tends to be more comfortable with these kinds of concrete attainments than with artistic accomplishments whose actual value, if any, cannot be determined without the strenuous exercise of intelligent critical judgment.

Which brings us to Dave Smith, a poet highly respected in the world of the creative-writing program. He might be described, indeed, as a model academic poet. He is prolific: in sixteen years he has published two books of fiction and twelve volumes of poetry, and this year alone has two new offerings—*The Roundhouse Voices: Selected and New Poems* and *Local Assays: On Contemporary American Poetry.*[1] He is a consum-

---

[1]*The Roundhouse Voices: Selected and New Poems*, by Dave Smith; Harper & Row, 182 pages, $16.95; and *Local Assays: On Contemporary American Poetry*, by Dave Smith; University of Illinois Press, 256 pages, $19.95. .

mate university man: as the biographical squib on the jacket of *Local Assays* informs us, he "is professor of English at Virginia Commonwealth University in Richmond" and "previously taught in the creative-writing programs at the University of Florida, the State University of New York at Binghamton, and the University of Utah." He has won numerous awards and grants: a Guggenheim, two NEA fellowships, a prize from the American Academy and Institute of Arts and Letters. And—ah, yes—he writes poetry.

It is, as one might expect, the sort of poetry which, in academia, currently has the greatest cachet. Indeed, as *The Roundhouse Voices* demonstrates convincingly, Smith has compiled—or, at least, at the age of forty-three, is well on his way to compiling—a body of work that is perhaps second to none in its ability to reflect the perverseness of the artistic criteria and professional priorities which constitute the "creative writing" sensibility.

Smith's poetry, written invariably in free verse (not a single poem in *The Roundhouse Voices* rhymes or follows a traditional form), typically consists of a gloomy, nebulous, rather burdensomely alliterative and assonant natural description, heavy with abstruse allegorical intent and often permeated by violence. In some poems an animal—a snow owl, a hawk—is at the symbolic center; in others it may be an oyster boat, a river, a pine cone, a duck pond. Sometimes the natural description is accompanied by a spotty memory from the poet's childhood or an anecdote about his own children; more often than not it yields some sort of murky epiphany or vague metaphysical speculation about passion, fear, reality and illusion, the passage of time, the triumph of death, the endurance of life. Whereas in another poet this nexus between the natural, the personal, and the cosmic might give the impression of being emotionally valid, in a typical Smith poem the connections between these elements appear to be arbitrary. The average Smith poem, indeed, seems held together not by the force of his love or distress or wonderment but by an act of will. One finds oneself imagining what would happen if one played mix-and-match with his verse—borrowing a description of a swooping hawk from the beginning of one poem, modulating into an anecdote about the poet and his father from another poem, and concluding with some epistemological musings from a third poem. Would this randomly rearranged set of words be any worse, look any more manufactured, than Smith's originals?

He has been compared to Keats, Whitman, Hopkins, Yeats, Thomas, and (most frequently, perhaps) Robert Penn Warren—all poets of feeling, of word-music. Unlike these masters, though, Smith appears to be guided only rarely by emotion. Most of his lavishly "sensitive" evocations of nature, childhood anecdotes, and philosophical *mots*, for instance, seem to reflect little more than a desire to be clever or forceful or dramatic. Imagery, in his hands, is often an academic exercise, his personification tending towards such clichés as "the sullen sun," "the shocking gray face of the sea," "the wind softly lick[ing] the wave." His most characteristic metaphors and similes are equally mechanical; parodic of sincere emotion, they run the gamut from the confusing to the ridiculous, their main purpose clearly being not to conjure up a vivid, emotionally authentic image but to weave exotic verbal tapestries. What defensible poetic purpose is served, after all, by describing a hawk as "com[ing] out of the strange clouded horizon like the dark of whipped / phone wires"? Or saying that a sundial "spreads time on the floor / like moss in a cove"? Or that a school of bluefish are like"[d]reams / graven on cold cell walls"? Or that a spot of blood on a palm is "red as the sun's first blink / of love"? Similes such as these are ubiquitous in Smith's poetry, and his use of them, in place of straightforward description, seems little more than an unfortunate tic. Even more exasperating are those similes in which he pointlessly compares physical objects to abstractions, the effect of which is to turn potentially sharp images into cryptic ones: an old toolshed is "eternal as guilt," a plunging hawk "as lethal as love," an arroyo "empty as memory." Again, one feels as if one could play mix-and-match without doing any real harm—why not, for instance, a hawk "as lethal as memory," a toolshed "as empty as love"?

What's especially strange about Smith's poetry is that it manages to be inert in spite of his patent attempts to be darkly, grandly passionate. One can almost always count on his headlamps being "huge" and "malignant," his rooms being "hopeless" and "hateful," his lakes being "ancient" and "black." Sometimes, in fact, it seems as though everything in his poetry is black, from "the black body of the river" to "the black streaks / of earth," from "the black / historical fact of life's event" to a "black shadow" crawling across a face. Manifestly, Smith yearns to create a vision of life as a Southern Gothic nightmare in the tradition of Poe (who, like Smith, was a Virginian). This may explain why dreams, dark and silent and terrible, occur throughout his verse, from "the dark / rotting dreams of your love" to "the black slough / that the dream has warned is love's terror," from "the killing dream" and "the dream-contending world" to "desire's black whirling dream" and "dreamed moments skidding like rocks / in the silence of a Wyoming midnight." This is a poetry that is trying very, very hard—but just not making it. Smith's hyperbole, alongside that of a Poe or a Swinburne, is pale and programmatic; it fails to generate real excitement, let alone erupt into a moment's glorious music. It doesn't even give the poetry that awful-but-interesting baroque quality that one might expect it to. Most of the time, despite Smith's efforts, the poetry just lies there, flat and forgettable.

The ultimate reason for the deadness of this verse, one suspects, is that the bulk of it was born not of spiritual but of professional necessity—Smith's need, that is, to produce poems whether he actually had poems in him or not. A more gifted and versatile poet of dreams, Randall Jarrell, once complimented Robert Frost by writing: "How little Frost's poems seem performances, no matter how brilliant or magical; how little things made primarily of words, and how much things made out of lives and the world that the lives inhabit." Smith's poetry gives the opposite impression. Like so much of the "creative writing" produced in the halls of ivy, it seems to be a series of performances made less out lives than out of words, a poetry that proceeds not along a line of feeling but, glibly and indelicately, along a chain of word associations. Words are, as a matter of fact, one of Smith's favorite themes. Time and again he talks about words *qua* words—their difficulty, their ambiguity, their limitation:

> ...I find myself
> unable to say a simple word
> true or false...
> We walk and find there are only a few words
> we want to say: water, root, light, and love...
>
> Think of the verbs by which they go: waddle, lumber, loll,
> shudder, slide, shuffle, wander—

On the face of it, of course, there is nothing wrong with Smith's word-infatuation; after all, some poets are capable of parlaying an obsession with language into very fine poetry indeed. But Smith is not one of them. The more he concentrates on his language, it sometimes appears, the more graceless it gets.

Amazingly, there are a handful of poems in *The Roundhouse Voices* that seem to have come into being the old-fashioned way—through genuine inspiration, or at least genuine feeling—and that are therefore genuinely effective. "August, On the Rented Farm" for instance, is a lovely poem about the poet's son entering, in an abandoned barn, "the showering secret of our lives"—that is, the knowledge of death. The boy stands among the spiders and crickets, and "the light fur of some-thing / half-eaten mats his hands." Later, father and son sit on a rot-ting pine log, enjoying the songs of birds. "Soon," the poem ends,

> in the yellow last light,
> we will begin again to speak
> of that light in the house
> that is not ours, that is only
> what we come to out of the fields
> in the slow-plunging knowledge
> of words trying to find a way home.

But such touching poems as this one are, in this collection, few and far between.

One turns from *The Roundhouse Voices* to *Local Assays* to find Smith, in Part I of this collection of critical prose, upholding as the paramount virtues of good verse precisely those qualities to which he seems, for the most part, indifferent in his own poetry. In a series of brief, discur-sive lucubrations upon the poetic art, this author of often obscure, con-voluted, inharmonious, and trendy poems speaks up, in turn, for clar-ity ("In so far as a poem is a coded organization of words, it is one the poet should be trying to decode"), simplicity ("Most of the poems of my generation seem to me like contemporary furniture, more veneer than wood, less built than bolted"), meaning ("The poem must mean or it is no poem"), music ("The music of poetry *is* poetry"), and tradi-tion (the past is "a continuously and powerfully affective force in ev-ery present moment"). He is, moreover, a strong defender of form— though not traditional form. To his mind, it appears, each poem should find its own shape, and the poet—the contemporary poet, anyway— who writes a sonnet, or villanelle, is copping out. "The artist," he in-tones, "follows no law other than the one he makes, though his law will be more strict, more demanding, more impossible to keep or to understand than any exterior law. The forms he creates act according to structures never acknowledged until the poem is complete." Poets who do follow exterior laws—who, that is, work in traditional forms—receive no praise in these pages; Smith (unjustly, to my mind) ridicules John Hollander and William Harmon, both formalists, as creators of "inert verse-clones." At the other end of the spectrum, he more defensibly takes to task such formal "innovators" as Charles Olson for replacing "verbal musics" with "verbal architectures."

Though one may be less than pleased by Smith's love of jargon (how can a poet who claims to revere language use a term like "verbal musics"?), one must admit that most of his observations are sound. The main problem, however, is that what he has put together here is, essentially, a collection of axioms. And though a few of them are interesting ("All poetry is...a retreat from unselective experience"; "Naked poetry is a contradiction in terms"), most might be described as simple, fine, true, and absolutely unsurprising ("The great poem simply tells us more, and tells it more profoundly, about what it means to be alive"). All too frequently, alas, these axioms are so simple, fine, and true that they strike one as hopelessly banal. ("Every poem comments on human experience: that is the poem's subject." The task of poetry is to "force back the borders of the unknown." "Poems do not occur organically as do lemons, worms, or uranium. [Since when is uranium organic?] Human deliberation which leads to a shaping of words, the mere intent to order, is the first step toward any poem's meaning.")

Because of Smith's inclination toward banality, reading Part I of *Local Assays* is something of a contradictory experience. On the one hand, one is pleased by the gravity with which he approaches his discussion; one tends to excuse many of his platitudes on the grounds that he is making an earnest and comprehensive attempt to map out the landscape of the *ars poetica* as he knows it—and the fact is that some areas of that landscape are more familiar, and less interesting, than others. On the other hand, though, one cannot help but be driven to distraction by his unmistakable gift, in prose as in poetry, for loquacity, abstraction, and hyperbole. All things considered, perhaps the fairest way to describe Part I of *Local Assays* is not as literary criticism but as a civilized compilation of a poet's thoughts on his craft. One is reminded of Somerset Maugham's far more accomplished book about the novelist's art, *The Summing Up*.

Part I, as it happens, represents Dave Smith the critic at his strongest. In the second and third sections of the book he offers reviews of May Swenson, Louis Simpson, James Dickey, and other contemporary poets, and his reluctance to make full use of the opportunity to deal specifically with specific texts is endlessly frustrating. As a critic, he is, as these reviews demonstrate once and for all, a maker of grand pronouncements rather than a builder of fine arguments. He speaks of Richard Hugo's occupying "the middle ground of discourse" without really explaining what he means. In one of two essay-reviews of Robert Penn Warren's poetry, he writes that

> No poet currently living has so resolutely wrestled with or turned to advantage the problem of form as has Robert Penn Warren. He has settled upon form as dialectic, as conversation between dramatic monologue and lyric speculation. The personality of men formally created by Warren exists in the citizen of intense passion, philosophical introspection, moral violation, and ethical study. This man acts and is acted upon by nearly blind forces, yet his mission is to know those forces, to recreate them in dramas of the self. Unlike the poet who demands we make it new and theoretically casts loose from the past, Warren seeks reality in the ever-newness of the past and his attitude toward form is essentially historic. He renovates form.

What does any of this mean? What does Smith see in Warren, and not in other poets, that makes him write such a paragraph? Presumably he has something in mind here—but he refuses to offer any examples for purposes of clarification, let alone support. Reading such a passage, one has the feeling that here, as in his poetry, Smith is more interested in effect than in meaning; he wants to impress us with the tortured complexity of his thought, wants to show us how many abstractions he can keep in the air at once. (One notices, apropos of this, that what Smith admires the most in Warren—or, at least, *quotes* the most—are those windy, orotund stretches about truth, beauty, energy, reality, passion, and blackness that represent Warren at his weakest.)

When Smith is not making puzzling pronouncements about one poet, he is breezily praising another in slushy, meandering prose. His piece on Sylvia Plath, which begins as follows, is representative:

> We know her. How odd it is to say that of a poet dead nearly two decades. It is certainly not the Truth, yet we feel we

know her and in important ways it is the truth to say we know her.... She is, almost, *the* American woman poet [!], yet she is featured in British anthologies of their poetry. No one knew Sylvia Plath less than she knew herself but *The Collected Poems* is, I think, beyond anything else the record of her struggle to know herself, which was the struggle finally to accept the self she was beyond all choosing and posturing. That is why we know her. If we do not really *know* her poetry, her prose, her letters—in the sense that one means when one has immersed oneself in another's written life, or even in the sense of the scholar who has "mastered the canon"—we continue to speak of her as if we do know her.... No one who invokes her name feels compelled to explain who she is. Or was. Can we really say *was* about Sylvia Plath? None of the women now writing poetry in America could have written as they have, not quite, without the example of Sylvia Plath. If they breathe poetry, they breathe that which has Plath in it....

And on and on he goes, in no discernible direction. Smith is chatting away, loving every minute of it. The passage provides a perfect example of the way literature tends to be viewed in the world of the creative-writing program—a world where two decades are an eternity, where the achievements of Wyatt and Surrey, say, are far less familiar than those of last year's Yale Younger Poet, where Sylvia Plath is something of a patron saint.

Plath, of course, isn't Smith's only touchstone. He is the kind of literary critic who extracts his truths from the lyrics of rock-and-roll songs (he reminds us: "Freedom, Janis Joplin's followers used to echo, 'is when you have nothing left to lose'"), who makes numerous references to popular television shows (he mentions *The Incredible Hulk* twice), and who, when searching for an example or an analogy, often finds it on the athletic field.

The song of the nightingale and the bellow of the moose may cause rapture but they are not poems. They are only sounds. Dandy Don Meredith may call O.J. Simpson's broken-field dash for a touchdown an example of poetry in motion, but he is wrong. No painting, symphony, movie, or prose is, precisely and actually, a poem.

M. Slotznick's *Industrial Stuff*...might...be poetry by, say, Howard Cosell, convinced of its clear thinking, its cures for social and industrial dilemmas, but dazzled into speaking a nonsense that is smart-alecky.

I am tempted to say [the poet who successfully handles the theme of adolescence] must be lucky and then to remark, as Jack Nicklaus did when told how lucky he was to sink a long putt, it is funny how constant practice makes a man lucky.

Smith takes sports very seriously. In the interview with Peter Balakian that closes the book he remarks, in all solemnity, that "Bill Heyen wrote me once that it was odd how all the best poets are ex-jocks." This is Smith's idea of a good theory. For once, he offers several examples of something, reminding us all that Jarrell played tennis, Ransom played baseball, Keats swam. (What about Emily Dickinson? Did she skip rope in the attic?) "And speaking of Ransom," Smith goes on, "he has a wonderful line: what a poet must have in the right order is the head, the heart, and the foot.... It is hard to believe that anybody could argue that the grace of the body is not absolutely necessary to the grace of a poem." It is unfair to blame poor William Heyen for this nonsense, of course, for he made his observation in a personal letter, not in a published interview, and probably meant it half-seriously at best. It is impossible, however, not to blame Smith for proffering such foolishness in the guise of thoughtful literary criticism.

One can understand, though, why this particular poet would suggest such a theory. One of Smith's major concerns, as *Local Assays* makes clear, is to be recognized as a "regular guy." It is the sort of motive one might expect from a poet habituated to the ways of the contemporary academy—an academy that, at times, appears ludicrously eager to align itself with the popular culture. Characteristically, Smith makes a point of his admiration of fishermen (which is manifested in a number of his poems) and remarks that this admiration "partially reflects my suspicion of the intellectual life—as a partial life." In other words, he doesn't admire the fishermen for themselves but *wills* himself to admire them in part because they serve his purposes as an anti-intellectual. His admiration for them is contrived. (This, of course, helps to explain why, from certain angles, his very persona seems contrived—which, in turn, helps to explain why his poetry is so contrived.)

In the fourth section of *Local Assays*, Smith gets more personal. Aside from the aforementioned interview (in which the prolific Smith asserts, among other things, that the sheer bulk of a poet's work is a measure of his importance), this section contains a handful of essays derived from his experience as a poet and a teacher of creative writing. In the most interesting of these pieces—"Notes on Responsibility and the Teaching of Creative Writing"—he mounts a defense of creative-writing programs. Part of his strategy in this piece, as the title suggests, is to present himself, as in Part I, as a strong believer in excellence, in high literary standards, in a responsible attitude toward the literary art as well as one's students. But his arguments in favor of creative-writing programs—to the extent that he offers any arguments at all—are unconvincing.

Not too surprisingly, the essay begins with a two-and-a-half-page anecdote about an inspiring football coach of Smith's acquaintance whose "task, the task of the writer and the teacher of writing, was to help people see what they were and what they might be, not as the hypothetical average, but as individuals in the living dramatic context." As it develops, this is, in essence, Smith's principal defense of the creative-writing program: it may not produce great or even good writers, but it "is one of the few formal opportunities in education for self-discovery and self-creation." What are we to make of such an argument? It is true, of course, that all art is to some degree a means of self-discovery, for its creator as well as its audience. But can a writer who is not good enough to enhance a reader's sense of self-discovery truly enhance his own? To put it another way, can a student with little or no gift for creative writing discover himself more profoundly by (a) entering a creative-writing program and learning to write bad poems, or (b) by taking courses in literature where he will read the work of such poets as Chaucer, Shakespeare, Swift, Keats, Browning, and Arnold? To choose (a), I think, is to view the writing of workshop poetry not as a bona fide literary act but as yet another postmodern method of life-style enhancement, like est or the Jane Fonda workout. It is, in short, to denigrate literature.

Smith's other major argument in favor of creative-writing programs is equally dubious. He defends the writing workshop as an institution

whose "historical pedigree...exists [sic] from the pre-Socratic philoso-
phers to the Scribler Club of Swift, Pope, Gay, etc., to Ransom, Warren,
Tate, and other Fugitives, to the Harlem Renaissance, to the Beats, to
Black Mountain, and unto university programs in creative writing."
This is, of course, ludicrous. No one can seriously compare a circle of
philosophers, a school of poets, or a writer's club—an organization,
that is, of professional artist or thinkers with a genuine affinity for one
another's work and ideas—with the big-money, amateur-oriented busi-
ness that is the university creative-writing program. The writing pro-
gram is descended, in truth, not from the Scriblerians and the Fugi-
tives but from such enterprises as the Famous Writers' School of
matchbook-cover fame, an operation that was founded not by artists
in search of truth and beauty but by businessmen in search of profit.

To be sure, Smith makes reference to the criticisms most often lev-
eled against creative-writing programs—that they have trained a gen-
eration of poets largely unaware of poetry's traditions and possibili-
ties, and have duped hordes of talentless students into wasting their
time and money. But Smith offers very little of substance to counter
these charges. Rather than confront them directly, he brands the critics
who raise them as irresponsible polemicists who, "in these generally
conservative times," have been seized by "a new and reactionary criti-
cal anxiety about the untidiness of the literary world." He is particu-
larly hard on Karl Shapiro for observing in *Poetry* that in creative-writ-
ing programs, "[r]eading itself is discouraged, perhaps in legacy of the
destruction of libraries in the Sixties and of the Yahoo cry for Relevance.
Not only is the student ignorant of craft and craftsmanship: he is igno-
rant of literature itself." Smith's response to this is to call Shapiro a
demagogue suffering from "the conservatism of aging poets." Yet in
another essay in Part IV, "Passion, Possibility, and Poetry," Smith him-
self, in the course of outlining his workshop method, confirms Shapiro's
main contention. "Most [poetry workshop] students," he says, "have
read very little, have at best a rudimentary understanding of poetry,
and have only in the rarest instances a vocabulary which permits the
articulation and exchange of helpful criticism."

Nonetheless, after a few semesters of sitting around discussing one
another's poems, these students will be graduated, given letters of rec-
ommendation, and sent on their way to other universities (which will
hire them to teach writing) and to little magazines and presses (which
will publish their work). It's a disturbing setup, which seems designed,
more than anything else, to frustrate the fortunes of American poetry

by drowning the handful of truly talented young poets in a sea of pro-
lific, well-connected, degree-certified mediocrities. If *Local Assays* and
The Roundhouse Voices have accomplished nothing else, they have es-
tablished Dave Smith as one of the principal exponents of this new
order in American poetry—a prime defender and practitioner, that is,
of Poetry-as-Business, Poetry-as-Self-Exploration, and Poetry-as-
Careerism. Those of us who still cling to the reactionary old habit of
thinking of poetry as literature cannot but be dismayed by it all.

DECEMBER 1985

TALK SHOW:
THE RISE OF THE LITERARY INTERVIEW

Yet from none of these men, in conversation, did I learn a critical thing.
—Donald Hall, *Remembering Poets*

My first interview took place when I was twenty-four, a graduate teaching assistant in English. I had the most tenuous possible claim to fame: I'd just published a newspaper op-ed piece—a modest forerunner to E.D. Hirsch's *Cultural Literacy*—in which I'd complained about how ignorant my undergraduate composition students were of even the most fundamental facts of history, geography, and the like. Somehow, the news director of the university radio station got wind of this article and decided to interview me on the air. "Controversial topic," he growled at me over the phone. "Hard-hitting." "Should I prepare anything?" I asked, in obsequious grad-student fashion. "Hell, no!" he barked. "Last thing we want is something prepared. Just talk off the cuff." When I showed up for the taping session, his only words of advice were, "Act natural."

Well, I acted natural, and I suppose it went well enough; my interviewer told me afterwards that I had come across as "very relaxed, very natural," and apparently this—along with the fact that my topic had been "controversial" and my approach "hard-hitting"—was all that mattered. Whether I had actually said anything worth listening to seemed to be relatively unimportant. In any event, once it was over, there were two things I knew for certain: first, that so far as I had managed to sound relaxed and natural, I'd been guilty of manufacturing an illusion; and second, that although most of what I'd said during the interview had indeed come off the top of my head, in those moments when I'd spoken to the point most clearly and succinctly there had been no spontaneity on my part whatsoever. On the contrary, I'd been working from a script—reciting from memory, that is, the words of my op-ed piece. This realization made me wonder why on earth radio listeners should be asked (and why, for that matter, they should be willing) to spend half an hour of their lives listening to an extemporaneous conversation on the subject of college students' ignorance—an interview that by the very nature of its form was bound to be characterized by inexact diction and needless repetition, among other infelicities—when they could instead, in the space of two minutes, read my article, in which I'd said everything I had to say on the subject in the best words I could find? In the twenty-eight minutes that the audience saved by reading the essay instead of listening to the interview, they could read half-a-dozen Wallace Stevens poems they'd never had time for, or listen to a recording of the Waldstein Sonata, or study a map of Eurasia or a diagram of the Krebs cycle or, for that matter, make love. Who was I to take up their valuable time with my unpremeditated yammering?

This was, I now realize, a foolish question. For it has become clear to me in the intervening years that, in these peculiar times, unpremeditated yammering—whether it is recorded on audiotape, videotape, or good old-fashioned paper—is one of those things of which we Americans simply cannot get enough. Interviews, in short, are hot. To glance at the television listings is to recognize that it is possible to spend upwards of ten hours a day watching almost nothing else. On a typical weekday in the New York metropolitan area, for instance, you can follow two hours of chatter on "Good Morning America," say, with an hour of "Geraldo" or of something called "The Morning Show," a half-hour of "Best Talk in Town," an hour of "Hour Magazine," an hour with either Phil Donahue or Oprah Winfrey (or both, if you choose to tape one for later viewing), and an hour of "Live at Five." In the evening, there's an endless stream of interview programs to choose from, including "Nightline" and "The Tonight Show"; for late-late television viewers, there are four straight hours of "CBS News Nightwatch"; and on the weekend, there's an endless stream of political interview programs, both national and local, along the lines of "Meet the Press." Although their titles may suggest that they consist principally of news or some sort of entertainment, these shows are mostly composed of interviews, one after another—interviews with TV stars and Vegas headliners, with public officials and opinion makers, with psychiatrists, sociologists, educators, clergymen, "experts" of every kind. And even, here and there, a few interviews with writers.

It doesn't seem much of an exaggeration, indeed, to say that, in America in the 1980s, the interview is an even hotter form than the music video. This is no less the case in the pages of the literary magazines than it is on the television screen. Forty years ago, in the heyday of the *Partisan* and *Kenyon* reviews, literary interviews were all but unheard of in the pages of serious journals; then, in 1953, George Plimpton founded the *Paris Review*, and nothing has been quite the same since. The second half of its title notwithstanding, from the very beginning the *Paris Review*'s editors held to a policy of not publishing critical essays or reviews. Instead, they ran literary interviews—a brilliant way to get the names of gigantically famous writers on the cover without having to pay gigantic fees for their work. And famous writers were, as it turned out, more than willing to cooperate. The interviews gave them an opportunity to promote their work, to settle old scores, to get their opinions into print without having to write about them. The interviews let them talk about themselves—and what could appeal more strongly to the average writer's ego? The first issue of the *Paris Review* contained an interview with E.M. Forster; another early number featured the now-famous conversation with Ernest Hemingway. These and other such interviews, published (usually) two to an issue, brought the magazine considerable early recognition at relatively little expense. In fact, they brought it a degree of fame that one cannot imagine it having attained on the basis of the poetry and fiction that have appeared in its pages. Other small-magazine editors took note, and during the sixties and seventies the *Paris Review*'s emphasis on literary interviews rather than critical essays was imitated widely.

Though scores of literary magazines nowadays routinely publish interviews with writers, the *Paris Review*'s contributions continue to be markedly more admirable than most. Part of the reason for this, I think, is that the *Paris Review* does something that might be considered cheating: it treats the interview transcript not as a sacred document to be presented verbatim, but as a piece of copy which, like everything else that goes into the magazine, is open to editing, tightening, revision. In addition to doing their own blue-penciling, moreover, the editors allow the writer being interviewed to make changes. The interview text itself, unlike most published literary magazine interviews, often represents more than one encounter between the parties; in many instances, if an interview is deemed too thin, the interviewer is dispatched a second time, and perhaps even a third, to post further questions.

The *Paris Review*, in other words, does not go in for what a friend of mine refers to as the "interview vérité." That's the sort of interview in which not only the subject's every word is dutifully transcribed, but also his sneezes, coughs, laughs, *um*'s, and *ah*'s are reverently recorded for the enlightenment of future generations. This sort of interview came into vogue in the sixties, thrived in the seventies, and has faded a bit in the eighties, though ludicrous examples of it may still be found here and there. Take, for example, this excerpt from an interview that the poet Tim Dlugos conducted with the poet Michael Lally for a 1980 issue of a magazine called *Little Caesar*:

> *TD: ...What's your favorite color?*
>
> ML: It's um, uh...I'm looking for a new one.
>
> *TD: (Laughs)*
>
> ML: It's obviously been blue. For a number of years. I remember in the Fifties, it was red and black. Then it was pink and grey. Then it was grey and black, with a little olive drab. Then it became blue, and it's been blue ever since.
>
> *TD: What's your favorite T.V. show?*
>
> ML: That's a good question. Old movies. But, obviously, they don't qualify as T.V. shows, let me think a second. (long pause) I don't have a favorite at the moment, except now it's just specials.
>
> *TD: What's your favorite food?*
>
> ML: It's always been chicken. That's easy to answer.
>
> *TD: Okay (laughs)*
>
> ML: What's my favorite gender? (laughs) What's my favorite...uh...(laughs)
>
> *TD: That's a good question. What's your favorite gender? (long pause) Well, which do you like better, going to bed with men or going to bed with women?*
>
> ML: (pause) Women...(pause) in terms of the whole procedure. (pause) In my fantasies, it's mixed...now. Although up until my thirties it was always predominantly, almost exclusively women. I find women easier in some ways to approach and get along with and I find the whole sexual encounter with them more familiar and more acceptable to my style and so on. I have difficulties with that too though, I mean I went to bed with a woman the other night

who's about as straight a woman as I've been to bed with in
a long time..."been to bed with"...I hate that expression,
but I don't know how else to put it...

Interviews vérités seem more often to involve poets than fiction
writers. Wendell Berry, in an astute essay on contemporary poetry for
the *Hudson Review*, makes a few observations that, though not explic-
itly concerned with the interview vérité, nonetheless help explain the
popularity of this subgenre among poets and their interviewers. To
Berry's mind, the "sudden rise and growth" of the literary interview
"suggests, as a sort of implied premise, that poets are of a different
kind from other people; hence the interest in what they *say* as opposed
to what they write." Berry speaks of "a class of what might be called
poet watchers," whose purpose in watching poets is not to hear what
they have to say about poetry but to "*examine* the poet, to *study* as
unobtrusively as possible whatever privacies may be disclosed by the
inadvertencies of conversation." The interview vérité is plainly a symp-
tom of this sort of writer-worship gone berserk; and the writer-wor-
ship is in turn symptomatic of that perverse post-Beat Generation men-
tality that views the poet less as an artist—a human being using his
craft, intelligence, and talent to create an ordered, controlled work of
art—than as a prophet, a visionary, a seer, whose every act and utter-
ance is taken to be of nearly scriptural significance. It's a mentality
that doesn't understand how enormous the difference is between writ-
ing and talking—a mentality that doesn't appreciate the thought, the
rewriting, the shaping that go into a coherent, unified literary compo-
sition.

Some of the best *Paris Review* interviews are so far removed from
the verbatim transcripts of the *Little Caesar* type that they might not
even be considered "interviews" at all, in the strictest sense. Though,
in the most recent edition of *Writers at Work: The Paris Review Inter-
views*, the majority of conversations are conventional in format—May
Sarton, Eugène Ionesco, Elizabeth Hardwick, Arthur Koestler, and
William Maxwell were each apparently interviewed in one sitting, and
Malcolm Cowley was interviewed twice—there are a number of de-
partures from this standard operating procedure. John Ashbery, for
instance, was interviewed once, with "a few additional questions...asked
and answered" on later occasions and "incorporated into the whole."
John Barth was interviewed on television by Plimpton, and the tran-
script of this exchange, being deemed "a bit short by the usual stan-

dards of the magazine," especially given that Barth was such a "master of the prolix" (!), was forwarded to Barth with additional questions to answer (although instead of complying, Barth shortened the text he'd been sent). Milan Kundera met with his interviewer, Christian Salmon, several times; but, as Salmon informs readers in his brief introduction, "instead of a tape recorder, we used a typewriter, scissors, and glue. Gradually, amid discarded scraps of paper and after several revisions, this text emerged." The interview with Raymond Carver was conducted partly by mail, and—most radical of all—the one with Philip Larkin entirely by mail.

What these last few incarnations of the *Paris Review* demonstrate is that a literary interview can come into being in any number of ways, so long as the end result reads like a conversation—preferably a spontaneous, informal conversation—between the author being scrutinized and the interviewer. Whether such a conversation ever took place is immaterial. Though there is something to be said, I suppose, for a strict constructionist's view of this modus operandi—for the argument, in other words, that a literary interview that is not the record of a real, live, face-to-face interview is not a bona fide interview at all—what's interesting to me is that, of all the above-mentioned interviews, the one that I consider by far the best is the one whose subject never even so much as met his interviewer. I refer to the interview with Philip Larkin, which Robert Phillips conducted by mail in 1981–82, and which contains this memorable exchange:

> INTERVIEWER: How did you arrive upon the image of a toad for work or labor?
> LARKIN: Sheer genius.

To say that such-and-such an interview is the best in the book, however, is to be confronted immediately with a not-so-easy question—namely, by what criteria do I deem this interview to be the best? Or, to put it more broadly, what critical standards should be brought to bear upon any literary interview? It's a fair question, for no one seems ever to have answered, in anything even remotely approaching a definitive manner, the intimately related and equally difficult question of just what a literary interview is. Is the literary interview, for example, itself a literary form? Can it be art? (An interesting distinction; in the epigraph to his book *Conversations with Capote*, a compilation of interviews with the late writer-celebrity, Lawrence Grobel asks, "Do you think that remarks can be literature?" Capote responds, "No, but they can be art.") Or is the literary interview at best only an entertaining hodge-podge of personality, public relations, and primary source material? Why do we read such things, anyway? Why *should* we read them—or should we perhaps take a cue from the editors of the very best literary magazines, such as *Poetry* and the *Hudson Review*, and not bother with them in the first place?

All of these complex questions can be summarized in one simple question: how seriously should we take the literary interview? Certainly the participants in many an interview take the form very seriously indeed. Again, this seems to be especially true of poets. Forty years ago, a poet with something to say about a poem, another poet, or poetry in general would write an essay; since the 1960s, however, it has become increasingly common for poets to air their literary opinions and theories not in essays but in interviews. With a few notable exceptions, poets don't *write* anymore. If you find it difficult to believe this, look at some of the books in the University of Michigan's "Poets on Poetry" series, the purpose of which is to present literary criticism by notable American poets. In one volume after another of this series, the interviews outnumber the essays; even extremely distinguished poets who have been publishing poetry for decades—some of whom I, for one, admire enormously—prove on inspection to have produced a shockingly small body of critical prose.

Frequently, in such para-critical (as one might call them) interviews, the questioner is also a poet, no less well known than his subject, and hardly any less talkative; sometimes no distinction at all is made between interviewer and interviewee, and the text is described not as an interview but as a "dialogue." Although these interviews may concern philosophical and aesthetic issues, one cannot get away from the fact that they are interviews, not essays; one is manifestly expected to excuse the repetitions, non sequiturs, logical inconsistencies, lapses in diction, and argumentative weaknesses because this isn't somebody writing but rather a transcript of two people talking.

Yet how profound these interview-happy poets try to sound! It's peculiar that the most brilliant and learned poet-critics of mid-century—people like Randall Jarrell and Delmore Schwartz—wrote essays on poetry that were lucid, engaging, and unpretentious; but many a third-rate poet of the present day seems unable to so much as talk about his art without pouring forth the most astounding banalities, couched in the most breathtakingly pretentious terms. Often the poet's purpose in these interviews seems to be not to convey an opinion or insight but to impress the reader with his vocabulary, learning, and ability to string together grandiose abstractions like beads on a string. Perhaps the most remarkable examples of the form are the ones in which both interviewer and interviewee go the pompous, verbose route. Take, for example, an interview that appeared in the fall 1986 issue of the *Seneca Review*. The interviewer is a poet named David Wojahn; the subject is David St. John, another poet. Let's join them *in medias res*:

> DS: ...I think every poem has to be alert to history, both the history of literature and the history of the world. Every poem has to be conscious of the culture in which it is framed, though that doesn't mean that every poem need exhibit an argument about topical matters. It seems to me the most interesting poetry is poetry that investigates the way the human mind performs and responds to history and experience.
>
> DW: One of my reasons for asking that question is a sense I have in your work that artifice is seen as the force that defines our universe, that mitigates our existence, and that prevents our experience from being tragic and overwhelming, and I sometimes feel that that very kind of needful embrace of artifice is what allows you to achieve success with strategies and stylistic techniques that in the work of other poets might seem strained or mannered.
>
> DS: Well, I hope that's true.

This sort of thing is not literary discourse—it's two poets showing off, pure and simple.

Every so often, to be sure, one comes across a literary interview that seems genuinely valuable—an interview that, if one were teaching an undergraduate course about the writer, one might well add to the reading list. A fine example is a brief interview that David Stern conducted with Robert Fitzgerald for *Sequoia* in 1976. It is a no-nonsense conversation in which Stern asks about Fitzgerald's method of translating Homer, about the development of the verse form used in his translations, about his opinion of other translations, and about the possible influences upon him of Pound and Stevens. Stern poses such questions as "What are the most important things to try to keep from the original Greek in an English translation?" Fitzgerald's answers are clear, taut, straightforward, carefully worded, and fitted out, where necessary, with well-chosen examples:

> D.S.: What kind of liberties did you feel you were allowed to take in your translations and what kind of liberties did you feel that you could not take?
>
> R.F.: Translating is finding equivalents. When I was at work on *The Odyssey*, I had to find them. For example, I had been puzzled, as everyone had for centuries, by the epithet given to Nestor—"Lord of Pylos, Warden of Achaeans." In what sense he was warden of Achaeans puzzled everyone. I found among the palace tablets a list of categories of people employed by the palace. When I saw that among these categories were coast watchers, I knew I had found the answer. Pylos was on the west coast of the Peloponnesus and we knew that sea raiders were very common in those centuries among those waters. What was more natural that there should be coast watchers detailed in the keeping of the palace? This was something for which a modern equivalent might be found. I found it in the list of titles of the commanding admirals in the Second World War. In England there was a whole command of destroyers and destroyer escorts operating out of their West Coast to spot German submarines in the sea lanes leading to the British Isles. The name of that command was "The Lord of the Western Approaches." So Nestor became "The Lord of the Western Approaches to Achaea," and I knew I had my equivalent for him.

Few literary interviews, alas, are this serious and useful. Far from providing reliable information, most subjects of literary interviews are congenitally foggy about names, dates, titles, and such. In a *Paris Review* interview, for instance, Tennessee Williams declares that William Inge wrote "an enormously brilliant work"—but Williams can't remember the title: "*Natural Affection*, or something like that." Errors of transcription are also common. Thus, in the Tennessee Williams interview, Hemingway's story "A Simple Enquiry" becomes "A Simple Inquiry," Sheilah Graham becomes Sheila, and Elinor Wylie becomes Eleanor. Of course, errors of this variety may be found in critical essays too; but they seem to occur more frequently in literary interviews and to be taken far less seriously by all concerned. Indeed, there seems to be an unspoken understanding among interviewers, editors, and readers that literary interviews should not be held to the same standards of accuracy as, say, literary essays. Even if an interview subject misrepresents the truth, his questioner will almost certainly not contradict him. Why not? Because he couldn't care less about the truth. What literary interviewers are after is not truth but sheer portraiture. So what, their logic seems to run, if the interview subject gets his facts wrong, contradicts himself, or fails to support an argument adequately? That's *him*—and to try to correct his facts, or to ask him to rethink his argument, would only be to stifle his individuality, to muck up the character portrait.

In many an editorial office, in fact, a writer's value as an interview subject seems to be directly proportionate to the outrageousness, immoderation, and irresponsibility of his remarks. So at least it would appear from the publication, in recent years, of two grotesque compilations: Lawrence Grobel's *Conversations with Capote* (NAL, 1985) and Robert J. Stanton and Gore Vidal's *Views from a Window: Conversations with Gore Vidal* (Lyle Stuart, 1980). Whatever one might think of Capote's and Vidal's fiction, it is obvious that they were made the subjects of such books not because their writings tower over those of their contemporaries but because both of them are notorious for saying sensational things. Even more than most writers, Capote and Vidal relish the interview as an opportunity to brag, to show off, to settle old scores and trash the competition with some *ad hominem* name-calling. The "literary criticism" in these two interview books, accordingly, is for the most part of the crudest variety (which is a marked contrast, one should add, to Vidal's often highly accomplished literary essays). In a chapter called "Contemporaries," for instance, Capote shoots spitballs at one after another of his fellow novelists: Kesey is "dead," Kerouac "was a joke," Bellow "is a nothing writer," Malamud is "unreadable." Updike? "I hate him." As for Joyce Carol Oates,

> She's a joke monster who ought to be beheaded in a public auditorium or in Shea or in a field with hundreds of thousands. (*Laughs.*) She does all the graffiti in the men's room and the women's room in every public toilet from here to California and back, stopping in Seattle on her way! (*Laughs.*) To me, she's the most loathsome creature in America...
>
> *Has she ever said or written anything about you to deserve such vituperation?*

> Yes, she's written me a fan letter. She's written me extreme fan letters. But that's the kind of hoax she is. I bet there's not a writer in America that's ever had their name in print that she hasn't written a fan letter to. I think she's that kind of person...or creature...or whatever. She's so...oooogh! (*Shudders.*)

So long as one is not on Capote's list of victims, this sort of thing makes for entertaining reading. But after a while the utter lack of substance wears one down, and Capote's cattiness seems merely depressing. Can this really, one wonders, be the testament of a major American writer? What is wrong with a literary scene capable of producing such a document? What warped set of values in America's editorial offices could possible have resulted in the placing of such nonsense between hard covers?

Cattiness, it should be noted, is not the exclusive province of American writers. Nearly all literary interviewees, foreign and domestic, have something to say about their fellows, and whereas young and ambitious writers tend to dole out more politic praise than tough criticism, many older writers specialize in snappy put-downs. In the course of her *Paris Review* interview, for instance, Rebecca West makes mention of Somerset Maugham, who "couldn't write for toffee, bless his heart"; of Leonard Woolf, who "had a tiresome mind" ("But he was certainly good to Virginia"); of Arnold Bennett, who "was a horrible mean-spirited hateful man"; and of George Bernard Shaw, who possessed "a poor mind, I think." As for Yeats,

> He wasn't a bit impressive and he wasn't my sort of person at all. He boomed at you like a foghorn. He was there one time when Philip Guedalla and two or three of us were all very young, and were talking nonsense about murderers in Shakespeare and whether a third murderer ever became a first murderer by working hard or were they, sort of, hereditary slots? Were they like Japanese specialists and one did one kind of murder, another did another? It was really awfully funny. Philip was very funny to be with. Then we started talking about something on the Western isles but Yeats wouldn't join in, until we fussed round and were nice to him. But we were all wrong. What he liked was solemnity and, if you were big enough, heavy enough, and strong

enough, he loved you. He loved great big women. He would have been mad about Vanessa Redgrave.

So much for the greatest poet of the century. This passage is of course vintage cantankerous, dotty old English literary lady, but in a sense it is a classic literary interview excerpt: one part valuable (the modest addition to the trove of Yeatsiana), one part ridiculous (the remark about how much less fun Yeats was to be with than Philip Guedalla), one part entertaining (the joke about murderers in Shakespeare), and one part utterly bizarre (the mention of Miss Redgrave).

It is rather refreshing to remember that for every know-it-all, like Capote or West, there is a *faux-naïf* like Larkin:

> INTERVIEWER: Is Jorge Luis Borges the only other contemporary poet of note who is also a librarian, by the way? Are you aware of any others?
> LARKIN: Who is Jorge Luis Borges?

To read an interview with a writer like Larkin is to appreciate the literary interview as a legitimate means of getting a glimpse of an extremely unusual personality—in this case, a personality that is crabbed yet somehow charming. Elizabeth Bishop is likewise an appealing interview subject, sensible and ladylike and truly modest: "There's nothing more embarrassing than being a poet, really." Isaac Bashevis Singer is also delightful, in the manner of a grouchy grandfather:

> INTERVIEWER:
> Sin is more interesting than virtue. That's what George Bernard Shaw said.
> SINGER:
> We didn't need George Bernard Shaw to say it.

William Goyen is gentlemanly and reflective, as demonstrated by this *pensée*, a part of his memory of his friend Carson McCullers's writing block:

> It was a murderous thing, a death blow, that block. She said she just didn't have anything to write. And really, it was as though she had never written. This happens to writers when there are dead spells. We die sometimes. And it's as though

we're in a tomb; it's a death. That's what we all fear, and that's why so many of us become alcoholics or suicides or insane—or just no-good philanderers.

William Maxwell, too, is a gentleman, just as sensitive, mild-mannered, and unpretentious as his wonderful novel *The Folded Leaf* might lead one to expect; one immediately likes him as much as one likes his work. But Maxwell is an exception; usually there's surprisingly little correlation between one's opinion of a writer's *oeuvre* and one's reaction to his personality as it comes across in a literary interview. However exquisite much of Capote's fiction may be, it is difficult to like him as a person; on the other hand, Stephen Spender is so genially candid about the weaknesses of his own work ("Auden was much better than I") that it's hard to dislike him. One can take the humble act too far, though: Kurt Vonnegut tries so hard to come off as a regular guy—telling dumb jokes, calling himself a "hack," and describing writing ostentatiously as a "trade"—that it seems a bit too much like slumming. But then one of the pleasures of literary interviews is watching writers (not all, but some) straining desperately to come off a certain way.

The foremost reason most writers agree so readily to grant interviews, of course, is that literary interviews are a splendid way to promote themselves. Many a big literary gun—the names of Vidal and Philip Roth, to mention two, spring instantly to mind—has developed this variety of media exploitation to a high art. (It might be convincingly argued, in fact, that it is in the fine art of publicity that such celebrity writers as these demonstrate their greatest gifts.) Far from merely using the literary interview, as movie stars use the television talk show, to plug their latest products, "name" writers like Vidal and Roth are out to establish the terms in which these products will be discussed by critics, to determine the criteria by which they will be judged. For example, when in the June 1987 *Interview* magazine Vidal discourses upon *Empire*—his historical novel set in America during the Theodore Roosevelt era—he seems eager to ensure that reviewers will dwell not upon its fictional artistry (or lack thereof) but rather upon its value as a history lesson. "I am the history teacher of the country," Vidal claims, adding that, in the series of novels of which *Empire* is a part, "I've redreamed the entire history of the Republic."

Not all interview subjects are as effective as Vidal at stage-managing their conversations. As often as not, interviewers retain the upper hand. Which topics they choose to dwell upon varies from one to the other. Some interviewers want to delve into what it means to be a woman writer, a black writer, an English writer, a homosexual writer. Daniel Stern asks Bernard Malamud: "Does this idea or theme, as you call it, come out of your experience as a Jew?" (And later: "Are you a Jewish writer?" Malamud: "What is the question asking?") Rebecca West's interviewer keeps asking questions that contain the word *woman* (and no wonder, because when one turns to the interviewer's biographical note, one discovers that she is the author of feminist studies of the Virgin Mary and Joan of Arc, and "is currently working on a study of female form in allegory"). More often than not, the interviewer is more interested than the interviewee in discussing such matters and tends to press on (as West's interviewer does) long after the author has clearly grown tired of the topic.

This is, needless to say, a mark of bad interviewing. One of the things a good interviewer must be able to sense is that it's time to move on. He must have good instincts, too, about the next turn the interview should take, must have the sensitivity and savvy to follow his subject's line of thought, and must be able to ask intelligent follow-up questions when the occasion arises. A good interviewer must know as much as possible about his subject, but must not wear that knowledge on his sleeve. He must have enough in common with his subject to make possible a meeting of the minds, but must be different enough to get something interesting going; he must balance sophistication with curiosity, respect with skepticism.

And he must ask the right questions. Naturally, most interview questions are familiar ones. Probably ninety percent of the conversations in ninety percent of literary interviews revolve around the same handful of topics: writing habits (What time of day do you write? How many drafts? Is it hard? Is it fun? Do you use a pencil, typewriter, or computer?); personal history (What was your childhood like? How autobiographical is your work?); other writers (What do you think of them? Which ones have influenced you?) and literature in general. And then there is that broad category of questions about the subject's social, political, ethical, and philosophical ideas. Usually, these are the questions that separate the men from the boys. Some distinguished authors, when they talk about non-literary ideas, are quite impressive; others are so blinkered, narcissistic, and just plain fatuous that they remind one of starlets holding forth on *The Tonight Show*. When Tennessee Williams praises Fidel Castro's regime, for example, it's plain that he's doing so mainly because, when he went to Cuba, Castro knew who he was, treated him with respect, and "introduced me to the Cuban cabinet.... When he introduced us, he turned to me and said, 'Oh, that *cat!*' and winked. He meant *Cat on a Hot Tin Roof*, of course. I found that very engaging." As for President Carter, the major fault Williams found with him was that he ran a dry White House: "We were only allowed to have one very small glass of what was purported to be a California chablis." And here—just to show Williams, in his *Paris Review* interview, attempting to develop a serious critical thought—is the complete text of a section of the interview entitled "The State of the Culture":

> Literature has taken a back seat to the television, don't you think? It really has. We don't have a culture anymore that favors the creation of writers, or supports them very well. I mean, serious artists. On Broadway, what they want are cheap comedies and musicals and revivals. It's nearly impossible to get serious work even produced, and then it's lucky to have a run of a week. They knocked Albee's *Lolita* down horribly. I've never read such cruel reviews. But I felt it was a mistake for Albee to do adaptations. He's brilliant doing his own original work. But even so, I think there's a way of expressing one's critical displeasures with a play without being quite so hard, quite so cruel. The critics are literally killing writers.

The principal emotion that one experiences when reading a passage such as this is embarrassment—embarrassment for Williams, for American drama, for literature. Would such silly, incoherent observations as these ever be allowed into print in any other context than a literary interview?

Complain as we may, the form continues to increase in prominence. In the past few years, whole volumes of literary interviews have proliferated. In 1984, Alfred A. Knopf published Charles Ruas's *Conversations with American Writers* (among the subjects, unsurprisingly, are Capote, Vidal, Mailer, and Williams); in 1987, the University of Illinois Press issued *Alive and Writing: Interviews with American Authors of the 1980s*. (Editing volumes of literary interviews is apparently developing into a favorite, and respectable, scholarly pursuit; one of the two editors of *Alive and Writing* is a Professor Larry McCaffery of San Diego State University, who has also co-edited *Anything Can Happen: In-*

terviews with Contemporary American Novelists.) The already-mentioned books of interviews with Vidal and Capote have been joined by an entire series of book-length "literary conversations" with individual writers (including Flannery O'Connor and Katherine Anne Porter) published by the University of Mississippi Press. A form of literary interview that has become especially popular in the 1980s is the sort in which the subject himself is not interviewed—or, at least, is only one of many persons interviewed. I am speaking of the "oral biography," in which the biographical subject is portrayed not by a single biographer, who has sifted through the primary sources and formed a coherent vision of one person's life and character, but by a number of people who knew the subject; on such projects it is the job of the "biographer" (if such a word can even be used) to record, transcribe, edit, and put into some order these people's taped remarks about the subject. Peter Brazeau's *Parts of a World: Wallace Stevens Remembered* (1983) is one example thereof; Peter Manso's *Mailer: His Life and Times* (1985) is another. Just as the interview form has, then, in the past couple of decades, taken the place of the critical essay in the *oeuvres* of many poets, it has likewise, in recent years, begun to move in on the territory of the literary biography. Taken together, all of these developments—anthologies of interviews, book-length interviews, and oral biographies—are an ominous sign that in the 1980s, even when the topic at hand is literature, real writing is increasingly giving way to talking disguised as writing.

In his introduction to volume four of *Writers at Work* (1976), Wilfrid Sheed notes that, in a review of volume two, he had complained "that the information contained therein was neither better nor worse than Hollywood gossip." But the complaint, he confesses, was "dishonest...in that I artfully concealed how much I enjoyed the volume—which meant it had some kind of value, if not the kind I was looking for. It was also an ingenuous piece because I did not yet realize that gossip is the very stuff of literature, the *materia prima* of which both books and their authors are made." (Note also Truman Capote in *Conversations with Capote*: "All literature...is gossip.") Sheed goes on to say that a literary interview is worthwhile because it affords us a glimpse of the author in the act of "self-creation," of fashioning his own image; and he claims that what distinguishes writers from Hollywood movie actors—and what therefore makes literary interviews, despite their preoccupation with trivial details, more valuable than interviews with movie actors—is that an author "knows, as movie actors do not, that such details can immortalize a character." This argument seems to me extraordinarily misguided: if there's anything that movie actors do know about, it is the manufacturing of images and the fixing of characters in the public consciousness.

As for Sheed's point that all literature is gossip, I suppose in the broadest sense this could be said to be true; but one must distinguish between the high gossip of *Hamlet* and the low gossip of Liz Smith's column, and one must recognize that the literary interview is closer to the latter than to the former. Whereas reading almost anything "literary" requires a certain level of concentration, reading literary interviews is mostly very much like reading Liz Smith, or for that matter watching television.

Yet Sheed does have a point. Literary interviews can be fun to read, and it would be dishonest not to admit, even while one is decrying the form for its vulgarities and pretensions, that one has been much entertained by them. And there's nothing *wrong* with being entertained by them. The important thing is to admit that most of the time, one is merely being entertained and not edified—to acknowledge that the majority of literary interviews fall squarely into the same category as movie-star biographies, literary party gossip, talk radio, and "Entertainment Tonight." And to recognize, even as one is enjoying oneself, that one's time would really be much better spent reading the fiction, poetry, or plays for which these people are famous than poring over a published transcript of their extemporaneous chatter.

SUMMER 1988

BRIEF ENCOUNTERS: CREELEY, SNYDER AND COMPANY

Poems have always been mirrors to Robert Creeley. While the rest of us look on from the sidelines, he stares down at the page and into himself in often perplexing private rituals of self-love and self-hate, self-reverence and self-punishment. As his *Collected Poems 1945-1975* (published last year by the University of California Press) makes abundantly clear, the theme Creeley has kept returning to throughout his career is the detachment of the Self: its isolation in a body, a place, a time—contexts which he is powerless to alter. "Here I / am. There / you are," he asserts laconically in a poem from the 1960s called "The Finger." In another Sixties poem, "Numbers," he insists: "You are not / me, nor I you." And in one of five poems titled "Here" (for Creeley recycles titles almost as frequently as he does themes) he declares, "No one lives in / the life of another— / no one knows."

As these quotations suggest, it is quite possible to come away from a Creeley poem without being too baffled. What *is* difficult is to come away sated. For, though there are occasional moments of interest (usually when Creeley breaks his rules against figurative language, grammar, syntax, description, and logic), most of those Creeley poems which do not come under the category of "cryptic" are simple trifling. *Mirrors* is, essentially, the mixture as before.[1] Most of the poems, to one degree or another, are minimalistic meditations upon the natural walls that divide Self from Other, present from past, here from there. Here is a characteristic entry *in toto*, including the title: "SHE IS / *Far from me* / thinking / her long / warmth, close- // ness, how / her face lights, / changes, how / I *miss* her, // *want no* / *more time* / *with out* / *her*." The book contains Creeley's second poem to be given the title "There," his third "Time," his second "Dreams" (if you don't count two earlier poems titled "Dream"), and his second "Echoes" (not to mention "Some Echo"; there are also three earlier poems titled "Echo" and one "Echo

---

[1] *Mirrors*, by Robert Creeley; New Directions. $6.95.

Of"). Choose a poem at random in this book, and you can not only trace its ancestry in the *Collected Poems*, you can hunt up its brothers and sisters elsewhere in *Mirrors*.

Age, death, and old memories seem to be increasingly on Creeley's mind (and when Creeley is writing about age, death, and memory, you can be sure there will be poems titled "Age," "Death," and "Memory"). In some of the poems in *Mirrors*, these preoccupations are expressed memorably. Here, for example, is the Williams-like "Memory, 1930":

> There are continuities in memory, but
> useless, dissimilar. My sister's
>
> recollection of what happened won't
> serve me. I sit, intent, fat,
>
> the youngest of the suddenly
> disjunct family, whose father is
>
> being then driven in an ambulance
> across the lawn, in the snow, to die.

If this poem is above-average Creeley, it's because, though it treads familiar Creeley territory, it does so in comprehensible human terms (and perhaps even with a dash of symbolism, against which the poet has railed extensively). Unlike run-of-the-mill Creeley, "Memory, 1930" is blessed with clarity, concreteness, and even a measure of music. That the poet appears in the poem as a child is also unusual; Creeley has heretofore published few poems about his childhood, his parents, or his own children. There are, however, a few such poems in *Mirrors*, and they seem to have taken the place of his hostile-husband and suffering-lover poems, which with their Berrymanesque combination of self-pity, contentiousness, and adoration (*vide* "Ballad of the Despairing Husband"), have more or less bitten the dust. Creeley, in short, seems to be mellowing.

Gary Snyder's last book was his Pulitzer prize-winning *Turtle Island* (1974), whose title, as he explained in an introductory note, was "the old/new name for the continent, based on many creation myths [in which the earth is seen as resting on a turtle's back] of the people who have been living here for millenia, and reapplied by some of them to 'North America' in recent years." Like *Turtle Island*, *Axe Handles* is about North America, in particular about the underpopulated, still unspoiled regions of the American West which Snyder has made his home.[2] It is an America of axes and water pumps, tortoises and woodchucks, Douglas fir and Ponderosa pine, Boletas and pennyroyal, an America free of TV sets, frozen dinners, and *The New Yorker*. The poet seems increasingly comfortable in this world, perfectly happy being a tiny component—"a naked bug / with a white body and brown hair"—of what he sees as an exquisitely ordered universe.

The title of the present book signals Snyder's heightened interest in tradition, culture, and family. The title poem begins with Snyder helping his son Kai (who, with his other son, Gen, plays an important part in this book) to make an axe handle. They carve the handle with Snyder's axe, and the poet remembers Pound's words: "'When making an axe handle / the pattern is not far off.'" The carving of the boy's axe handle with his father's axe comes to represent, for Snyder, the passing on of knowledge and skills from one generation to the next— which is, in fact, the dominant theme of the book. Snyder derives great strength and security from the recognition that his sons are his "gifts to the future / to remember us." Because of this strength and security, Snyder is more successful in *Axe Handles* than in most of his earlier works at avoiding the temptation to deal in the angry abstractions ("Freedom," "Nature," "the People") which filled *Turtle Island*, or to beat the drum for his Zen-Amerindian-Marxist philosophy. He reads like a man who has found tranquillity: the form of his poems has grown more regular, the language more conventional, the tone more pensive, less self-conscious, and never hysterical or pretentiously nutty or shrill. He is still a man of convictions, but they are for the most part (the relatively blunt "For / From Lew" is an exception) communicated implicitly through simple, significant dramatic episodes. Some of these episodes are real-life encounters (complete with exact dates and settings) with his children; others are encounters with the land—which, like his sons, represents to Snyder a link with eternity. He rhapsodizes the earth—not only the American West but Japan, the homeland of his wife's family—in a number of poems whose shape and sound (and even typeface) recall the most Oriental of Pound's *Cantos*.

---

[2]*Axe Handles*, by Gary Snyder; North Point Press, $12.50 cloth, $7.50 paper.

Indeed, so tranquil is Snyder that even when he makes a point of noticing the various computer-age (or even industrial-age) phenomena which do intrude into his world from time to time, he perceives them not as symbols of evil (as was his practice in *Turtle Island*) but as exotic manifestations of his revered natural order. Snyder does, however, come upon a few phenomena which he has trouble fitting into the natural universe as he has come to understand it. One such phenomenon is a Strategic Air Command jet. Yet even this emblem of destruction does not incite his wrath toward the "Amerika" which he described in his previous book as a nation of "invaders" who stole Turtle Island from the Indians and "who wage war around the world." Lying in a sleeping bag in the Sierra Nevada and watching the lights of a SAC jet streaking across the sky, the poet muses:

> These cliffs and the stars
> Belong to the same universe.
> This little air in between
> Belongs to the twentieth century and its wars.

Quietly, gently, *Axe Handles* conveys a luminous, poignant vision of a life afforded joy and strength by recognition of the essential things which give it meaning. It is, to my tastes, Snyder's finest book.

Stephen Sandy's taut, precise poems describe—in relentless, often cryptic, symbolic terms—the way in which one human generation succeeds another.[3] His natural symbols, among them lights, roots, rain, shade, macadam surfaces, and the branches of saffron trees, occur in poem after poem, sometimes memorably, sometimes quite confusingly. Until one has picked up Sandy's private language, a good deal of his poetry is nearly incomprehensible. "Family Album," for example, a poem about frayed-edged Polaroids in a photograph album, states: "These sculptures are volcanic rock / Carved to look like corrugated card / The silly grin means they were once aflame." These three lines contain two of Sandy's major symbols: rocks and fire. Fire symbolizes life, of which such things as photographs (represented by volcanic rock) are the inert records. Rocks appear with such frequency in *Riding to Greylock*, always with the same thematic significance, that it might be

---

[3] *Riding to Greylock*, by Stephen Sandy; Knopf, $11.95 cloth, $6.95 paper.

fairly said that they constitute the book's central conceit. The fine, "Ozymandias"-like opening poem, "End of the Picaro," describes the remains of an "Edifice once of stunning proportions—decked / With mottos of obedience, loyalty, pomp," which has been reduced to rubble, its inscriptions made unreadable by "tendrils [which] grip / The scattered letters broken to unbreakable / Code. The trail stops here. / Or here. And here. / Or so: it merely fails in brakes where kudzu / Wild grape and raspberry lashes rope and knot." Thus new life, in the form of sprawling vines, obliterates the records of past lives. The closing poem, "Returning to Eagle Bridge," describes not a once-grand edifice but a once-grand stone marker, the letters of which are in the process of being erased by creeping myrtle:

> It is time for the inaccessible again,
> To lose the place, and all that had taken place.
> On the terrace the myrtle is creeping on the marble
> Slab we unearthed by the barn and planted here
> Face-up so its buried words would see the light,
> "H. Pratt" and "Fecit, 1 8 7 8."
> The grooves uneven, graved by an amateur,
> Seem fainter now after seven years of rain,
> Just legible—before the myrtle had begun
> Its evergreen erasure. Names everywhere
> Here; everywhere lost track of...

Although these poems are purportedly about human life, the human context is sometimes lost in them, and the true poetry of which Sandy is capable is choked out by unmusical phrases like "bouffant catafalque," "viridian micro-scape," "latticed creel," and "deep-tunneled loggia," which seem to please Sandy's ear as much as they displease mine, and by a persistent and sometimes impenetrable symbolism which comes to seem rather mechanical. If the poems about becoming a father in part two of *Riding to Greylock* are pleasing out of all proportion to their actual literary value, it is because finally Sandy is expressing his generational theme in human (rather than geological, botanical, or meteorological) terms. After reading several poems in which human beings, when they appear at all, play supporting roles to "granite plates / And mica glintings" and the like, it is refreshing to see a baby described as the "paradise / of generation verified; *now* made minutely visible!" This is not to deny the force of the symbolism that dominates such fine poems as "Groupings," "Oyster Cove," "Summer Mountains," and "Winter Mountain"; it is merely to suggest that Stephen Sandy could use some men to match his mountains.

C.K. Williams is, among other things, a storyteller.[4] Each of the seventeen long and lovely and lush poems in *Tar* presents a personal anecdote, a "small history" drawn from the poet's life. These poems (which are as reminiscent of the stories of, say, Flannery O'Connor or Peter Taylor as they are of the work of any contemporary poet) recall Pound's dictum that poetry must be as well written as prose: their language is rich and resonant, their sentences beautifully composed. Their lines may be long—between fifteen and twenty or so words apiece—but they are far from Whitmanesque; Williams's lines are quieter than Whitman's, radiating not energy so much as warmth and intensity of feeling, and reflecting not egotism but an exquisite sensibility which is as sensitive to the distresses of others as to its own.

For Williams is not only a storyteller but a portraitist. His poetry is engagingly, magnificently human, and one has the feeling, unusual when reading today's poets, that he is truly interested in the lives around him. He has known alienation and misery—but he also knows that other people have known them at least as intimately as he. The paraplegic Vietnam vet who tumbles out of his wheelchair onto the sidewalk while the poet watches from his upstairs apartment in "From My Window"; the "shabby, tarnished" woman who walks her wretched, drooling dog past his house in "The Dog"; the old lady refugee with the "frightening yellow" feet "horned with calluses and chains of coarse, dry bunions" in "Combat"; the small-town teenager in "Neglect" who is "afflicted with a devastating Nessus-shirt of acne / boiling down his face and neck—pits and pores, scarlet streaks and scars": it is with such pathetic, near-grotesque victims of war and poverty, time and nature, that Williams's poems are concerned. Some of these poems communicate, and quite effectively too, his dismay over the Vietnam War and nuclear power and the decay of American cities; but the strength of these poems lies in Williams's resistance of the temptation to write shrill, preachy protest verse or to escape into the mountains to commune with (and list) every flower, bird, and tree in sight.

---

[4]*Tar*, by C.K. Williams; Random House, $10.00 cloth, $5.95 paper.

People—not issues, ideas, or inert images—are at the center of his poetry.

Among the best poems in *Tar* are "Waking Jed," a vivid, three-page description of the poet's son (one assumes) coming to consciousness in the morning, and "The Color of Time," which seems to derive from the poet's childhood. The latter poem (which is told entirely in the third person, but which one cannot help reading as a memory poem) illustrates Williams's rare gift for unostentatiously bringing out every bit of beauty and meaning in a simple, seemingly unremarkable episode. A boy, home alone, lies in bed in a "late, dull, stifling summer dusk," clad "in briefs and T-shirt, his limp sheet disarrayed," and listens to the cries of an anguished woman in the opposite apartment. "'I can't go on,'" she drones, her voice "harsh but affectless." Another voice accuses her of being drunk, and she replies: "'I'm beating my head.'" The boy remembers having seen her "out back, by the trash." "Something about her repels the boy, maybe the nightgown, maybe that their eyes never meet." The argument quiets down; the next thing the boy knows, he has awakened after drifting off to sleep. Some nights, he knows, he wakes up screaming, with his father or mother holding him:

> He never remembers the scream, just the embrace, usually
>   not even that, but once, he knows,
> he called out, his father came to him: *Listen*, the boy said,
>   *Outside, there are babies crying.*
> *Cats*, his father, angry beyond what the occasion seemed to
>   imply, had whispered, *Go to sleep,*
> jerking roughly, irrationally, the boy had thought, the sheet
>   up nearly over the boy's head.
> Although it's quiet now, not a sound, it's hard—the boy
>   doesn't know why—not to cry out.
> He tries to imagine the bar of warm glow from his parents'
>   room bisecting the hall
> but the darkness stays stubbornly intact and whatever it is
>   shuddering in his chest keeps on.
> I hope I don't cry, he thinks; his thighs lock over his fists:
>   he can hold it, he thinks.

With every line, *Tar* reminds us not only what poetry is all about, but what life is all about. It is a beautiful book.

The guiding philosophy of James Schuyler's fifth collection of verse, *A Few Days*, is indicated at the beginning of its lengthy, concluding title poem.[5] A few days, writes Schuyler,

> are all we have. So count them as they pass. They pass
>   too quickly
> Out of breath: don't dwell on the grave, which yawns for
>   one and all.

This twenty-five-page-long poem, with its long lines, is atypical; all but one or two of the other poems in *A Few Days* are as short, and as short of line (and, for that matter, as unprobing and colloquial), as Robert Creeley poems. Schuyler's *modus operandi* is simple: he totes up his days, at least those he feels like toting up, in chatty, offhand, stream-of-consciousness fashion, with each poem (except the quasi-epical title poem) covering no more than a single day's events, thoughts, emotions. We get dates, weather reports: "It's a hot day: / not so hot / as the days before: / it's *that* July, / the one in 1981, the hot one." Or: "it's / February first, 1982, / and they say (on the radio) / torrents of rain will / descend and the temperature / drop to well below / freezing." We get reports on Schuyler's moods ("I really / love this day"), descriptions of his surroundings (the flower on his desk, the view outside the train window), and rundowns of his daily activities (walking the dog, watching *The Jeffersons*). We also get plenty of confidential, if utterly unrevealing, details (his Blue Cross number, his monthly rent). And we get confessions—extremely personal ones. In several poems, for instance, the middle-aged poet (Schuyler was born in 1923) bewails his unrequited love for his young, blond secretary, whom he names in full:

> Tom, Tom, Tom
> why do you not lie beside me
> I mean to say, why
> Oh, tell me why
> why do you not lie beside me
> entwined in one another's arms
> my head upon your pliant marble shoulder
> you asleep and me awake,

[5]*A Few Days*, by James Schuyler; Random House, 91 pages, $14.95 cloth, $8.95 paper.

decked beside me
body pressed body to body?
Tom Tom Tom Tom, Thomas Paul Carey
I love you so: forever and forever and forever
            and a day
through all eternity
and yet beyond that

Characteristically, this sentimentality is undercut, in the succeeding lines, by a slangy parenthetical flippancy: "(when the inspiration / to write this poem / came to me / en route to see my shrink / I envisioned / twenty or so pages and this is only six: oh well, can't win 'em all)."

Schuyler aims, it is clear, to experience every facet of life with the freshness and vigor of a child, and to render it with a child's brash, no-holds-barred honesty. Like a child, he is quick to declare his love— whether for a man or a woman, the month of October or his notebook from Italy—and his poetry, as a result, is often marked by a primitive charm and sweetness. The principal consequence of his approach to poetry, however, is a want of nobility, depth, intelligence, and linguistic beauty; all too frequently, his verse seems to skate sloppily across the surface of life, grabbing at the first locution to come along. While its energy and feeling are incontrovertible, then, one can't imagine anyone being enchanted by its music, captivated by its play of ideas, or lost in the world it creates.

Though Herbert Morris is a member of Schuyler's generation, his poetry could not be more different form Schuyler's. The poems in his first collection—the widely acclaimed *Peru*, which he did not publish till 1983—were long, elegant narratives written in restrained, pensive blank verse; devoted, for the most part, to the remembrance of things past, they were inspired by childhood memories, old photographs, and history, and they conjured up an exquisite memory-world of ghosts, shadows, and luminous dreamscapes. The twelve poems of Morris's second volume, *Dream Palace*, are essentially more of the same.[6] "Boardwalk," for instance, describes in elaborate and affectionate detail a snapshot of the four-year-old poet-to-be on a holiday with his parents, and

---

[6]*Dream Palace*, by Herbert Morris; Harper & Row, 87 pages, $16.95 cloth, $8.95 paper.

purports to fill in the history of that now-mythical long-ago day; "Road Construction Workers, Westerwald 1927: A Photograph by August Sander" describes a photograph of a German road crew, and attempts to read the story behind the photograph in the faces of the young workmen (many of whom, Morris reasonably implies, doubtless went on to become Nazi soldiers in World War II). "Sackets Harbor, 1866" and "The Park Hotel, Munich, 1907" are both extremely well-executed dramatic monologues; in the former, a 19th-century spinster unburdens herself to a visitor, and in the latter an elderly Sigmund Freud explains a fainting spell to a young Munich physician, and discourses upon the necessity of (among other things) a "belief in the possible":

> allow me, if you will, to entertain,
> at least a little longer, the idea,
> extravagant as it may very well be,
> that, as a young man, you may still be open
> to possibility, to variation
> in human life, to some remnant of music,
> if you will, to those things, as one grows older,
> one seems eager to close off in oneself,
> almost as though one struggled to ward off
> too vigorous an onslaught by those forces
> which would keep us accessible to feeling,
> to passion, to the poetry in us,
> all things unprecedented, unexpected.
> And without that conviction, Doctor, without
> that belief in the possible, what are we?

These poems are so admirably written that when one comes across an error (e.g., "awhile" for "a while") one can hardly believe it; perhaps their major flaw, indeed, is that they are sometimes too composed—not only in the sense of "made," but in the sense of "placid." There are no great, inspired lines here; there is nothing quirky or surprising; and there is little versatility of tone. Nor is Morris's poetry characterized by an overabundance of humor. But these are relatively minor objections. On the whole, *Dream Palace* is a lovely accomplishment, the work of a consistently effective poetic craftsman of entrancing gifts.

Brad Leithauser and Richard Kenney are both young poets whose debut collections—*Hundreds of Fireflies* and *The Evolution of the Flight-less Bird*, respectively—were mightily acclaimed by critics upon their publication in 1984. Both poets have received numerous grants and prizes, and, like Morris, have begun to develop widespread reputations as masters of form. Each has now put together a second full-length volume of verse.

Leithauser, in an introductory note, asks us to regard his new collection, *Cats of the Temple*, "as a sibling companion" to *Hundreds of Fire-flies*.[6] This is not too difficult to do, for like its predecessor the book is a slender rural travelogue of poetic technique marked by extensive internal rhyme and alliteration, elaborate imagery, and a highfalutin, flowery diction that often seems out of place. While *Fireflies* tended to hover about the Michigan countryside, *Cats* takes us to Ireland, Guam, Nova Scotia, and—especially—Japan, whose poetry would seem to have influenced Leithauser's highly visual, compressed lines. (Japan was, by the way, the setting for his run-of-the-mill first novel, *Equal Distance*, published last year.) Some of Leithauser's descriptions of nature are quite accomplished. Too often, though, there appears to be little or no real emotion beneath the highly polished surfaces. Here, for instance, is the beginning of "Seahorses":

> Kin to all kinds
> Of fancied hybrids—minotaur
>   And wyvern, cockatrice,
> Kyrin and griffin—this
> Monkey-tailed, dragon-chested
>   Prankish twist of whimsy
> Outshines that whole composited
> Menagerie, for this sequined
>   Equine wonder, howsoever
>   Improbably,
>
> Quite palpably
> Exists! Within his moted
>   Medium, tail loosely laced
> Round the living hitching post
> Of a coral twig, he feeds at leisure
>   As befits a mild, compromising

---

[6]*Cats of the Temple*, by Brad Leithauser; Knopf, 70 pages, $14.95 cloth, paper $7.95.

Creature with no arms of defense
Save that of, in his knobby
    Sparsity, appearing
    Unappetizing.

Leithauser wants to achieve a tone of wonder here, but it doesn't come off; the enthusiasm strikes one as forced, the diction as unduly precious; the poem is a sparkling but largely soulless exercise in versification. Similarly, the abstruse metaphysical conclusions he supposedly draws from his observations of flora and fauna in such poems as "The Buried Graves" and "Two Suspensions against a Blacktop Backdrop" seem facile.

The weakest part of *Cats in the Temple*, however, is the brief section devoted to "minims" (that's Leithauserese for "light verse"). These verses are so slight and witless that their inclusion in this volume is puzzling. Here, for example, is "Manifest Destiny":

Now if, somehow, offered a brand-new New
World, an endless, arable *tabula rasa*,
Wouldn't we dedicate that one, too, to
The billboard, the smokestack, the shopping plaza?

It is perhaps in these "minims" that Leithauser's major flaw is most manifest: he simply has nothing to communicate that is original or interesting or vital. One comes away from his poems impressed with his technical facility, but one *feels* nothing.

Richard Kenney's new book, *Orrery*, takes its name from an eighteenth-century instrument that plots the orbits of the planets.[7] Indeed, the book is not only named after the orrery; it is, as Kenney explains in an extensive prefatory note, supposed to *be* an orrery—metaphorically speaking, of course. How so? In the sense that the book, like an orrery, takes the yearly cycle as its organizing principle. The poems in its main sequence, "Apples," which relate episodes occurring over a period of several years in the lives of three people on a contemporary Vermont cider-milling farm, are not ordered in true chronological sequence but, instead, are arranged seasonally—from fall to summer—as if they

[7]*Orrery*, by Richard Kenney; Atheneum, 108 pages, $17.50 cloth, $10.95 paper.

chronicled a single twelve-month period. Why has Kenney chosen to do this? Because, as he tells us in his note, he thinks this is the way the memory actually works: we associate events in our past not with a specific year but with a season.

Though I'm not sure I agree with this notion, I could admire a well-executed book based upon it (as, for example, I can admire the theory-ridden poems of Yeats). But it can't really be said that *Orrery* is a well-executed book. Kenney is altogether too strongly in the grip of something that, as one reads along, looks less and less like an insight and more and more like a bad gimmick. The entire book, one comes to realize, hinges upon that prefatory note: a reader who failed to study it before reading the poetry would be totally at sea—and that's a serious weakness. (Even Yeats's poetry, for all his devotion to bizarre cycles, can be appreciated without such preparation.)

The "Apples" poems themselves—most of which are rhythmic, low-voltage, telegraphically brief atmospheric pieces about harvesting apples, repairing chimneys, and observing the stars and the weather—are competent enough. But few are sufficiently strong to stand on their own. (Of the sixty-seven poems in the section, only twelve have appeared in periodicals; the best of these include "Inertia," "Starling," and "The Starry Night.") Many are obscure and tiresomely descriptive—by the end of the book, one feels as if one has learned altogether too much about cider-making—and most are cluttered with ugly, esoteric words like *chert, scry, coign,* and *retrodict.* And the redundancy! Even the titles repeat: there are two poems apiece called "Solstice," "Shadow," "News," and "Orrery." and no fewer than six entitled "Dream," one of which reads as follows:

> I seem to juggle green apples
> in the crown pane;
> a dream of new breath tippled up
> on stems of green champagne,
> where bubbles rise the glassy flue
> like notes blown off a reed,
> or once and future zeroes through
> the ephemerides.

Orrery's two other sections—between which "Apples" is sandwiched—are "Hours" and "Physics." The former comprises seven pages of text, each of which contains two "sonnets" separated by a quatrain in dimeter; the latter consists of fourteen poems, in iambic dimeter, of twenty-eight lines apiece. Kenney's explanation for these formal choices is more baffling then enlightening. Suffice it to say that the poems in both of these sections essentially form an abstract comple-ment of the concrete "Apples"; in them, Kenney philosophizes, often very ambiguously, about "the simple solar systematics / all our lives involve alike." In general, "Hours" is the best-written part of the book (and, not coincidentally, is also that which most clearly betrays his sty-listic indebtedness to James Merrill); in a representative passage, he rejects Einstein, saying:

> I'll keep Sir Isaac Newton's
> world, all crankcase cogs and whirring gears; Ikhnaton's
> axletree's a god, here; sunlight's light, not curd-
> and-whey. Who keeps the time in Janus space? Oh,
>   blinkered
> eye! What curvatures we're knotted in!

This passage, in its renunciation of Einstein—and, by extension, the twentieth century—is emblematic. But Kenney's rendition of old-fash-ioned farm life is ultimately dull, simplistically nostalgic, even conde-scending.

There are, then, some interesting passages in *Orrery*. Kenney is, indeed, a good poet. But what this peculiar book demonstrates more dramatically than anything else is that he, like Leithauser, seems to be grasping at themes.

As its opening poem, "Lines at the New Year," makes plain, *The Sun-set Maker*—Donald Justice's fifth collection in twenty-eight years, and his first book since *Selected Poems* (1979)—is preoccupied with the re-membrance of things past: "The old year slips past / unseen, the way a snake goes. / Vanishes, / and the grass closes behind it."[8] Suffusing most of the twenty-four poems, two stories and one prose memoir that compose this graceful volume are the author's affectionate memories of events and people—including his own younger self—that have van-ished, with the lost years, into the high grass. Solemn and stately, taut

---

[8] *The Sunset Maker*, by Donald Justice; Atheneum, 73 pages, $16 cloth $8.95 paper.

and tender, these writings are nonetheless often startling in their raw response to the fact of mortality: *"The dead,"* runs the refrain in "Nostalgia and Complaint of the Grandparents," *"don't get around much anymore."*

In another poem, "Nostalgia of the Lakefronts," Justice recalls a setting associated with his long-gone youth, and—as he does continually in this book—links natural phenomena to memory, to history: "Nostalgia comes with the smell of rain, you know." Time and again he contrasts the blithe naïveté of the young, in regard to their own mortality, and the sad knowledge that has come to him with age; in "Children Walking Home from School through Good Neighborhood," for instance, he compares a group of boys and girls to "figures held in some glass ball, / One of those in which, when shaken, snowstorms occur; / But this one is not yet shaken." Yet the youngsters are fated to go the way of all flesh; in a striking image, Justice describes them, running in their bright sweaters, as "a little swirl of colors, / Like the leaves already blazing and falling farther north." Time holds them green and dying, though they sing in their chains like the sea.

Poems with titles like "Young Girls Growing Up (1911)" thus coexist in *The Sunset Maker* with poems entitled "Purgatory" and "Cemetery"; the poet shifts easily—or, rather, with a sad unease—from images of innocent youth to reflections upon death and decrepitude. In several poems he elegizes loved ones, including (in "Psalm and Lament") his mother, after whose passing "the yard chairs look empty, the sky looks empty, / The sky looks vast and empty." The quietly insistent repetition is characteristic of the poems in this book, and seems designed to reflect the repetitiousness of the daily routines and natural events (e.g., sunsets) which persist despite a loved one's death:

Out on Red Road the traffic continues; everything continues.
Nor does memory sleep; it goes on.

Out spring the butterflies of recollection,
And I think that for the first time I understand

The beautiful ordinary light of this patio
And even perhaps the dark rich earth of a heart....

Let summer come now with its schoolboy trumpets and fountains.

But the years are gone, the years are finally over.

His mother's passing, then, has turned the poet's own existence into a sort of death-in-life. Yet this state is not without its consolations, bittersweet though they may be. For one thing, he now has a deeper understanding of life and a more profound appreciation of the simple beauties around him. He also has nature, which—even as it seems to mock his mortality or, alternately, to grow old and weary itself—can, with its ever-returning spring, awaken his long-dormant memories of other, happier springs. Finally, he has his art, by means of which he— the sunset maker, the God-mimic—can bring his affections, his memories, and his very self to life for those who choose to read him.

This is presuming, of course, that he continues to be read—a score on which Justice is less sanguine than Emily Dickinson, who boasted in one famous poem that she could fashion two sunsets to the Almighty's one, and who ridiculed publication as "the Auction / Of the Mind of Man." Unlike Dickinson, Justice considers an audience necessary to the artist. In one elegy, he memorializes "the Unknown Poet, Robert Boardman Vaughn"; in the title poem and a pendant story, "Little Elegy for Cello and Piano," the speaker notes that nobody but he remembers the works of his late composer friend Eugene Bestor— and since he recalls only one six-note cello phrase from the entire *oeuvre*, he thinks of Eugene "as surviving through this fragment." He reflects that after his own death, "nobody will recall the sound / These six notes made once," and then Eugene will be truly dead. Unless, of course, the poem and story (in both of which those notes are preserved) continue to be read.

Music occupies an important place alongside poetry in this book; several poems, as well as the memoir, "Piano Lessons," recall Justice's boyhood music teachers. Two of the poems are subtitled "A Song," and indeed, whether Justice writes in prose, free verse, or form (this book includes two villanelles and several sonnets), his work has a manifest musical quality. Justice's ear is perfect. Much of one's joy in his poetry derives from his consistently delicate patterning of sounds, particularly from the wonderful half-rhymes that fill poem after poem— for example, "Villanelle at Sundown"—with a multitude of similar sounds that echo softly off each other:

Turn your head. Look. The light is turning yellow.

> The river seems enriched thereby, not to say deepened.
> Why this is, I'll never be able to tell you.
>
> Or are Americans half in love with failure?
> One used to say so, reading Fitzgerald, as it happened.
> (That Viking Portable, all water-spotted and yellow—
>
> Remember?) Or does mere distance lend a value
> To things?—false, it may be, but the view is hardly cheapened.
> Why this is, I'll never be able to tell you.

Justice's work is memorable not only for its music, though, but for its visual imagery. It does not seem to be a mere coincidence that the title poem mentions a painting by Bonnard, for many a Justice poem—dense with words like "diaphanous," "vague," "wisps," "misty," "ghostly," "blurred," "hints," "glimmerings"—sets a soft-focus, pastel-colored, Bonnard-like canvas before the mind's eye. Justice is a verse Impressionist, an Intimist of the written word.

If one has any reservations about *The Sunset Maker*, it is that the stories and memoir are not up to the poetry. Though it is interesting to see Justice rework a poem's material into prose (something he does twice in this book), it is very much a poet's prose: fastidiously composed and exquisitely contemplative, but structurally weak and short on action and conflict. Yet this is a minor cavil. On the whole, *The Sunset Maker* is a deeply affecting volume—a beautiful, powerful meditation by a modern master upon the themes of aging, lost innocence, and the unalterable, terrifying pastness of the past.

Born in 1926 (a year after Justice), W.D. Snodgrass won fame as a confessional poet. His Pulitzer-winning first book, *Heart's Needle* (1957), influenced the colloquial, personal manner of the pivotal *Life Studies* (1959), whose author, Robert Lowell, wrote to Randall Jarrell that Snodgrass was "incomparably the best poet we've had since you started."

An auspicious beginning. Yet since then Snodgrass has settled into a marginal, ambiguous position on the poetry scene. He continues to be identified with Plath and Sexton; the *Selected Poems 1957-1987*—which contains a variety of work: nature poems, poems about famous paintings, poems in form and free verse—seems intended to change all that.[9] The poems from *The Fuehrer Bunker* (1977) and its two sequels concern the last days of the Third Reich and take the form of first-person testimony by Hitler, Goebbels and company; the most recent poems, in the section entitled "Kinder Capers," chronicle the adventures of a fanciful version of the poet, called W.D., and feature energetic rhythms, multiple rhymes and pert parodies ("My hat leaps up when I behold / a rhino in the sky") reminiscent of the later Delmore Schwartz.

Snodgrass's work is almost invariably readable and lucid, and often witty and touching; drawn to the extremes of human nature and emotion—love and hatred, joy and horror, saintliness and evil—he dwells with equal fascination upon moral corruption and children's innocence. His is an interesting mind, and an exuberantly original talent. Yet one cannot avoid the conclusion that this talent, at its strongest, lies squarely in the confessional realm, that Snodgrass's particular gift is for trapping a raging personal emotion within the confines of a rigorous form. Arguably, his best poems are those from *Remains* (1970), a sort of contemporary *In Memoriam* that charts the poet's reaction to a loved one's death. In "Disposal," for example, having distributed the deceased's good, never-worn clothes, he reflects that

> We don't dare burn those canceled patterns
> And markdowns that she actually wore.
> Yet who do we know so poor
> They'd take them? Spared all need, all passion,
> Saved from loss, she lies boxed in satins
>
> Like a pair of party shoes
> That seemed to never find a taker;
> We send back to its maker
> A life somehow gone out of fashion
> But still too good to use.

John Ash is over twenty years younger than Justice or Snodgrass, but he is already on his fifth book. *Disbelief* contains more than fifty poems and prose-poems by the Englishman-turned-New Yorker, and a wildly

---

[9]*Selected Poems 1957-1987*, by W.D. Snodgrass; Soho Press, 270 pages, $19.95 paper.

uneven batch it is.[10] Ash doesn't seem to know a good poetic idea from a bad one, and follows both varieties up with equal enthusiasm and lack of discipline. The resulting poem's success depends on whether the original idea was valid, the inspirational energy unflagging, and the rhythm in his head strong and true, as in "Memories of Italy":

> I loved the light of course
> and the way the young men
> flirted with each other.
> I loved the light,—
>
> the way it fell out of sky like a painting,
> or perhaps like the ground (if this
> is not too paradoxical a way of
> putting it) for a painting,
>
> and the way the young men stood in the station
> wearing jeans that were the colour of the sky
> or the sea in a painting...

And on it goes, the lines growing ever longer, like a spiral of words spinning out from the center of the poet's consciousness. These are indeed stream-of-consciousness poems, whose value is entirely dependent upon the swiftness and smoothness of the particular stream in which Ash happens to have found himself; the line breaks, the diction and the details all patently came at once, and are either inspired or awful. Ash is out to shock (with daring forms, outlandish images and a matter-of-fact pansexuality), to impress (with his French, his knowledge of the cafés and squares of foreign capitals, and his cosmopolitan ennui: "I am tired of Paris today"), and to be frightfully clever and frivolous ("There are still more hairs on my head / than there are croissant outlets in Seattle"); he is very much a Wildean poseur, a glib, condescending dandy, and the pose itself is a conscious part of his poetic strategy. Certain poems seem designed to show the boundlessness of his daring: in "A Lithuanian Mantilla" (one of his many exotic, Stevens-like titles) all fifty-six lines rhyme; in "The Sky My Husband," all seventy-nine lines consist of the words "The sky my" followed by one or

---

[10]*Disbelief*, by John Ash; Carcanet, 127 pages, $9.95 paper.

more common nouns, such as "piano" and "mother." Such poems are less *tours de force* than they are *jeux d'esprit*—and vapid ones, at that.

There is, of course, a philosophy behind all this. *Disbelief* probes the consequences of disbelief in God, in the perfectibility of man, and in the ultimate significance of life, which Ash describes in one poem as "a festive marching to no purpose." If life means nothing, runs his implicit argument, one might as well forgo seriousness and have some fun—be as superficial, sloppy and extravagant as one likes. And yet many of his poems strike one as acts of faith. One of his prose poems is called "Every Story Tells All," and Ash seems desperately to want to "tell all," to sum life up in a single piece of writing, to believe that poetic truth is arrived at not through labor but by means of inspirational flashes (more an American than an English notion, surely, which might help explain why Ash has relocated to these shores). The expectation that words might prove to be a principle of meaning and organization in a godless cosmos seems to inform poems like "Romanza"—"Some days the whole of living / is like a phrase you overheard in the subway"—and "Rooflines and Riverbells"—"Some evenings / there are no other songs / that so open the possibility / of summing the whole thing up." Such poems as these, in which a genuine longing shines sweetly and affectingly through the mesh of tired flippancies, are by far Ash's most promising.

SEPTEMBER 1984, MARCH 1986, JANUARY 1988

PUSHKIN BY THE BAY

Let me begin by making it clear what *The Golden Gate*, the new "novel in verse" by Vikram Seth, is not. It isn't great poetry: it doesn't have (or attempt to have) the requisite depth or density; it isn't rich in metaphor or other poetic devices; to examine it alongside a contemporary book-length narrative poem like Alfred Corn's *Notes from a Child of Paradise* is to recognize that the two works are so utterly different in kind as to make comparison pointless. Nor is *The Golden Gate* a great novel: there can be little doubt that, had it been written in prose, its characters would have come across as rather insignificant, its plot as less than compelling.

What this book *is*, however, is an extraordinarily accomplished work of narrative verse—one that has all the cardinal virtues of the genre, and has them in abundance. It's engaging, well-paced, technically mesmerizing; indeed, one of Seth's most remarkable achievements is that he makes us forget about those mainstays of contemporary literature, poetry and the novel, and reminds us how enthralling it can be to watch a prodigious versifier triumph, line by line, over an extremely challenging form—all the time developing a charming story, sustaining a sardonic yet sympathetic tone, and flourishing a marvelous wit. Seth has done something a good deal more difficult than compose a respectable contemporary novel or long poem: he has given new life to a genre that, for no good reason, has in the present literary climate come to be considered passé, retrograde, even infantile. The result of his efforts is one of the most delightful new books in recent memory.

The Golden Gate is composed in the *"Eugene Onegin"* stanza, the form invented by Pushkin a century and a half ago for his classic novel in verse. Each of Seth's 590 sonnet-length stanzas of iambic tetrameter—like each of the 400 stanzas of *Eugene Onegin*—follows the rhyme scheme aBaB ccDD eFFe GG, with lower-case letters denoting feminine rhymes and capitals denoting masculine rhymes. (Perhaps the number of stanzas in *The Golden Gate* should actually be reckoned at 594, because Seth's acknowledgments, dedication, table of contents, and author's note are also written in the *"Onegin"* stanza—thus outdoing Pushkin, whose work was prefaced only by a dedication in verse.) Like Pushkin, Seth addresses his audience as "Gentle Reader," divides his book into chapters, and numbers each stanza. In stanza 5.5 he acknowledges his debt to Pushkin:

> Reader, enough of this apology:
> But spare me if I think it best,
> Before I tether my monology,
> To stake a stanza to suggest
> You spend some unfilled day of leisure
> By that original spring of pleasure:
> Sweet-watered, fluent, clear, light, blithe
> (This homage merely pays a tithe
> Of what in joy and inspiration
> It gave me once and does not cease
> To give me)—Pushkin's masterpiece
> In Johnston's luminous translation:
> *Eugene Onegin*—like champagne
> Its effervescence stirs my brain.

Seth has taken more than his form from Pushkin. Like *Eugene Onegin*—and like Byron's *Don Juan,* which strongly influenced Pushkin—*The Golden Gate* describes, with amiable irony, the romantic adventures of a privileged, rather naïve young man who takes himself perhaps a bit too seriously. He is in this regard the direct opposite of his creator, for Seth, like Pushkin and Byron, never takes anything too seriously, himself least of all; on the contrary, he pokes playful fun at nearly everything available—his poem, his hero, even the conventions of verse to which he is scrupulously conforming. Like Pushkin, too, Seth is a meticulous and sensible observer of the place and time in which he has found himself: the manners, means, and mores of contemporary America fascinate him. (He is not, however, one of those writers who make a career out of listing the names of cars, television programs, or product brand names; he puts all such paraphernalia in their proper place.) It is indicative of the Sethian sensibility that the chain of events in *The Golden Gate*—in which the lives of several people are changed utterly—is set in motion by a misguided frisbee:

To make a start more swift than weighty,
Hail Muse. Dear Reader, once upon
A time, say, circa 1980,
There lived a man. His name was John.
Successful in his field though only
Twenty-six, respected, lonely,
One evening as he walked across
Golden Gate Park, the ill-judged toss
Of a red frisbee almost brained him.
He thought, "If I died, who'd be sad?
Who'd weep? Who'd gloat? Who would be glad?
Would anybody?"

So it begins. Our hero, John—a "chaste, ambitious" executive with Datatronics, a Silicon Valley defense contracting firm, whose "plastic name tag hangs around / His collar like a votive necklace" and whose friends "claim he's grown aloof and prim"—suddenly finds himself tormented by his solitary life. He "feels an urgent riptide drawing / Him far out, where, caught in the kelp / Of loneliness, he cries for help." But no one hears. He tries to lose his newfound sorrow in rock music, but it doesn't work:

He goes home, seeking consolation
Among old Beatles and Pink Floyd—
But "Girl" elicits mere frustration,
While "Money" leaves him more annoyed.
Alas, he hungers less for money
Than for a fleeting Taste of Honey.
Murmuring, "Money—it's a gas!...
The lunatic is on the grass,"
He pours himself a beer. Desires
And reminiscences intrude
Upon his unpropitious mood
Until he feels that he requires
A one-way Ticket to Ride—and soon—
Across the Dark Side of the Moon.

Reading doesn't help either. The "pensive prose" he wraps himself in ("*Life's Little Ironies* by Hardy, / The gloomier sermons of John Donne, / The *Zibaldone* of Leopardi, / *The Queen of Spades*") sinks him even

335

deeper into "the crevasse of melancholy."

Finally, John presents his problems to his former girlfriend, Janet Hayakawa. She is, we learn, a sculptor whose work the art critics consistently savage:

> Blind mouths! They spew their condescension:
> Miss Hayakawa, it appears,
> Lacks serious sculptural intention.
> Where has she been these thirty years?
> Are Moore's and Calder's use of medium
> Unknown to her? The languid tedium
> Of lines too fluid to show pains
> Reflect this artist's dated chains:
> Derivative, diluted passion,
> *A facile versatility....*
> With smooth and blinkered savagery,
> Servile and suave, obsessed by fashion,
> These chickenhearted chickenshits
> Jerk off their weak and venomous wits.

In her seemingly effortless dexterity and indifference to artistic trends, Janet is plainly something of an alter ego for Seth himself (who may well be suggesting, in the above lines, the sort of critical reception he expects *The Golden Gate* to receive from faddish critics). It is she who comes up with the solution to John's problem: behind his back, she places a personal advertisement on his behalf in the *Bay Guardian*. John, irritated, berates Janet for pulling such an underhanded stunt ("Why did you choose to loose this host / Of bacchantes on me through the post?"), but eventually agrees to look over the responses to the ad. So it is that he ends up meeting and falling in love with a sweet and lovely young San Francisco attorney named Liz Dorati.

In its early stages, Liz and John's romance is appealingly corny, rather in the way romances in Rodgers and Hammerstein musicals are meant to be. On their first date, "They look, half smiling, at each other, / Half puzzled too, as if to say, / 'I don't know why I feel this way.'" On the second date, John can't decide if Liz is "A woman, or divine illusion?" Before long they are exchanging nothing but baby talk:

Their diction has, alas, become
Incomprehensible and numb.
Their brains appear to be dissolving
To sugary sludge as they caress.
In lieu of fire, force, finesse,
We have a ballet now involving
A pretty pas de deux instead,
With common Walkmans on their head.

This pas de deux—which, unfortunately, soon develops into something of a *mano a mano*—is not the book's only love story. In due course we meet, and watch a romance blossom between, Liz's brother Ed and John's friend and former colleague Phil Weiss. Ed, twenty-three, works in advertising; Phil, thirtyish, divorced, with a young son named Paul, has recently quit his job designing missile guidance systems at Datatronics because "To go on would have been high treason / To common sense and humankind." Though the two men are in love, their affair is doomed by the fact that Ed, every so often, falls into a "godly mood," wherein he feels a pious contempt for his homoerotic urges and wonders: "can he / Make Phil consent to chastity?" Phil has no patience for this part-time piety: "Your religion / Doesn't square too well with your lust. / I wonder which first bites the dust!" Ed tries to talk Phil into a Platonic friendship:

If lovers cannot cease caressing,
Isn't it that they long to find
Their bodies' unity expressing
A truer unison of mind?
For us this oneness is reality.
Can't we dispense with the banality
Of intermediary ends?
Phil, let's just—why can't we be friends—
And find this craved complementation
Of our true selves in its true form,
The love that keeps our spirits warm
Through the shared touch of conversation?

But Phil isn't having any of it. "Does earthly beauty just exist," he asks,

For contemplation? Why, unduly,
Would God create a perfect form
If not to make our lives more warm?
It seems to me a curious fashion
To give a man an appetite,
Then tell him a starvation ration
Is all he's due for. I don't quite
Get why religion makes you grateful.
I would say, Ed, that it's a hateful,
A pretty odious-spirited trick
To make you as you are, then stick
The pin of infinite damnation
Into you....

Neither of these romances, then, is a model of mutual compatibility. All four lovers must make the journey through discord to reach harmony.

For all the discord, though, the world of this book is one in which everybody—with the notable exception of a few cruel and distant art critics—is essentially decent. There are no villains here (no *human* villains, anyway). Instead, the principal conflicts tend to arise out of the characters' irritation with each other's quirks and foibles (which, to a reader at least, are mostly quite amusing). John, for instance, employs Yuppie metaphors ("The Dow-Jones of my heart's depressed," he tells Janet) and indulges in self-dramatization ("I die! I faint! I fail! I sink!"); Janet, a connoisseur as well as perpetrator of hard rock, says things like "You are the DJ of your fate"; and Liz pursues gestalt therapy, practices "holistic / Modes of ingestion," and is neurotically devoted to her nasty old cat, Charlemagne. Yet Seth's affection for all of his characters is incontrovertible—and contagious.

Affection, in fact, is what his book is all about. Its ultimate lessons are wonderfully simple ones: that love and friendship are the finest things on earth; that life being short, youth evanescent, and the world unstable, human attachments should be cherished, not repudiated; and that the silly, arbitrary ways in which people come to discover and care about one another does not gainsay the beauty and dignity of their devotion. In *The Golden Gate*, even the nuclear-weapons issue is secondary to love and friendship. Seth devotes several stanzas to an angry debate on this topic between John and Phil, in which he prefer radically on this great life-and-death question of the day—the two young men, at the close of the argument, remain friends; and this, to Seth, is what's most important.

Although he keeps his own politics out of the debate between John and Phil, Seth, like Pushkin and Byron, is far from reluctant to draw attention to himself. He makes a Hitchcock-like cameo appearance as "Kim Tarvesh" (an anagram for "Vikram Seth") at Liz and John's house-warming party, and, à la Pushkin and Byron, digresses amusingly from his narrative on several occasions to inject an ironic observation or autobiographical tidbit:

> A week ago, when I had finished
> Writing the chapter you've just read
> And with avidity undiminished
> Was charting out the course ahead,
> An editor—at a plush party
> (Well-wined, -provisioned, speechy, hearty)
> Hosted by (long live!) Thomas Cook
> Where my Tibetan travel book
> Was honored—seized my arm: "Dear fellow,
> What's your next work?" "A novel..." "Great!
> We hope that you, dear Mr. Seth—"
> "...In verse," I added. He turned yellow.
> "How marvelously quaint," he said,
> And subsequently cut me dead.

The man, of course, was right. Seth's book *is* marvelously quaint, in the best sense of the word—which is to say that it's clever, elegant, and decidedly untrendy. Indeed, in an age when the work of some of the most widely touted young poets and novelists is numbingly soul-less and torpid—and even, quite frequently, technically inept—the sweetness, wit, imagination, facility, and sheer joy of creation that shine out from every line of *The Golden Gate* are glorious to behold.

MAY 1986

FORMAL POETRY IN THE LAND OF THE FREE

Recently I spent three days at a private high school in New England, doing something that, given my considerable unease over the rise of the creative-writing establishment, I had thought I would never do: I taught a poetry workshop.

Not, mind you, that a poetry workshop is necessarily a terrible thing. Some of my best friends teach poetry workshops. And I would never contest the proposition that the guidance of a certain type of poet can be of real value to a certain type of student. Surely one can imagine a gifted, intelligent fledgling poet profiting from the experience of working closely with a more mature poet who loves his art, has a technical mastery of it, knows its history, and, while maintaining high standards of discipline, discrimination, and technique, is open-minded enough to allow the student to develop in his own direction—and who, moreover, has the time, energy, sensitivity, and dedication to help him find that direction.

But unblinkered veterans of creative-writing programs know that this ideal is seldom approached, let alone attained. More often, students are encouraged to view poetry not as an art but as a profession; encouraged not to aspire to excellence but to tailor their work to a marketplace that exalts blandness and mediocrity; encouraged not to work hard at poems over a substantial period of time, but to churn them out like assembly-line products. Moreover, as the poet David Dooley observes in his recent essay "The Contemporary Workshop Aesthetic," workshops tend to produce students who write pretty much the way their teachers do—which means, at least nine times out of ten, that they manufacture tame, slack, and highly derivative free-verse lyrics consisting mostly of (a) jejune personal confession that the poet has made little attempt to render interesting or meaningful, and by means of which he advertises his sincerity and sensitivity; (b) familiar surreal imagery whose putative virtue is presumably its quality of freshness, surprise, and subversiveness; and/or (c) lackluster, undiscrimi-

340

nating descriptions of foliage, land forms, and such, the point of which is to demonstrate the poet's responsiveness to nature and his attention to detail.[1]

Formal poetry? Forget it. If traditional form and meter are covered at all in workshops, they tend to be treated at best as exotic options, at worst as quaint historical curiosities—things that a contemporary poet should know about in the same way that scientists should know about alchemy or Lamarck's theory of acquired characteristics. Even teachers who harbor an affection for form and meter are likely to place little emphasis on these matters in class, partly because they know that formal poetry (despite somewhat greater acceptance in recent years) is still not smiled upon by most American poetry editors, but even moreso because, in the small amount of time that these teachers are able to devote to any one student, the best they can hope to do is to help him to avoid outrageous mistakes—to help him, that is, to *look* professional, so that he'll get published and, in turn, get hired to teach creative writing elsewhere. These teachers know that the best way to keep a young poet's middling or underdeveloped talent from showing through is to teach him to write—well—tame, slack, derivative free-verse lyrics; and they know, conversely, that the *last* thing to do is to introduce him in any serious way to the demands of form and meter, which, aside from being regarded by many poets as repressive and retrogressive, have a funny way of exposing a poet's deficiencies.

Though many creative-writing teachers will concede the truth of these criticisms in conversation, few will do so in print. Which is why it was refreshing to find Wayne Dodd, in an interview with Robert Bly in the latter's book *American Poetry: Wildness and Domesticity*, confessing that while he makes his living as a teacher of creative writing,

> I always feel uncomfortable with a workshop situation
> because it seems to me to be such an essentially negative, or
> to borrow your metaphor, domesticating, function....Often
> it [the workshop] teaches you how *not* to do certain things.
> It teaches you how not to make gross mistakes that are go-
> ing to be unacceptable....But is that the same as learning to
> write poetry?

---

[1]David Dooley, "The Contemporary Workshop Aesthetic." *The Hudson Review*, 43:2 (Summer 1990), pages 259-80.

Bly's answer: No. Both poets go on to admit that, as Bly puts it, "[t]here's some kind of lie that the workshops, and visiting poets, are involved in. I'm involved in it."

Why, then, when an invitation came from friends of mine to teach at a three-day "writer's conference" for aspiring high-school poets and short-story writers, did I agree to become a part of this "lie"? Part of the reason was that I figured the experience would do me good: as a veteran of two or three undergraduate writing workshops, and as a longtime observer and critic of the creative-writing industry, I figured that I should take the opportunity to look at things, for once, from the teacher's end. But the determining factor was that I saw this also as an opportunity to do something seditious—namely, to get a crack at these teenagers before the undergraduate workshops and M.F.A. programs did, and to encourage them to write in *form*.

I would, I decided, teach a workshop on the sonnet. During the first three-hour session I would give them a handout containing one sonnet apiece by Wyatt, Shakespeare, Wordsworth, Coleridge, Frost, Thomas, and Lowell, as well as two recent sonnets by young contemporary poets—one by Phillis Levin about Rilke, and one by Molly Peacock about lawn mowing. There wouldn't, of course, be time to give any of these poems its due; but the students would at least be forced to confront the fact that a variety of poets through the centuries, with very different sensibilities, concerns, and voices, have nonetheless chosen, for some reason, to work in sonnet form; they would come to recognize how flexible the sonnet form was, would notice the wonderful variations in theme and tone and diction that these nine sonnets displayed, would hear the distinctive sound of the rhymed pentameter line in the hands of each of these nine poets. Or, rather, seven poets—for Lowell's sonnet is in iambic tetrameter, and Levin's doesn't rhyme.

The students would see, too, that in choosing to follow a general iambic scheme, a poet is not forcing himself into a metronomic straitjacket, but establishing a background pattern, rather like a regular drumbeat behind a guitar solo; they would see that the sonnet form, when skillfully employed, makes possible a witty, playful tension between the poles of structure and freedom, a tension not unlike that between the melody of a familiar popular song and a jazz musician's interpretation of it. They would see that to write a sonnet is to place oneself in the context of every other sonnet ever written, and that those sonnets become the subtext of one's own poem. In short, they would see that, to a true poet, form is no enemy but a friend, no prison cell but a set of wings.

The students who were to be in my workshop had submitted from one to three poems apiece along with their application materials, and these manuscripts were forwarded to me a few weeks before the conference. When I examined them, I was surprised to find the poems considerably worse than I had expected. Only two or three of them featured rhyme or traditional forms (wasn't it just yesterday that teenagers thought poems *had* to rhyme?), and those that did were stiff, lifeless doggerel—even worse than the free-verse poems. The notable exception was a promising villanelle, which proved to be the work of a senior at the private high school where the conference was taking place. Once the conference had begun, it did not take long for me to realize that this boy and his schoolmates were vastly more sophisticated and articulate than the other students, who attended local public high schools.

And this, it should be said, was no coincidence. That private school impressed me enormously: it had small classes, twelve-hour class days, and an intensive arts-oriented curriculum; the students were taught out of original texts, not dumbed-down textbooks, and the older ones taught classes themselves. They read the classics of literature and philosophy, played Bach on the harpsichord, Chopin on the piano, Mozart in chamber groups; in the school atelier they painted and sculpted and drew, and in the school theater they put on polished productions of Molière in French. They were, it appeared, the products of as fine a liberal-arts education as money can buy in the United States in 1990. Nor was any of this surface learning: their education had given them a real understanding of the principles of art, and—it had been made clear to me—of the way form functioned in symphonies, paintings, and plays. When I thought of my own more pedestrian public-high-school education, it all seemed quite overwhelming.

Which is why it struck me as all the more extraordinary, on the opening day of the conference, that the students—even the ones from this magnificent school—simply couldn't understand something that I had understood, I think, at the age of twelve: the purpose of poetic form and meter. For all their wide reading, they had given little thought to the function of form in poetry. Why, they asked, after I had handed out the copies of Wyatt, Shakespeare, et al., and had begun talking about the sonnet, would a poet write in a traditional form? Why would he want to restrict his expressiveness in such an unnatural way? It was a puzzlement to them, a matter of frustration. And it frustrated me, too—for if these students, with their extraordinary training in art, music, and culture, didn't have a clue as to why someone would write in form, then what hope was there for more ordinary students at more ordinary schools?

The brightest student in my workshop—the villanelle-writing senior from the host school who (I had been told) wrote compelling essays on art and philosophy, played piano and cello, taught tenth-grade math, had exceptional talent as a visual artist, was fluent in French and German, and had performed splendidly in the title role of *The Misanthrope*—this paragon was the most persistent of all. It exasperated him that he couldn't understand the purpose of poetic form. This surprised me, not only because he had written that villanelle (apparently as a class exercise), but also because, when asked the name of his favorite poet, he had unhesitatingly said, "Blake." Presumably, then, he liked *some* poems that used rhyme and meter, and he knew how to use them himself if he wanted to. But he couldn't see *why* he should want to. To him, as to the others in the class, composing such a thing as a sonnet seemed a pointless exercise—a game, like a crossword puzzle, that had nothing to do with the free-verse effusions they all enjoyed writing.

And that was the problem: they did enjoy writing poetry. But they didn't enjoy it, I gathered, in the same way that they enjoyed painting or playing the piano. For in art and music, they took for granted the idea of formal and technical principles, and knew the exhilaration and the challenge of struggling to master them. Somehow or other, though, they had gotten the idea that poetry was different. Poetry, to them, was patently something of a holiday from those more disciplined arts— a chance to express themselves without restraint, to pour out their romantic agonies, their irritation with their parents, their anguish over not being children anymore. If they had come here to work on their own free-verse poems, it was not to improve them in a technical or formal sense, but simply to make clearer and more coherent the unfettered expression of personal feeling. They did not disguise the fact that my determination to have them write sonnets made them look upon me as a killjoy, out to ruin their pleasure and thwart their self-exploration. That form and meter might help to take them beyond the rudimentary level of their current efforts in verse did not occur to them.

Indeed, it was not until the villanelle writer asked me for the third time to explain the reason for writing in sonnet form, and I launched into my third explanation—this time, in desperation, drawing an analogy with sonata form—that a light began to come into his eyes. He was, I felt, beginning to catch on.

Yet none of them was entirely convinced. And they were, I sensed, impatient with all this chatter about other people's poems: they wanted to discuss their own. At my direction, they tried to write sonnets before our second meeting; but they did so half-heartedly, and none were comfortable enough with what they had written to share them with the rest of us. Consequently, we spent our last three meetings talking about the poems they had submitted with their applications. We didn't even get to consider that villanelle; the author vetoed that idea, choosing instead to have us examine the two free-verse poems he had submitted, the longer of which was addressed to Allen Ginsberg and began with these memorable lines: "I stay home / and moan your poetry / till it gives me an erection."

If the poems had their flaws, however, the discussions went beautifully. These teenagers who couldn't quite fathom the justification for writing in traditional form and meter had a near-expert knowledge of how to take apart a free-verse poem and put it back together again. Plainly, most or all of them had extensive poetry-workshop backgrounds. The villanelle writer was particularly impressive, putting his finger immediately on the fundamental problems with his fellow students' poems. He was excellent at elucidating and simplifying obscure passages, at noticing connections, at seeing logical contradictions between lines that were half a page apart, at noting inconsistencies in point of view, and at pointing out weak lines, explaining why they were weak, and offering changes for improvement. Yet the more brilliantly he performed, the more troubled I was by the fact that even he could look at a contemporary sonnet and shake his head in bemusement.

It was disconcerting. I had come to this conference hoping that, in a very small way, I might buck the creative-writing establishment; but I hadn't counted on the influence of that establishment having extended so widely that even the smartest senior—and, it appeared, the most serious writer—at a first-rate liberal-arts high school would have so much trouble understanding why a novice poet should want to compose a sonnet. Returning home on the Boston-New York train, I wished only that I had been prepared for such massive resistance, and that I had been more successful at communicating to this boy why form and meter mattered to me, and why I thought they should matter to him.

I can only wish now that I had been able to hand him a copy of Timothy Steele's new book *Missing Measures: Modern Poetry and the Revolt against Meter*.[2] For this critical and historical study, whose author is himself a very gifted formal poet (*Uncertainties and Rest, Sapphics Against Anger*), might well have been written to explain to an intelligent novice poet why form and meter should be important to him. Steele places the modernist revolt in the context of the history of poetry, arguing forcefully that the revolt's emphasis on free verse made it a unique event and that this singular emphasis, and the continuing dominance of free verse in our own time, have proceeded from grievous misconceptions on the part of the revolutionaries and their successors, and have turned poetry into something those revolutionaries would never have wanted it to become.

Steele reminds us that poetry has always had its revolutions, which have generally been led by relatively young poets who feel that the poetry of their elders has grown stale, stuffy, tired; he notes that Euripides, Horace, Dryden, Wordsworth, Villon, and the Symbolists, among others, all led revolts of this sort, and declares that such periodic upheavals are needed to keep poetry fresh and vigorous. But these have always, he points out, been revolutions in language, never in meter; poets may have rejected the formal or metrical choices made by their elders and made others instead (as the Romantic dropped the heroic couplet and took to the sonnet and blank verse), but they never entirely repudiated form and meter. What makes literary modernism unique, Steele argues, is that it was the only poetic rebellion many of whose leaders saw form and meter as an inextricable part of the problem with their predecessors' poetry, and accordingly chose to write in free verse.

How did this come to pass? Steele traces the free-verse revolt back to Kant and the doctrine of aestheticism, whose stress on the individual consciousness and on the poem as a self-contained object "freed poetry not only from ethical and rational understanding, but from its

<hr>

[2]*Missing Measures: Modern Poetry and the Revolt against Meter*, by Timothy Steele; University of Arkansas Press, 340 pages, $22.95 cloth, $12.95 paper.

own history." Furthermore, Steele argues audaciously that the modernists—and he focuses especially on the critical writings of Eliot, Pound, and Williams—"misunderstood meter." They grew up, he writes, in

> a world in which Swinburne was the chief poet and in which Swinburneanism was the mode most obviously available to the young poet. Swinburne was a dead end... because of the numbingly emphatic quality of the verse. It was because the metrical effects of the verse... insisted on themselves as metrical effects in the absense of serious and vital subject matter. It was because the verse almost seemed to preclude mature and flexible expression.

If Swinburnean verse was a dead end, however, late Victorian prose fiction was vibrant and colorful—which, Steele notes, may explain Pound's declaration that "poetry must be as well written as prose," a precept which in any previous era would simply not have made sense, since it had always been prose that sought to mimic the techniques of poetry, never the reverse.

Steele also cites J.V. Cunningham's interesting argument that the problem lies in the modernists' elementary-school educations. Cunningham says that when English poetry began to be taught in the schools during the late nineteenth century, students were taught to read it aloud in a singsong, metronomic manner, in order that they might be able to identify the underlying metrical patterns. It was this practice, Cunningham suggests, that incited the modernist rebellion against meter, and prompted Pound, in his famous list of Imagist principles, to ordain that poets should "compose in the sequence of a musical phrase, not in sequence of a metronome."

This dictum of Pound's is often cited approvingly by opponents of formal verse; yet his musical analogy has always seemed to me misbegotten. Its obvious implication is that conventional meter makes it impossible to write poetry that flows like music—which leads one to wonder how Pound accounts for the fact that musical phrases can themselves be divided into conventional measures. Indeed, just as a piece of music can be written in 4/4 time, say, and yet flow naturally, so (as Steele puts it) "conventional versification accommodates personally distinctive rhythm within the norm of measure." Pound's deliberate vagueness on this point is denoted by his odd, blurry use of the word "sequence" to mean both "surface movement" and "underlying pattern." It is interesting to realize that if he had been more precise in spelling out his analogy, the fallacy at the heart of it would have been more evident.

To say such things about Pound or the other modernists, of course, is not to condemn modernism *tout court*, or to suggest that Steele does so. On the contrary, he writes about Eliot, Pound, and company with respect, acknowledging that they "abandoned meter out of a genuine wish to renovate verse and reconnect it to a real world and a real audience." His complaint is simply that, to a great extent, the effect of this abandonment of meter "has been to deprive poetry of resources that enable it to examine human experience appealingly, distinctively, and meaningfully." In other words, if poetic revolution was once a cyclical affair—a recurrent, generation-by-generation process of self-renewal—modernism's rejection of meter, though revitalizing in the short term, proved eventually to be destructive, the beginning of a downward spiral in which each new generation of poets would revolt against its predecessors not by energizing the language of verse but by moving progressively further from the rigors of traditional form and meter, and writing poems that were ever more slack and shapeless.

Steele recognizes that the modernists would have been the first to deplore the situation of poetry today, and notes that, in fact, they expressed concern in later years "that their revolution was not followed by a period of consolidation, but by increasingly casual and incoherent experiments with poetic form." He cites Eliot's 1947 remark that "[w]e cannot, in literature, any more than in the rest of life, live in a perpetual state of revolution," and quotes from a letter that Eliot wrote in 1950: "I was shocked when my grand-niece presented me with some verses that she had written as school exercises to find that little girls in an American school were *encouraged* to write in vers libre."

What would those high-school students I met at the "writer's conference" have made of Eliot's shock at this discovery? They would, I think, have been very perplexed—unable to reconcile Eliot's enthusiasm for vers libre with his displeasure at its being taught in school. What makes this confusion possible, of course, is that these students live in an age when poetry *does* look upon itself as being in a permanent state of revolution, and when the headquarters of that revolution, furthermore, have long since been relocated to the academy; paradoxical though this alliance of academy and poetic revolution may be, even the brightest of teenagers today have never known any other set of circumstances, and so it is difficult for them to see, as Eliot did, that such an alliance is destined to foster a poetry establishment dominated by inert, insular, and technically inept rebels without a cause—a poetry establishment which, for all its stagnancy and need for revitalization, is ironically all the more difficult to overthrow than previous establishments precisely *because* it has taken possession of the very idea of revolution.

Of course, creative-writing teachers today can dismiss Eliot's objections to the institutionalization of free verse as the grumblings of an elitist snob, a man from St. Louis who turned himself into an Englishman; the great appeal of free verse, for many of them, is that they view it as inherently American, and meter and form as British. They derive this idea largely from William Carlos Williams, whom contemporary free-verse poets tend to look upon as their founding father. Steele rightly criticizes this schematic view, arguing that "[m]eter has nothing in particular to do with...England," being "common to the poetries of many different societies [going] back to prehistoric times," and that it is similarly wrongheaded to "talk of an 'American' tradition in poetry, as if this were a single massive flood upon which every poet in our country is obliged to launch his bark." Besides, as Steele points out, even Williams, in his later years, was displeased by younger poets' absolute renunciation of form and meter, complaining in "The Poem as a Field of Action" that "the tiresome repetition of this 'new,' now twenty years old, disfigures every journal," and protesting in 1953 that "[t]here is nothing interesting in the construction of our poems, nothing that can jog the ear out of its boredom....I among the rest have much to answer for....Without measure we are lost. But we have lost even the ability to count."

As for the absurd but widespread notion that free verse is somehow democratic and traditional form and meter elitist, Steele advises that those who hold this view should keep in mind that Pound and Wyndham Lewis were Nazi apologists. He observes, too, that "throughout most of literary history, readers and listeners have loved and venerated verse more" than prose, and that "[i]ts primacy has derived from meter"—which, given the fact that the rise of free verse has seen poetry lose its general audience, makes it seem more reasonable to identify free verse as elitist and metered verse as democratic than to do the reverse.

Steele presents, in short, a splendid argument for the continuing value of traditional form and meter. I fear, however, that it won't change the minds of many unadulterated free-verse poets or of the academic critics who champion them and malign formalism. Steele founds his defense of meter and traditional form on the fact that they have been a consistent part of Western civilization since its Greek beginnings; but to many free-verse poets and their critical champions it is precisely this civilization that is suspect. Fervent anti-formalists despise the Western tradition, and one cannot imagine them looking upon Steele's marvelously erudite display of classical learning with anything other than bemusement or contempt; indeed, they often condemn poets of Steele's ilk as reactionaries who are out to undermine the anarchic freedom of contemporary poetry, to silence subversive voices, and so forth—all the usual rhetoric, none of which has anything to do with the making of art.

Steele, needless to say, knows all this: he knows that poetry has, in large part, fallen into the hands of anti-intellectuals who have little interest in literary history and who, as he puts it, "confus[e] what is extrinsic to poetic structure with what is intrinsic to it," reducing "formal poet" (if they acknowledge such a concept at all) to a mere subcategory along with all sorts of artistically meaningless groupings based on politics ("feminist poet") or ethnic background ("black poet") or sexual orientation ("gay poet"), and defending the most confused and undisciplined free verse by saying that "we should write in a crazy fashion because our times are crazy." As Steele observes, such poets don't realize that all times feel crazy to those who live in them, or that by expressing in their poetry a glibly nihilistic philosophy they may "be inviting us to collaborate with the very forces we should resist."

There are times, to be sure, when even this enthusiastic reader does not agree entirely with Steele. I think he's a bit unfair to Robert Lowell, for example, whose explanation, in his *Paris Review* interview, of his decision to "break forms" in *Life Studies* moves Steele to unnecessary sarcasm. (My own feeling is that Lowell was a better poet after he loosened up—but I also think that he, like other ex-formalists, made a good free-verse writer largely because his experience as a formalist gave his best free-verse poems a tautness, a sense of shape and rhythm, that many other free-verse poems don't have.) One also feels from time to time—for instance, during Steele's discussion of aestheticism—that he is too inclined to view the ancient Greeks as the ultimate authorities, and to view everything that came afterward as an aberration precisely to the degree that it departs from Greek theory and practice.

But for every time that one differs with Steele, there are a dozen times when one nods fervently in agreement. And it should be emphasized that Steele is not proposing that free verse be abolished; he is merely demonstrating that form and meter are valuable tools which have served the aims of poetry well for millennia, and that these tools are inadequately appreciated by many poets. To be sure, there are doubtless many free-verse poets who, regarding poetry mainly as a means of self-expression, are in the habit of identifying the poem with the self it expresses, and consequently are inclined to see arguments for the value of form and meter as a hostile act against the free-verse poet's self—an attempt to confine, to stifle. Steele, in the final words of his book, implicitly addresses this contemporary poetic emphasis on the poet, and on the ephemeral gratifications of tossed-off, undisciplined verse, by shifting emphasis to the reader, and to the deeper, long-term pleasures that memorable, well-crafted poetry can provide. "Only the poetry of our time," he writes, "can offer the prospect that, after we and those we love have returned to dust, some reader somewhere will be moved by lines that bear witness to us and will commit our words to heart and mind that we may live again." These words strike at the essence of what poetry is, or should be, all about, and in their passion, seriousness, cadence, and amplitude epitomize the very qualities that are most wanting in contemporary free verse.

NOVEMBER 1990

ABOUT THE AUTHOR

Born in New York City in 1956, Bruce Bawer received a Ph.D. in English from the State University of New York at Stony Brook in 1983. He served for ten years as literary critic for *The New Criterion* and for four years as the *American Spectator*'s film critic. His book *The Middle Generation: The Lives and Poetry of Delmore Schwartz, Randall Jarrell, John Berryman, and Robert Lowell* (1986) was named an Outstanding Academic Book of the Year by *Choice* magazine; his volumes of literary essays, *Diminishing Fictions* (1988) and *The Aspect of Eternity* (1993), prompted reviews that called him "a literary essayist for the ages" (*Kirkus Reviews*) and "a critic of the first order, one of the best we have today" (*Commonweal*). His other books include a textbook on writing, *The Contemporary Stylist* (1986); a collection of film criticism, *The Screenplay's the Thing* (1992); and a collection of poems, *Coast to Coast* (1993), which received attention by the *Dictionary of Literary Biography Yearbook* as "the finest first volume of poetry of the year." Bawer's 1993 book *A Place at the Table: The Gay Individual in American Society*, which was praised in the *Detroit Free Press* as "one of the most sensible assessments of the gay rights movement that's ever been written, as well as one of the most eloquent arguments for acceptance of gays that's ever been made," was for several months the #1 best-seller in gay bookstores and received a Lambda Book Award nomination. Bawer lives in New York City with his partner, Chris Davenport.

A former director of the National Book Critics Circle, Bawer reviews books frequently for *The New York Times Book Review*, *The Washington Post Book World*, and *The Wall Street Journal*. He has also published essays and reviews in *The American Scholar*, *The Nation*, *Connoisseur*, *The Hudson Review*, and *Newsweek*. His poems have appeared in the *Paris Review*, *Poetry*, and other journals.